THE BORDER

THE BORDER

A JOURNEY AROUND RUSSIA

Through North Korea, China, Mongolia, Kazakhstan,
Azerbaijan, Georgia, Ukraine, Belarus, Lithuania,
Poland, Latvia, Estonia, Finland, Norway,
and the Northeast Passage

ERIKA FATLAND

Translated from the Norwegian by Kari Dickson

PEGASUS BOOKS
NEW YORK LONDON

THE BORDER

Pegasus Books, Ltd.
148 West 37th Street, 13th Floor
New York, NY 10018

Copyright © 2017 Kagge Forlag AS
English translation copyright © 2020 by Kari Dickson
Maps © Kagge Forlag
Photographs © Erika Fatland

First Pegasus Books paperback edition March 2022
First Pegasus Books cloth edition February 2021

ISBN: 978-1-64313-949-4

10 9 8 7 6 5 4 3

Printed in the United States of America
Distributed by Simon & Schuster
www.pegasusbooks.com

PLACE NAMES

Many of the place names in the book have been transcribed from other alphabets. The names and spellings used in the book are those that are most commonly used in English. This has been done for the sake of familiarity and readability, and has no political connotations whatsoever.

For my mother,
who gave me wings

CONTENTS

THE CAUCASUS

EUROPE

LIST OF ILLUSTRATIONS

Kazakhstan

21/22 Paradise on earth: Roma hopes that the whole world will one day come to Poporechnoye in the Altai mountains.

23 After months inland, the briny breeze of the Caspian Sea was almost intoxicating.

24 My visit to the cosmodrome in Baikonur had been agreed months in advance, but this was as close as I got to seeing a rocket.

Caucasus

25 The flame at Ateshgah Temple outside Baku burns eternally.

26/27/28 The many faces of war, from dismal border crossings to bombed blocks of flats. Dato Vanishvili woke up one morning to find himself in another country.

29 Gori: the modest dwelling where Stalin spent his early years is now housed inside a somewhat less modest building.

30 Georgia is still a "wonderland", as it was in Hamsun's day.

31 The Gergeti Monastery in Stepantsminda on an exceptionally clear and beautiful evening.

Ukraine

32 The victims of war are ever-present in Kiev.

33 In a panic, I deleted all my photographs from Donetsk as I approached the Belarusian border. This picture of me with Vladimir, a professor of history who retrained as a tank driver when the war broke out, is the only memory I have from there. (© Christopher Nunn)

34 Holodomor: the famine in Ukraine in 1932–3 was devastating. Bare millstones surround this hungry little girl, who clutches a precious ear of corn.

35 The Chernobyl disaster as a tourist attraction: the physical remains of the catastrophe should not be touched.

Belarus

36 Lenin still stands on his pedestal in front of the parliament building in Minsk, but the square has been renamed Independence Square.

37 Head of state on a minimum pension: Stanislav Shushkevic told me about his role in the dissolution of the Soviet Union.

38 Maia Levina-Karpina, one of the few survivors of the Germans' grotesque extermination of the Jewish population in the Minsk ghetto.

The Baltics

39 The land around Nida on the Curonian Spit has passed through the hands of many nations.

40 Narva lies so close to the border that you can see Russia on the other side of the river.

41 The Ligatne Bunker in Latvia. In the event of a nuclear war, the surviving leaders were expected to talk on a number of different telephones.

42 The monument to the Singing Revolution in Tallinn.

Finland & Norway

43 The symbolic Three-Country Cairn, where Norway, Finland and Russia meet. Walking around the cairn is prohibited.

44 The Finnish border guards keep an eye on their neighbours to the east from impressive watchtowers.

45 In summer 1969, Soviet tank guns on the far side of this bridge were aimed at Norwegian border troops for four nerve-racking days, until they disappeared as suddenly as they had appeared.

THE OCEAN

*"Human beings have an irrepressible need to
explore all parts of the world"*
Fridtjof Nansen

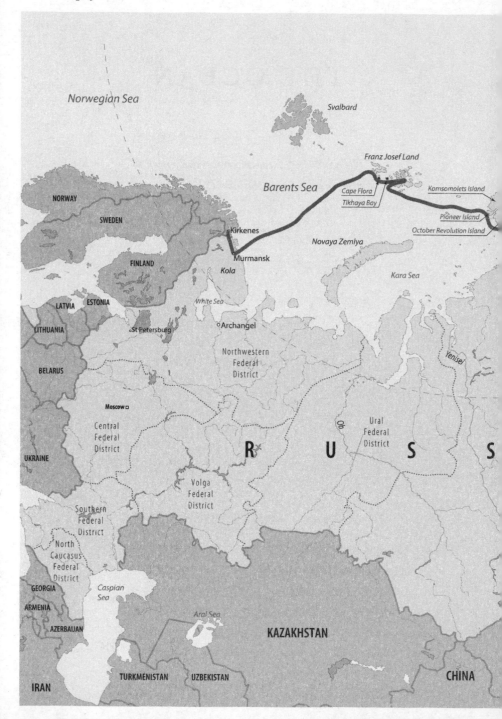

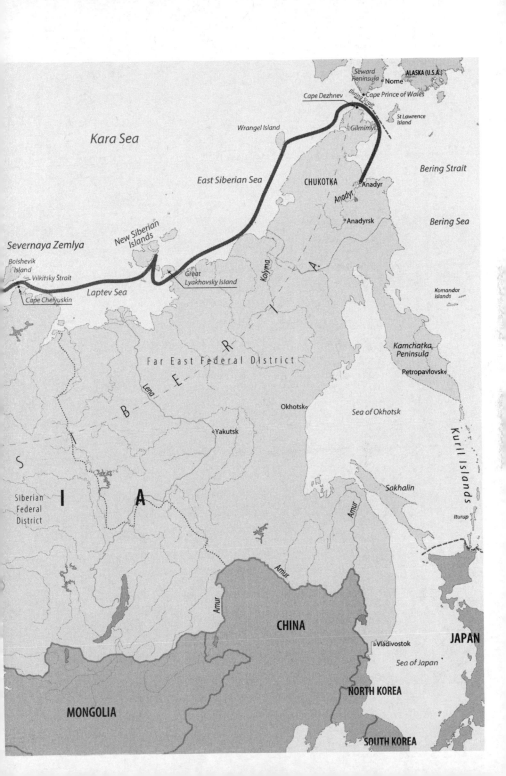

Arctic Summer

Cape Dezhnev is the easternmost point of the Eurasian continent. It is 8,500 kilometres from Moscow, more than 6,500 kilometres from New York, and less than 90 kilometres from Cape Prince of Wales in Alaska, on the other side of the Bering Strait.

I climbed up the rocky hill to the small lighthouse. It looked so indescribably lonely standing as it did, surrounded by steep green slopes and precipitous cliffs. I turned and looked out at the grey ocean. Here, right here, is where Asia and mighty Russia end. On the front of the lighthouse, facing out over the strait, is a bronze plaque commemorating Semyon Dezhnev. The Cossack explorer and tax collector sailed across the Bering Strait in 1648, a feat that was repeated eighty years later by the Danish naval officer Vitus Bering. By then everyone had forgotten Dezhnev, and the account of his journey was gathering dust in an archive in Yakutsk, more than five thousand kilometres east of Moscow. The Russian Empire was so vast that even the tsar was not sure where it ended, and no-one had an overview of former explorers' discoveries.

Just below the lighthouse was a huddle of grey, weathered, crooked wooden huts: the old Soviet border station. The Americans had a similar installation on the other side of the strait, and so, year after year, they sat on either side of an invisible iron curtain, watching each other's every move with binoculars and radars as big as tower blocks.

Not far from the lighthouse lay the ruins of a Yupik village. The Yupiks are an indigenous people closely related to the Inuit in

Alaska and on Greenland, and there are only about seventeen hundred of them left in Russia. Scores of round, largely collapsed foundations dotted the slopes. Long, sharp walrus tusks, on which they used to hang their traditional walrus-skin boats to dry, had been thrust into the ground between the houses. Were it not for the odd frying pan and some abandoned plastic jerrycans, it would be easy to assume that the ruins were hundreds of years old. But the inhabitants of the village, which was called Naukan, had in fact been forced to leave relatively recently, in 1958. The official reason was that it was too hard to get supplies to the isolated and exposed village. But its location on the edge of the Bering Strait, less than ninety kilometres from the western coast of Alaska, presumably played a part.

The inhabitants of Big Diomede Island, which lies in the middle of the Bering Strait and is Russia's easternmost territory, had already been evacuated during the Second World War, before the Iron Curtain fell between the two countries. The Inuits who lived on the island were never allowed to return. The sound between Big Diomede and Little Diomede, which is part of Alaska, is barely five kilometres across, but the International Date Line runs down the middle. In winter, when the sound is frozen, it is in theory possible, though of course strictly forbidden, to walk from the U.S.A. to Russia, from yesterday to tomorrow. An invisible but very real border lies between the two islands, which are so close in the natural world, and yet belong to two completely different man-made worlds, divided by the same thin line on any map that separates East from West, system from system, date from date.

The Russian border is not just long; at 60,932 kilometres it is the longest in the world. By way of comparison, the circumference of the earth measures 40,075 kilometres. Almost two thirds of Russia's border follows the coastline from Vladivostok in the east to

Murmansk in the west, a colossal area inhabited by very few people that is covered in ice and snow for most of the year. This stretch of coast was one of the last regions on earth to be explored and mapped. Severnaya Zemlya was the last archipelago in the world to be discovered in 1913, and was not mapped until twenty years later.

More than three-quarters of Russia's enormous landmass lies in the east, in Asia. The greater part of this vast territory was not conquered by the tsar's army but by fur trappers, hungry for profit. In the mid-sixteenth century, a wealthy merchant from the Stroganov family was given the tsar's blessing to colonise the regions to the east of the Ural mountains, for the fur trade. Semyon Stroganov was not only exempted from paying tax, he was also given permission to organise his own private army to conquer the territory. Demand for fur in Europe and Asia was insatiable, and thanks to the Stroganov family's colonisation of Siberia, Russia was for a long time the world's biggest fur exporter. The hunt for fur drove the Stroganovs further east with every passing day. These fur trader colonies eventually became more official and state-like, with forts and fortresses. The Cossacks, a group of free hunters, warriors and adventurers, were given the task of collecting *yasak*, contributions, for the tsar from his new subjects, who were often nomads. The contribution, or tax, was largely fur, which of course was the driving force behind the expansion.

Semyon Dezhnev was one of the Cossacks who collected such contributions. He was born in 1605 in a village by the White Sea, not far from Archangel, and started to work as a tax collector for the tsar in Siberia when he was a young man. It was a demanding and dangerous job. Many of the nomads did not know that they were considered subjects of the Russian tsar, so did not realise that they had to make a contribution to him. It was not always easy to make them understand that they were obliged to supply a stranger – a man who lived far, far away – with fur.

Accounts of Dezhnev's life are inadequate and divergent. He was apparently a very gifted diplomat and on several occasions managed to negotiate peace between warring tribes. It was because of these skills that he was sent further and further east to find new peoples who could pay tribute to the tsar. Together with a small group of merchants, trappers and Cossacks, he headed north-east. When they came to the Kolyma River in north-eastern Siberia, they heard from the indigenous people about another river, the Anadyr, where there was an abundance of walruses and fur-bearing animals, so they decided to find it. Their first attempt to travel further east was unsuccessful, due to ice, but the following year, in summer 1648, they tried again. A party of about ninety people set off into the unknown in seven kochs, a type of Russian sailing boat that was designed for difficult sea conditions with lots of ice. Two of the boats were immediately lost in a storm and never found again. Two more disappeared along the way and no-one has ever managed to discover what happened to them. But on September 20, the crew on the remaining boats spotted a stone formation which they later described as a "great, rocky projection" – the cape that is now named after Dezhnev. Here they stopped and visited the Inuits who lived there. They also went ashore on Big Diomede Island. Presumably without knowing it, Dezhnev had proved that North America and Asia were two separate continents.

The expedition ran into a powerful storm south of the strait that is today called the Bering Strait but should of course be called the Dezhnev Strait, and the three remaining boats were separated. Dezhnev's boat, with a crew of about twenty on board, was ship-wrecked south of the mouth to the Anadyr River, which was their destination. It is not known what happened to the two other boats: perhaps they sank with everyone on board, or perhaps any survivors were killed by the hostile and fearsome Chukchi people. One questionable but enduring theory is that the survivors made it ashore in Alaska, where they established a small colony.

After ten strenuous weeks wandering through the wilderness, Dezhnev and his exhausted men reached the mouth of the river, where they bunkered down for the winter. Only thirteen of them were still alive when spring came. Later that year, Dezhnev established the Anadyrsk trading post, about six hundred kilometres upriver. He must have liked it there, because he stayed for twelve years. Twenty years after he had left Yakutsk to travel south in search of new tribes who could pay tribute to the tsar, he returned with an enormous amount of walrus ivory.

Over time, however, the memory of Dezhnev's expedition was lost, only to be rediscovered piece by piece in the Yakutsk archives by German historian Gerhard Friedrick Müller nearly ninety years later. It was not until 1898, two hundred and fifty years after Dezhnev's expedition, that the Russian Geographical Society decided that the name of the easternmost point of the Eurasian continent should be changed from East Cape to Cape Dezhnev. Strictly speaking it should have been named after the Yupik people who already lived there when Dezhnev and his men turned up, but that is the way of the world: the atlas is full of the surnames of courageous European men who set sail in small, unsafe vessels to discover what had already been discovered long ago.

*   *   *

The final leg of my long journey around Russia had started in Anadyr some days earlier in July 2017. Not in Dezhnev's Anadyrsk, but in the town that was established at the mouth of the river in 1889, six hundred kilometres from the simple settlement where Dezhnev and his men had spent more than a decade killing thousands upon thousands of walruses, and had built up a tower of ivory.

The quayside was dirty and bare. A group of fishermen were wading in the shallows further along the shore, and in the distance I could see clusters of colourful apartment blocks. The water was full of curious seals, and every now and then the glistening, arched back of a beluga whale broke the surface.

For the next four weeks, I would sail through the Northeast Passage from east to west in an old Soviet research vessel called *Akademik Shokalsky*, named after the Russian oceanographer Yuly Shokalsky, together with forty-seven other passengers. The voyage would cover 5,650 nautical miles along the northern coast of Russia, all the way to Murmansk.

The trip had been fully booked for more than a year, and I had been lucky to secure one of the very last places. I had spent considerable time wondering who my fellow passengers would be. Who was willing to shell out twenty thousand dollars to spend four weeks on a relatively small boat on which you had to share cabins, with showers and toilets out in the corridor, the only entertainment going ashore on remote, windswept islands?

A bevy of wrinkly, stooped men and women shuffled up the gangway, dressed in bright Gortex rain jackets, equipped with expensive binoculars and even more expensive cameras. I was not taken aback to discover that most of the passengers were pensioners, but the average age did surprise me. Many of them were so old that their ancient frames shook and they needed help to get down the steep stairs on board. Some were there with their spouses, but a good number were already widowed and travelling alone.

The conversation at dinner was all about travel. It was the perfect place for anyone wanting travel tips. There was not an island or obscure, autonomous territory that at least one of the pensioners had not visited. Somaliland? Of course, been there several times. Bhutan? Interesting place, the less-visited eastern part, in particular. Yemen? Fascinating culture, such a shame about the war. It soon became clear that I was the only one who had not been on an expedition to Antarctica. Most had been there a few times; some had even been on the same trips and knew each other already.

The aged globetrotters continued to chat at the breakfast table the following day. During lunch, the initial pleasantries gave way to personal and detailed questions about border crossings, visa regulations and alternative travel routes. Then it was time for the first activity of the trip: an excursion to the bird cliffs in a Zodiac, a rigid inflatable boat.

"This is exciting!" I said enthusiastically to Elie, the eighty-five-year-old, determined Dutchwoman with whom I was sharing a cabin. She had packed her own clothes hangers, multi-socket adapters and clothes with logos from her many previous trips to the Arctic.

"Exciting?" She gave me a baffled look. "Why?"

"I've never been in a Zodiac before," I said.

Elie was wide-eyed with surprise: "I've been on hundreds of Zodiac excursions. Hundreds!"

The sea was rough and the Zodiacs by the side of the ship rocked up and down. If you wanted to avoid falling in the water, you had to jump on board just before the rubber boat disappeared behind the crests of the waves again. One pensioner after another mustered their strength and fell onto the bottom of the rubber boat with a defiant smile and a look of concentration.

"I realise that time is running out," said Alyson, a tall American in her seventies, with a hoarse, contagious laugh. "In the past year alone, I've lost five friends."

Thousands of black-legged kittiwakes and guillemots swirled above our heads as we approached the high, vertical bird cliffs. The bird calls were accompanied by the furious clicking of cameras with metre-long lenses; the veteran explorers hung over the sides of the boats in daring, acrobatic positions to capture the birds from the best angle. No-one, apart from me, and I come from a long line of fishermen and sea folk, appeared to be the slightest bit bothered by the choppy waves. I could feel the bile pushing up in my throat, there were spots in front of my eyes, and the tears welled up. In the end, I let go of my pride and crawled to the back of the small boat by the outboard motor, where there was slightly less movement.

Twenty-seven days left. The final leg.

One night, three and a half years earlier, I had dreamt that I was wandering around on a vast map. My footsteps followed a wavy red line: the border of Russia. I wandered from country to country, with the mighty Russia always to the north or east. When I woke up, I knew straightaway that this would be my next book, a journey along the Russian border from North Korea to northern Norway.

I immediately started planning my route. I would start in Pyongyang and slowly travel west, homewards, towards Europe and Norway. The democratic and pluralistic Norway and the totalitarian, closed North Korea do not have much in common, except that both countries border on Russia. As do China, Mongolia, Kazakhstan, Azerbaijan, Georgia, Ukraine, Belarus, Lithuania, Poland, Latvia, Estonia and Finland. Only China has as many neighbours as Russia – fourteen in all.

Now on board the *Akademik Shokalsky*, surrounded by the Arctic Ocean, the greater part of my adventure was over. For eight months, I had travelled along the southern and western borders of Russia, from Pyongyang to Grense Jakobselv, with one question in mind: what does it mean to have the world's largest country as your neighbour?

Along the way I had discovered that there is no single answer to the question; there are at least fourteen, as many answers as there are neighbouring countries. Though in truth there must be millions of answers, one for each person who lives along the border, each with their own unique history.

Following the dissolution of the Soviet Union, Russia was on its knees in terms of its economy, military power and politics. The drunkard Boris Yeltsin was at the helm, and had the thankless task of tidying up after many years of economic mismanagement. In the chaotic Nineties, hundreds of investors made enormous profits buying up cheap government bonds, while the majority of the population struggled to make ends meet. Inflation was out of control, and criminal gangs and anarchy prevailed. The U.S.A. celebrated victory over communism, while in Russia people mourned all that was lost: welfare benefits and the dream of utopia.

And, not least, the loss of an empire. In the course of a few months, the population shrank from 300 million to 140 million. A fifth of the territory was gone, divided into fourteen independent nations. Among these were Kazakhstan, Azerbaijan, Georgia, Ukraine, Belarus, Lithuania, Latvia and Estonia, countries which had all been part of the Russian Empire and then the Soviet Union, and now were Russia's new neighbours. The Eastern European satellite states were no longer under Moscow's control either. Over the centuries, Russians had got used to numerous peoples and nations dancing to Russia's tune, but now the tune had changed, and all that was left was a final exhausted wheeze.

In his annual speech to parliament in 2005, President Vladimir Putin described the collapse of the Soviet Union as "the greatest geopolitical catastrophe of the twentieth century". He was naturally referring to the territorial dissolution, but also to the 25 million Russians and people with Russian as their mother tongue who suddenly found themselves outwith Russian territory. Many of them now live in the neighbouring countries, on the other side of Russia's extensive border.

But Russia is still enormous, and slowly expanding. Over the past decade, with Putin in power, Russia has once again taken a dominant position on the world stage. The economy is on track and the military has been significantly upgraded. Its neighbours can no longer sleep easy at night. In some places, they do not sleep at all, but spend the nights in cold, dark cellars, sheltering from the shells that light up the sky like distress flares.

Being Russia's neighbour has never been easy. Norway is the only one of its fourteen neighbours that has not been invaded or at war with Russia in the past five hundred years. While other great European powers such as France and Great Britain had overseas colonies, Russia just continued to expand its boundaries. One nation after another, one ethnic group after another, was swallowed up by the empire and became subjects of the tsar, and still there was room for more. To this day, there are nearly two hundred different ethnic groups within the boundaries of the Russian Federation, from the Tuvans, nomadic reindeer herders in Siberia, to the Pontic Greeks on the fertile shores of the Black Sea. Unlike France and Great Britain, Russia has few natural boundaries; the landscape is largely flat, open and limitless, so the empire could spread in all directions. Already in the seventeenth century, in the Cossack Dezhnev's day, the country stretched from Moscow to the west of the Ural mountains all the way to the Pacific Ocean in the east.

Huge tracts of Russia are covered by tundra, taiga and forest: hard to defend, easy to invade. Russia's size and enormous distances have been its best defence over the centuries. Even though the terrain west of Moscow is flat, without any major mountain ranges or other physical barriers, no-one has yet managed to conquer Russia

from the west. Before the armies have even reached Moscow, supplies and soldiers have been exhausted. The main routes east have
proved too long and the freezing temperatures too extreme. But
that does not mean there have been no valiant attempts: Poland,
Sweden and France all tried, as did Germany, twice, in 1914 and
1941, with catastrophic results.

Russia's bold expansion started in the sixteenth century with the
defeat of the Muslim Kazan Khanate to the east of Moscow
and subsequent colonisation of Siberia and the Far East, which was
initially driven by trappers. When the twenty-two-year-old Mikhail
Fyodorovich became Michael I, the first Romanov to be crowned
tsar in 1613, the country was already so big that no-one had a
complete overview of how many people lived there, or how many
different ethnicities the tsar ruled over, or even where the outer
boundaries were.

A hundred years and six tsars later, there was still uncertainty
as to where Russia ended. Were America and Asia connected? Peter
the Great, otherwise known as Peter I, was perhaps the most energetic and westward-looking of the tsars, and a great reformer. He
was also passionate about ports and maritime navigation. One of
the last things he did was to send an expedition to Russia's
outposts to map the coastline. The Danish mariner Vitus Bering,
who like a great many other Danish and Norwegian sailors served
in the Russian navy, was appointed captain of the expedition.

Bering set out for the Pacific coast in 1725, the same year that
Peter the Great died. The expedition east, which would cover close
to ten thousand kilometres, was strenuous, to say the least. Long
stretches of the journey passed through terrain where no-one had
ventured before, and they often had to build bridges and boats in
order to cross the wide, raging torrents they encountered. A good
deal of the journey was over marshland, where many of the horses
and some of the people died from infections, owing to innumerable

insect bites. Those who survived the swarms of mosquitoes were rewarded with the perishing cold of winter. It took two years for the expedition to reach Okhotsk on the Pacific Ocean. From here, they sailed to the Kamchatka Peninsula, which had been conquered a few decades before, but was still an unexplored wilderness, inhabited by hostile tribes. It took the entire winter for Bering and his men to reach Kamchatka, first by boat and then by sled. They arrived at the small Cossack settlement on the southern end of the peninsula in March 1728, three years after they had left St Petersburg. It was then that the real expedition could begin. But first they had to build a ship. Finally, when summer came, Bering and his crew were ready to sail north into uncharted waters.

On August 16, after a month at sea, Bering sailed through the strait that now bears his name. There was thick fog and visibility was appalling. Bering could see one of the Diomede Islands, but the other lay hidden, as did the continent on the other side. The intention was to carry on east towards the New World, but the weather was so bad and the self-made boat so unsuited to high seas that they turned back, on Bering's orders.

In 1730, five years after he had left the Russian capital, Bering returned to St Petersburg. Straightaway, he started to prepare for the even longer and more ambitious Great Northern Expedition, the largest and most expensive exploration enterprise ever, with the exception perhaps of the moon landings. The purpose was to map the Arctic and East Siberian coastline, to explore America and Japan (with which Russia had had no previous contact), and to undertake ethnographic, zoological, botanical, astronomical and geographical studies in Siberia. Historians have calculated that a total of ten thousand people were involved in the expedition in one way or another, and it is estimated to have cost 34 billion euros at today's prices, a seventh of the total annual Russian government budget at the time. The expedition was divided into three main groups, with multiple sub-groups, which together mapped the greater part of Russia's northern coastline.

Bering himself, who had overall responsibility for the expedition, went east again. For a number of logistical reasons, it took him five years to get from St Petersburg to Okhotsk. And it was only at the start of June 1741, eight years after they had left St Petersburg, that Bering and his seventy-strong crew were ready to set sail from the Kamchatka Peninsula. Their aim was to find a sea route to the east, to America.

In mid-July, they caught sight of land to the east: high, snow-capped mountains and a pointed volcano, presumably Mount St Elias, which lies on the border between what is now Alaska and Canada. Their mission was complete. The following day, Bering gave orders to return to the Russian mainland. Georg Steller, a German doctor and scientist who was part of the expedition, begged for more time, but to no avail. He had had no more than a day ashore in the New World. But in that one day he managed to describe a considerable number of new plant and bird species in detail, and this work in itself would have immortalised him. Of course, one day was far from enough to explore the unfamiliar surroundings where no European had set foot before. In his diary, Steller remarked: "Ten years the preparation for this great undertaking lasted, and ten hours were devoted to the work itself."[1]

Supplies on board were running low and several crew members were already showing symptoms of scurvy, including Bering himself, which may go some way to explaining why he had no interest in exploring the new continent.

Scurvy was the curse of all sailors. We now know that the illness is caused by a lack of vitamin C, one of the vitamins the body cannot produce, which therefore has to be supplemented by diet. Early symptoms of scurvy include tiredness, apathy, breathlessness and aching limbs, as well as changes in personality. This is followed by bleeding gums and loss of teeth. Internal bleeding is also usual, and the cause of death is either internal bleeding or starvation. If, however, the patient manages to eat or drink something that is rich in vitamin C, the symptoms will recede after a week or two, and the patient normally recovers. One of the earliest descriptions of the disease was given by Hippocrates; later, it afflicted the crusaders. It was a serious problem on all long expeditions, when scurvy would often kill half the crew. In the eighteenth century, more men in the British navy died from scurvy than in battle.*

The first of Bering's men died from the dreaded disease at the end of August, not far from the Alaskan coast. On the return voyage, the ship was caught in several prolonged storms, and eventually only a handful of the crew were able to stand upright and work. September turned into October and one storm followed another; in the end, sailors were dying every day, and the water supply was almost dry. It was not until early November, two months after they had left Alaska, that they caught sight of land. "It is impossible to describe how great and extraordinary was the joy of everybody at this sight," Steller wrote in his diary. "The half-dead crawled up to see it and all thanked God heartily for this great mercy."[2]

The joy, however, was short-lived. As they got closer, it became apparent that they had not reached the Russian mainland, but rather an uninhabited, treeless island, with steep unwelcoming cliffs and mountains. The ship ran aground as they were trying to land, so they were forced to spend the winter there. Many of the crew were by now so weakened by scurvy that they could no longer eat; their gums were reduced to open, bleeding sores with shreds

---

* The fact that Norwegian sailors were spared scurvy could not be explained at the time. Today we know that this was thanks to the supplies of cloudberries and ligonberries normally kept on board, which are rich in vitamin C.

of flesh hanging down over the few teeth they had left. Of the seventy-five sailors who had left Kamchatka in the early summer, twenty-eight were now dead or dying. The remaining men spent the winter building a new boat from the wreckage, and in spring 1742 they finally made it back to Kamchatka.

But it was too late for Bering. His condition was critical; he could no longer stand up, so lay, apathetic, on the ground and let the sand blow over him. Georg Steller tried to brush the sand off, but Bering stopped him. "Let me be," he murmured. "The deeper in the ground I lie, the warmer I am; only the part of me that is above ground suffers from the cold."[3]

Two hours before dawn on December 8, 1741, Vitus Bering died. He was sixty.[*] The island on which he died is now also named after him. Bering is remembered as Russia's Columbus, the man who discovered America from the west. His name was immortalised in 1776 when Captain James Cook named the strait between Russia and America the Bering Strait.

Steller's name has also gone down in history. The barren island where they ran aground had a rich animal life, perhaps because humans had never been there before. Steller was kept busy. Some of the species that he discovered and described now bear his name, including Steller's sea lion and Steller's sea eagle, and, perhaps the most famous of them all, Steller's sea cow. The sea cows on Bering Island were one of the few surviving species of mammal from the last ice age; they could grow up to nine metres long and weigh nearly ten metric tons.

The discovery of the sea passage to Alaska led to the creation

---

[*]   In 1991, Bering's grave was discovered by a Russo-Danish expedition, and his remains were taken to Moscow. Close investigation showed that Bering had not died of scurvy after all. It was also possible to recreate his appearance, on the basis of his skeleton, and it turned out that the most famous portrait of him was in fact not the Danish seafarer, but in all likelihood Vitus Pedersen Bering, his great-uncle, who lived from 1617 to 1675. The remains were returned to the island in 1992.

of the state-supported Russian-American Company. The company was established in 1799, more than fifty years after the Bering expedition, its mission to colonise Alaska, trade with the locals and, most importantly, get fur. The natives, who were forced to work with the Russians, died by the score from illnesses introduced by the incomers, just as millions of native Americans further south had died from influenza, measles and whooping cough a couple of decades before. The company's southernmost outpost was in fact in Fort Ross, California.

Alaska was an anomaly in Russian history: it was the only mainland territory that was not attached to the rest of the empire. There were never very many Russians in Alaska – only eight hundred or so ever settled in the colony. The stock of precious fur-bearing animals declined through the nineteenth century, at the same time that the Americans were winning more and more of North America. In 1867, when the Russian-American Company was doing relatively well and considering the possibility of expanding into timber, minerals and gold, Tsar Alexander II sold Alaska to America for 7.2 million dollars. The person driving the deal on the American side was the then Secretary of State, William H. Seward. The sale was a bargain, and without a doubt could be described as the best real estate deal in history, yet the American press called Alaska "Seward's folly" or "Seward's icebox". Only when gold was discovered in Klondike in 1896 and a few years later in Nome did his critics fall silent. The Russians, on the other hand, never quite got over the fact that Alexander II had sold Russia's only overseas territory for so little. To this day, some marginal right-wing extremists in Russia still cherish the dream of reclaiming Alaska, one hundred and fifty years after the Americans bought it for the equivalent of four dollars per square kilometre.

Georg Steller's detailed descriptions of the fauna on Bering Island paradoxically led to the extinction of many species. It did not take long for fortune hunters to come and help themselves to the natural riches. Already by the mid-1750s the sea otter – Steller had estimated there were close to a million on the island – and the northern fur seal, of which there were approximately two million, were almost extinct. The last sea cow is said to have been killed in 1769, only twenty-seven years after Steller had been on the island.

Steller himself died on the way back to St Petersburg, at the age of thirty-seven, disillusioned and bitter, without knowing that the book manuscript he had sent ahead to St Petersburg a few years earlier would make him famous. He was buried in Tyumen, to the north of Kazakhstan. As Steller was a Protestant, the local monks refused to bury him in the orthodox cemetery, so a shallow grave was made for him in a remote spot by the river Tura. The grave and body were desecrated by grave robbers, mutilated by dogs, then washed away by a flood and wiped from the face of the earth, like Steller's sea cow.

* * *

Thick mist rolled in over the Bering Strait. Cape Dezhnev disappeared behind an impenetrable, grey wall and suddenly visibility was no more than a few metres, as it must have been when Bering himself sailed through the strait nearly three hundred years earlier. Then, just as quickly as it had come, the mist disappeared again and we had no problems rounding the cape. The ocean was steely blue, with barely a ripple. And no ice in sight.

The conversation at the dinner table continued to be about extreme destinations, followed by extensive studies of the atlas – the most popular book in the ship's library – in the bar afterwards. Peter, a retired British commercial lawyer, had taken it to the extreme. He had been travelling constantly since he retired and had rented out his home in Sydney, as he was never there.

"I'm homeless, but not penniless," he said.

Peter could spend hours at a time studying the atlas and making detailed travel plans. The following year, 2018, was already full. He was going to go to Nebraska and Kansas in the U.S.A., the only two states he had not yet visited, as well as Mexico, the U.K., Germany, Belgium, Turkey, a couple of places in India and a number of Ebola-infected countries in West Africa. He was also going to cross Russia on the Trans-Siberian railway and hoped to squeeze in a quick visit to Birobidzhan, a Jewish autonomous oblast by the Chinese border. On the table in front of him he had a notebook full of travel plans that was organised by month. He was constantly making small adjustments, dropping a town or country, moving one trip up and delaying another. He was a member of The Travelers' Century Club, and was ranked number eighty-two on mosttraveledpeople.com. The website lists 875 different territories, of which Peter had visited 530.

"By the end of next year, that number will be five hundred and seventy," he told me. "And my ranking may increase to seventy-five. But you have to remember that the others on the list also travel a lot."

He pulled out a map of the various territories in Russia.

"Do you know if it's possible to get to South Ossetia from North Ossetia? And would three weeks be enough to visit all the republics in the European part of Russia, south of Moscow, or should I perhaps make two trips? The territories are so close in the European part that you can score lots of points; the problem is, I can only get a visa for thirty days, which makes it a bit more complicated. So I have to make a detailed travel route. And do you think September is a good month to travel in the Caucasus?"

"September is perfect, it should still be nice and warm," I said.

"No, wait, September isn't possible, that's when I'm sailing the Northwest Passage!" He scratched his head. "I think October is still free. What do you think about October?"

"October is a good month as well, but not quite so good if you are intending to sunbathe."

"I never sunbathe," Peter said, and jotted down *Caucasus?* under October in his notebook. "I have been looking forward to this trip," he added with a sigh. "It's nice to relax in one place for a while. Though, relax is perhaps not the right word. At least I don't need to carry my suitcase anywhere!"

The ship had its own rhythm. The route passed through nine time zones, so the clock was put back an hour at appropriate intervals. There was no Internet or mobile coverage on board; for four weeks, we had no contact with the outside world and floated around in our own little universe, a universe that soon settled down into routine and ritual. There were two dining rooms on board, and after no more than a few days, people went to the same places at the same table with the same people in the same room. Breakfast was at half past seven, lunch at half past twelve, and dinner at seven. On the port side, we could see the Russian coast, a low, dark strip of land that was partially hidden by grey fog, and on the starboard side we had the open sea. Every now and then we caught a glimpse of white sheet ice or bare, rocky islands.

If we had taken the fastest route to Murmansk, without any detours or stops, the voyage would have taken between one and two weeks – the record is six and a half days. But we went ashore as often as we could, onto windswept islands that were inhabited only by seabirds, lemmings and huffing, puffing walruses. The word "Arctic" is derived from the Greek ἀρκτικός, *arktikos*, which means "near the bear" and refers to the constellation Ursa Major, the Great Bear, which is clearly visible in the northern hemisphere. It could, of course, also refer to the very real bears of the animal kingdom – we saw polar bears, or signs of polar bears, on every island where we went ashore. For this reason, we always stayed together in a group. This was the home of the polar bear, and we were guests. Once we saw more than two hundred polar bears in a single day, which is one per cent of the total population. From on board the ship they looked like sheep in the distance.

Even when you think you have no expectations, as the place is utterly unknown, the journey so different from any other, you still have subliminal expectations about what you might see and experience, not least about what you will *not* see and experience.

I had not expected so much rubbish. I have never seen so many rusty oil drums as I did in the Arctic, thousands upon thousands of old drums, stacked up on top of each other, or just lying around on the tundra; a very concrete reminder of the Soviet Union's ambitious investment in the north. At its peak, there were more than a hundred weather stations along the northern coast, which were staffed, as a rule, by three or four people who lived there in isolation, in all kinds of weather, through the long, white nights of summer and the long, black nights of winter, often for years at a time. The first polar stations were built soon after the creation of the Soviet Union, before any ships had managed to cross the Northeast Passage without getting stuck in the ice for at least one winter.

Until 1920, only three expeditions had successfully negotiated the Northeast Passage. The Finnish-Swedish explorer, Adolf Erik Nordenskiöld, was the first to complete the voyage from the coast of Norway to the Bering Strait in 1878–9. The feat was not repeated until forty-five years later, in 1914, by the Russian naval officer and hydrographer Boris Vilkitsky – only this time the journey was made from east to west. It was in fact Vilkitsky who discovered Severnaya Zemlya, which lies roughly in the middle of the Northeast Passage, north of the Taymyr Peninsula and Cape Chelyuskin. Vilkitsky named it Emperor Nicholas II Land. In 1926, the archipelago was given the more neutral name Severnaya Zemlya, meaning "northern land", and when the area was mapped in the 1930s, the islands themselves were given edifying names such as October Revolution, Bolshevik and Komsomolets, which today sound as outdated as Emperor Nicholas II Land must have sounded in 1926.

The last of the three explorers, Roald Amundsen, set sail in 1918, and thus became the first person to sail both the Northeast Passage and the Northwest Passage. Nordenskiöld, Vilkitsky and Amundsen all got stuck in the ice and were forced to winter in the frozen wasteland. Nordenskiöld's ship, *Vega*, froze into the pack ice only a hundred nautical miles from the Bering Strait and was stuck for ten months, whereas Vilkitsky's two ships got stuck in the ice about three hundred kilometres east of Cape Chelyuskin. And Amundsen did not reach Alaska until 1920, two years after he left Norway, as his ship got caught in the ice twice.

The Northeast Passage, or Northern Sea Route as the Russians call it, is reckoned to be one of the most difficult, and not without reason. It covers a distance of more than three thousand nautical miles, from Murmansk to the Bering Strait, across five seas: the Barents Sea, the Kara Sea, the Laptev Sea, the East Siberian Sea and the Chukchi Sea, which are all part of the Arctic Ocean. In winter, the greater part of the route is covered in thick sea ice, as the waters are often very shallow, barely more than five or six metres deep in some places. The breakthrough came in 1932, after many attempts and almost as many catastrophes and dramatic rescue operations. The Russian scientist Otto Schmidt successfully completed the journey from Murmansk to the Pacific Ocean in only ten weeks, without being forced to winter en route. As a result of Schmidt's success, the Soviet Union invested heavily in the Arctic region, and Schmidt was appointed director of the newly established Directorate for the Northern Sea Route. Weather stations, navigation bases and military posts popped up along the entire coastline and people started to cherish the dream of developing the Northern Sea Route for commercial transport – a dream that was then set out in ambitious five-year plans which were never realised.

The only evidence that remains of these past dreams and ambitions are the buildings: deserted, dilapidated, with books by Stalin and Lenin on the bookshelves, shoes, chairs, beds and insulation strewn around, and the occasional typewriter for writing reports. Most of the weather stations were abandoned following the collapse of the Soviet Union and have been replaced by satellites, but a handful of people continue to live and work in some of them.

After a week at sea, we landed at Great Lyakhovsky Island, one of the New Siberian Islands. There were some abandoned houses from the 1930s, which nobody had bothered to demolish, as well as two new buildings where the meteorologists now live and work. The inhabitants were standing waiting for us on the beach when we arrived. Three tall, thin men and a young woman with a pallid complexion and round glasses. Her name was Anya. She was twenty-two, and had been on the island for five months.

"The worst thing is the boredom," she said. "There's nothing to do here. We don't have the Internet, or newspapers, just a television, and nothing ever happens."

Four thick-coated guard dogs hid behind Anya's legs and watched us with darting eyes. They had never seen so many people together at once.

"What do you do when you have finished work for the day?" I asked.

Anya shrugged.

"We watch television. In summer, we go fishing. Sometimes we go for a walk." She laughed. "But there aren't many places to go."

The island was not large, and there was detritus everywhere: old equipment, cars, boats, the wooden frames of outside toilets, boathouses, observation stations. And in between all the old rusty oil drums lay new blue barrels. The circle was not closed, but had expanded into the new century.

"Isn't it lonely here?" I said, and immediately realised how ridiculous the question was.

"The fewer people there are in the station, the higher the wages," Anya said, and shrugged again. "As a recent graduate, I would find it almost impossible to get a suitable job in Novosibirsk."

Anya was a newly qualified meteorological assistant. She had originally studied business and marketing, but her husband, Yury, was the warden on the island and had already been there for two and half years. In the end, the waiting became too much, and Anya dropped out of her course, applied for an intensive three-month course in meteorology, then followed him.

"It is hardest in winter," Yury said. He was twenty-eight, but looked at least ten years older. "It is dark all the time and we never see the sun."

"And I'm sure it's very cold."

"Minus thirty-five, or thereabouts," he said. "But that's fine. Novosibirsk is very cold as well."

"How long will you be here?" I said.

"In theory, we can go home once a year in October, on the icebreaker, but the company has no-one to cover for us, so we will be here for another two years, I guess," Anya said.

On the opposite side of the island, which took a few hours to sail around, was another weather station, which had opened in the 1920s and then been abandoned after the collapse of the Soviet Union. The ruins of big and small buildings remained, as well as a rusty tracked vehicle and, as always, rusty oil drums. There was a used condom by the outside toilet, and in one of the houses we found the remains of white bread, an open jar of chocolate spread covered in mould, an open packet of macaroni and a collection of D.V.D.s. The bread could not have been more than a few weeks old.

"Mammoth tusk collectors," Yevgeny, one of our Russian guides, told us.

"Mammoth tusk collectors?" I repeated.

"Yes, mammoth tusks are big business! When the weather warmed up after the last ice age, lots of mammoths fled to the New Siberian Islands, so there are mammoth tusks all over the place. Now that the permafrost is melting, erosion is speeding up and more and more tusks are being found. Some collectors hire helicopters and boats to get here. There is a lot of money to be made – we are talking millions. This is probably one of the areas in the Arctic where there is most human activity. Customs officers and soldiers are involved, obviously, as there is so much money to be had. The Chinese are insatiable!" Yevgeny laughed. "They grind them to powder, which they use as an aphrodisiac."

"Water" would have been a more suitable name for our planet. "Earth" is as misleading a name as Greenland. Sometimes the ocean was turquoise, almost emerald green, and at other times it was a muddy brown. Some days it was metallic blue, almost black, framed by golden-white skies. Other days the difference between water and air was erased and the sea and sky blended into one. The days spilled into a purple dusk before the sun rose again, having dipped briefly below the horizon. An elderly French couple were on the bridge from early morning until evening, forever watching seabirds, taking only short breaks for breakfast, lunch and dinner. Every observation was logged in a squared notebook, and reported at the Bird Club meetings which took place every evening in the bar. Other than the seagulls that trailed the boat, there were not many species to report; most had already migrated south.

Over the course of the morning, a storm blew up. The boat rocked from side to side and it was hard to keep your balance. The pensioners stumbled from wall to wall. Nausea squeezed my ribs like a tight yellow belt, and only when I lay absolutely still did the seasickness subside; my balance was as ephemeral as morning mist. At lunch, I stumbled into the dining room and my usual table; people were conspicuous by their absence. Every second chair was empty. A queue of ashen faces waited outside the ship doctor's office.

"This is nothing compared to the Antarctic," said the jovial Australian who was standing beside me.

"This is a walk in the park compared with the Antarctic," his wife said.

"Do you remember that evening, darling, when it took us half an hour to get up the stairs and back to our cabin?"

"The boat was moving so much that all we could do was cling to the banister!" his wife laughed. "They gave up serving food for several days, just put out sandwiches for those who could stomach it, and we had to strap ourselves into our berths so we wouldn't fall out."

"Sounds like a wonderful trip," I muttered.

"Oh, it was unforgettable!" the man said. "A once-in-a-lifetime experience. You must go to the Antarctic if you get the chance, but don't take one of the short trips. Take a long one, so you see it all."

"The long ones are best," his wife agreed.

It was not until late in the evening that the wind dropped. But then we hit ice, lots of it. The captain had to concentrate as he navigated the pack ice, which boomed and slowly cracked open to let us through. A polar bear sow and her two cubs lay wrapped around each other on a melting iceberg and observed us with black, watchful eyes. We were already just over halfway to Murmansk, and the most difficult stretch lay ahead: Vilkitsky Strait, the northernmost strait along the Northeast Passage. The strait is fifty-five kilometres wide, and relatively shallow with strong currents. The surface of the water is generally covered with pack ice throughout the year. All night long, the ship pressed through the thick ice; it bumped and humped and crunched as we crept towards Cape Chelyuskin, the northernmost point on the Eurasian continent.

The cape is feared by sailors because of the difficult weather conditions. When the ice is not lying thick, there are terrible storms, and if, against all odds, the wind is not blowing, the desolate landscape is covered by dense fog. It was not until one hundred and fifty years after Semyon Chelyuskin had discovered and mapped the cape on land that Nordenskiöld successfully navigated the northernmost point of Russia. Many had predicted that Cape Chelyuskin would be the death of him, and for that reason the Swedish naval minister, Carl Gustaf von Otter, was against the expedition, as he believed it was too risky. But Nordenskiöld set sail in 1878 all the same. *Vega* rounded the dreaded cape without any drama, but Nordenskiöld was not impressed by what he saw: ". . . which was the most monotonous and the most desolate I have seen in the High North."[4]

The border guards would not let us ashore on the cape, so we had to be satisfied with a trip along the cliffs in a Zodiac. When we got close to land, it was easy to see why the Russians did not want us there. Cape Chelyuskin is an environmental catastrophe, a parody of Russian decline and poor maintenance. Not hundreds, but *thousands* of rusty oil drums lay in haphazard piles. Small streams of old fuel ran into the ocean from some of the drums. There were scrapped cars, pieces of airplanes and helicopters, unidentifiable metal objects and empty apartment blocks with gaping, broken windows and cracked facades full of holes. The settlement was simply an enormous Soviet rubbish tip. There was not a flower to be seen, not even a blade of grass, just shades of grey, muddy brown and rusty red. The only sign of life were the three soldiers who suddenly set about repairing a radar on one of the roofs and pretended not to be keeping an eye on what we were doing in the boats.

Rugged, black cliffs formed a shield around Eurasia's northernmost point. Right out on the edge of the cliffs was a small graveyard. Down by the water, a cairn had been built to commemorate Roald Amundsen, and somewhere else there was a memorial for Nordenskiöld. Beside the graveyard was a single Russian border marker in red and green, just as dirty and tired as the rest of the base.

One day at sea was much like the next, and yet they were unlike any other days. For the first few I wandered endlessly up and down the corridors, up and down the stairs, round and round the decks, but slowly the restlessness subsided and was replaced by a kind of peace, or perhaps it was resignation. The ship was moving, I stood still. The pensioners slept. Not all the time, of course, but they seemed to get more and more tired with each degree of longitude we moved west. They slept after breakfast, after lunch and after dinner, and often took a short nap during the evening lectures on polar history.

However, Anatoly, one of the Russian passengers, did not waste his time on board with sleep. For hours on end he energetically marched round and round the lower deck; some days he might walk for six or seven hours at a stretch. He was somewhere in his fifties, with a little pot belly, and intensely present in all that he did. Whenever we went ashore, he always had his iPad with him. "Dear friends, I am now standing on a piece of history. It was here that Nansen met Jackson, and numerous other expeditions have met," he proclaimed to the camera as soon as we stepped onto dry ground at Cape Flora on Franz Josef Land, one of the busiest meeting places in the Arctic in the era of the great explorers.

In the evenings, the Russian passengers sometimes broke into spontaneous singing orgies that went on for ever, one song after another, and all of them, absolutely all of them, knew all the songs and sang with great gusto. The British and Australian pensioners regarded the Russian mixed choir with reserved, anxious smiles from the other end of the bar as they sipped their milky tea before discreetly retiring to their cabins to sleep some more. The Russians, meanwhile, enjoyed their wine, not to mention vodka, and it never took long before Yevgeny, the Russian guide, got out his guitar and played melancholy tunes. As the contents of the vodka bottle dwindled, it became ever easier to persuade him to play just one more. Even Anatoly was quiet when Yevgeny sang his sad songs about the loneliness of life on the tundra. Konrad, the German ship's doctor, intensified the mood by singing East German love songs in a minor key.

When we got to Champ Island, which is also part of Franz Josef Land, we had to rejig the day's itinerary. One of the Rosatomflot atomic icebreakers, full of tourists who had just been to the North Pole, was anchored out in the bay, and we had to wait patiently until all the polar explorers were on board again before we could go ashore and admire the enormous, perfectly symmetrical stone spheres. These days, if you have the money, you can go on a cruise to the North Pole, eat caviar, drink champagne and take selfies in the frozen wilderness before getting back on the icebreaker and treating yourself to a drink at the bar to celebrate your accomplishment.

The situation was very different a hundred years ago. Polar history is still a relatively new subject: Franz Josef Land, which comprises nearly two hundred large and small islands, was not officially discovered until 1873 by an Austro-Hungarian polar expedition led by Julius von Payer and Karl Weyprecht. As with many other expeditions and explorers, Payer and Weyprecht had aimed for the North Pole, which at the time many people believed was a large, magnetic stone surrounded by open sea. Their vessel, the polar ship *Admiral Tegetthof*, got frozen in the ice and drifted north to the archipelago, which they named after the Austrian emperor. Unlike Emperor Nicholas II Land, the islands have kept their name, even though the Austro-Hungarian Empire and royal family entered the history books long ago.

Franz Josef Land quickly became the preferred starting point for international expeditions with ambitions of reaching the North Pole. Many felt the call, but none were chosen. There were nearly as many rescue operations as there were expeditions. The islands are scattered with lonely graves. Everywhere we went, we saw signs of heroic courage and tragedy.

At the foot of a rocky outcrop at Cape Heller on Wilczek Land, we discovered the modest grave of the Norwegian Bernt Bentsen, who died there in 1899 at the age of thirty-eight. He had been part of the Fram expedition, Nansen's legendary attempt in 1893–6 to reach the pole, and after only a year back at home in Norway, Bentsen was hired for another expedition, led by the American journalist Walter Wellmann. Not far from the grave stood the remains of the stone-and-turf hut where Bentsen wintered with a fellow Norwegian, Paul Bjørvig, in 1898–9. They had been asked to guard the supply depot that would be used for the expedition to the North Pole the following summer, while the rest of the expedition spent the winter at the main base, further south.

"On Saturday, October 22, Baldwin, Emil and Olaf travelled to Cape Tegetthof," Paul Bjørvig wrote in his diary.[5] "Bentsen and I remain in the hut. God knows if we will ever see them again. God willing. [. . .] There is no means of heating the hovel whatsoever. We only make food twice a day in order to save fuel. In the evenings, we read a magazine. We only have the one, so have to be frugal with this too. While one reads, the other has to tend the moss lamp. Eight days have passed since we were left here on our own, and thus far all is well, though our sleeping bags have been sodden since we left Cape Tegetthof. They are now frozen. The reason for this is that Baldwin has treated us like dogs. Where we slept, we were exposed to the snow and wind, while he himself always took the best and driest places. He would lie there eating chocolate and other delicacies, while we ate walrus meat."

Before long, Bentsen fell ill. It started with a sore throat, but the symptoms quickly worsened: "Monday, November 12. Storm from the east, minus twenty-eight. Bentsen is extremely unwell. It would seem he can no longer get out of his sleeping bag. He is unable to get up from the bunk. It is his stomach that is weak. His faeces are mostly blood."

As the weeks went by, Bentsen got steadily worse. Bjørvig had to keep the polar bears at bay and look after the dogs, making sure that they had food and drink. In the polar nights, it was "as dark inside as it is out", but every now and then the sky was illuminated by the magnificent Northern Lights. Bjørvig had more than enough to deal with, however, and had neither the time nor the energy to admire the colour play.

"My friend has started to hallucinate," he wrote in December. "All he wants is for us to go back to Tromsø, we can get there quickly, he says. He sees people and talks with them, and is astonished that I cannot see them or talk with them too. [...] I now have all manner of tasks to do. I look after the dogs, clear the snow and nurse the patient, not least, though without any kind of medicine whatsoever. Thus I need not fear that I will use the wrong kind."

Bentsen was still alive on Christmas Eve; Bjørvig thought that he might even be getting better. Their Christmas celebrations were nothing to write home about: "It must be the dullest and saddest Christmas Eve experienced by anyone. We are two lost souls, lying here at the end of the world, in the most inclement place on the planet, in the far north in a tiny snow hut."

On the night of January 1, the two Norwegians entertained each other with songs. Bentsen even joined in with two verses of "Fairest Lord Jesus".

"A better song could not be sung under such circumstances," Bjørvig wrote. The two then fell asleep. When Bjørvig woke up at dawn, all was quiet in the wretched turf hut. "I thought he was still asleep so did not want to wake him. I struck a match and then saw that he was dead. I had long known that this was where it would end and had in many ways accepted it. But the reality felt so different. [. . .] I got up and melted some ice, then washed his face and hands and left him in the sleeping bag where he had died. When we were left on our own in the autumn, we had agreed that if either one of us was to die, the other would keep the body in the shelter until the expedition came north, to keep it safe from the bears and dogs."

Bjørvig kept his promise. "It was a little sad to lie beside the deceased," he wrote in a pragmatic entry. "It was cold to lie in the sleeping bag with him when he was alive, but it feels even worse now that he is dead. I must take things as they come."

It was not until two months later, on February 27, that Wellmann and the rest of the expedition came to relieve the Norwegian.

"How are you?" Wellmann asked. "And where is Bentsen?"

"I am well, but my friend is dead," Bjørvig said.

"Where have you buried your friend?"

"I have not buried him, he is lying in there," Bjørvig said, and pointed at the shared sleeping bag at Wellmann's feet. Bjørvig recalled that Wellmann was silent for a long time. Later, once a grave had been dug for Bentsen, Wellmann, Bjørvig and the rest of the small expedition attempted to travel north, but they had to give up after only a few weeks, and returned to the base at Cape Tegetthof.

Bjørvig took part in many more polar expeditions on Spitsbergen and in Antarctica. He spent the winter of 1908–9 as a watchman

on the north-western coast of Spitsbergen with the experienced
Arctic skipper Knut Johnsen, once again working for Wellmann.
One May day, Johnsen fell through the ice and was gone. This time
Bjørvig was on his own for a month before help came. Wellman
later tried to persuade Bjørvig to go back to Svalbard, but Bjørvig
had had his fill: "The Arctic has given me enough sorrow," he
wrote in his diary. "But if one has no sorrows, one has no joy."

He died in 1932 at the age of seventy-five.

The meteorologist Evelyn Briggs Baldwin, who, according
to Bjørvig, had guzzled chocolate while he and Bentsen had had
to eat walrus meat, returned to the Arctic in 1901. On that occasion
he was sponsored by the American baking powder millionaire William Ziegler, who paid for three polar expeditions, each more
expensive than the last, but all equally unsuccessful. Baldwin's expedition was forced to winter on Alger Island, one of the southernmost
islands in Franz Josef Land. The remains of the timber hut where
they kept their supplies are still there, and in astonishingly good
condition.

"We are doing everything we can to save valuable historical artefacts and record everything before it disappears," said Yevgeny
Yevmonov, the young historian leading the work to document
the polar history of Alger Island. "Twenty years ago, the hut was
forty-five metres from the water. But now, as you can see, it is
only two metres away, and the water is rising faster and faster.
The permafrost is melting, and the coastline is being swallowed up
by the ocean. We are working as fast as we can. Back then, in 1901,
things looked very different here. Baldwin's ship was anchored
about where yours is now, but in the midst of thick ice."

Akademik Shokalsky was anchored a few hundred metres from
the shore, surrounded by still, deep green water. There was not a
crystal of ice to be seen.

Polar history is literally crumbling and being eroded. The Arctic is one of the regions where man-made climate change is most dramatic and visible: the north is warming at double the global average, and it is accelerating. Since measurements began in 1979, the ice in the Arctic has shrunk by 91,000 square kilometres *per year*, and the sea ice that is still there is getting thinner and younger. It is a vicious circle, as thick white ice reflects the sun's rays back into the atmosphere, whereas thinner ice and the ocean absorb them. In 1980, four per cent of the sun's heat penetrated through the ice into the water. In 2010, that figure was eleven per cent. Climate experts believe that the Arctic has not been as warm as it is now for 44,000 years, if not more.

The voyage through the Northeast Passage on *Akademik Shokalsky* would have been unthinkable without an icebreaker only a few years ago. And future passengers may perhaps not even encounter sea ice at all. The landscape we travelled through is disappearing. The Arctic, as we know it, will soon be gone. Forecasts indicate that the Northeast Passage will be ice-free in summer within twenty years, if not sooner, and the average temperature is expected to have risen by as much as five or six degrees Celsius by 2080. The warming of the Arctic region will have enormous consequences for life on land and in the water, and will also affect wind cycles and ocean currents. Furthermore, warm water is less able to absorb CO_2 than cold water, which will result in a dramatic increase in the CO_2 in the atmosphere, which in turn will speed up global warming. An even more frightening scenario, if that is possible, is the melting of the permafrost in the Arctic and Siberia. This will lead not only to more erosion, but also to the release of greenhouse gases that have been stored in the permafrost for thousands of years. In 2016, a twelve-year-old boy and 2,300 reindeer died following an anthrax outbreak on the Yamal Peninsula in Siberia. The bacteria were stored in the permafrost and came back to life as the frost melted. No-one knows what other viruses and bacteria may lie hidden in the melting permafrost.

Only the Russian government and those in the shipping and oil industries have reason to celebrate such alarming prospects. The Arctic holds perhaps as much as a fifth of the world's oil and gas reserves, which will become more accessible as the ice melts. The route along Russia's northern coast from China and Japan to Northern Europe is about a third of that via the Suez Canal. The Chinese have already invested in icebreakers, which they may soon no longer need. And the nineteenth-century polar explorers' idea that the North Pole was an enormous area of open water may shortly be reality.

The dramatic consequences of climate change open up a potential gold mine for the Russian authorities. Not only will it be easier to access the reserves that lie hidden in the seabed, they will also have jurisdiction over the fastest route between Asia and Northern Europe. Even if future traffic along the Northeast Passage is only a fraction of the traffic through the Suez Canal, it will still make the northern regions so important that the traditional view of geography will be turned on its head. Russia's hopelessly remote ports, which until now have lain inactive through much of winter, could soon be busy and lucrative.

As a result of global warming, a new northern era is freeing itself from the ice.

*　*　*

No sooner had we stepped ashore at our final stop, Tikhaya Bay on Hooker Island, than there landed a helicopter full of Russian border guards. It must rank high on the list of the world's most expensive passport control.

Following the stagnation and decline of the 1990s, Russia is once again investing in the Arctic. Military bases that were shut

down have been given a facelift, and border stations, nature reserves and weather stations are now staffed again. Russia recently
submitted a claim to the U.N. for 1.2 million square kilometres
of the Arctic seabed, including the underwater Lomonosov Ridge,
which lies between Russia and Canada, and stretches to the North
Pole. Denmark and Canada have also laid claim to the same area,
so now it is up to the U.N. to decide who is the rightful owner
of the contested seabed.

Unlike in the Caucasus and Ukraine, Russia has largely followed
international rules in the Arctic, and, given the size of its territory,
will no doubt gain from this strategy in the long run. Compared
with that of Russia's other border areas, the history of the Arctic
is relatively peaceful. In the frozen north, conflicts are resolved
by law rather than by weapons, even though it might take time.
In 2010, Norway and Russia finally agreed on a boundary line in
the so-called Grey Zone in the Barents Sea. Negotiations had been
going on for forty years and ended with both countries getting
equal portions of the disputed maritime area.

Three days at sea were all that was left between us and
Murmansk. The Barents Sea had a kick to it, and, again, many
were missing from the dinner table. Peter was quieter than usual,
not because of seasickness, but because ice made it impossible to
visit Novaya Zemlya, the archipelago where the Soviet authorities
had a nuclear test site during the Cold War.

"Do you think there's an airport there?" he eventually asked me.

"I have no idea," I said. "You could ask the Russian park rangers."

The whole of Franz Josef Land is a protected nature reserve,
and all tourists are accompanied by Russian rangers. Two of them
had hitched a lift with us back to Murmansk. The season was
over and they were going home.

Peter nodded enthusiastically and almost dragged me over to
the wardens' table, so that I could translate.

"The airport is used only by the military," Nikolay, the older of the two, informed us. "But they are planning to build a hotel at the northern end, so in a few years' time I'm sure it will be possible to get there in some way or another. There's no point in building a hotel if there are no guests."

Peter lit up and put a reminder in his densely written notebook: *Novaya Zemlya 2020?*

Our four weeks in the Arctic were coming to an end. Four weeks without mobile coverage, without Internet, without any outside contact. No emails to answer, no Trump tweets to get exercised about, no Norwegian election campaign, no Facebook updates or pointless discussions to follow; the ship and its small universe were all that existed. Travelling must have been like that in the past; when you were away, you were away, and home was nothing more than a memory, a parallel world, out of reach – unlike now, when it is always in your pocket.

My long journey along Russia's border had started two years earlier in a similar news vacuum in North Korea, also on a group trip. Now, more than sixty thousand kilometres later, I was at the end of my journey. Since I left school, I have been drawn to Russia, to its culture, literature, history and language, and, not least, to the people, the so-called Russian *dusha*, the Russian soul, and I have spent many years of my life trying to understand the vast country and the people who live there. This time I had taken a different approach: is it possible to understand a country and its people from the outside, from the perspective of its neighbours, or, as now, from on board a ship?

A border is both very real and highly abstract. In the course of the four weeks at sea, we had crossed Russia's maritime border many times; we had moved in and out of Russian territorial and international waters, back and forth across dotted lines that were visible only on the captain's sea charts and G.P.S. The Russian border guards had to be alerted at least four hours in advance of whenever we crossed the invisible line. The border did not actually exist, and yet it was an absolute and awkward reality.

The same is not true of borders on land. They are often very real, watched by cameras, protected by fences, a no-man's-land with buffer zones where it is forbidden to loiter. The father of Norwegian social anthropology, Fredrik Barth, developed a famous theory based on the idea that you can only see yourself, your people and your culture in relation to "the other". It is at the border and in relation to the unknown that identity and cultural differences arise.

Russians often claim that they are neither European nor Asian, nor anything in between; they are *Russians*. The argument is often presented as self-evident, with something akin to smugness, as though Russia were a world in its own right. But, naturally, Russia does not exist in a vacuum. The gigantic country is surrounded by neighbours on every side, except for here in the north; some are big and powerful, like China, others small and wilful like North Korea and Georgia. Has Russia, past and present, been shaped by these neighbours?

If the answer is yes, then the same must be true of the neighbouring countries: just as large parts of Russia have been created by its borders, the neighbouring countries have also been shaped and worn by their geographical proximity to the great country in the north and east.

On a globe, countries are neatly defined, often in different colours, like pieces in a puzzle. In reality, the land mass is continuous: there are no borders in nature, just transitions. It is people who have divided the world up into different colours, separated by lines on the map. Some of these stretches are so new that border agreements have not yet been completed – for example, the border between Estonia and Russia has still not been ratified.

Other borders have been, but are dissolving, as is the case in Eastern Ukraine, where no-one knows any longer where Russia ends and independent Ukraine starts.

The history of Russia's border is the history of modern Russia, with all its new neighbours, but it is also the history of how Russia came into being and, of course, what Russia is. It remains to be seen whether it is also the history of Russia's future. When I started to dream about following the Russian border three and half years ago, Putin was still in favour, the 2008 war with Georgia had been forgiven, if not forgotten, and the Winter Olympics in Sochi were about to begin. A few weeks later, Russia annexed the Crimean Peninsula and soon after war broke out with Eastern Ukraine. The Russian border had moved again.

The border to the north may also move, depending on what the U.N. decides. In contrast to the gun-toting separatists in Ukraine, their only concern is that the legal conditions be correctly interpreted. For the moment, continental shelves and underwater conditions trump political agitation and mindless nationalism.

The pensioners on board the *Akademik Shokalskiy* slept more than usual in those final days. And the Russian choir reached new heights in the evening. One afternoon, we got company. We were suddenly surrounded by hundreds of harp seals and minke whales. I snapped hundreds of pictures with frozen fingers, and none of them were any good. In the end, I put my camera away and simply enjoyed watching the playful seals and waving flukes of the whales.

Sea and sky, that was all there was. The Arctic summer light shifted from white to grey to golden. In the evening, the sky was streaked with pinkish-purple wisps. Each day was like the last, even though we were never in the same place. It felt as though we were standing still; we kept to the same cabins, the same tables, the same chairs, and so the days rolled into one another.

Time stopped and yet passed too quickly, and suddenly we were at the end.

On the final evening, Anatoly sat hunched over his iPhone calculator with a concentrated expression on his face.

"Four hundred and fifty thousand steps," he said, triumphantly. "Has anyone done more?"

The colour drained from his cheeks moments later when he discovered that he had forgotten to turn on the sound when recording videos, and that he therefore had hours of silent footage from the voyage through the Northeast Passage.

Peter was, as always, thinking about his future travel. He was already far advanced in his plans for 2019 when Murmansk appeared in the distance. Monstrous, dirty-grey apartment blocks towered up on the horizon. After four weeks when abandoned weather stations had been the only sign of human civilisation, the buildings were almost overwhelming.

My mobile phone started to vibrate angrily.

We had arrived.

ASIA

"Although we now live in separate countries and speak different languages, you couldn't mistake us for anyone else. We're easy to spot! People who have come out of socialism, are both like and unlike the rest of humanity – we have our own lexicon, our own conceptions of good and evil, our heroes and martyrs."

Svetlana Alexievich

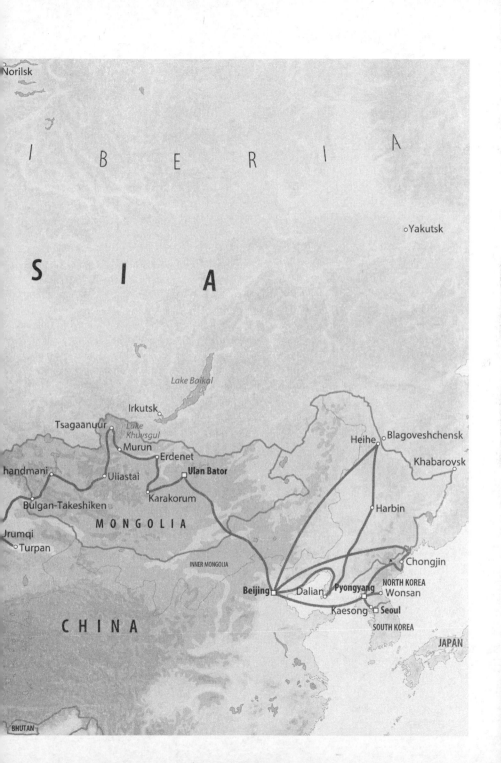

Map of North and South Korea

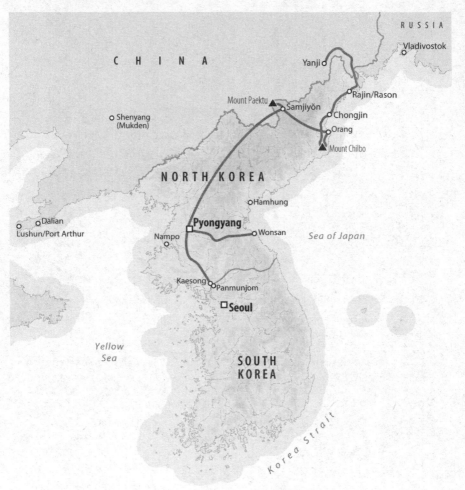

RUSSIA

Vladivostok

C H I N A

Yanji

Rajin/Rason

Mount Paektu   Samjiyŏn

Chongjin

Shenyang
(Mukden)

Orang

Mount Chilbo

N O R T H   K O R E A

Hamhung

Dalian

Pyongyang

Lushun/Port Arthur

Nampo

Wonsan   Sea of Japan

Kaesong

Panmunjom

Seoul

Yellow
Sea

SOUTH
KOREA

Korea Strait

The Art of Bowing without Bowing Down

From the viewing platform, we could look into both China and Russia without any hindrance. On the Russian side, there was nothing. No fence, no watchtower, no houses or fields, just a rusty railway bridge and a hazy, flat landscape. The Tyumen River, which marks the border between North Korea and Russia, is neither particularly deep nor particularly wide. It looked as though it might even be possible to wade to the other side.

The North Korean border with Russia is the shortest of them all, barely nineteen kilometres, and yet there are few countries on which Russia has had greater impact, albeit indirectly, than North Korea. Kim Jong-un would not have been a dictator today had it not been for Stalin. Korea was under Japanese rule from 1910 until the Second World War. In 1945, the peninsula was divided by the U.S.A. and the Soviet Union. Stalin needed a loyal, local leader in the new satellite state, and his choice was Kim Il-sung, who had spent the war years in a Soviet military camp. However, Kim Il-sung proved to be anything but an obedient puppet for Moscow. Instead of following Soviet policies, he and his successors have gone their own way. The Kim family has developed into a dynasty of brutal autocrats, with a personality cult unlike any other in modern times. The Kims have become god kings in the bizarre, insulated bubble that is this backward country.

The bus driver set off for the Chinese border; a two-week group tour of the world's worst dictatorship was coming to an end. I had been allowed in under the guise of being a tourist; I had said I worked as a secretary in the family meat business. Getting a press visa for North Korea is a long and time-consuming process, and journalists are, as a rule, only allowed to visit Pyongyang. I wanted to see as much as possible.

Thanks to the packed and well-choreographed itinerary of the Korean Tourist Company, a North Korean government agency, I had certainly seen a lot. I had been up and down to the north and south, had visited revolutionary museums, inspected enormous statues, watched school performances by the score and had travelled to places and towns that had only recently been opened to tourism. Even though everything we were shown had been carefully curated, and the guides had never been more than a few metres away, this staging had itself been revealing at times. And sometimes it came apart at the seams. The further away we got from Pyongyang, the more visible the cracks became.

But now the only thing we had left to do was to reclaim our passports from Miss Ri, who had gathered them up two weeks earlier, and leave the bubble.

"First of all, let me wish you a warm welcome to Korea!" said the young woman who had taken up position at the front of the bus. "My name is Miss Ri, and I will be your guide in Pyongyang. Mr Kim," here she nodded at a serious, middle-aged man, "my colleague, will be working with me. If you have any questions, please ask Mr Kim or myself."

Miss Ri then proceeded to list all the things we could not do, smiling all the while: "You must not take photographs of people without asking permission, and you must never, under any circumstances, photograph soldiers. If you want to take pictures of statues of Kim Il-sung or Kim Jong-il, be sure to take the whole statue, not just parts of it. If we say that you cannot take pictures of something, then you cannot take pictures, is that understood? To be on the safe side, it is always best to ask us first. Mr Kim and I will always be nearby. Please have your passports to hand, as I will come down the bus now to collect them."

She laughed when she saw the faces of some of the tourists, even though she must have seen the same reaction a hundred times before. "Please do not worry, they will be returned to you when you leave. But as long as you are in Korea, it is best that I look after them. You may lose them and then we would have all sorts of problems."

A couple of tourists made a feeble attempt to protest, but Miss Ri ignored them and snapped up their passports with a smile. The roads we drove along from the airport into Pyongyang were dark and deserted. At regular intervals, we passed gigantic portraits of Kim Il-sung and his son, Kim Jong-il, North Korea's first leaders. The two despots quite literally lit up the night. Otherwise, everything was dark, but not as devoid of people as I had at first thought. People walked and cycled in the dark, armed with torches that cast weak beams of light onto the pavements. There were people everywhere, if one just looked.

"You must not go out alone," Miss Ri warned us. "Koreans are not used to foreigners and they do not speak English; if you venture out on your own, you may end up in trouble. If you would like to get some air when the day's programme is finished, you can go for a walk in the parking lot outside the hotel. But there is no need to worry, you will not be bored, as there is plenty to do in the hotel!"

I guessed from the wide boulevards and tall buildings with no lights in the windows that we were already in the city centre. To the right lay a large, open square. There were rows and rows of seated children on the ground; there must have been thousands of them. All were wearing white shirts and navy blue trousers or skirts, and they were all sitting there quietly in the dark.

"They are practising for Party Foundation Day on October 10," Miss Ri told us.

"Can we take a photograph?" asked one of the group.

Miss Ri nodded. There was a frenzy of clicking on mobile phones and cameras.

"Oh, and please remember to change your clocks," Miss Ri said. "In August, only a few weeks ago, we got our own time back, so we are no longer in the same time zone as the Japanese imperialists. The time is now 20.55, Korean time, half an hour ahead of China."

The hotel where we were going to stay lay very handily on a peninsula in the middle of the Taedong River, which splits Pyongyang in two. If anyone did dare to break the rules and go out into town alone, they would first have to sneak unnoticed over the wide, empty bridge that led into the centre.

"The four-star hotel has forty-seven floors and a total of a thousand rooms. There is a restaurant on the top floor that turns round and round!" Miss Ri told us with great enthusiasm as we swung into the car park, which was packed with tourist buses. We were then led into the hotel lobby and eventually into an enormous dining room, where we were served fish, luke-warm rice and North Korean beer. I had a couple of mouthfuls before I staggered over to the lift, ready to drop after nearly forty-eight hours of travel.

The hotel room was decorated in various shades of brown and there was a strong smell of mould and damp. Only one of the lights worked, a wobbly steel lamp with a crooked shade. A small legion of mosquitoes and moths swarmed below the ceiling. I stood and looked down at the city for a short while. Apart from the odd monument here and there that was illuminated, the city of more than a million lay in the dark. It felt as though I was in a war zone in blackout. Out of habit, I checked my mobile phone, but there was no coverage, naturally. In theory it was possible to buy a local SIM card, but it cost 120 dollars, included only twenty text messages and was blocked for calls to North Korean numbers. For an extra ninety dollars, fifty megabytes were added for surfing on the Internet.

I set my mobile to airplane mode, and put it away.

The next day, I was woken at six o'clock sharp by Miss Ri's wake-up call. The day's itinerary was breathtaking, a conscious strategy on the part of the tourism department: if tourists do not have freedom of movement, they have to be kept busy from early morning to late evening. Not a free moment. No empty spaces. No breaks along the way. Total exhaustion.

"I apologise for the poor state of the roads," Miss Ri said from her place at the front of the bus. "Would you like me to sing a traditional Korean song for you?"

She had a beautiful voice, pitch perfect and clear, but the P.A. system on the bus did not do it justice.

Once we were out of the city centre, we had the wide, bumpy, concrete road to ourselves. We passed rice paddies, fields of maize, and, every so often, a small cluster of houses. The few people we saw were either on bicycles or on foot, or squatting by the side of the road, armed with scissors and trowels. There was a narrow bed of pink, purple and white flowers by the verge, on both sides of the road.

Two hours and 170 kilometres later we came to some lush, rolling hills.

"It is no coincidence that the museums are here," Miss Ri said. "Kim Jong-il chose this place specifically because of the beautiful surroundings."

A visit to the International Friendship Exhibition is part of the standard package; no tourist can avoid it. More than two hundred thousand gifts from well-wishers at home and abroad, spread over more than one hundred and fifty rooms. Originally there was only one museum building, but as the number of gifts increased, the authorities realised that they would have to build another, a mirror image of the first, to house them all.

Two massive bronze doors opened into a dark, marble hall. A beautiful young woman in a traditional long silk dress led us down a long corridor. On the walls were framed pictures of all the flowers and animals that Kim Il-sung had been given as gifts over the years. Partly out of politeness, and partly out of curiosity, we stopped to admire each picture, much to the irritation of the young lady, who eventually gave us a long speech in Korean.

This was translated by Miss Ri as: "Hurry, hurry!"

We were whisked from one room to the next, each bigger and grander than the one before. The gifts, which varied from watches and cameras to barbecue sets, Karl Marx coffee cups and dusty books, were all presented in glass cases, sorted by country, with the sender's name carefully noted. Every time we entered a new hall, Miss Ri shouted out the countries that she thought might be relevant to the group: "Switzerland!" "Belgium!" "Sweden!" "Italy!" "Great Britain!" It felt a bit like the Eurovision Song Contest. Norway was also represented: the communist party in Østfold had been particularly generous. The glass cases were largely filled with gifts from marginal communist party branches and friendship associations, rarely from governments or heads of state. I assumed that the exhibits were primarily intended for a home audience, an assumption that was bolstered by the many groups of North Koreans that marched past us at regular intervals.

When we walked over to the new wing, the museum guide took the opportunity to put some questions to Heinrich, the only German in the group. I was right behind them, so overheard what was said.

"What do you think of our museum?" Miss Ri translated.

"Very big and very impressive," was his diplomatic answer. The guide nodded, obviously pleased.

"Do you have similar museums in Germany?" she asked.

"No, we don't," Heinrich said.

The young woman smiled.

"Do you have historical museums in Germany?" she said.

"Yes, we do," Heinrich replied.

"Oh." The museum guide sounded disappointed. "I didn't think you had historical museums in Germany," she said quietly.

One of the main attractions in the new wing was the airplane that the Communist Party of the Soviet Union gave to Kim Il-sung in 1958. The impressive gift exemplified the warm but unequal relationship between the Soviet Union and North Korea. No country gave North Korea more economic and technical support than the Soviet Union during the Cold War. Over a forty-year period, Soviet experts built about seventy large factories in the country, and in 1990 Soviet-built power stations accounted for seventy per cent of North Korea's electricity. Even though it behaved like an independent country, North Korea was in fact a Soviet satellite state.

One by one, we climbed up the narrow steps and peered in at the green sofas in the cabin. But the absolute highpoint was saved until last.

Miss Ri ordered us to form two queues, and we did as we were told. The silent, ever-watchful Mr Kim inspected each one of us carefully. What he saw did not please him.

"You cannot have your arms crossed," Miss Ri said. "It is disrespectful."

Mr Kim pointed at one of the Belgian tourists.

"You cannot have your sweater tied around your waist," Miss Ri said. "It is disrespectful. Put your sweater on. And you cannot keep your sunglasses on your head. Please put them in your pocket. Is anyone chewing gum?"

A Spaniard sheepishly put up his hand. Miss Ri pulled a paper napkin from her bag and did away with the disrespectful sub-stance. Only when we were deemed to be radiating the necessary respect were we allowed into a dimly lit room. At the far end, a life-size wax figure of a smiling Kim Il-sung stood in a meadow of artificial flowers. Solemn music played in the background. We were asked to stand in a line and to bow deeply. I could not bring myself to bow to a dictator, so remained straight-backed, as did the French members of the group. Mr Kim sent us a disapproving look, but said nothing. Then we moved on to the next room, where we were met by a smiling Kim Jong-il, who was also full size. He was standing on North Korea's holy Paektu Mountain; the famous blue lake glittered in the background. Finally we were ushered into the room of Kim Jong-suk, Kim Il-sung's wife and Kim Jong-il's mother, North Korea's answer to the Virgin Mary.

The wax figures in the Friendship Exhibition were the support act. The following day was North Korea's national day, and we were going to visit the holiest of holies.

The travelator proceeded slowly down the grey marble corridor in Kumsusan, the Palace of the Sun, in Pyongyang. Walking was not permitted; it was *meant* to take time. The walls were decorated with photographs from the ever-smiling Kim Il-sung's eventful life. A long line of North Koreans, standing four abreast, rolled towards us on the other side of the corridor, the men in stiff uniforms, the women in long, colourful silk dresses. None of them appeared to even notice the hotchpotch group of European and American tourists who had at least tried to dress up. As the Koreans passed, I saw that they were looking at us discreetly, even if their heads did not move.

When we had been transported a long way and then some, we came to an escalator. Slowly we rose up into an enormous hall. Two huge wax statues of Kim Il-sung and Kim Jong-il dominated the space. We were again instructed to form a neat line and to bow in front of the statues. We then had to file through a dust-blowing machine to remove any dust, dead skin and loose hairs before stepping, pure and clean, into a hall that was bathed in red light. Sombre horn music poured out from the loudspeakers. The Eternal President lay in state in a glass sarcophagus in the middle of the room. His body was covered by a red cloth and only his suit-covered shoulders and head were visible. His features were stiff and plastic-looking. Even in the intense, deep red light, the Eternal President's skin looked yellow and wan.

There was a long queue to see the body, and we were taken round the sarcophagus at a brisk pace. We were told to bow three times, once on each side, and once by his head, but not, at any cost, by his feet. The Koreans who were behind us bowed so deeply that their heads almost touched their knees. We were then taken into a room where we could admire Kim Il-sung's 144 medals, a striking number of which were from Arabic or African countries. From here we were fed onto an escalator that took us down to another slow travelator, flanked by photographs of a smirking Kim Jong-il. We eventually came to another dust-blowing machine and another hall bathed in red light. In the middle lay Kim Jong-il, who, unlike his father, looked frighteningly alive; his face had a healthy brown hue, and in many ways the lame dictator who suffered from diabetes looked better in death than in life. The art of embalmment had clearly developed and improved from when Kim Il-sung died in 1994 to when his son was laid to rest in 2011.

The bright sun blinded us when we were released into the daylight again. It was almost thirty degrees in the shade and my clothes stuck to my skin.

"Boys and girls, we have to move on!" Miss Ri called, with an enthusiastic clap. "We can't be late for the traditional dance."

Hundreds of dressed-up university students were waiting in Kim Il-sung Square, ready to dance. Group dancing is a North Korean speciality. The men were wearing suits, white shirts and red ties, and the women were dressed in the traditional long silk dresses. These are cone-shaped, almost doll-like, and come in all possible colours: bright yellow, pastel pink, mint green, sky blue. In other words, the square was a colourful sight.

"Find a space on the steps and please join in the dance if you feel like it," the smiling Miss Ri said.

The steps were already packed with tourists from other groups. The students danced energetically for an hour in various circle formations. When I later looked through the hundreds of photographs I had taken of the show, I discovered that none of the dancers were smiling. They all stared straight ahead as the sweat formed on their brows in the heat.

Pyongyang means "flat country" or "peaceful country", and the first meaning could not be more appropriate: the North Korean capital is located on a flat steppe, which is divided by the Taedong River. Most of the apartment blocks are from the 1960s, when the country was rebuilt at top speed following the war with South Korea in the 1950s. Millions of people needed somewhere to live. The result was cheap but functional housing blocks, twenty to thirty storeys high. Most of the blocks have lifts, but many are permanently out of order. Even when they do work, few people risk using them as power cuts are a regular occurrence. The de-mand for flats in the lower storeys is therefore huge and a large proportion of Pyongyang's elderly are in effect imprisoned in their flats. There is often no water in the top flats, which is why many of them stand empty.

The futuristic Ryugyong Hotel, North Korea's tallest building, towers over the centre of the city. It looks like a pyramid crossed with a rocket. Building started in 1987, and the hotel was supposed to have 105 storeys and 3,000 rooms. It was estimated that construction would take two years. In 1992, the North Korean economy collapsed in the wake of the dissolution of the Soviet Union, and construction work came to a halt. As the framework was com-plete, it stood like an empty shell in the centre of the city for sixteen years. Work did not start again until 2008, and in 2011 the exterior, which is largely blue glass, was completed. The intention was that the hotel would be opened in 2012, on the centenary of Kim Il-sung's birth, but that did not happen. There was then a rumour that the luxury hotel chain Kempinski was going to take over the building, but neither the partial opening nor the Kempinski plans materialised. At 330 metres, the Ryugyong is currently the world's tallest, unoccupied hotel.

A grey polluted sky hung low over Pyongyang the week that I was there; it was like a morning mist that never lifted. Even though many of the concrete apartment blocks were painted in cheerful colours, the mist and greyness drained them of any joy. In several places, building was under way on new projects, but for the most part people appeared to spend a lot of time standing around. Every day we saw large gatherings of people from the bus windows; nearly every square in the city seemed to be full of people in white shirts who were either standing in carefully thought-out formations, often with flags or pompoms in their hands, or sitting idly on the ground waiting for things to get started. Pupils, students, workers. Whenever I asked Miss Ri what they were doing, I always got the same answer: "They are practising for the celebrations to mark the anniversary of the party's foundation on October 10."

Then there were all the men in brown uniforms. They were

everywhere. They cycled, marched, controlled parades, and sat in the back seats of polished Mercedes. Who were they? Party members? High-ranking military personnel? It seemed that fashion had stopped sometime in the Fifties. The men who were not dressed in brown uniforms generally wore dark trousers and light cotton shirts, and the women had on knee-length skirts, light-coloured blouses, perhaps a matching cardigan or blazer, and heeled court shoes. They all had a red badge on their chest, with a portrait of Kim Il-sung or Kim Jong-il on it, or both.

Pyongyang is the country's showcase, and access to the city is strictly regulated. Even though egalitarianism is at the heart of communism, the North Korean authorities have never been particularly concerned about equality. On the contrary. At the end of the 1950s, Kim Il-sung devised *songbun*, an ingenious hierarchy or caste system that places everyone in the country in one of three main categories: "the core" or the loyal class, reserved for those who supported him actively during the fight for liberation, took part in the resistance against the Japanese imperialists or distinguished themselves during the Korean War. The greater part of the population belong to "the wavering" class and have to be watched carefully; lastly, there is "the hostile" class. These three main classes are then divided into more than fifty subcategories. Seven thousand bureaucrats and party members were given the task of investigating every citizen's family background in order to determine their *songbun*. This work was completed in 1965, and, since then, the individual's *songbun* has been inherited through the father's line. A person's *songbun* determines what kind of house they live in, their food rations, which schools and jobs he or she can access, and their access to medical treatment and even shops. Pyongyang, for example, is largely reserved for people from "the core", and a few "waverers", who all provide services for "the core". If a person flees the country or breaks any of the rigid regulations, this breach will not only affect him and his own *songbun*, but also that of his family, including future generations.

On our tours of Pyongyang, we came so close to the city's inhabitants that we could have reached out and touched them. Some young people smiled and waved at us in the buses, but, as a rule, only eyes turned discreetly in our direction. What did they think of their country and leaders? What did they actually know of the world beyond? Never have I found it so hard to get under the surface of a place. We moved around the same city as them, we walked the same streets, breathed the same polluted air, but we might as well have been visiting a zoo. Look, but do not touch. Here, but no further. One of the more absurd highlights of the trip was therefore a visit to the metro. Pyongyang metro opened in 1973 and has two lines and sixteen stations. The tracks are some of the deepest in the world, 110 metres underground, and the stations double up as nuclear bunkers. Until recently, tourists were only allowed to visit two of the stations. We went to six.

The stations were all clean and ornate. Massive chandeliers hung from the ceilings and the walls were decorated with colourful murals of happy workers and gigantic portraits of the ever-smiling Kim Il-sung. Even when there was a power cut, his portrait was illuminated. The day's newspapers were displayed in glass cases on the platforms and lots of passengers used the waiting time to catch up on Kim Jong-un's latest achievements.

The green and red carriages, with leather seats along the sides, brought back memories from Berlin, which is perhaps not so strange, as the carriages came from there. The graffiti has been removed and replaced by photographs of the two deceased leaders.

Four guards in stiff uniforms made sure that the passengers and trains moved as they should, and gave the signal when the trains were ready to leave. There was not much room inside the carriages. For the first time on the trip, I found myself close to ordinary people. Some stared, but mostly they kept their eyes on the floor. The others from the group were standing further down the carriage and for a moment I pretended that I was there on my own.

It is possible to visit North Korea alone, on a so-called individual tour, but even those who pay to travel without a group are accompanied by two guides from morning to night, and follow the same daily regime as group tours. This extreme control of tourism means that travelogues from North Korea are often very similar, as everyone experiences more or less the same things and is escorted by guides who have practised the same speeches. I am neither the first nor the last writer to travel to North Korea under false pretences, but most of the other tourists in the group were just that: tourists.

So who are these people who are willing to pay for a holiday in the world's worst dictatorship? None of the twenty people in the group was the typical package-holiday type, and yet a surprising number of them had chosen to travel in North Korea precisely because the tour was organised. They preferred group travel, ideally to unusual places. Many of them lived and travelled alone, and in the group they could never be lonely. I would guess that about half of them had chosen North Korea as a destination because they were drawn to the aesthetics of the dictatorship; they were quite simply fascinated by the iron discipline, the shameless propaganda and the displays put on for us.

Everything we saw was staged, even the people. On the metro, when I was hemmed in by bodies, I was still a member of the audience, and the Koreans were involuntary extras in a carefully staged show.

When we reached the end station, we took the escalators up to the grey mist. The coal dust stung my nose and throat with every new breath. An unusually large crowd of people had gathered on the other side of the road, both adults and children, all in white shirts. They stood in different formations and shouted slogans as they moved rhythmically. There must have been thousands of them.

"What are they doing?" I asked.

"They are practising for the celebrations to mark the founding of the party on October 10," Miss Ri said.

Some years before, when I had travelled in Turkmenistan, which is sometimes called the North Korea of Central Asia, I was surprised by how open some of the guides were. Several of them had strong opinions about the regime and nothing but disdain for Turkmenbashi, who had ruled the country like a sun king from the break-up of the Soviet Union until he died in 2006. Miss Ri, on the other hand, never lost her composure. Not once did she let her mask slip. If there was a question she did not want to answer, she giggled, put her hand to her mouth and said: "I don't know."

"How much does an ordinary Korean earn per month?" I asked as we walked down the wide street.

Miss Ri giggled and put her hand to her mouth. "I don't know."

"Well, what is the average wage then?" I persisted.

Miss Ri laughed. "I don't know. I really don't. I guess it varies."

"Is there a minimum wage?"

"I don't know." She giggled. "I have no idea what other people earn."

I was not going to give up. "How much do guides earn, then, for example?"

Miss Ri tittered. "I don't actually know."

"You don't know how much you earn?"

"I have no idea, Miss Erika! I really don't! But most people do not earn very much, because we get everything we need from the state. Jobs, flats, even clothes."

"What about mobile phones, do you get them from the state

as well?" I asked. I had noted that lots of Koreans, including Miss Ri and Mr Kim, had fancy Chinese mobiles. North Korea started to allow mobile telephone services in 2008 and already had more than three million contracts.

Miss Ri shook her head. "We have to buy our own mobile phones."

"How much does a mobile cost?"

"I don't know, Miss Erika. I really don't know."

North Korea is not only the world's most authoritarian regime, it is also the most corrupt. For the past twenty years, the country has lain at the bottom of Transparency International's Corruption Perception Index and it is decades since North Korea was governed according to purely socialist principles, if that was ever the case.

As already mentioned, the break-up of the Soviet Union in 1991 caused a major economic crisis in North Korea. The governing authorities in Russia had more than enough to deal with at home in the 1990s – North Korea was not high on their list of priorities. The generous financial support, camouflaged as loans, suddenly dried up. When Kim Il-sung died in 1994, the regime no longer had the wherewithal to feed the population. Nor were they able to do anything to curtail the catastrophe. According to the North Korean authorities, 220,000 people died from starvation, which is a high figure, but foreign experts believe that the number of deaths was even greater – perhaps as many as three million people starved to death. The famine at the end of the 1990s changed North Korea for ever. People learned that they could not rely on the state to look after them, and started to take measures them- selves. A grass roots economy developed alongside the socialist system, led by women, who were not obliged to work for the regime to the same extent as men. Housewives and grandmothers sold whatever they could in order to put food on the table. When the famine started to ease, many women continued to buy and sell on the black market to supplement the family finances – not unlike the extensive black market that developed in the Soviet Union after Stalin's death.

In 2009, Kim Jong-il made an abortive attempt to break the parallel economy once and for all. On November 30, it was announced that two zeros would be struck from all banknotes: with a stroke of a brush, 10,000 won became 100 won. The exchange limit was initially set at 100,000 won per person, equivalent to 30–40 dollars, but this was then raised to 150,000 won in cash and 300,000 in bank deposits, which is still an absurdly low amount, even by North Korean standards. Many people lost all their savings overnight and the country was thrown into financial crisis. To make the chaos complete, it was decided that pay for employees in state factories and institutions would remain the same, so a worker who previously earned 4,000 won should still be paid 4,000 won, but food prices would be adjusted to the new won. A kilo of rice that had previously cost about 2,000 won would now cost 22 won. In practice, this meant that the country's millions of state employees got a ten thousand per cent pay rise. The result was galloping inflation, and very soon the new won was worth as little as the old. The regime has not attempted any currency revaluations since, and the illegal market economy is now tacitly accepted. It has become so usual to supplement official earnings with money from illegal market trade that the authorities are suspicious of families where *no-one* is involved in this kind of business.

The regime has gone to great lengths beyond the country's borders to supply its pleasure-seeking elite with currency and luxury goods. For decades, North Korean embassies have carried out illegal activities, such as the sale of alcohol in Muslim countries and the smuggling of ivory and drugs. There was a high turnover in spirits and cigarettes at the North Korean embassy in Oslo before it was closed down in 1994. In a Congressional Research Service report in 2008, American researchers estimated that approximately a third of North Korea's export revenue came from illegal activities of this sort. Following Kim Jong-il's death in 2011, the import of luxury goods has more than doubled, despite the import restrictions introduced by the U.N. in 2006 following the country's first nuclear weapons test.

Money and income were obviously on the guides' list of taboos. When it came to questions about family life, however, Miss Ri's answers were far more illuminating.

"When do people normally get married?" I asked.

"Women are usually between twenty-six and twenty-eight when they get married, and men are between twenty-eight and thirty," Miss Ri said. Her answer was in line with Kim Il-sung's "special instruction" in 1971, when he urged men to delay marriage until they were thirty and women until they were twenty-eight, so that they could serve the motherland first.

"How many children do people normally have?"

"One or two."

"Are arranged marriages or marriages for love more usual?"

"Marriages were arranged before, but now love marriages are more usual," Miss Ri said. "Young people decide for themselves."

"Can you marry who you want, regardless of status?"

"Yes."

"Is it possible to live together without getting married?"

"No."

"Is it easy to get a divorce?"

"It's not usual here," Miss Ri said. "When you get married, you are expected to get married for life. Family is very important to us Koreans."

"What happens if a woman has a child without being married?"

Miss Ri giggled.

"I don't know. I have never heard of that happening."

"Never?"

She shook her head.

"Is abortion legal?"

"Abortion?" Miss Ri clearly did not understand.

"When you terminate a pregnancy."

"Yes, of course it is legal," she said. "You go to hospital to have it done. It is quite usual. How do you spell abortion?"

I spelled it out for her, and she memorised it. Then she smiled at me. "I have learnt a new word now. Thank you!"

Great Leaders

"On April 15, 1912, the great leader Kim Il-sung was born in this house," the museum guide said with great reverence, and pointed at one of the simple, straw-roofed houses that had been seriously renovated. We could see into the small houses through the open doors and windows. A number of household goods, apparently original, were exhibited on the bare floor. The paths between the houses were cobbled and flanked by flowers; everything was so quaint and pristine that it was hard to imagine that anyone had ever lived there.

Kim Il-sung came into the world on the same day that the Titanic sank, two years after the Japanese had colonised the Korean peninsula. He was born in the village of Mangyongdae, outside Pyongyang. His parents, who were both Christians and active in the church, were neither rich nor poor. They christened their first-born son Kim Song-ju. He took the name Il-sung, which means "rising sun", when he was fighting in the Korean resistance. In about 1920, the family fled to Manchuria in northern China. The Japanese regime in Korea was brutal. Any opposition was severely punished, and people were sentenced to hard labour; the Korean language was forbidden and Koreans were forced to take Japanese names. Hundreds of thousands of Koreans therefore fled to northern China, and while some only fled so they could get food, others went to join the fight against the Japanese colonial regime they so despised.

In Manchuria, Kim Il-sung went to a Chinese school and quickly became fluent in Chinese. In 1931, when he was nineteen, he joined the Chinese Communist Party and became actively involved in the guerrilla war against the Japanese in northern China. He rose swiftly through the ranks and was given responsibility for a battalion just shy of two hundred men. In June 1937, he had his greatest military success when his battalion managed to seize within a few hours Pochonbo, a small, Japanese-occupied town on the border between China and Korea. The Japanese did what they could to stamp out the Korean resistance; in the years that followed, many of the guerrilla soldiers in Kim Il-sung's battalion were traced and killed. In 1940, Kim crossed the Amur River with the remaining soldiers and fled to the Soviet Union. The Soviet authorities took charge of the Korean soldiers and sent them to a military base near Khabarovsk for further training.

On August 8, 1945, the Soviet Union declared war on Japan. One week later, on the same day that Japan capitulated, the Red Army marched into Pyongyang, having met almost no resistance along the way. North Korean schoolchildren are taught that Kim Il-sung and his troops drove the Japanese from Korea more or less single-handedly, but the truth is that Kim Il-sung did not take part in any combat in his homeland. When the Russians liberated Pyongyang, he was still in a military camp in the Soviet Union. It was only a month after Japan's capitulation that Kim Il-sung and the sixty or so soldiers who had fled with him sailed to the port town of Wonsan on the Soviet ship *Pugachev*. On September 19, they landed on Korean soil, still dressed in Soviet uniforms, and went to eat noodles and drink beer in a local restaurant.

Already, then, the fate of the Korean peninsula was sealed. Shortly after Japan's capitulation, it was divided in two along the 38th parallel. Soviet forces kept control of the north, and the Americans were given control of the south. Stalin needed a lackey to run his half, and his choice was the thirty-three-year-old

Kim Il-sung. Kim was selected because he spoke good Russian and because he had had no contact with the somewhat nationalistic communists in Korea, as he had lived elsewhere for most of his life. But given all those years abroad, his mother tongue was now rusty. Before Kim Il-sung could deliver his first speech to the people in October 1945, Soviet envoys had to give their protégé Korean lessons.

Three years later, on September 9, 1948, the Democratic People's Republic of Korea was officially established in Pyongyang, with Kim Il-sung as leader. Kim Il-sung remained in power until he died in 1994, almost half a century later. Not only did he outlive six Soviet general secretaries, but also the Soviet Union itself.

"And now you can drink water from Kim Il-sung's well," the museum guide told us. "Kim Il-sung himself drank water from this spring." She reverently pulled up a bucket of water. Those who wanted to could hold out their hands or bottles. A couple of people followed the example of the locals and drank straight from the communal cup that was sent round. When everyone who wanted to drink the miraculous water had done so, it was back to the bus. The next stop on our ambitious programme was the war museum, and we had, as usual, no time to lose.

The guide at the war museum, a young woman in a pristine military uniform, took us straight over to the neat rows of American tanks, airplanes, jeeps and helicopters, all trophies from the Korean War.

"In 2012, Kim Jong-un decided that a new war museum should be built, and no more than ten months later, it was ready," the guide boasted, as we walked up the wide steps that led into the museum. The building was lavish, with marble walls, thick pillars and polished surfaces. As it was only three years old, there were no signs of wear and tear. The guide pointed at maps and installations and recited information about America's defeat and Korea's victory, emphasising times, dates and figures. Hard facts, in other words. Only, nearly all that she told us was lies. It was not the Americans who attacked first – Kim Il-sung had been itching to invade South Korea from the moment he was appointed leader and had repeatedly tried to persuade Stalin to attack. But Stalin was not so keen to go to war with the U.S.A., the world's only nuclear state and South Korea's close ally. It was only when the Soviet Union also developed an atomic bomb in 1949 that Kim Il-sung managed to persuade Stalin. In spring 1950, the North Korean leader travelled to Moscow to discuss the details. He stayed there for several weeks and returned home with the following agreement: if Mao Zedong of China promised to send reinforcements should the Americans get involved, then Kim Il-sung had Stalin's permission.

North Korea attacked on June 25, 1950. Kim Il-sung had assured both Stalin and Mao that he had many supporters in the south, and that victory would therefore be swift, three days at most. Two days later, the U.N. Security Council voted to send military forces to South Korea, a resolution that was supported and followed up by the U.S.A., which also sent troops. It was the first time that the U.N. had voted to provide military assistance in a conflict, and the resolution might easily have been stopped had the Soviet Union vetoed it. The Soviet Union was currently boycotting the U.N., however, as it would not recognise Mao Zedong and the communists as China's leaders, so the Soviet representative was not present at the Security Council meeting.

U.S. and U.N. military support was relatively modest to begin with, and by August 1950 North Korean forces were in control of ninety-five per cent of South Korean territory. In mid-September, U.S. and U.N. troops started a major military offensive against the port of Incheon, close to Seoul, forcing the North Koreans to retreat. Soon after, the North Koreans were driven out of Seoul and American troops crossed the 38th parallel and advanced into North Korea. The Chinese warned the U.N. and U.S.A. against entering North Korea and, in particular, against closing in on Chinese territory. The American general Douglas MacArthur, who was leading the U.N. forces, saw the warning as a ploy to increase pressure, and firmly dismissed the possibility of Chinese military intervention, even though President Harry S. Truman had urged the general to show restraint. Within a few weeks, the North Korean troops had been as good as annihilated and U.N. forces and American soldiers had advanced far into North Korea, so close to the border with China that they became involved in skirmishes with Chinese soldiers. MacArthur wanted to cross the border into China in order to cut supplies to the North Korean army, but before he was able to do that, Mao fulfilled his threat: at the end of November, several hundred thousand Chinese soldiers joined the North Korean forces, thus tipping the balance of power again. The Soviet Union also stepped up its military assistance, but sent only airplanes, as Stalin wanted to avoid direct combat with the Americans.

Following some major battles, the front lines stabilised through spring 1951, around the 38th parallel. In April that year, President Truman relieved the bullish MacArthur of his post as supreme commander. The war continued for another two years, with fighting in the trenches and frequent bombing raids.

On July 27, 1953, the various factions signed an armistice agreement. The three-year war had cost the lives of more than three million people, most of them civilians. Among those killed was Mao's eldest son, Mao Anying. North Korea may have suffered the greatest losses, but South Korea also lay in ruins. And the border along the 38th parallel remained as good as unchanged.

In North Korean mythology, the war against South Korea has

been rewritten as a national triumph. Little mention is made of the significant contributions from the Soviet Union and China. The war is also used as a warning as to what could happen if North Korea gives up its newly acquired nuclear weapons. Many now believe that capitalists hate socialism so much that the Americans would immediately march straight into Pyongyang.

Before we hurried on to the enormous statues on Kim Il-sung Square, the next item on our itinerary, I overheard a conversation between an American woman and her guide:

"Why do you spend so much money on museums when your farmers are still digging the earth with hoes and spades?" the woman asked.

"Every country has its own farming methods," the guide said calmly. "The museum is also an important educational institution."

The border to the south was disappointingly ordinary. It took a while before I realised that the long, blue barracks were in fact built across the borderline. It is hard to know what I had expected. Barbed-wire fences? Horn music?

Six or seven North Korean soldiers stood to attention outside each barrack. There was no-one to be seen on the South Korean side. To the left of us, the South Korean flag fluttered soggily in the drizzle; Freedom House, the South Korean border building that is shaped like a modern pagoda, rose up behind the barrack. Other than that, there was only forest as far as the eye could see.

It had taken us three hours to travel 168 kilometres to the so-called demilitarised zone. The name is deceptive, because the border between North and South Korea is one of the most heavily militarised borders in the world. North and South Korea are technically still at war: the two countries have never signed a formal peace agreement. The 1953 armistice still applies, and the de facto border runs along the front lines of the war at the 38th parallel.

However, the truce has been broken a number of times and several hundred soldiers have been killed on duty in the demilitarised zone in the past few decades.

"Normally, we can go into the middle barracks to see the actual borderline," Miss Ri told us. "It is the highpoint of the trip. But not today. The barracks are closed."

"Why?" I said.

Miss Ri shrugged.

"South Korea has the key. The door was open yesterday, today it is closed. We never know why. They must be angry about something."

As there was no access to the Internet, I had no way of finding out why South Korea was angry. It was a slightly claustrophobic feeling. At home we get news from North Korea almost every day, but here, at the heart of the conflict, I was in a vacuum.

* * *

When Korea was divided by the Soviet Union and the U.S.A., one of the oldest and most ethnically homogeneous nations in the world was split in two, divided by two rival superpowers. Korea was united as one kingdom in 668, and even though dynasties came and went through the centuries, and foreign powers – gen-erally China and Japan – invaded the peninsula more than once, Korea remained one nation, one ethnic group and one territory until the end of the Second World War. When the peninsula was divided, the Soviet Union was in many ways given the better deal, as the Japanese had chosen to invest in heavy industry in the north, rather than in the more populated south, which was perceived to be an agricultural backwater. In 1945, some twenty million people lived in the south and about nine million in the north. More than one million North Koreans, primarily Christians and opponents, defected south during the first years of Kim Il-sung's reign.

South Korea still has a higher population, with more than fifty million inhabitants, which is at least twice as many as North Korea. Until the mid-1970s, the G.D.P. per capita was the same in both South and North Korea, whereas now it is about thirteen times higher in the south than in the north. Today, the countries represent two extremes: the North Korean government continues to believe in Stalin's planned economy and isolationism, and rules with an iron hand, whereas South Korea is among the world's most developed market economies. The countries are divided by political ideology – and a green belt that is four kilometres wide.

The border between North and South Korea is 250 kilometres long and protected on both sides by a two-kilometre buffer that constitutes the demilitarised zone. Access to the zone is highly regulated and there are only a few, very small settlements there. The absence of human activity has made the area a haven for many threatened animal species. Several hundred species of birds live there, including the extremely rare Japanese crane. The amur leopard, Asian black bear and almost extinct Siberian tiger have also taken sanctuary in the buffer zone. Some people say that the Korean tiger, one of the rarest tigers on the planet, is to be found in the demilitarised zone. There has been talk of making the area into a nature reserve, but these nascent initiatives from the south have been actively boycotted by the authorities in Pyongyang.

The Juche Tower is the tallest building in Pyongyang and was built in 1982 to commemorate Kim Il-sung's seventieth birthday. The 170-metre tower was apparently designed by Kim Jong-il and the structure is said to contain 25,550 granite stones, one for each day of Kim Il-sung's seventy years, not including supplementary days for leap years. At the top of the tower, above the observation deck, is a twenty-metre-high metal flame, which weighs forty-five metric tons.

Juche is the name of North Korea's state ideology, which was devised by Kim Il-sung after the Korean War. Juche can be translated as "self-reliance" and is a mixture of Marxism–Leninism, Stalinism, Maoism, Confucianism and traditional Korean social systems. The ideology made it easier for Kim Il-sung to distance himself from the Soviet Union after Stalin's death. The North Korean leader was strongly opposed to Khrushchev's liberal reforms and personally preferred Mao's uncompromising leadership style. Citing the Juche ideology, North Korea refused to become a member of Comecon, the Council for Mutual Economic Assistance, based in Moscow, the aim of which was to improve economic cooperation between communist countries. The key doctrine of Juche is self-reliance in terms of the economy, defence and politics, with no assistance or intervention from other countries. However, North Korea continued to be dependent on financial support from the Soviet Union. The North Korean regime has yet to achieve the goal of Juche, a kind of exalted independence; from its inception, the country has relied on help from outside, and still does.

Juche was launched as a "third way" to communism. In con-trast to Marxism–Leninism, Juche ideology regards the people as the driving force of history. However, the masses need a great leader, which is where Kim Il-sung comes in. In the 1980s, the heir-apparent, Kim Jong-il, removed all references to Marxism–Leninism from Juche theory and instead introduced the concept of "Kimilsungism". After his father's demise, this concept was expanded to include himself: "Kimilsungism–Kimjongilism". And thus, in the momentous year of 1991 when the Soviet Union collapsed, the authorities in Pyongyang could answer why, thanks to Juche: it was because Marxism–Leninism had not been adapted to suit local conditions, as it had been in North Korea with Juche.

Juche still permeates North Korean society at every level. A

Juche calendar has been devised that starts in 1912, or Juche 1, the
year Kim Il-sung was born. Juche is taught to all children, from
their first day at school, and at university one fifth of the students'
time is spent studying Juche, no matter what their chosen degree.

* * *

A lift took us to the observation platform at the top of the tower,
directly beneath the red metal flame. From up here, 150 metres
above ground, Pyongyang looked like a rather ordinary, slightly sad,
Asian concrete city.

"No photographs of the river!" Miss Ri shouted. "That is strictly
forbidden!"

I looked down at the brown water. All I could see was a handful of sorry riverboats.

Our allocated five days in the model capital were over. The
inhabitants of Pyongyang were well groomed and presentable,
and there was no visible poverty, but the control was absolute. The
broad, frozen smiles of the leaders were never far away. Everything
about our stay was marked by routine and control; some six
thousand Western tourists visit North Korea every year, and most
of them see only Pyongyang. Our minder, Miss Ri, never put a
foot wrong: she stuck to the script, she never slept in, she ferried
us here and there, and was always cheerful and energetic under
the ever-watchful eye of the silent Mr Kim. One morning a couple
of the tourists in our group tried to go for a short walk around
the hotel, but no sooner had they left the car park than they were
stopped by vigilant hotel staff. We were prisoners of the sightseeing
programme. Bussed back and forth at breathtaking speed, we were
always rushing on to the next place, and when evening came, we
were ready to collapse. On a couple of occasions, I thought it looked
as though someone had rummaged through my suitcase while I
was out, but I could not be sure; everything seemed to be where I

had left it. But if that were so, what were they looking for? Did they suspect that I was not a receptionist for the family meat business? It would have been easy enough to find out – a quick Google search would have been enough. Even the chambermaids worked in pairs, like the guides. They were watching each other.

A Sensitive Matter

The morning shift arrived at the airport at the same time as us. Long lines of workers dressed in blue overalls, marching in time, ready for the fight. At the front walked a man waving a large red flag. Orange sparks from welding torches rained down on workers in blue overalls already dangling from the roof. The new main terminal, built in true dictator style, was so new that it was not yet finished. Everything was shining white and clean, but a disloyal, pervasive smell of damp, mould and solvents betrayed the fact that the materials were not of the best quality.

There were six departures that day: three to Beijing, one to Zhengzhou, one to Vladivostok and one to Samjiyŏn – our charter plane. The only people at the airport other than us were wealthy North Koreans, the chosen few who had their papers in order and enough money to leave the country. A gigantic globe dominated the centre of the departure hall, a reminder that the world is, after all, big.

The tiny Air Koryo propeller plane was of the old-fashioned kind, with curtains and open luggage racks. We could sit wherever we liked, and no fuss was made about seat belts, emergency exits or oxygen masks. From the window, we could see the vibrant green forests below. An hour and a half and 384 kilometres later, we landed on the runway at Samjiyŏn.

The air in the north was noticeably cooler. Two tired buses carried us through the empty pine forest to Mount Paektu, North Korea's highest and most sacred mountain. We were now well above the treeline, and the landscape was desolate, stony and moonlike. There were swarms of soldiers at the foot of the myth-ical mountain, all dressed in thick jackets with large hats on their heads. Miss Ri disappeared off the bus with our passports and papers. She returned beaming.

"You are very lucky," she announced. "Kim Jong-un was here earlier today! He has just left."

As the funicular railway was not working, we were given special permission to drive almost to the top. Kim Jong-un had walked up on his own two feet, we were told. We, on the other hand, were only allowed to walk the very last stretch, otherwise we would be short of time. A flock of North Korean tourists came running towards us, euphoric after their trip to the holy mountain, shouting and laughing like children.

From the top there was a view of a circular, green lake. Our mobile phones suddenly awoke from their slumber, and started to beep and vibrate frantically. Half of the lake lay in China; we were close enough to the border to get coverage. We were all engrossed in our text messages and taking photographs of each other from every possible angle when Miss Ri hastened over to us.

"Can you hurry up, please? I said that you only had twenty minutes, and now nearly half an hour has passed. We have a lot to see today, we need to move on."

The next stop on the itinerary was Kim Jong-il's supposed birth-place, a wooden cabin deep in the forest about an hour's drive from Mount Paektu. According to myth, Our Dear Leader was born here under a double rainbow. A new star also appeared in the sky to mark the occasion. "Even the white February snow cel-ebrated his arrival," wrote his anonymous biographer, in *The Great Man Kim Jong Il*, which I had bought in one of the tourist shops in Pyongyang.

In fact, Kim Jong-il was born to the east of the Soviet Union, in a village called Vyatskoye, close to the military base in Khabarovsk. And he was named Yury Irsenovich Kim.

The guide who showed us around – once again a beautiful young woman – talked with great empathy about the hard life of Kim Jong-suk, Kim Jong-il's mother. During the war with Japan, she had gone into hiding. But the cabin where she had hidden was not discovered until the 1960s, on the instructions of Kim Il-sung. When it was found, only a few of the original timbers remained. The cabin was rebuilt in the 1980s and upgraded to a national monument. There were two other cabins in addition to Kim Jong-suk's original hideaway that had been rebuilt based entirely on imagination. According to our guide, they had served as the main base for Kim Il-sung's guerrilla soldiers.

There was quite a crush in the three wooden cabins. A steady flow of Korean soldiers was bussed in to learn about the country's fictive fight for independence. There is, however, no doubt that Kim Jong-suk had a very difficult life. Like Kim Il-sung, her family fled to Manchuria at the start of the 1920s, when she was five. As a teenager, she lost both her parents in rapid succession and eventually joined one of the anti-Japanese guerrilla groups. In 1940, she married the leader of the group, Kim Il-sung, and together they had two sons and a daughter: Kim Jong-il, who officially came in to the world on 16 February 1942, three decades after his famous father (according to Soviet and Western historians, he was actually born in 1941), Kim Pyong-il, who was born in 1944, and Kim Kyong-hui, who was born in 1946. Kim Pyong-il later drowned in a swimming pool in Pyongyang, when he was only three years old. Two years after this tragic accident, Kim Jong-il's mother, Kim Jong-suk, died in labour.

Kim Il-sung then married his secretary, Kim Song-ae, during the Korean War, and had another two sons and a daughter with her.

The eldest son was named Kim Pyong-il, after the boy who had drowned, and is today ambassador to the Czech Republic.

* * *

The following morning, we continued our journey east to the coast, in the same old airplane as the day before. The roads in the north are in such poor condition that driving was not an option.

"No photography from the bus," Miss Ri ordered, once we had safely landed again. "You can take pictures of the beautiful landscape, but not of the people, is that understood?"

The people here looked poorer than they had in the south. Their clothes were simpler; many people wore brown or blue uniforms. There were practically no private cars; most people cycled or sat packed like sardines on the back of a truck. Many also walked, often carrying heavy loads on their backs. Behind the neat rows of white, pink and purple flowers that lined the road were ditches full of rubbish. The houses were of a much simpler standard than in Pyongyang. And the wall paintings of happy socialists were peeling off in great, colourful flakes.

For a change, we were not staying in a hotel, but in a so-called "homestay village". The village was situated by an idyllic beach, and all the houses were new and well maintained, the one identical to the other. When I "checked in", my host, a young woman who had only a smattering of English, handed me a welcome pack that consisted of toilet paper and a toothbrush. I saw no more of her.

Before supper, which was to be served in a large communal dining room, and not with "our families", we went for a walk on the beach. The sun was setting, and both the sea and sky positively glittered. I dipped my toes in the clear, blue water. It was not at all cold.

What surprised me most about North Korea was how beautiful it was. Not the towns, which were every bit as ghastly as I had

imagined they would be, but the countryside. When I had tried
to imagine what North Korea would be like, I had subconsciously
pictured it in black and white, as if the regime had stolen all the
sunsets and chlorophyll. Whereas, in reality, the beaches were just
as beautiful as those in Vietnam. On our way here we had stopped
to look at dark green, mountainous landscapes that stretched as
far as the eye could see, broken only by the red slogans carved
into the rock face. Not even the mountains had escaped the ever-
present propaganda machine.

When I got back to my room, I discovered that I had lost my
iPhone, so I went back to the beach to look for it. For once, we were
allowed to move around on our own, as long as we did not cross any
bridges. Crossing bridges was strictly forbidden.

It was almost dark by the time I got back to the beach. A woman
and two boys were sitting in a rowing boat that had been pulled
up onto the sand. Four or five dogs were circling the boat. The
dogs started to growl quietly as soon as they saw me, but left me
alone. I retraced my footsteps, but did not see the phone anywhere.
Eventually, I went over to the woman and the boys in the boat.

"Phone?" I said, holding my hand up to my ear, as though I
was talking on the phone. Then I made a questioning gesture with
my hands. They did not say anything, just continued to stare at
me blankly. I turned around and started to walk back. But when
I had gone only a few metres, the woman called after me and
pointed to one of the boys. Reluctantly he pulled the iPhone out
from under his T-shirt. As I took it, I felt a sharp pain in my calf.
The woman's eyes widened; clearly afraid, she tried to order the
dogs away. They pulled back a little, but were still growling. The
woman said something in Korean and gestured that I should
leave. I turned and walked as calmly as I could back to the road,
trying not to provoke the dogs. They snarled aggressively, but did
not follow. Even when I had retreated so far that it was no longer

possible to hear the dogs, I imagined them snarling and barking right behind me. It was only when I was safely back in my room that I stopped shaking. My brief independent adventure in North Korea had ended with bite marks on my trouser leg. My calf was bruised bluish-yellow, but still intact; I had escaped with nothing more than a scare.

Only a truly dedicated few were continuing further north: Linda, a single British woman; a middle-aged Danish couple; Marcel, a retired Swiss pilot; and Dmitry, an overweight Russian from Moscow. Dmitry had come to experience the last remnants of communism in action. "They're making the same mistakes as we did," he frequently muttered to himself. "Exactly the same mistakes . . ."

Miss Ri and Mr Kim went back to Pyongyang with the rest of the group. Those of us who were carrying on got new guides: Mr Nam, a jovial, broad-shouldered man who could not speak a word of English but did speak French, and Mr Gong, who had just qualified as a guide. Mr Gong was thin as a stick, and he was so nervous that he was dripping with sweat before he even got on the bus. He had only been studying English for four months, so it took a while to get used to his peculiar pronunciation. On the seat next to the driver at the front of the bus sat an older man in a dark uniform. We were never told his name, and he never said a word.

As we were about to drive off, a man came running over to the bus. He was holding a thick, worn paperback in his hand, one of Ken Follett's historical novels. He gave the book to Mr Gong, said a few words in Korean and nodded towards Linda.

"You forgot this," Mr Gong said to Linda.

"No, I left it behind on purpose," Linda explained. "I've finished reading it, so I don't need it anymore."

"It is best you take it with you," Mr Gong insisted.

NORTHEAST PASSAGE

Above: Polar explorers are more frail these days, and the Northeast Passage is no longer what it was.

Left: Cape Dezhnev, the most easterly point of the Eurasian continent.

Below: A reminder of the Soviet Union's ambitious plans for the most northern sea route.

NORTH KOREA

Pyongyang: pastel colours only partially disguise the bleakness of a dictatorship that, like the pollution, blankets the city.

Chongjin: poverty is more visible in the north than in the capital. This picture was taken surreptitiously.

Mass dancing on Kim Il-Sung Square on September 9, North Korea's national day.

A soldier guards the entrance to the North Korean side of the border barracks in the so-called demilitarised zone.

The metro in Pyongyang is not long either, but it runs on time and has some beautiful public art.

The more peaceful border with Russia. A shallow river is all that separates the two worlds.

The hut at the foot of Mount Paektu where Kim Jong-il was supposedly born in 1942. In fact he was born Yury Irsenovich Kim in a village close to Khabarovsk in the Soviet Union, in 1941.

CHINA

Left: Harbin was known as the Orient's Moscow. St Sophia's Church, which miraculously survived the Cultural Revolution, is now a museum.

Above: The influx of Russian day trippers has been slowed by sanctions and the financial crisis. The shopping malls of Heihe are empty.

China has invested one trillion dollars in building the new Silk Road, which consists of several modern communication routes between China and countries to the west.

MONGOLIA

Yurts have not changed for centuries, though the means of transport and power supply are very definitely twenty-first century.

Aragalan Tsagaach lives with his reindeer herd all year round. His family fled from the Soviet Union to Mongolia in the 1950s.

The mysterious Deer Stones from the Bronze Age are a reminder of how little we know about people from that time.

Mongolian throat singer Dashdorj Tserendavaa gave us an unforgettable, intimate concert in his yurt.

The sprawling *ger* districts around Ulan Bator expand by many yurts a day.

Genghis Khan may have been a small man, but the monument that honours him is unquestionably based on the scale of his achievements.

The Buddhist monastery in Kharkhorin: this was the site of Karakorum, the Mongolian capital.

"But I don't need it any longer," Linda said. "Can't they just throw it away?"

"It is best you take it with you," Mr Gong repeated, and put the book down in her lap.

For most of the journey, Mr Gong sat hunched over the guidebook. Every now and then he wiped the sweat from his brow with the back of his hand. After a couple of hours, we stopped to see a monument to the revolution. The location was magnificent; the white cliffs could rival those on Corsica or the Amalfi coast. And apart from a couple of fishermen, we had the place to ourselves.

"Kim Il-sung visited this village in 1947," Mr Gong told us in his frantic English, pointing to a white stone with red inscriptions. "The people here were so poor they couldn't even afford to buy salt. Kim Il-sung taught them how to work together and harvest salt from the seawater! After that, they never lacked salt again! This memorial stone was erected to mark the event."

The shoreline was littered with similar memorial stones.

"Kim Il-sung was photographed here, together with his wife," Mr Gong informed us by another white stone. And at the next one: "Kim Il-sung ate breakfast here." He looked around in anguish. No-one was listening. Some people were chatting, others were taking photographs of the picture-postcard views; the Danish couple had taken off their shoes and were paddling in the Sea of Japan, or the Korean East Sea, as it is called in North Korea. Mr Gong continued feverishly from stone to stone, clutching the guidebook to his breast. His blue shirt was flecked with sweat.

Mr Nam was sociable and chatty, a completely different type. But as only Marcel, the retired Swiss pilot, and I knew any French, his choice of who to speak to was limited. Marcel had taken a seat right at the back of the bus, and was sullen and silent, as the bus was so rickety. Mr Nam sat next me. To my surprise, he wanted to discuss politics.

"The situation is a little tricky right now," he said, "because North and South Korea are still divided. Everything will be better after reunification."

"Do you really think reunification is likely?" I asked.

"Of course," he replied, confidently. "We will have two systems and become one federal state, with Pyongyang as the capital. But right now, as I said, times are hard. Sanctions make it very difficult for us to develop."

"The sanctions would be lifted immediately if the authorities stopped the nuclear weapons programme," I pointed out.

"Unfortunately, that is not possible," Mr Nam said sadly. "If we did not have nuclear weapons, the U.S.A. would attack us. They have already done so once, after all."

We stopped at yet another white stone with red inscriptions, yet another monument to Kim Il-sung's good deeds. And though I am sure that Mr Gong told us what it was, I have forgotten.

"What do they say about North Korea where you come from, in Western Europe?" Mr Nam asked, when we were back on the bus.

"Do you want to know the truth?"

He nodded.

"We say it is the world's worst dictatorship."

"Oh." He was quiet for a while. "What do they say about our leader then, about Kim Jong-un?"

"Do you really want to know the truth?"

He nodded again.

"They say . . ." I searched for the right words, without finding them. "Gosh, how shall I put it?"

"Is it a sensitive matter?" Mr Nam asked, helpfully.

"Yes, you could say that."

"I dream about meeting him one day," Mr Nam said. "Just once."

As the density of buildings increased, I realised we were approaching Chongjin, the third largest city in North Korea. The journey had taken longer than estimated because the roads were in such a sorry state, and it was late afternoon by the time we got there. Compared with the narrow, potholed roads here in the north, the asphalt roads of the south were luxurious highways.

"We are now passing the steelworks on our right!" Mr Gong shouted, and pointed to an enormous factory. Black smoke spewed out of the great fat chimneys.

As in Pyongyang, the houses in Chongjin were painted in cheerful pastel colours, yet the city seemed much greyer than Pyongyang. There was hardly any traffic here; people either cycled or walked. Many people carried heavy loads of firewood on their shoulders, as they did in the villages, while others pushed their loads in wheelbarrows. Nearly one fifth of the inhabitants here starved to death during the North Korean famine in the 1990s, twice as many as anywhere else in the country. I tried to read their faces as we drove by. What had they seen and experienced? How had they survived? Did they still believe the regime's lies, or had they lost faith a long time ago?

"Hurry, hurry!" Mr Gong shouted, when the bus driver stopped outside an ugly concrete building.

"What are we supposed to do here?" Marcel asked, grumpily.

"Buy sweets for the children." Mr Gong danced impatiently on the pavement as we piled out through the narrow bus door. "We can't arrive empty-handed!"

"Which children?" Marcel asked.

"The children in the kindergarten, of course," Mr Gong replied. "They have been rehearsing a show for us. They are sitting waiting for us right now, we must hurry!"

We were bustled into a combined souvenir and sweet shop. The shelves behind the counter were full of bags of colourful boiled sweets and toffees, which we dutifully bought for the kinder-garten children who were waiting nervously for us.

"No, not the small ones, buy the big ones!" Mr Gong ordered. "There are lots of children, everyone must get something!"

When we got back into the bus, the aisle was full of bags of sweets. Famine was a thing of the past. A few minutes later, we stopped by a large, open square.

"Please leave your bags on the bus," Mr Gong said sternly. "No sunglasses, no chewing gum, no jackets tied around your waist, is that understood?"

We nodded feebly. We all knew what was coming.

We filed out into the large square, and Mr Gong led us over to two gigantic statues of Kim Il-sung and Kim Jong-il. They were remarkably similar to the statues in Pyongyang, which is perhaps not so strange, as they are all produced by the same company. We were instructed to line up and bow respectfully. The local guide, a beautiful young woman dressed in a long, pink silk dress explained briefly how important the city was to these great leaders.

"Kim Il-sung visited Chongjin as many as fifty times!" She clapped her hands in delight, with a charming smile. "The city also meant a lot to Kim Jong-il, who visited twenty times!"

Then on we went to the next item on our itinerary. Mr Gong ran ahead, frantically waving his arms.

"Hurry, hurry! The small children are waiting!"

"Can't we just go straight to the children then?" Linda, the single British woman, asked.

Mr Gong looked at her, perplexed. "No, that is not possible. First we must go to the Revolutionary Museum."

Inside the museum, there were long lists of all the places where Kim Il-sung's guerrilla forces had apparently won decisive battles against the Japanese during the war. When the guided tour was over, Mr Gong rushed to the exit.

"Hurry, hurry, we have to go to the library!" He sounded harassed. "The children are waiting!"

"Why don't we go straight to the kindergarten?" Linda suggested again. "We've already been to see the library in Pyongyang, so we don't really need to see another one."

"The library first!" Mr Gong set off across the square, past the gigantic statues of Kim Il-sung and Kim Jong-il, over to the library that lay on the other side, opposite the Revolutionary Museum. There were two long rows of computers in the library. And in front of every screen, sat a child in school uniform, either writing or playing a simple game.

"We have many more computers in other rooms, many, many more than you can see here," the librarian boasted.

"Why are you not taking photographs?" Mr Gong asked, impatiently. "Please photograph the computers, quickly."

We obediently took some pictures. The children behaved as if we weren't there, and just carried on with whatever they were doing.

Finally, we were ready to go to the kindergarten.

I have no idea how many children's performances we saw in the fortnight we were in North Korea. In every town we visited, new children were waiting to do a show for us, the one very much like the other. In my mind, they have blurred into one endless line of perfectly choreographed tiny children with stiff smiles, made up and dressed in colourful costumes, who played, danced and sang about life in the socialist paradise with well-rehearsed movements. They never made a mistake, there was never an accident. When we asked the teachers how long the children had been rehearsing, they generally shrugged. Not that long. A couple of weeks, perhaps. Even the teachers' answers were the same.

When we got to the hotel, the atmosphere was strained. There was no hot water in any of the rooms; in fact, in several, there was no water at all, and in some, the plugholes had even been filled with cement. Mr Gong ran back and forth in distress, his face ashen grey. Marcel was even more petulant than usual.

"I don't want green tea, I want *black* tea!" he thundered. "Can that be so difficult? Black tea is perfectly normal in most countries around the world, there is nothing special about black tea. Why don't they have black tea in this stupid country?"

I noticed that I was a bit irritable myself. Here we were, in Chongjin, a city only recently opened up to tourists, so not many foreigners had been there before, and all we had seen was two statues, a revolutionary museum, a library and a kindergarten.

"Could we go for a walk after supper?" I asked Mr Nam. "We've been sitting on the bus all day. It would be nice to stretch our legs and get a little fresh air."

Mr Nam shook his head firmly.

"No, it's not in the programme."

"Just a short walk?" I begged.

"Impossible!"

"Please?"

Mr Nam sighed.

"I will see what I can do, but I can't promise anything, O.K.?"

He got up from the table and went over to talk to the mysterious man in uniform. Just then, Mr Gong came running in to the room.

"You have hot water! You can shower now! But you have to hurry, because it may not last long! Who wants a shower? Why are you just sitting there, why don't you go and shower?"

"There are two types of people: those who shower in the morning and those who shower in the evening," Marcel said, grimly. "Very few people shower in the morning and the evening. I belong to the first group. In other words, I have already showered today and do not intend to shower again."

Mr Gong gave him a bewildered look.

"You don't want to shower? But there is hot water in the rooms now, I got it fixed."

Marcel grunted something and left the table. His green tea was untouched. Fifteen minutes later, Mr Nam reappeared.

"I have good news, Miss Erika! You are allowed to go for a short walk after supper. It was not easy, there was opposition, it is not in the programme, as I said, but I can never say no to a beautiful girl . . ."

Four of us seized the opportunity of this extraordinary evening walk. The streets were pitch dark, even though it was no later than eight, but there were still lots of people around.

"Watch out for stones and holes," Mr Gong warned us. "Be careful, so you don't fall and hurt yourselves!"

We walked past a small kiosk, then crossed the road. At the end of the next block, Mr Nam led us into a kind of improvised basketball court. It was barely fifty by fifty metres and fenced in on all sides; there was a basketball hoop at each end. We were the only people there.

"This is a good place for stretching your legs," Mr Nam declared, happily.

"Can't we just keep walking down the street?" I asked.

"That is not possible," Mr Nam replied. "Here, but no further, is that understood?"

"But wh—?"

"Why? *Be-cause*, Miss Erika, because *it-is-not-possible!*"

After we had wandered around the enclosure for about ten minutes, we went back to the hotel.

"Can we carry on a little further in the other direction?" I asked. I felt like a four year old who was testing the grown-ups' limits.

"You can walk around the car park a little, if you would like," Mr Nam sighed. He shrugged. "I'm sorry, but those are the rules. We've done as much as we can."

"I have never experienced anything like it," I grumbled. "Even in Turkmenistan I was allowed to walk around as I pleased."

"This is not Turkmenistan, Miss Erika," Mr Nam said.

"I know," I muttered.

"We Koreans are very disciplined," Mr Nam said. "But perhaps," he then added, "perhaps tourists will be able to walk around freely after the reunification of Korea."

Capitalism Lite

Miss Pan and Mr Kang, our new guides, led us solemnly up the steps to the Golden Trial Bank, the only bank in North Korea where foreigners are allowed to change money. The bank had a high ceiling, lots of counters and very short queues.

"Be careful not to exchange too much money," Miss Pan said. "Remember that it is forbidden to take won out of the country. You have to use it all while you are here."

I changed one hundred Chinese yuan, about twelve British pounds, and was handed 125,000 won in crisp new 5,000-won notes. Mr Kang raised an eyebrow when he saw how much I had changed.

"The normal monthly salary is a hundred thousand won," he said, when he was sure that Miss Pan would not hear him. Miss Pan was the strictest guide we had had so far. She was in her forties, always immaculately dressed and spoke English with a British accent. If she noticed anyone taking pictures of things she had not approved in advance, she made sure that the photographs were deleted immediately. Mr Kang was also in his forties, but he was calm and relaxed, and made no effort to hide his curiosity about life in the West, and about pay and prices in particular. "How much does a loaf of bread cost?" he might ask when Miss Pan was out of hearing. "How much does a flat cost? What does a teacher earn?"

When we emerged from the bank, there was military music blasting from loudspeakers all over the city. When the march faded, an earnest woman's voice took over. The woman spoke for a long time, with exemplary sincerity and vigour.

"What is she talking about?" I said.

"Nothing." Miss Pan pulled a face, as she tended to do whenever she did not want to answer a question.

"She's giving the day's news," Mr Kang said, when Miss Pan was out of earshot.

Our next stop was a bar. Some of the new won notes flew straight back out of my pocket. A pint of imported Czech beer cost 25,000 won. Apart from a small group of American tourists, we were the only people there.

We had arrived at the final and northernmost destination in North Korea: Rason, a special economic zone on the border with China and Russia. About two hundred thousand people live in this zone. Ordinary North Koreans do not have access to the area, certainly not without bribing someone. The zone was established by Kim Jong-il and serves not only as a place where the authorities can experiment with capitalism and the free market, but also as a controlled, contained area where the regime can attract sorely needed capital.

Following our visit to the bar, Miss Pan took us to a textile factory where we could witness for ourselves the wonders of the North Korean work ethic. Young women in blue uniforms sat in long rows sewing yellow fishing vests. Each of them was responsible for a tiny part of the vest and repeated the same, mechanical movement over and over again.

"Employees work from eight in the morning until six in the evening, with breaks," the foreman told us. "It is piece work and they earn about a hundred dollars a month."

That was ten times more than what Mr Kang had said was the average monthly salary.

"Is it alright to take photographs?" Linda asked.

"Take as many as you like," Miss Pan said graciously.

"Who buys the vests?" I asked.

"Mainly the Chinese," the foreman said.

"But surely because of the sanctions you are not allowed to sell North Korean products in China?" Marcel said.

"That is true, which is why we do not mark the clothes as *Made in DPRK*, but, rather, *Made in China*," the foreman said, cheerfully.

Outside, there were clothes hanging up to dry all around the factory.

"Everyone contributes to helping the flood victims," Miss Pan said. "The North Koreans help each other, that's just the way we are."

"Is it alright if I take a photograph of the clothes that are out to dry?" I asked.

"That is not something worthy of a picture," Miss Pan said, and pulled a face.

A few weeks earlier, the region had been hit by violent storms and flooding. More than five hundred thousand people had lost their lives and more than thirty thousand houses had been destroyed or damaged by the floods. Entire villages had been washed away. According to the opposition newspaper *Daily NK*, which is based in South Korea, many of the victims were found with portraits of Kim Il-sung and Kim Jong-il clutched to their chests.

The next item on our programme was a visit to a school for particularly gifted children. As soon as we entered the classroom, the students stood up and greeted us politely. We introduced ourselves, and said a little about where we came from. The pupils listened attentively. Then they got some chairs and invited us to sit at their desks, so we could have more private conversations, one to one. My allocated partner was a serious twelve-year-old boy.

"What is your name?" he asked. I told him and he followed up with a long list of trivial questions: "How old are you? Do you live in a house or a flat? How many rooms are there in your flat? Do you have a living room? Do you have a kitchen? What are your hobbies?"

I told him a bit about my flat and my hobbies.

"I also like watching films," the boy said. "Korean films. Especially films about my country's history and culture."

"What else do you like to do in your free time?" I said.

"I like to play football in my free time," the boy answered in perfect English. "When do you go to bed in the evening?"

"About midnight," I said. "When do you go to bed?"

"I go to bed at ten o'clock," the boy said. "When do you normally get up?"

"About eight," I said. "And you – when do you normally get up in the morning?"

"I get up at four o'clock to do my morning exercises and then I do my homework."

"What do you want to do when you leave school?" I asked, expecting him to say that he wanted to be teacher, or perhaps a doctor.

"I am going to join the army and be a soldier."

"And how long will you be in the army?" I said, trying to hide my surprise.

"Ten years." His reply was immediate.

As a step towards self-reliance, Kim Jong-il introduced the "Military First" doctrine in 1994. North Korea currently has the largest army in the world with more than 1.3 million soldiers. Ten years is standard for compulsory military service, and many of the soldiers are in practice free labour for the state.

"Why do you want to be a soldier?" I said.

The boy hesitated.

"Wait a moment, please, just a moment." He stood up and went over to the teacher. When he came back, he had his answer ready. "I want to be a soldier so I can defend our country!"

The teacher, who had never been far away to begin with, now hovered round us.

"What is your favourite colour?" the boy asked.

"Red," I said.

"Mine too," the boy said and pointed at the pioneer scarf round his neck. He almost smiled for the first time. "What is your favourite food?" was his next question.

"I love Italian food – pizza, for example," I said.

"What is pizza?" the boy asked, with curiosity.

I was about to explain when the teacher beat me to it.

"It is a kind of pancake."

"My favourite food is cold noodles," the boy said. "It's the best thing I know."

"Would you like to travel, to see the world?" I asked, when the teacher was out of earshot.

"No." Again, there was no hesitation.

"Why not? You are studying languages, after all."

"Our country is the best in the world!" the boy declared. "Why would I want to go anywhere else?"

Our conversation faltered. The boy got out his notebook and showed me the dialogues he had copied with such care from a textbook. The conversations all took place in Australia and were largely about the species to be found there and meteorological conditions. To pass the time, I got out my mobile phone and showed him photographs of my family and of Norway. He gave me his full attention. The waterfalls in particular made an impression. "Magnificent!" he exclaimed, clearly impressed, when I showed him the 612-metre-high Langefoss, which is close to my home. I carried on, showing him pictures from some of my travels, from Rome, Paris, Istanbul.

"That is a very beautiful building," the boy said and pointed at the Blue Mosque.

"Yes, it is a very famous mosque," I said.

He looked at me, bewildered.

"It is where Muslims go to pray," I said. The boy stiffened and glanced fearfully over his shoulder. We had been given *strict* instructions not to discuss politics or religion. Fortunately, the teacher was at the other side of the classroom. I moved quickly on.

To finish off our visit, a couple of the pupils performed a selection of the dialogues from the Australian textbook. They knew them off by heart and rattled through them without any mistakes, and without any feeling.

How are you doing today, my friend?

Jolly good, thank you. The weather is very nice today, isn't it?

Yes, the weather is very nice today, indeed, my friend.

On the way to the port the next day, Miss Pan seemed unusually agitated. It did not take long before she told us why.

"Over breakfast, I read in the newspaper that Kim Jong-un visited the region affected by floods yesterday," she said, as the bus pulled out of the hotel car park. Her voice trembled with emotion. "It is the first time that our leader has visited Rason. I was so touched when I read it that I almost started crying."

She looked down and wiped a tear from the corner of her eye.

"I find it strange that you know so little about your leader," Mette, the only Dane, said. "Do you know how old he is, for example?"

Miss Pan shook her head.

"We know nothing about his private life," she said. "I know that he is married, but I don't know whether he has children or not. Some tourists once told me that he went to a famous school in

Sweden. Sweden is close to Denmark, isn't it? Have you heard of the school?"

"It is in Switzerland, not Sweden," I said. "A friend of mine went to the same school."

"Really?" Miss Pan lit up. "A friend of yours?" She moved to the seat next to me and bombarded me with questions: "What does your friend do now? How old is he? Was Kim Jong-un a good student? He was, was he not? Switzerland is very beautiful, is it not? Is it true that the school is very famous?"

Kim Jong-un was born on January 8, 1984, and is Kim Jong-il's youngest son. For a long time, it was assumed that Kim Jong-nam, Kim Jong-il's eldest son and Kim Jong-un's half-brother, would take over, but then he fell from favour. In 2001, he was stopped at Narita Airport in Tokyo with a forged Dominican passport and was deported to China. Kim Jong-nam never returned to North Korea, but divided his time between China and Macao, keeping a low profile.

The middle son, Kim Jong-chul, was never favoured as an heir, because his father apparently thought he was too effeminate. The choice fell instead on the youngest son, Kim Jong-un. Even though he was only twenty-six when his father died, Kim Jong-un swiftly mastered the brutal power play required at the top. After only a short while in the driving seat, he saw to it that several of the most powerful generals in the party were executed. No-one can feel safe under his leadership, not even close family members. In 2013, Kim Jong-un's uncle, Chang Song-thaek, who many believed was the second most powerful man in North Korea, was executed. It is not known if Kim Kyong-hui, Chang Song-thaek's wife and sister of Kim Jong-il, is still alive, or if she was also killed.

In February 2017, the family black sheep, Kim Jong-nam, was poisoned with the nerve agent VX at Kuala Lumpur international airport. VX is one of the most poisonous substances ever to be produced, and the former heir died in hospital soon after. The attack was carried out by two young women from Vietnam and Indonesia, but it is presumed that Kim Jong-un was the brains behind it.

"Do you know what grades Kim Jong-un got?" Miss Pan asked, as we drove into the port area.

"No, I am afraid I don't," I said. "My friend did not know Kim Jong-un personally. I'm sorry."

"I am sure he got very good grades," Miss Pan said.

"I am sure he did," I agreed.

Miss Pan smiled happily. Her cheeks were flushed. She was sitting beside someone who knew someone who had gone to school with Our Dear Leader.

It was clear that there were major refurbishments going on in the port, even though there was no sign of activity when we were there. In 2008, Russia signed a leasing contract with the North Korean authorities that guaranteed them access to the port for the next fifty years. The Russian authorities plan to transport goods by rail from Vladivostok, which will then be transferred to ships in Rason, which, unlike Vladivostok, is ice-free all year round. Even though more than two thirds of Russia's border is maritime, the country has very few deepwater ports. This desire for warm-water ports has been the cause of several wars in Russian history: Peter the Great, Catherine the Great, Nicholas I and Nicholas II all stopped at nothing in their attempts to make the enormous empire a maritime superpower. A leasing agreement with the world's worst dictator is one of the less dramatic steps Russian leaders have taken to guarantee the country an ice-free port.

The port area was quiet and dead. Not a single ship to be seen, either Russian or Korean. There was an oil refinery on the far side of the port, but there was no sign of activity there either.

"It has not been in operation since the 1990s," Mr Kang said. "The Americans do whatever they can to hurt us. They hate communists."

"You don't think that North Korea is responsible for the situation it finds itself in?" Marcel, the Swiss pilot, said.

"All we want is reunification with South Korea, so that we can be one country again," Mr Kang said.

"So North Korea is not to blame at all?" Marcel said.

"From the very beginning, the Japanese and American imperialists have tried to break us," Mr Kang said. "Sanctions have made things very difficult for us."

I eventually lost patience and interrupted: "The reason for the sanctions is that you have nuclear weapons, not that you are communists. No nuclear weapons, no problems!"

"Erm, now we're talking politics . . ." Mr Kang mumbled and looked at his watch. "I do believe it's time to move on!" He turned on his heel and headed for the bus.

Before our last dinner in North Korea, we had time to visit the evening market in Rason, the only market in the country that foreigners are allowed to see.

"Watch out for pickpockets," Miss Pan warned us before we went into the hall.

I was surprised. "Do you have pickpockets in North Korea?"

Miss Pan pulled a face and did not answer. She and Mr Kang escorted us into the citadel of capitalism. It was like stepping into another world. Even though it was a big building, there was not much space. The market stalls sold shoes, hats, clothes, underwear and whatever other cheap Chinese product your heart might desire. People pushed forward and bartered with fervour. It was noisy, hot and humid in there. One woman tried her best to sell us some brown cloth shoes, another tried to interest us in felt hats with red communist stars sewn on. The won we had left flew out of our purses, though everything here cost a fraction of what it had in the tourist shop.

For a short while it felt like being in a normal country.

The Rusty Friendship Bridge

The road to the Chinese border was bumpy and narrow. Miss Pan used the opportunity to go through all the photographs we had taken in Rason, one camera after another, and took the liberty of deleting any photographs she did not approve of. Most of my photographs passed her critical eyes, but the photograph of a sailor in dirty clothes that were full of holes made her frown.

"I said only beautiful things," she told me and resolutely pressed the delete button.

The very last thing on our extensive sightseeing programme was the Russian–Korean Friendship House. It was beside a rusty railway bridge, the so-called Friendship Bridge, which crosses over into Russia. Large photographs of Kim 1, 2 and 3 flanked by Russian delegates hung on the walls.

Following the annexation of the Crimean Peninsula and subsequent sanctions from Western countries, the Russians have shown more interest in their Asian neighbours. Only a few months after the annexation, the Russian authorities decided to write off ninety per cent of North Korea's debt to Russia, the majority of which derived from the Soviet era. A ferry route between Vladivostok and Rason was recently opened. The Russian state railway is carrying out extensive upgrades on the North Korean rail network and has already invested 300 million dollars in infrastructure improvements for its neighbour. The quid pro quo is exclusive access to North Korea's mineral mines. This, combined with access to the Russian port in Rason and the resulting increase in traffic, may also contribute to stronger economic ties between Moscow and Pyongyang in the future. But at present, China is still North Korea's most important trading partner, by a long shot. Business with China accounts for more than sixty per cent of foreign trade. By way of comparison, business with Russia accounted for only one per cent of North Korea's total import and export in 2013.

Russia and North Korea celebrated the Year of Friendship in 2015. The Russian Ministry of Foreign Affairs said in a statement that the aim was to elevate ties "to a new level". In February 2016, Russia signed an agreement to return any North Korean citizens who had entered the country illegally, on condition that they not risk imprisonment or torture in their home country. In theory, this means that Russia cannot send any North Korean refugees back, but the chances of them securing the legal right to remain are slim. Between 2011 and 2015, sixty-eight North Korean citizens sought asylum in Russia. Only two of them were granted refugee status. However, a large number of North Koreans do live in Russia; in recent years some fifty thousand North Koreans have been granted visas to do manual work. They are supervised by the North Korean guards who accompany them and most of their wages are commandeered by the North Korean authorities, who earn considerable sums by hiring out cheap labour to countries in Asia and Africa as well.

The friendship between Russia and North Korea has, however, cooled; in 2016, the North Korean regime carried out two nuclear tests, which led to harsher sanctions from the U.N., including the introduction of a total ban on the import of coal and minerals from North Korea. The frequency of missile and nuclear tests intensified through 2017, with increasingly dangerous bombs and more powerful missiles. President Putin has criticised the test programme and loyally backed U.N. sanctions. He has also warned against President Trump's aggressive rhetoric, as well as against military intervention and further sanctions, which he argues will have no effect whatsoever on the North Korean regime. It is of course not in Russia's interest that its small, unpredictable neighbour to the east should have the possibility of developing precise weapons of mass destruction, and the authorities want to avoid a brutal and devastating war in their backyard at all costs. Furthermore, the Russian authorities have, as mentioned, invested huge sums in the country's infrastructure and also want to protect its precious warm-water port.

Few could have believed that the North Korean regime would survive the turbulent 1990s. One communist state after another toppled and fell. When the Soviet Union foundered, many expected the North Korean government to be caught up in the slipstream. But rather than opening up the country, Kim Jong-il let hundreds of thousands of people starve to death.

How much longer can the dictatorship survive? Unlike China and the Soviet Union, North Korea has become a hereditary dictatorship. Kim Il-sung's grandson, Kim Jong-un, has built amusement parks, ski resorts and a shiny new airport, it is true, but little has changed: North Korea is still steering its own course, with a focus on nuclear testing rather than on more conventional diplomacy. The surveillance and control of the population are without parallel in human history. At the same time, the gap between the haves and have-nots is growing. While the Kim family enjoys French cognac and an expanding middle class lives in relative comfort in the capital, a fifth of all children under the age of five are malnourished, according to the U.N., and between 80,000 and 120,000 people are forced to live in inhuman conditions in labour camps. Often their only crime is that they have tried to leave the country.

South Korea has a ministry that deals solely with the question of unification, but the number of South Koreans who favour reunification shrinks each year. The unification of East and West

Germany was far more expensive than anyone had anticipated – it is estimated to have cost between one and a half and an eye-watering two billion euros. Germany was divided for forty-five years, and East Germany was never as closed as North Korea. The Korean peninsula has been divided along the 38th parallel since 1953. The cost of unification between the two countries would make the price of German *Wiedervereinigung* pale in comparison.

The financial aspect of a possible unification is one thing, the culture shock is another altogether. Even though contraband D.V.D.s and U.S.B. sticks have allowed more and more North Koreans to get a glimpse of the world outside, the few thousand that have managed to flee to South Korea have found it overwhelming. Many of them never manage to adjust to living in the capitalist south.

But most refugees never get that far. However, more than two hundred thousand North Koreans stay in China illegally, and live in constant fear of being sent back. The Chinese authorities have recently raised barbed-wire fences and installed surveillance cameras along the border to make it harder for North Koreans to escape. The key to Pyongyang's future no longer lies in Moscow, but in Beijing. But as long as it is in China's interest to avoid a mass immigration of poor North Koreans, the regime is likely to survive.

The North Korean border guard was even more thorough than Miss Pan. He was zealous in his review of my photographs, of which there were more than six hundred. He deleted all the pictures of people who looked poor, and all pictures of men in military uniforms, of which there were a number. Fortunately, I had been smart enough to do a back-up.

When the guard was finished with my camera, he was obviously bored, as he went through everyone else's photographs far more quickly. He did not bother to look at our mobile phones. But he did check all our purses and wallets, and he confiscated the won that Marcel had not managed to spend.

There was a group of overweight, loud Chinese people behind us. They were laden with plastic bags full of North Korean herbal medicines. Of the two hundred thousand or so tourists who visit North Korea every year, the majority are Chinese day-tourists on shopping trips. In North Korea they can buy dried snakeskin and teas that can cure almost anything, from cervical cancer to impotence, for a fraction of the cost in China.

A small bus transported us to the Chinese border post. None of the guards could speak English, but after much discussion, they eventually decided to stamp our passports and let us into China.

The Chinese roads were wide and luxurious, without a single pothole, with traffic moving in the opposite lane and streetlights. Neon advertisements glared at us.

203 Hill

A forest of steel, glass and exclusive emporiums flashed by: Bulgari, Prada, Chanel, Gucci . . . North Korea was only a short train journey away, but I was already in another world, far from the family dictatorship, in every sense. I was in Dalian. The name is derived from the Russians' name for the town – Дальний, *dalny* – which means "remote" and stems from the brief period when the town was under Russian rule towards the end of the 1800s. Dalian is now one of the fastest-growing cities in China, with about seven million inhabitants, and it was recently heralded by *China Daily* as the best city to live in in China.

I was travelling on to the neighbouring city, Lushun, formerly known as Port Arthur. The story of how Port Arthur fell into Russian hands in 1898, only to be lost again seven years later, is complicated, but key to understanding Tsar Nicholas II's gradual fall from power and the end of the Russian Empire. Imperial Russia's expansion eastwards stopped here, in this relatively insignificant Chinese port, after nearly three hundred years of incredible growth. From the time that the Romanovs came to power in 1613, the Russian Empire grew by an average of one hundred square kilometres *every day*. In other words, Tsar Nicholas II did exactly what his predecessors had done: he tried to make Russia even bigger. But he started to lose touch with reality and the young, inexperienced tsar fantasised about winning Manchuria, Korea and Tibet, and why not Persia, while he was at it?

To begin with, Nicholas was successful in his Asian ambitions, not least thanks to the weak position of the Chinese emperor. In the mid-seventeenth century, the Aisin Gioro clan from Manchuria, an area now in north-east China, forced the Ming dynasty from the throne and established the Qing dynasty. The Manchus ruled China for more than 250 years until 1912, and established a strictly hierarchical system based on ethnic divisions in which the Han Chinese were subservient to the Manchus.

The Qing dynasty expanded fast – the Manchus conquered vast territories in Mongolia to the north, Turkestan to the west and Tibet and Burma to the south. They also made considerable technological advances and the population grew rapidly. But all this progress was reversed in the nineteenth century and challenges to both domestic and foreign policy started to surface. The population grew faster than food production, and national opposition movements sprang up all over the empire. Foreign powers also started to cause problems. Great Britain demanded that more Chinese ports be opened for trade, but the emperor refused. One of Britain's most important and profitable exports was Indian-produced opium, but trade in opium was strictly forbidden in China, because of its harmful effects. When the Chinese seized stockpiles of smuggled opium in 1839, the British responded with military force. The war that followed has gone down in history as the First Opium War. The Chinese lost, and had to cede Hong Kong to the British and open five ports for trade. The British, however, were not satisfied. They wanted opium to be legalised and British merchants to be given access to the whole of China. The Second Opium War started in 1856 and, this time, the French fought with the British, as they too wanted greater access to the lucrative Chinese market.

The Russians realised that their moment had come. In 1858, while Emperor Xianfeng was struggling to deal with the French and British in the south, Russia gathered its troops along China's northern border and forced China to accept the Treaty of Aigun, a border agreement that was extremely favourable for the Russians. At a penstroke, Russia acquired the region to the north of the Amur River and increased its empire by 600,000 square kilometres.

The Treaty of Aigun replaced the 1689 Treaty of Nerchinsk, the first border agreement between Russia and China. Russia had conquered large territories in Siberia and therefore was a neighbour to the Chinese Empire for the first time. Border relations between the two countries had never been negotiated and the Manchu emperor did not like the fact that Russian pioneers had started to settle along the Amur River, which he deemed to be his territory. This was the cause of intermittent fighting and protracted negotiations between the two empires. It could take a year for a letter sent from the imperial palace in Peking to reach the tsar's palace in St Petersburg, and when it did eventually arrive, there were not always translators available to read its contents. Finally, in summer 1689, emissaries from the two empires met in the small town of Nerchinsk, which lies north of what was then the border between Mongolia and China, but is now Russian territory. The Russians had hoped that they would gain the area to the north of the Amur River, as above all else, they wanted to secure access to the Sea of Japan. However, the Manchu emissary was accompanied by more than ten thousand soldiers, five times as many as the Russian emissary, who swiftly abandoned Russia's ambitious territorial demands.

The Aigun Treaty of 1858 finally gave Russia control of the area. And two years later, they gained access to the Sea of Japan, when British and French troops stormed Peking and set the imperial summer palace on fire. The Russians forced the considerably compromised Chinese emperor to sign yet another border agreement, the Convention of Peking. This time the Chinese had to cede the area to the east of the Ussuri River to Russia. Thus Russia gained not only a further 400,000 square kilometres of Chinese territory, but also a coastal border with the Sea of Japan. Nikolay Muravyov, the chief negotiator for Russia, had not originally intended to confiscate the Chinese coastline down to Korea, but justified this later decision as follows: "If the area were to remain in Chinese hands, the British would take it."[6] That very year, the foundations were laid for the port town of Vladivostok, which means "Ruler of the East". The name left little doubt as to their ambitions.

The border agreements that were signed in the wake of the opium wars are known as the "Unequal Treaties" in China. The Chinese still believe that the Western superpowers used these treaties to exploit China's disadvantage in an unjust and dishonourable manner, and for a long time hoped that the treaties would be renegotiated as soon as China regained its strength. Great Britain and France withdrew from Chinese territory a long time ago, but the Sino-Russian border remains more or less the same as the one decided by the agreements of 1858 and 1860.

In 1894, Japan joined in the fight for power. Having pursued a policy of isolationism for centuries, the Japanese Empire modernised its army and society at record speed and turned its focus west. They were concerned by Russia's swift expansion to the Pacific Ocean, and were particularly alarmed by the construction of the Trans-Siberian railway, which started in 1892. When the railway was completed, it would stretch from Moscow in the west to Vladivostok in the east, and cover a total of nine thousand kilometres. The Japanese emperor feared that the Russian tsar's appetite for expansion would not be satisfied until he reached Japan, and therefore quickly established a buffer zone. On August 1 that year, having first sent eight thousand soldiers to Korea, Japan declared war on China. The goal was to gain control of the

Korean peninsula, which had been a Chinese vassal state since the seventeenth century.

The war ended in victory for the Japanese emperor: Taiwan and the Liaodong Peninsula, and Port Arthur, fell to Japan. The kingdom of Korea, which had had to pay tribute to the Chinese Qing emperor for centuries, was independent for a brief period.

The Japanese victory was, however, short-lived. Russia and the European colonial powers were not pleased that an Asian country had started to make inroads into what they perceived to be their domain. Six days after this victory, France, Germany and Russia forced the Japanese to give up the Liaodong Peninsula. In 1896, Russia entered into a secret military and economic alliance with China against Japan. The agreement cemented Russia's right to extend the Chinese Eastern Railway through Manchuria. The railway line, which was linked to the Trans-Siberian line, would considerably shorten the journey time to Vladivostok. The Russian Empire had become so vast that a shortcut would be an advantage.

The taking of Vladivostok meant that the Russians finally had access to a port on the Sea of Japan, but as it froze over in the winter months, it was still far from ideal. Port Arthur, on the other hand, named after a British naval officer from the Second Opium War, was on the end of the Liaodong Peninsula and ice-free all year round. In 1897, the Russians occupied Port Arthur, and the following year forced the Chinese to give them a twenty-five-year lease on the port. Russian engineers immediately started to build a railway line to link Port Arthur with the Chinese Eastern Railway and the Trans-Siberian Railway.

One of the few sensible ministers in Tsar Nicholas II's government, the Minister of Finance Sergei Witte, was concerned that what was in practice the occupation of Port Arthur might have a serious impact on relations with Japan. "This fatal step will have disastrous results," he warned. Tsar Nicholas II, on the other hand, was very pleased with the way things had turned out. "At last we have a real port that doesn't freeze. I'm thankful the occupation was peaceful. This gives me real joy! Now we can feel safe out there for a long time," he wrote in a letter to his mother in March 1898.[7]

A year later, in 1899, the Russians founded the town of Dalian. At the same time, the Boxer Rebellion broke out. This was a Chinese rebellion led by boxers from "the Righteous and Harmonious Fists" movement. The rebellion was initially targeted at Chinese Christians and foreign missionaries, but subsequently was against any imperial Western influence. Local authorities supported the Boxers, who attacked foreign embassies and companies, including the Chinese Eastern Railway.

The tsar deployed 170,000 soldiers to defend Russian interests in Manchuria. Japan, Great Britain, France, the U.S.A., Germany, Italy and the Austro-Hungarian Empire also sent military forces to quell the revolt, which cost the lives of many thousands of Boxers, Chinese soldiers and civilians. In autumn 1901, China was coerced into signing the Boxer Protocol, in which they agreed to pay more than 300 million dollars in war reparations, and to allow foreign troops to be stationed throughout the country. More than half of the Russian soldiers remained in Manchuria, thereby forcing the Chinese to surrender Manchuria to Tsar Nicholas II and Russia. This antagonised the Japanese, but they made an offer: Russia could keep Manchuria if they got Korea. The tsar was not willing to accept this compromise, however favourable: "I do not want Korea for myself, but nor can I accept that the Japanese put foot in the country. If they attempt to do so, it will be a *casus belli*." Witte argued that this posturing was "child's play that would end in catastrophe", but no-one listened.[8]

Japan repeatedly offered an agreement, but Nicholas did not even see fit to reply. In the end, Japan had had enough. On the night of February 9, 1904, Japanese torpedo boats launched a surprise attack on the Russian fleet in Port Arthur while the tsar enjoyed an opera about the water nymph Rusalka in the fashionable Mariinsky Theatre in St Petersburg. The next day, Tsar Nicholas II declared war on Japan. It was not until two days after the initial attack that Japan officially declared war on Russia.*

The surprise attack was carefully planned – the Japanese knew very well that it would take the Russians a long time to mobilise more forces. The Trans-Siberian Railway was almost finished at the time, with one important exception: the stretch by Lake Baikal had not been laid yet. A temporary track had been installed over the ice, but could only bear the weight of one horse-drawn carriage at a time. The troops would have to march across the ice carrying all the necessary equipment, causing a considerable delay to any deployment. Not only that, there was only one rail track, and no more than a handful of places where meeting trains could pass. And the trains could not travel at high speed. The track had been laid quickly, at an average rate of two kilometres a day, and as cheaply as possible, using soldiers and prisoners as labour. On the longer stretches, the average speed was less than ten kilometres an hour. It would therefore take fifty days to transport a regiment to Port Arthur. The empire was by then so vast that it was no longer able to defend itself effectively.

Tsar Nicholas II had been caught off guard.

The bus journey from Dalian to Lushun took one hour. When we turned into something that resembled a main street, I got off, pleased that I had managed to take a bus on my own in a country where I was, in effect, an illiterate deaf mute. I had made a feeble

* In 1941, the Japanese applied the same tactics, only on a larger scale, when they attacked Pearl Harbor. Japan did not declare war on the U.S.A. until the attack was officially acknowledged. Perhaps they hoped they could repeat the success of 1904 in 1941.

attempt to learn survival Chinese before I embarked on my travels, but never got further than the sounds. Instead, I had to do my best with notes of the addresses that hotel receptionists had given me, if they understood English in the first place, or put my trust in the English–Chinese dictionary app that I had downloaded before I left Norway. I hailed a taxi and showed the driver the address that the receptionist had written down for me. The driver, an old, toothless man, soon stopped trying to converse. He drove away from the centre of town and stopped by a large, empty car park. We had arrived. I bought an entry ticket to the hill, which is now described as a scenic viewpoint by the tourist board, but had once been the site of some of the most brutal battles in the Russo-Japanese war for precisely that reason.

The fighting around Port Arthur continued throughout 1904. At the start of the summer, the Japanese managed to blockade the harbour, but they still did not have full control on land. The Russians had used the time to build trenches and forts in strategic positions, and held their ground. One of the main problems that the Japanese faced was that they did not have a good enough over-view of the harbour, and the Russians exploited this disadvantage by constantly moving their ships around. Through the summer and autumn, the Japanese took control of more and more hills around the harbour, but the Russians still had the most important one, 203 Hill, whose peak is exactly 203 metres above sea level. The Japanese attempted to take control of the hill in September, but were unsuccessful. They made another attempt towards the end of November. In a matter of days, eight thousand Japanese soldiers and more than six thousand Russian soldiers lost their lives. The stench of blood, excrement and gunpowder must have lain heavy on the hillsides – and over the harbour.

I wandered up the slope in the sun. I was the only tourist and the hillside was green and peaceful. When I got to the top, I understood why it had been so important a hundred years earlier. I had a panoramic view of the harbour. A cannon stood aimed at the ships down on the water. Beside the cannon, the Japanese had erected a rather tasteless monument to commemorate their victory in the battle for the hill: the huge cartridge is made from metal taken from weapons used during the fighting. A sign from the Chinese tourist authorities informs visitors that the monument is now seen as "a monument of shame".

On January 2, 1905, a few weeks after the Japanese had taken control of 203 Hill, Port Arthur fell. The war continued for another six months, however. At the end of February, more than half a million Russian and Japanese soldiers clashed at Mukden, which is today known as Shenyang, about four hundred kilometres north of Port Arthur. The battle, which many historians believe was worse than any that had gone before it, cost the lives of an estimated fifteen thousand Japanese and eight thousand Russians.

And still it continued. The year before, on October 15, 1904, the Russians' Second Pacific Squadron had left the Baltic with twelve thousand soldiers on board various warships. The voyage started badly. On October 21, in the mist off Dogger Bank, the Russians thought they were being attacked by Japanese torpedo boats. They opened fire and killed two British fishermen. At the start of May 1905, seven months after they had set sail from the Baltic, the Russian fleet reached the Indian Ocean. And on May 27, they clashed with the Japanese fleet in the Tsushima Straits between Korea and Japan in the biggest naval battle since Trafalgar. The Russians were utterly destroyed. Approximately five thousand Russians were killed and a further six thousand were taken prisoner. Twenty-one Russian ships were sunk. In contrast, the Japanese lost only 117 men and three torpedo boats.

This marked the end of the war and Russia's humiliating defeat. It was the first time in history that a European country had lost a war to an Asian country. Sergei Witte represented Russia in the peace negotiations, which were formally led by the American president, Theodore Roosevelt, in Portsmouth. Witte had clearly done his homework and performed well, as Russia got off remarkably lightly: they did have to relinquish Port Arthur, the Liaodong Peninsula and the southern half of Sakhalin Island to the Japanese, and withdraw from Manchuria, but they did not need to pay war reparations and were allowed to keep the northern part of Sakhalin Island. Even though he was not personally present during the negotiations, President Roosevelt was awarded the Nobel Peace Prize for his efforts. He was the first (but by no means the last) American president to be given the highly esteemed prize.

The year 1905 proved to be a very busy one for both Tsar Nicholas II and Sergei Witte. The war had cost them dear on the home front as well. In addition to the many thousands of soldiers who had been killed far away in a war that very few understood, it had also resulted in food shortages in the major cities. On January 22, several hundred peaceful demonstrators marched on the Winter Palace, demanding reform, better working conditions and an end to the war with Japan. In their hands, they carried icons and pictures of Nicholas II. The tsar was not at home himself, but his uncle, Grand Duke Vladimir Alexandrovich, who was head of the security police, ordered guns to be fired at the demonstrators. More than 130 people were killed in what has gone down in history as "Bloody Sunday". This, in turn, led to strikes, protests and revolt throughout the empire. In the autumn, following Russia's humiliating defeat by the Japanese, all the major cities were brought to a standstill by a general strike. The tsar was forced to take action and Witte was appointed prime minister, with extended powers. In what later become known as the October Manifesto, Witte pledged that all men would be given the right to vote, and that all citizens would benefit from basic civil rights, including freedom of speech. A legislative assembly was formed, the State Duma, which was to be responsible for about half the national budget. Men from all social classes could in principle be elected to the Duma. This paved the way for a fairer and more democratic Russia, but the empire's absolute ruler was reluctant to accept these changes and prorogued both the first and the second Duma, which he thought were too radical. Nicholas II's inability to accept the fact that times were changing, and that the days of the autocrat were numbered, would cost him dear.

The Martyrs' Cemetery, the largest graveyard for foreigners in China, lies not far from the centre of Lushun. Two thousand Russians are buried here. Many of the graves are from the Russo-Japanese War, but some of them are more recent, from the liberation of Manchuria at the end of the Second World War. The graves are well organised, but rather unloved; many of them are decorated with red stars and the inscription "Hero of the Soviet Union". The Second World War did not end with Hitler's suicide on April 30, 1945. Three days after the atom bomb had been dropped on Hiroshima, on August 9, one and a half million Soviet soldiers marched into China to drive out the Japanese occupiers, who had been in Manchuria since 1931.

The Japanese ended up losing everything they had gained in 1905, including South Sakhalin Island and the Kuril islands, which were given to Russia at the Yalta Conference. They also lost control of the Korean peninsula, which was divided by the Soviet Union and the U.S.A. Russia and Japan are still squabbling about the three small islands of Iturup, Kunashir and Shikotan, as well as the islets of Habomai. Japan claims that these do not belong to the Kurils, whereas Russia maintains that they are included in the spoils of war that legally fell to them at the end of the Second World War. The disagreement about these small islands, with some ten thousand inhabitants, is the reason why Japan and Russia still have not formally signed a peace treaty to mark the end of the war.

The Soviet army remained in Port Arthur for ten years. In 1955, the soldiers withdrew peacefully, in line with the Treaty of Friendship that Mao and Stalin had signed five years earlier. (It should be noted that the withdrawal did not happen until Stalin had died and his successor, Nikita Khrushchev, was at the helm.) All that remains in Port Arthur of Russia's and Japan's great dreams of power are a few dilapidated buildings and monuments from the war, a cemetery, a prison and a small, turquoise wooden railway station. Russia never managed to extend the Chinese Eastern Railway here, as planned. The small station is in operation today, but is administered by China Railways.

Such time when the Chinese needed help from the Russians to expand their railway network is long gone. China Railways has experienced explosive growth in recent years. In the past decade, the number of train passengers has nearly doubled, and the Chinese rail network is now the second largest in the world, after that of the U.S.A. Two and a half million passengers travel on Chinese trains every year, a figure which is all the more impressive when you take into account that the *average* journey is more than five hundred kilometres. The expansion of Chinese railways and the express trains that run between the major cities are telling examples of the dramatic improvement in the Chinese economy, which has, quite literally, been high speed.

The Orient's Moscow

In no more than a few hours, the high-speed train took me from Dalian to Harbin, more than eight hundred kilometres further north. Clusters of identical, modern high-rise blocks sped past the train window and disappeared. Every now and then a field, maize plants. Then more high-rises.

Before I went there, I had been warned that China was like India, minus the stomach upsets. I had therefore steeled myself, but the people who warned me had clearly never been to India. To be fair, there were people everywhere in China, everything took time, and the traffic more often than not was at a standstill – if one did not travel by express train, that is, which was almost as expensive as flying. But if one looked past the pollution that hung like a grey lid over the cities, the Chinese towns were generally both clean and well planned. Queues were long, but disciplined. Almost no-one jumped the queue. Everything appeared to be efficient and organised. The same cannot be said of Indian cities.

However, these well-organised, tidy towns were devoid of character, and full of square, shabby concrete buildings or smooth, modern glass houses, and oceans of neon lights. It was not easy to distinguish one town from another; they were all the same, with one notable exception: Harbin. Harbin is a curiosity indeed, a Chinese city with character.

The town was founded by the Russians in 1898, as an administrative centre for the Chinese Eastern Railway. The name Harbin is a Manchu word that means "place to dry nets". It was originally a poor fishing village. The Russians were certainly not lazy, and soon there were shopping streets and churches along the riverbanks. Only a few years later, the town had thirty thousand inhabitants. St Nicholas' Church was completed in 1900, only to be pulled down during the Chinese Cultural Revolution. St Sophia's Church, which was built in the 1930s, is still standing, despite its vulnerable central location.

The green, onion-shaped cupola looks so out of place, surrounded as it is by Chinese signage. St Sophia's used to serve as a warehouse for one of the nearby department stores, a fate shared by many churches under communism in Russia. Then, about twenty years ago, it was given a token restoration in the hope that it might attract tourists to the city, and it now houses the city museum. Photographs hang on the flaking whitewashed walls that show what Harbin looked like before the Russians came. There are pictures of poor farmers in worn clothes bending over home-made fishing nets, and portraits of Europeans dressed in the latest fashion.

In the 1920s, Harbin was called the Paris of the Far East and was China's undisputed capital of fashion. But the Russians in Harbin did more than just go to church and sport fashionable clothes. In 1903, there were eight distilleries in the town, which, combined, produced a total of ten thousand litres of cherry vodka for the town's many thirsty inhabitants. The Russian railway employees not only had a taste for cheap Russian spirits, but also for cheap women. Sexually transmitted diseases were rampant in the Paris of the Far East in those early years. It is said that Chinese girls did not wash for fear that they might wash away their good luck. The railway company tried to improve hygiene standards by importing prostitutes from Japan. But as the Japanese ladies charged as much as those in Vladivostok, they did not stand a chance against the local workforce.

Following their defeat against Japan in 1905, the Russians lost control of the Chinese Eastern Railway. The majority of Russians moved away from Harbin, but the city continued to attract foreigners. Harbin became an international metropolis over the next few years, as 160,000 people from scores of different countries moved to the city. Then, during the Russian Revolution and bloody civil war that followed, hundreds of thousands of political refugees fled to Harbin, making it a largely Russian city again. Since many of the Russians who sought refuge here were Jews, it had the largest Jewish population in the Far East in the 1920s. The Jews had their own banks, libraries, hospitals, schools, old people's homes, soup kitchens and twenty or so newspapers, most of them in Russian, so helped to replenish the city's coffers and increase trade.

There are no longer any Jews in Harbin, nor any descendants of the original Harbin Russians. The Japanese invasion of Manchuria and establishment of the puppet state of Manchukuo in 1932 marked the beginning of the end for China's Paris, or the Orient's Moscow, as the city was also known. Some of the worst war crimes committed in the last century took place in a complex that was simply called Unit 731, only a few kilometres outside Harbin. A museum has been built so that no-one can forget the cruelties that took place there. The sombre, black building brings to mind the Holocaust Museum in Berlin.

The Japanese quickly realised that they would not win a war against the Western superpowers with conventional weapons, so they started intensive research into biological warfare towards the end of the 1930s. In Unit 731, which was the largest research facility in Manchukuo, experiments were carried out with all manner of things, from salmonella to dysentery, and anthrax to tuberculosis. They used rats, hamsters and horses to host bacteria colonies, which they then tested on prisoners of war and the local population. Among other things, the Japanese contaminated wells in

Mongolia with cholera and typhoid and then followed closely to see the effect this had on the nomads. Research was carried out with more than fifty different bacteria and viruses, and literally tons of bacteria colonies were produced in Unit 731 in the time it was operational. The doctors routinely carried out vivisection in order to study the progression of the infection in victims. To make the experiments as realistic as possible, prisoners of war were sometimes bound to stakes out in the fields and bacteria bombs were then released nearby; the prisoners were dressed in metal suits to protect them from the blast itself, so they would not be killed. Experiments were also carried out to study the effect of extreme cold on the human body.

It is unlikely that the biological weapons developed at Unit 731 were ever used, not even during the dramatic but relatively unknown border dispute between the Soviet Union, Mongolia and Japan in the summer of 1939. On May 11, the Japanese attacked a group of horsemen who they claimed had crossed the border into Manchukuo illegally. The conflict quickly escalated and developed into undeclared war between the Soviet Union and Japan. Hundreds of thousands of soldiers were involved in the fighting, which lasted four months. More than fifteen thousand soldiers were killed on the Mongolian–Chinese border that summer. The Japanese in particular suffered considerable losses and eventually had to withdraw from Mongolia, having gained nothing. The conflict was instrumental in Stalin's decision to sign a treaty of non-aggression with Hitler in August the same year. Stalin wanted at all costs to avoid a double-fronted war with Germany and Japan, who were allies, and the treaty gave him room for manoeuvre in both the east and the west. Japan never tried to attack the Soviet Union again.

Research continued at Unit 731 until the summer of 1945. Tens of thousands of people lost their lives as a result of the barbaric experiments, both inside and outside the walls of the much-feared facility. Before the Japanese withdrew from Manchuria in late summer 1945, they destroyed all the buildings where these grotesque experiments had taken place. But instead of killing the plague-infected rats, they released them. The epidemic that ensued killed more than twenty thousand people.

In August 1945, the Red Army entered Harbin and the circle was complete. Like the rest of the population, the local Russians had suffered during the Japanese occupation. But when the Red Army marched in, the situations worsened for many of them. Thousands of Harbin Russians were accused of being anti-communist or of having collaborated with the Japanese, and were sent off to camps in the Soviet Union.

In spring 1946, the Soviet Union surrendered Harbin to Mao's forces, the People's Liberation Army. Thus Harbin became the first major city to fall into the Chinese communists' hands. The Russians who were still left in the city were persecuted by the Chinese communist government, and by 1960 most of the Russians and Jews had left the city to seek their fortunes elsewhere.

But their houses are still there. The pastel-coloured buildings in the pedestrian streets of the old town are reminiscent of those in St Petersburg, even though most of them were in fact rebuilt or totally renovated long after the Russians had left town. The "Russian pedestrian zone" is categorised as a "free open-air museum" by the tourist authorities. It felt slightly absurd wandering past the archetypal buildings, surrounded by Chinese signs and people. There was not a Russian to be seen, and yet the shops all sold Russian chocolate powder and instant coffee, fur hats, vodka and wooden matryoshka dolls. The Russian heritage includes not only the buildings but also the food. Harbin is the only place in China where it is usual to eat bread every day, and the people who live here are also great consumers of ice cream and kvass, a slightly alcoholic drink made from fermented rye bread.

In order to avoid the aggressive souvenir vendors in the open-air museum, I went down one of the many stairways leading to Harbin's underworld. A network of streets underground makes it possible to cross the centre of town in any direction without seeing daylight or breathing fresh air.

The underground street network is a legacy from the Cold War. The relationship between China and the Soviet Union deteriorated dramatically in the 1950s owing to disagreements over ideology and which country should be the leading superpower in the communist world. Khrushchev believed that peaceful co-existence with the capitalist world was possible, which Mao regarded as pure revisionism. After Khrushchev's famous speech in 1956, when he denounced Stalin, the front lines were increasingly hard, and on several occasions in the years that followed, the countries were on the verge of war.

The most serious confrontation took place in the vicinity of Damansky Island, an uninhabited border island in the Ussuri River in 1969. In Chinese it is called Zhenbao Island. Its name, which can be translated as "rare treasure island", is very misleading: the island is no bigger than 0.74 square kilometres and contains nothing of any financial worth, and when the river runs high, the island is submerged. It is in fact more of a sandbank than an island. In March 1969, Chinese soldiers went ashore on Damansky Island and opened fire on the Soviet border guards. Several hundred Chinese and Russian soldiers lost their lives in the subsequent clashes.

In 1991, Damansky Island was formally handed over to China, which prompted strong reactions in Russia. Those who protested of course understood that the island was of no financial import-ance to Russia, but that was not the point. They believed that it was not *right* that the Chinese should have the island, given everything they had done to the Russians in 1969.

I tried for weeks to get permission to visit the disputed island, but none of the travel agencies I contacted even bothered to answer.

In the 1960s, many people feared that the conflict between the Soviet Union and China would lead to outright war. The Chinese feared that the Russians would then use nuclear weapons. The network of streets under Harbin was built with this in mind – the inhabitants needed a refuge. As Harbin was close to the Soviet border and therefore vulnerable, Mao moved any important industries further south. In other words, the chances of nuclear war were seen to be very real; there were even calculations of how many lives might be lost if the Soviet Union did attack. The Central Military Commission considered it not unlikely that 300 million people could die in the initial stages of any war. On the bright side, however, according to these calculations there would still be about 500 million people alive once the mushroom cloud had dispersed. And they would be ready to fight a sustained war against the enemy. It was regrettable that some hundreds of millions would die early on, but China would win in the end, and that was the only thing that really mattered to Mao and the generals.

There was no nuclear war, and the bomb shelter is now an enormous, underground shopping centre, one of the largest of its kind in the world. It is possible to buy everything from toilet seats to cheap clothes in the kilometre-long narrow passages, which form a labyrinthine city under the city, complete with signs and maps, shopping streets and places to eat. And it is no doubt very practical in winter, when temperatures can fall to minus thirty degrees Celsius. Harbin is the coldest city in China.

I personally could not cope with more than a few minutes in the cramped confines before I had to go up again for fresh air and daylight.

*

"The Russians are way behind us," said Tom, a young Chinese man who had studied Russian in Vladivostok in the early Noughties. A Norwegian friend of mine who had studied in Vladivostok at the same time had put us in touch. Like so many Chinese people, he had adopted a Western name in addition to his Chinese name.

"When I lived in Vladivostok, I felt that they were thirty years behind Harbin," Tom said. "Russia has agricultural land and energy. And China needs both things, so our leaders maintain a good relationship with the Russians. It is as simple as that. Personally, I would never go back to Russia."

Before he went, Tom had been warned what the Russians could be like. For a long time, everything was fine. On a couple of occasions, strangers came up to him and told him to go back to China, but never anything more serious. Not until the Chinese Mid-Autumn Festival, or Moon Festival.

"I and five other Chinese students had been out celebrating," Tom told me. "It was eleven o'clock in the evening and we were walking down the street. I was at the back. We were by the university and since there are no streetlights there, it was pitch dark. Without warning, someone started to throw bottles and stones at us. It all happened in silence, under cover of darkness. They said nothing, just threw hard objects at us. Then they attacked us in person. There were women with us, otherwise we would not have run away. How can anyone attack a woman? One of the girls ran in the opposite direction from the rest of us – she thought she could get away if she didn't follow the crowd. The attackers caught up with her and punched and kicked her in the face and stomach. She got a terrible black eye and the next day there was blood in her urine. I was hit on the shoulder, from behind. If you are going to attack someone, you should do it from the front, I think. Not from behind, under cover of darkness, without saying anything."

"Did you see who the attackers were?" I asked.

"No. I concentrated on running. I ran as fast as I could."

Tom made me promise not to use his Chinese name or say where he worked. He had run away. He should have fought back.

"After that experience, I stopped going out in the evening or at night," he said. "It was the end of my social life in Vladivostok. I have heard about many others who were attacked, it was not an isolated incident. So no, I do not like Russians." He smiled and shrugged. "And now Russia is on the way down, and China is on the way up."

Before I left Harbin, I visited the Russian Style Town. The advertisement promised dancing and exotic fantasies: "Russian Style Town has many European villas and chalets. The dancing of the blonde girls, the romantic love songs of the blue-eyed boys and the foreign charm placed people in exotic fantasy."

The Chinese are masters at recreating European towns. A true copy of Venice opened recently in Dalian, complete with canals and gondolas. There are also copies of Austrian and Swiss alpine villages, as well as miniature versions of London and Paris, with replicas of Tower Bridge and the Eiffel Tower. The Russian Style Town in Harbin was on Sun Island, a recreation area in the middle of the river that divides the town. At the entrance, I was met by a Putin matryoshka and a sculpture of a Russian farmer's wife. No sooner had I bought my ticket than a giggling Chinese girl asked if she could take a selfie with me. I was happy to oblige.

Inside the gates they had built an idyllic nineteenth-century Russian village, with timber houses, a bakery, a chocolate shop, a vodka shop and geese. Most of the houses were disguised souvenir shops, but some were actually furnished like a museum of a nineteenth century life that had never existed. I went into one of them and was effusively welcomed by an old woman with a wrinkly face, kind eyes and photogenic shawl over her shoulders. "*Zdravstvuyte!*"

I greeted her in return, and she realised straightaway that I was not Russian, but was all the more excited by the fact that I could speak Russian.

"My name is Tanya." The old woman gave me a long embrace and pinched my cheeks. "This is incredible," she mumbled to herself. "A foreigner who speaks Russian!" She clapped her hands in delight.

Tanya was from Vladivostok, and had moved to Harbin when her husband died three years earlier.

"It is impossible to live on a pension in Russia," she said. "Not if you are alone. The tiny amount of money they give us can hardly be called a pension! Here I get two thousand yuan a month with free board and lodging. And during the high season, I can earn one hundred and fifty yuan more each day from photographs."

When I thanked her for her time and was about to leave, Tanya slipped into a side room and came back with a pile of photographs. Her daughter-in-law, her grandchild, her late husband.

"Life here on the island is a bit monotonous," she said. "I speak no Chinese, so I spend all my time here in the village with the other Russians. Luckily there are a few of us old ladies from Vladivostok, so we keep each other company."

As we chatted, there were frequent little explosions of delight at the fact that I spoke Russian. When I told her that I was an author, she almost wept with joy. Before I left, she held me tight and planted a wet kiss on each cheek.

"Promise that you will write to me, promise!" She handed me a crumpled piece of paper with her email address on it. "We do not have Internet here, so I will not be able to read your emails until the spring, but I so look forward to hearing from you."

I had to hand over more yuan to get into the show area where the blonde girls entertained their audience with romantic songs about blue-eyed boys. The posters had shown shapely Russian girls in fishnet stockings and saucy stilettos, but the reality did not live up to my expectations. Five young Russian women sang and danced on a low, home-made, open-air stage for an audience of about ten. None of the women could sing, and they were not particularly good dancers either. They also looked as though they were bored to distraction. The shabby but respectable costumes were nothing like the sexy outfits on the poster. But the Chinese audience whooped and clapped enthusiastically after every number. When the show was over, the men leaped up onto the stage to be photographed with the girls. Every picture cost five yuan.

When I left the Russian Style Town, I sat down on a bench for a short rest. The autumn air was crisp and clear, and the bushes that edged the grass were cut like matryoshkas. In the ten minutes that I sat there, three Chinese people came over and asked if they could take a selfie with me. I explained to them that I was not Russian, but that did not seem to matter. I was fair-haired, blue-eyed and exotic, and that was good enough for them.

On the way back to the hotel, I wandered down an avenue of big, green trees. A sign informed me that I was in Stalin Park. All that remains of the Orient's Moscow is a theme park with hired Russians, a street of souvenir shops, a couple of churches that serve as historical museums, and a thin, rectangular park named after the worst despot of the last century.

As well as bread, kvass and ice cream.

Restaurant Putin

The flight from Harbin to Heihe took a little more than an hour, but when the small propeller airplane landed, I found myself in a different world. The Siberian northerly stung my cheeks as soon as I stepped out of the plane. The Chinese characters looked out of place in the familiar, northern landscape, with kilometres of orange birch trees and evergreen pine forest.

Heihe means "black river". It is a small provincial town, with roughly two hundred thousand inhabitants, on the banks of the Amur River by the Russian border. On the opposite side of the river is a mirror image of the Chinese town, the Russian town of Blagoveshchensk. It is more or less the same size as Heihe and is considered a city in that part of Russia. Heihe, on the other hand, barely qualifies to be called a town by Chinese standards, even though it has as many shopping streets, shopping malls and beautifully maintained parks as towns with three times the population. This is because the Russians from Blagoveshchensk can visit Heihe without a visa. According to the articles I had read, thousands of Russians streamed over the border every day, armed with shopping bags and yuan, ready to buy cheap Chinese goods. After a couple of weeks in China, where even ordering a cup of coffee was a considerable linguistic challenge, I was looking forward to meeting some Russians.

But first I had to get from the airport into the centre. I could only find the English name and address of the hotel I had booked on my booking app. The taxi driver drove me to five different hotels without finding the Hanting Express. Looking pretty desperate, he eventually dropped me off in the middle of a crossroads. The signs above the shops were in both Chinese and Russian. I stood there on the lookout for Russians who knew the town, but did not see a single fair-haired person. As far as I could tell, I was the only foreigner in Heihe, yet no-one graced me with a look, no-one wanted to take a selfie with me. They made their money from fair people, so I was no rarity there. But where were they, these hordes of suitcase shoppers who crossed the Amur River every day?

I stopped a couple of taxis, but the drivers did not understand where I wanted to go, so drove on without me. It was even colder here, close to the river. I blew into my hands and tried again to look it up on on my mobile. Eventually I managed to find the Chinese address for the hotel. The taxi driver I stopped gave me a strange look, but he let me get in, turned on the meter and off we went. The Hanting Express was a couple of hundred metres from the crossroads where I had been dropped.

I checked in, put on the warmest clothes I had and walked back to the river. On the other side I could see red and blue apartment blocks, low concrete buildings and church spires. Autumn leaves. The pale-blue sky and white clouds arched over the flat landscape.

In an attempt to please the Russian daytrippers, the local council in Heihe had put out matryoshka-shaped rubbish bins. It was a huge mistake. The Russians were furious. How dare the Chinese equate their culture with rubbish? The new bins were quickly left on the scrapheap, and, instead, statues of dancing bears now line the street along the river.

Aigun, the fort where the Chinese were forced to cede the area to the north of the river to the Russians, was thirty kilometres away. For more than 150 years, Russia has ruled over the forests and frozen steppes north of Heilongjiang, as the Amur is called in Chinese. Only slightly more than six million people, about a third of the population of Moscow, live in the whole of the Russian Far East region, an enormous area that lies to the east of Siberia and shares borders with China, the Pacific Ocean and the Arctic Ocean. This sparsely populated area covers a third of Russia's total territory. By way of contrast, about 40 million people live in the Heilongjiang district, on the Chinese side of the border, an area that is ten times smaller than the Russian Far East region. And so it has been since the seventeenth century: Russia has more land, China has more people.

Since large areas of arable land in eastern Russia lie fallow, Putin has decided to make the Far East region a priority. One initiative has been to offer all Russians who move there a hectare of free land. Some fifty thousand people have taken up the offer of free land so far. And the Chinese are also tempted by Russian soil. In recent years, Chinese companies and farmers have signed lease agreements for more than 600,000 hectares of land in Siberia and the Far East region, and if the Russian authorities were to give them free rein, they would gladly pay for access to more arable land. The local Russians are ambivalent: as the situation stands, large areas lie unused because there are not enough people to cultivate them. Incomers bring with them growth and development. On the other hand, the Russians are afraid that they will end up in the minority, surrounded by the Chinese. The Russian authorities, clearly aware of the problem, are therefore trying to balance Chinese investment in the region with increased settlement by ethnic Russians.

No more than eight hundred metres of water and sandbanks separate Heihe from Blagoveshchensk. No other Chinese town lies so close to Russia. During the Cultural Revolution, enormous loudspeakers were erected along the riverbank. The Russians on the other side of the river were bombarded day and night with loud Maoist propaganda. But during the Boxer Rebellion in 1900, the bombardment of Blagoveshchensk was far worse. According to legend, the town was saved from complete annihilation by the icon of Our Lady of Albazin. The people prayed to her night and day for the entire fortnight that the town was bombarded. As revenge for the attack, the head of police in Blagoveshchensk decided that the town's Chinese population, which was around four thousand at the time, should be banished. They were transported to the narrowest point of the river and forced to leave Russian soil. Those who refused were chased out into the water with axes and pistols. Since not many of the Chinese could swim, only a few made it over to the other side alive.

The animosity lasted a long time, even after the collapse of the Soviet Union. It was only in 2008 that Russia and China finally signed an agreement that delineated their 4,300-kilometre border, and thus put an end to the dispute. This had been kept alive by two contested islands, Tabar Island and Bolshoy Ussuriysky, which lie along the confluence of the Ussuri and Amur rivers. In 2008, the Russians agreed to transfer Tabar Island to the Chinese, and China accepted that they would only get half of Bolshoy Ussuriysky, not the whole island as they had demanded.

Blagoveshchensk has one of the largest Chinese populations of any Russian town, thanks to the 1994 duty-free trade agreement with Heihe. The construction of a bridge between the two towns is currently in its final stages, which will further facilitate trade. As a result of the sanctions imposed on Russia by the West following the annexation of Crimea, trade between Russia and China has increased considerably. China and the Netherlands are Russia's most important trading partners. Russia is the biggest supplier of crude oil to China, and work started in 2015 on a 4,000-kilometre gas pipeline from Siberia to Shanghai, via Heihe. The relationship between the two countries is far from balanced, however: China is significantly more important to Russia than Russia is to China. China's trade with the E.U. and the U.S.A. is still ten times greater than its trade with Russia.

My teeth were chattering as I walked over the bridge to the island that the Chinese call Tomazhnya, after the Russian word for "customs". The ferry to Blagoveshchensk leaves from the end of the island, hence the name. A few years ago, the Chinese built two big shopping malls on the island, which is on the Chinese side of the border, in order to satisfy the Russians' hunger for a bargain. Now all the Russians have to do is take the ferry to Tomazhnya, shop and then take the ferry home again, without having to set foot on the Chinese mainland.

A couple of empty taxis drove past, but other than that I was the only person on the bridge. I had wrapped myself in all the woollen base layers and winter clothes in my suitcase, but still the Siberian wind blew straight through me. It was only October, and Mongolia and Kazakhstan lay ahead. I was starting, literally, to get cold feet.

At the end of the bridge, a faded Russian flag fluttered on the roof of a long-shut bar. The enormous, almost empty car park was edged by two huge, grey shopping centres. I tramped over to the newest one, the Yuan Dun Centre. The windows were full of fur and leather jackets, but the building was dark and the entrance was locked.

The other mall, which was smaller and shabbier, was open. I walked through the glass doors and came into a hall of drawn curtains. Only a few of the shops were open; the others were closed and waiting for better times, the display stands and any goods that were left were hidden behind colourful textiles. Most of the booths sold tea, fur hats, pharmaceuticals, bags or fur coats – goods that were popular with the Russians. A handful of Chinese people were wandering around, but there was not a Russian to be seen. The booth holders perked up when they saw me.

"*Devushka*, very cheap!" they shouted to me in Russian with a thick Chinese accent. "Great offer! You want a bag? Chinese tea?"

"Where are all the Russians?" I asked a woman who sold traditional herbal medicines.

"The rouble . . ." she said, sadly. "The rouble has fallen!"

"Before, one yuan was worth five roubles," said the man next door, who specialised in cheap bags. "Now one yuan costs ten roubles. Not many Russians come here now, just look around."

The next floor was even more deserted. All the shops were closed apart from one selling fur coats, which had somehow managed to stay open.

"How old are you?" the assistant asked in rudimentary Russian.

It turned out we were the same age.

"Are you married?" she asked.

I nodded.

"Where do you live?"

I told her where I lived. There was no end to her questions: "Do you live in a house or a flat? How big is your flat? How many rooms do you have? Do you own it or rent it? What is your job? How much do you earn per month? How long are you staying in Heihe?" I barely managed to answer before she asked the next question. This must be what it is like to travel in China, if you can understand Chinese.

"Do you have children?" she asked.

I shook my head.

"I have a six-month-old baby. Having children is wonderful, you should try," she said. "Give it a go."

I promised to think about it, then made my way out of the semi-closed shopping centre. Desperate sellers called out as the glass doors closed behind me. "*Devushka*, very cheap! Great offer! Only ten yuan! How about some Chinese tea?"

There was a large amusement park behind the shopping centre, with carousels, bumper cars, kiosks and all the fun of the fair. But judging by the piles of rotting leaves that had gathered in the gondolas on the Ferris wheel, it was a long time since it had last gone round.

In the evening I went to Restaurant Putin, supposedly Heihe's best restaurant. Other than having the menu translated into Russian, the owner had not made any noticeable effort to link the name to the interior. The name itself was clearly enough, because there were four mature Russians sitting in the corner, eating and drinking. Finally! I sat down at a neighbouring table and it did not take long before I was on first-name terms with Victor, Oleg, Ludmilla and Natasha.

"We used to come here a lot before, but it is three years now since the last time," Victor said. "Everything is twice as expensive now because of the crisis."

"We used to come here when we wanted to get out and about," Ludmilla said. "Otherwise, we have everything we want at home in Russia. It's a good life. We have our flats and our dachas. And the standard of living is higher."

"They seem to have pretty good living standards here as well," I said.

"Only a few years ago, everyone cycled in China," Oleg said. "Now they all have cars. But their flats are small. We have big flats."

"And we have such a good president!" Ludmilla crowed. "His name is Putin. He doesn't drink. He keeps in good shape, even though he is over sixty."

The waitress appeared with perfect timing and filled their glasses with vodka. They raised their glasses to international friendship.

"Putin was in the region not long ago," Victor said. "He killed three tigers with his own bare hands!" He demonstrated how the president had killed the big cats. "Why don't you come over to our side? We have bears and tigers and ..."

"Don't frighten her!" Ludmilla said.

"I've mainly been in Moscow and St Petersburg," I admitted.

"Moscow and St Petersburg!" Victor snorted. "That is not Russia, that is Europe!"

"I have been to the Caucasus quite a lot as well," I said.

"That is certainly not Russia!" Victor roared.

"Very definitely not!" Oleg said.

I promised that I would visit the real Russia as soon as I could.

"Come soon!" Oleg said, and raised his glass of vodka again. "We will show you everything, the bears and tigers and ..."

"Shush, Oleg!" Ludimilla cried. "Don't frighten her!" She turned towards me, raised her glass and beamed. "We have a good life in Russia. It is much better at home than here."

Disney on the Border

"Number twenty-one." The conductor did not even bother to look at my ticket, she just waved me into the carriage. Her assistant followed me down the narrow corridor to the only compartment with an open door, and pointed to the bottom berth on the right.

"Number twenty-one."

A few minutes later, the train left Beijing railway station. I soon realised that I had not only the compartment to myself, but the whole carriage. The only thing the conductor and her assistant had to do was to look after me. This sense of being alone was a taste of what was to come: I was on my way from the world's most populous country to one of the least populated. Mongolia is the eighth largest country in the world in terms of area, twice the size of Turkey, but only about three million people live there.

The simplest way to travel overland from China to Mongolia is the express train from Beijing, so I had gone south again to the Chinese capital. I had been careful to book a ticket on a Chinese train to Ulan Bator, not on one of the many Russian trains that continue on to Moscow. If there was one thing I had learnt on my previous travels in the former Soviet Union, it was to avoid Russian trains at all cost. The Chinese train was wonderful: clean and tidy, new and modern, with a pastel-blue colour scheme. Soon we had left the grey smog of Beijing behind and were speeding through a landscape of green, pointed hills. These got lower and lower and the landscape flattened out. The hours passed. I had made delusional plans of how much I would read and write on the train;

instead I sat there staring out at the misty countryside. I wandered down to the restaurant car a couple of times for a simple meal.

When we got to the Mongolian border, this idyll was promptly shattered. Four Chinese guards in uniform knocked on the door and took away my passport. A short while later, the conductor and her assistant ordered me to leave the train. They were playing soothing Disney music on the bare, almost deserted station platform – soft flutey music on a loop. As I walked towards the building, the train reversed out of sight. The Chinese tracks meet the standard international gauge of 1.435 metres, whereas the Mongolian tracks follow the Russian standard, which is 1.52 metres. The carriages had therefore to be adapted before we could continue our journey into Mongolia. There was nothing to do other than while away the time in the spartan waiting room. Minutes ticked into hours. It was well past midnight by the time the train rolled back alongside the platform and I could be reunited with my lonely compartment.

Knock, knock.

The uniformed delegation handed back my passport and marched on to the next carriage.

Knock, knock.

A Mongolian customs officer popped his head in.

"Customs declaration, please!"

"Customs declaration?" I said, confused. "What customs declaration?"

The officer let out a deep sigh and carried on.

Knock, knock.

A friendly Mongolian woman appeared in the doorway.

"Passport, please."

She came back half an hour later, handed my passport back with a smile, and wished me good night before gently closing the door. A few moments later, we started to move. I lay there and listened to the soporific sounds of the train. *Ta-tam-tatam-ta-tam-tatam.* I eventually fell asleep. I woke up in the early morning and thought I should get up and look out of the window to catch a glimpse of the Gobi Desert, but my mind was befuddled and my body lulled by the rhythm of the train. When I woke up again, the landscape was entirely different, with low hills, like waves of hard-packed sand everywhere. There were herds of horses here and there, the odd camel. A small, square house, a lonely tent. Otherwise, nothing.

Later in the afternoon, the hills got higher and more undulating, with patches of snow. Exactly twenty-seven hours after our departure from Beijing, we drew into the station in Ulan Bator. The cold winter air hit me as soon as I stepped down onto the platform. I was immediately surrounded by a gaggle of women, armed with brochures. Did I need somewhere to stay? Was I looking for a tour operator? I took their brochures and went out into the street to find a taxi. A cheerful woman driver in her forties stopped. She spoke a little Russian and a little English, and a rather confusing mixture of both, peppered with Mongolian phrases. When she was not speaking, she sang Mongolian songs for me. The flat I had booked was only two kilometres from the station, but it took us more than half an hour to get there.

The congestion in Ulan Bator was even worse than in Beijing. The traffic was at a standstill.

A Living God, a Mad Baron and a Red Hero

"Excuse me!" I turned and came face to face with a red-haired European, who must have been about thirty-something. He was sporting a hipster beard and hiking gear. "You should be more careful," he said in English, and pointed at my camera, which was dangling down my back. "Things disappear round here. Keep an eye on it."

I thanked him and took a firm hold of the strap.

Later on in the evening, I met him again in the state department store, one of Ulan Bator's landmarks.

"Sorry if I frightened you," he said. "But there were two men walking behind you, and one of them was eyeing up your camera. After I warned you, they followed me for about fifteen minutes. I have heard so many stories. You have to keep your wits about you, especially in the streets around here."

The guidebook had warned that Ulan Bator was notorious for pickpockets, but I was still in a bubble having spent weeks in North Korea and China, where there is practically no crime against Western tourists. In the centre of the city, in amongst all the coffee bars and sports shops, it was easy to forget that Mongolia is still a poor country. To be fair, it is one of the former communist states that has managed the transition to democracy best, and everything seems to be pointing in the right direction – poverty is decreasing and life expectancy and education are increasing – but more than one fifth of the population still live below the bread line. Some of the poorest live on the outskirts of Ulan Bator.

In the past few decades, the Mongolian capital has grown, without any kind of town planning or even the most basic upgrade in infrastructure. Following the fall of the communist regime in 1990, the population of Ulan Bator has increased threefold, from half a million to one and a half million. Most of the newcomers are nomads who have come to build a new life in the city. Many of them had no choice. Every five years or so, Mongolia is afflicted by what the Mongols call *dzud*: an unusually hard winter in which a significant proportion of the livestock dies. There are five permutations of this catastrophe: *tsagaan dzud* (white *dzud*), which is caused by substantial snowfall that makes it difficult for the animals to feed; *khar dzud* (black *dzud*), when no snow results in a lack of drinking water; *khuiten dzud* (cold *dzud*), when it has been extremely cold for several days in a row and the animals cannot eat because they are using all their energy to stay warm; and *tumer dzud* (iron *dzud*), when a warm period in the middle of winter is followed by a cold period, so the snow melts, then freezes again and covers the ground with a layer of impenetrable ice. Sometimes more than one kind of *dzud* can strike in the same winter; such a combination is called *khavarsan dzud*. These catastrophes have occurred relatively recently and have hit hard. In 2010, Mongolia suffered the worst *dzud* in living history. Eight million animals died, nearly a fifth of the total livestock.

As the state does not have the capacity to offer compensation, the victims of a *dzud* must find other ways of earning a living. Many move to the city in the hope that they will find work of some kind. Ex-nomads rarely have the means to pay for a flat, so the majority live in yurts, or *gers* as they are called here, in informal settlements that are dotted across the city. More than half of Ulan Bator's inhabitants live in the *ger* district.

One afternoon I left the centre and went up to one of the hillsides covered in white yurts. It was not easy to get there. The road was so bad that the taxi driver eventually refused to go any further. There was nothing more than a hard-worn path between the rows of yurts. The air clawed at my throat, even though it was only October and many people had not started burning fires yet. The only way to heat a yurt in winter is to keep the wood burner stoked around the clock. Whereas nomads out on the steppes generally use dried dung as fuel, most people in the *ger* district use coal. In winter, when temperatures can fall to minus forty Celsius, Ulan Bator is not only the world's coldest capital, it is also the most polluted. Scientists estimate that at least ten per cent of deaths in the city are the direct result of air pollution.

My footsteps were accompanied by angry barking from the hundreds of dogs that guarded their limited territory behind high, improvised fences. Unlike in the wild, the inhabitants had made sure to protect their small plots of land. Brightly painted simple houses had been built next to the yurts, a sign of how permanent the tent settlements are. More than a million people live in the *ger* district, a third of Mongolia's total population, but they lack almost any infrastructure. Most of the yurts have electricity, but very few of them have access to mains water and there is no sewage system up on the hillsides. When it rains, the risk of land-slides is high. It is every man for himself.

The *ger* district on the edges of Ulan Bator is growing by about forty thousand people each year. Most of the people who come to settle here stay for the rest of their lives.

From the beginning, Ulan Bator has been a place with more tents than houses, inhabited by nomads passing through. Origin-ally the town itself kept moving. Ulan Bator, or Ikh Khüree ("big camp") as the town was then called, was established as a nomadic yurt monastery in 1639 for the Mongols' spiritual leader, Jebtsund-amba Khutuktu. As the town grew, the camp moved less often, and in 1778 the Mongolian capital became fixed in its present location. The Mongols continued to live in yurts, whereas the Chinese, who ruled Mongolia until 1911, built administrative buildings and shops. In the latter half of the nineteenth century, when China was forced to open up for trade with other nations and foreign merchants, the Russian population in the town grew.

The American naturalist Roy Chapman Andrews, who was in Mongolia towards the end of the First World War, described the Chinese and Russian influence in Urga, as the town was known in the West back then: "Three great races have met in Urga and each carries on, in this far corner of Mongolia, its own customs and way of life. The Mongol *yurt* has remained unchanged; the Chinese shop, with its wooden counter and blue-gowned inmates, is pure Chinese; and the ornate cottages proclaim themselves to be only Russian. [...] We never tired of wandering through the narrow alleys, with their tiny native shops, or of watching the ever-changing crowds. Mongols in half a dozen different tribal dresses, Tibetan pilgrims, Manchu Tartars, or camel drivers from far Turkestan drank and ate and gambled with Chinese from civilized Peking. The barbaric splendor of the native dress fairly makes one gasp for breath."[9]

Andrews was both attracted to and repulsed by the Mongols: "In the careless freedom of his magnificent horsemanship a Mongol seems as much an untamed creature of the plains as does the eagle itself which soars above his *yurt*," he wrote with great admiration. He was, however, less impressed by their hygiene. "When a meal has been eaten, the wooden bowl is licked clean with the tongue; it is seldom washed. Every man and woman usually carries through life the bodily dirt which has accumulated in childhood, unless it is removed by some accident or by the wear of years. One can be morally certain that it will never be washed off by design or water." He describes with horror the way in which corpses were abandoned outside the town to be eaten by eagles and wild dogs. He was not particularly impressed by their sexual morals either: "A man may have only one lawful wife, but may keep as many concubines as his means allow, all of whom live with the members of the family in the single room of the *yurt*. Adultery is openly practiced, apparently without prejudice to either party, and polyandry is not unusual in the more remote parts of the country." Andrews concluded that the Mongol "lives like an untaught child of nature".

When Andrews visited Mongolia in 1918, it was a country in transition, squeezed as it was between two mighty neighbours. It was still formally attached to China, but was striving for freedom and independence. Mongolia had been a part of China since 1368, when the Ming dynasty drove the Mongolians out of China and destroyed their capital city, Karakorum. Prior to that, the Mongolians had ruled an empire that stretched from the Sea of Japan in the east to Kiev in the west, including what is now China. Kublai Khan, Ghengis Khan's grandson, united China into one kingdom and founded the Yuan dynasty in the thirteenth century. When the Mongols were finally thrown out of China in 1368, they had ruled for more than a hundred years. They were driven back to their original territory, the inhospitable steppes and deserts to the north of the Great Wall of China. In the centuries that followed, there was a lot of internal conflict between the various Mongolian tribes. At the end of the seventeenth century, Mongolia was invaded by the Manchu Qing dynasty and formally became a part of China. The Manchus divided Mongolia into two administrative areas: Outer Mongolia to the north and Inner Mongolia to the south. Any revolt was brutally suppressed, in Inner Mongolia in particular.

In 1911, when the Qing dynasty buckled under the ongoing Xinhai revolution and eventually fell, Outer Mongolia grasped the opportunity to declare independence from China. A delegation travelled to St Petersburg to ask the tsar for help. Nicholas II, still smarting from damage done by the war with Japan six years earlier, did not want to get involved in another armed conflict in Asia, but he did agree to give Mongolia diplomatic support, which was later extended to include loans and weapons. Even though the new Chinese regime refused to recognise Outer Mongolia as an independent country, the spiritual leader of the Mongols, the eighth incarnation of Jebtsundamba Khutuktu, better known as Bogd Khan, was installed as monarch. Bogd Khan was born to a poor family in Tibet in 1869, a year after his predecessor, the seventh incarnation, had died. The Dalai Lama and Panchen Lama, the only two lamas higher than Jebtsundamba Khutuktu, identified the child as the eighth incarnation, and at five years old he was sent to Mongolia to lead the deeply religious locals. When he was crowned king, Bogd Khan was almost blind, but this did not prevent him from becoming a real leader for the Mongols, who worshipped the new monarch as a living god.

In 1919, while civil war was raging in Russia, the Chinese seized their chance and re-established their rule over Outer Mongolia. About fourteen thousand Chinese soldiers invaded the country and soon gained control of the capital. Bogd Khan was deposed, only to be reinstated two years later in March 1921, by Baron Roman von Ungern-Sternberg, an eccentric Baltic German who had sworn loyalty to the Romanovs during the Russian Civil War and on his own initiative led a crusade against the Bolsheviks in the Russian Far East, and later against the Chinese in Mongolia. Baron Ungern was deeply fascinated by eastern mysticism and the monarchy as an institution and his dream was to recreate the Mongols' great Asian empire. He ruled Outer Mongolia for a few months together with the blind khan and was happy to be declared a khan and demi-god.

There were also forces fighting for a communist revolution in Outer Mongolia. In 1920, the year before Baron Ungern took over, the leaders of the Mongolian communists, Damdin Sükhbaatar and Khorloogiin Choibalsan, went to Russia to ask for help. This time it was the Bolsheviks who were asked for military and material assistance in the fight against the Chinese. Outer Mongolia was not initially a priority for the Bolsheviks, but when Baron Ungern took control of the capital, things changed. In summer 1921, Sükhbaatar's Soviet-supplied soldiers defeated the eccentric baron and the remaining Chinese troops, and on July 11 Outer Mongolia once again declared itself independent. Baron Ungern was executed on September 15 following a summary trial.

Bogd Khan remained on the throne until he died in 1924. After the holy lama's death, the revolutionary Mongolian government declared there would be no more Jebtsundamba Khotuktu incarnations, and announced the establishment of the People's Republic of Mongolia. The capital, Urga, was renamed Ulan Bator, which means "red hero", in honour of Sükhbaatar, the young nation's revolutionary father, who had recently died.

Although Outer Mongolia was now in effect independent, both Inner and Outer Mongolia were still officially a part of China. Stalin's cunning is largely to be thanked for the fact that Outer Mongolia is an independent country today. At the Yalta Conference in February 1945, the Soviet Union's leader persuaded the allies to agree to the following formulation: "The status quo in Outer Mongolia (The People's Republic of Mongolia) shall be preserved." The Chinese government, which was not invited to Yalta, understood this to be a formal recognition of Chinese supremacy over Outer Mongolia. This is presumably what Franklin D. Roosevelt and Winston Churchill also thought. However, that was not what Stalin meant at all. In his meeting with Chiang Kai-shek, the leader of the Kuomintang, the party that ruled China from 1928 until the communist takeover in 1949, Stalin pointed to the formulation "The People's Republic of Mongolia" and said that *that* was what he had intended should be preserved. Negotiations with the Chinese were difficult, but Stalin did not waver and rolled out a map to demonstrate the strategic importance of Outer Mongolia for the Soviet Union. In reality, Chiang Kai-shek had no choice: the Red Army was standing ready to invade Manchuria with one and a half million soldiers to force the Japanese out. The Chinese were cornered. In order not to lose face, Chiang Kai-shek insisted that there should be a referendum. Stalin agreed to this, and on October 20, 1945, the Mongols went to the polls to vote whether Outer Mongolia should continue to be part of China or not. According to the Mongolian authorities, 487,285 people voted, in other words 98.6 per cent of those with voting rights, many dressed in their best clothes and carrying a Stalin flag. *Every single one* voted for independence from China.

China formally recognised Outer Mongolia's independence in January 1946. But for decades after, Outer Mongolia, which was now simply called Mongolia, continued to be included as a part of China on Chinese maps. Whenever there was a discussion about Mongolia possibly joining the United Nations, Taiwan vetoed it, on behalf of China. Mongolia was not able to become an independent member of the U.N. until 1961. In practice, however, the country continued to be a Soviet satellite state until the communist government was overthrown by popular protest in 1990.

In 1921, when Mongolia was granted de facto independence, it was one of the poorest countries in Asia. The population was a little more than 600,000 and infant mortality was so high that population growth was negative. There was no industry, eighty per cent of the livestock was owned by feudal lords, and ninety per cent of the population was illiterate. The world's second communist state was dependent on support from its brother in the north from birth.

The Soviet regime invested heavily in the development of the People's Republic of Mongolia. They built roads, apartment blocks, hospitals and schools, and sent medical teams and talented engineers to the towns there. By the 1980s, population growth in

Mongolia was the highest in Asia; the population had tripled and illiteracy had almost been eradicated, with the traditional Mongolian alphabet slowly being replaced by Cyrillic.

The Soviet authorities did not, of course, do this simply to help. As Stalin had pointed out in his meeting with Chiang Kai-shek in 1945, Mongolia's position was of great strategic importance to the Soviet Union. This became very apparent during the border conflicts with China in the 1960s; when these were at their most intense, the Soviet Union had more than seventy thousand soldiers stationed on Mongolian territory. Mongolia is also extraordinarily rich in iron and minerals. The Soviet Union helped the Mongolian authorities to exploit these resources, but were given a sizeable percentage of the profits in return.

Very little remains of the dirty, smelly and deeply religious town that Andrews described a hundred years ago. There are no camel drivers from Turkestan, and no tribal costumes to be seen. The current fashion is the same as you might find in Minsk or Beijing. More often than not, the men wear jeans and leather jackets, and the young women totter around on heels, wearing miniskirts and tight T-shirts. (The tourists, on the other hand, march around in high-tech, finely calibrated outdoor gear, ready to climb K2 at a moment's notice.) The bars are full of gaggles of girls giggling and chatting over cocktails and illuminated telephone screens; there is a high-speed Internet connection everywhere and most people speak some English. The same artists are played over the loudspeakers as anywhere else: Adele, U2, Lady Gaga.

As darkness fell over the traffic queues, the grey concrete buildings and the colourful *ger* district, it was only the presence of one man that reminded me that I was in the capital of Mongolia and not in any other Asian city.

And he was omnipresent.

World Rulers

No-one who visits Mongolia these days need doubt that they are in the home of Genghis Khan, or Chinggis Khaan, as the Mongolians spell it. Anyone arriving by airplane will land at Chinggis Khaan Airport. Those with more money may check in to the Chinggis Khaan Hotel, Mongolia's first four-star hotel. And as evening draws in, they may be tempted by a Chinggis Khaan beer at the Chinggis Khaan bar in the centre, where they may get chatting to students from Chinggis Khaan University. And for those who prefer something stronger, there are shots of Chinggis Khaan vodka, best enjoyed with a couple of deep drags from a Chinggis Khaan cigarette. Payment is in tugrik, the local currency. Inflation has been high, so you may as well get out a 20,000 tugrik note, which is adorned with the thoughtful face of Genghis Khan, even though there are no historical records of what he actually looked like. On the way back to the hotel, it is worth taking a detour past the parliament, where a general sits alone on horseback in illuminated majesty in a specially made monument, surrounded by elegant pillars, looking out over Chinggis Khaan Square.

Despite the name of the square, the statue is *not* of Genghis Khan, but of the hero of the revolution, Damdin Sükhbaatar, Mongolia's answer to Lenin. It was not until 2008 that a statue of Genghis Khan on horseback, which is to be found fifty kilometres from the city centre, was given to the Mongolian people. It is the world's largest statue of a horseman, a stainless steel monstrosity that stands 40 metres high and weighs 250 metric tons. The statue

was financed by Mongolia's then newly elected president, businessman and judo champion, Khaltmaagiin Battulga.

"It is a very popular attraction," said the young guide at the
visitor centre, which was situated under the statue. "Being proud
of Genghis Khan was not allowed under communism. We were not
even supposed to talk about him. After all, the Mongols conquered
Russia, didn't they? Now finally we can be proud again. Thanks to
Genghis Khan, everyone has heard about Mongolia!"

"Why was the statue put here, so far from the city?" I asked.

"When Genghis Khan was seventeen, he fought against the
Merkit tribe who had stolen his wife, and he found a horse whip
here," the guide told me, enthusiastically. "Finding a horse whip is
very auspicious in Mongolian culture. So it was here, more than
eight hundred years ago, that Genghis Khan decided to unite the
Mongol tribes into one nation."

An escalator took visitors up through the horse's stomach to a
viewing platform by the mane, between Genghis Khan's mighty
thighs. From here I could see the general's broad face. The firm,
determined gaze was fixed on the place where he was born, two
hundred kilometres to the east. The landscape was open in all directions, brown, barren and empty. The stainless steel flashed in the
sunlight.

It was in this landscape that Genghis Khan's army was raised
and cultivated, an army so powerful, efficient and well organised
that it conquered a seventh of the world's surface. On horseback.

Sometime in the middle of the twelfth century, a small caravan
crossed the Mongolian steppes. They were heading north, to the
homelands of the Merkit tribe. One of the horsemen was Chiledu, brother of the Merkit chief. In a camel-pulled carriage sat a
woman called Hoelun. She was from the Olkhunut tribe, and had

just married Chiledu and was now on her way to her new home. Yesügei, the chief of the Kiyad tribe, was out hunting with his falcon when the entourage passed. He happened to catch a glimpse of the woman in the carriage – a chance happening that changed the world. Yesügei was so taken with the young woman's beauty that he decided to steal her. He rushed back to find his brothers, and with them chased off the rest of the caravan and took Hoelun home with him. In 1162, Hoelun gave birth to a son. He was given the name Temüjin, iron man, but he is best known by the honorary title he was given as an adult: Genghis Khan.*

When Temüjin was eight or nine years old, his father arranged for him to marry Börte, a girl from the Olkhunut tribe, who was one year older. True to local tradition, it was decided that the boy would live with her family for a few years and serve the head of the household. When Yesügei was returning from Temüjin's new family, he was poisoned by an enemy tribe and died a few days later. But before he died, he managed to call Temüjin home. After Yesügei's death, his two wives and their seven small children were abandoned by the tribe and left to fend for themselves, which was as good as a death sentence. But the two women managed to feed their children, against all odds, by hunting, fishing and gathering berries and roots.

As mentioned, very little is known about Genghis Khan's early life. A chronicle known as *The Secret History of the Mongols* was written shortly after his death. The original manuscript was lost long ago, but, thanks to serendipity, the work has survived. At the end of the fourteenth century, the Chinese transcribed the history into Chinese characters and used it to learn Mongolian. Four hundred years later, a copy of the Chinese transcript was

---

*   There is some uncertainty regarding the year in which Genghis Khan was born. Some scholars believe he was born in 1167.

discovered in someone's private papers and transcribed back into Mongolian. This manuscript is the only written source that describes Genghis Khan's childhood. The author of the work is unknown, but was presumably close to the man and his family. The book is unreliable as a historical source, to put it mildly, and must, like all hagiographies, be read with a degree of cynicism. However, *The Secret History of the Mongols* does not contain only flattering stories but also events that could, with some goodwill, be called youthful mistakes. When Temüjin was thirteen years old, two of his half-brothers stole a small fish and a bird that he and his full brother, Khasar, had caught. In retaliation, Temüjin and Khasar killed one of the half-brothers. Naturally, the mother was beside herself, and her long tirade is included in *The Secret History of the Mongols*.

The nomadic society in which Temüjin grew up was fraught with violent tribal feuds. Loyalties changed, wrongs were avenged, an eye for an eye. As a teenager, Temüjin was taken prisoner by members of the Taichiyud tribe, who were old enemies of his father. This meant certain death, but after a couple of weeks in captivity, he managed to knock his guard unconscious and escape. When he was sixteen, Temüjin married Börte, the girl to whom he had been promised. Shortly after the wedding, Börte was kidnapped by the Merkit tribe, presumably as revenge for Temüjin's father having stolen Hoelun many years before. If Temüjin was to have any chance of leading the nomads, he had to get Börte back. He managed to drum up an army of more than ten thousand men, largely herdsmen and nomads, and with their help rescued her.

In the years that followed, Temüjin's reputation as a leader grew, and many of the disparate Mongolian and Turkic tribes allied themselves with him. Tribes that did not do so voluntarily were subjugated by force. Temüjin, the once outcast, unsupported young boy, was now a man with a clear goal: to unite and rule over all the nomadic tribes of the Mongolian steppes.

In 1206, after decades of alliance-building, intrigues and battles, Temüjin, who was probably forty-four by this point, achieved his goal. At a ceremony at which all the tribes were represented, he was declared leader of all Mongols and given the honorary title Genghis Khan, meaning "fierce", "hard" or "tough" ruler.

Genghis Khan had spent much of his life uniting the warring nomadic tribes, and in the process had gathered an enormous army. Once all the tribes had submitted to his leadership, he perfected the structure of his army. He introduced conscription for all men fit for military service. Senior positions were filled according to personal merit rather than family allegiances. And the army was organised using a decimal system, with base units of ten that were subordinate to larger groups of a hundred, then a thousand, and finally ten thousand men. Genghis Khan also had the Uighur alphabet of their Turkic neighbours adapted to the Mongolian alphabet in order to facilitate communication, though he remained illiterate himself.

But this enormous army needed something to do. As no Mongols paid tax, the soldiers lived off the spoils of war. It was therefore only natural that they should turn their attention to their wealthy neighbours in what is now northern China. The Mongols had never previously conquered towns and cities, but they were quick to learn. Once the disciplined, and soon adept, army had taken a town on horseback, they went through the town on foot, plundering and killing all the inhabitants. The women on the Mongolian steppes soon became accustomed to wearing luxurious silk clothes and expensive jewellery. But the soldiers not only stole clothes and jewellery, they also acquired and learned to use weapons such as catapults and gunpowder, and thus Genghis Khan's great army became invincible. In 1215, Beijing fell. In just under a decade, the Mongols had conquered two thirds of modern-day China.

If the sultan who ruled over Khwarazm, Muhammad II, had been wiser and responded differently, history might have been very different. Muhammad's rich empire stretched over much of what is now Afghanistan, Iran, Uzbekistan and Turkmenistan, as well as the southern part of Kazakhstan. Genghis Khan wanted to establish trading links with Muhammad in order to gain access to the beautiful glassware made by Muslim craftsmen. In 1218, he sent the following message to his counterpart in the west: "My greatest wish is to live in peace with you. I will look on you as my son. You are of course aware that I have conquered China and all the tribes of the north. You know that my empire has a surplus of warriors and a silver mine, and that I have no need whatsoever to win more land. It is in our mutual interest to develop trade relations between our two peoples."

Genghis Khan reinforced this promise of friendship by sending to Otrar, which lies in the southern part of what is today Kazakhstan, a caravan of five hundred camels laden with luxury goods such as gold, Chinese silk, white camel hide and jade. Otrar was at the time a very wealthy and important town on the Silk Road, with bathing houses to match those in Rome, and one of the largest and best libraries in the Muslim world. The caravan was attacked and plundered as soon as it reached the city, and it is said that only one of the original 450 merchants survived. It is unclear whether it was Muhammad himself who had given the order to attack the caravan, as some historians claim, or whether the governor of Otrar acted on his own initiative.

Genghis Khan let this doubt favour the sultan and sent a small delegation to Khwarazm, with the request that whoever was responsible for the attack be punished. Muhammad responded by killing the three envoys.* Genghis Khan was so furious that he mobilised an army of more than a hundred thousand men and headed west. Three years later, Central Asia lay in ruins.

It is impossible to calculate exactly how many people were killed during these brutal campaigns. At least half the population of towns that did not surrender were routinely killed, if not more. In Merv, one of the wealthiest and most sophisticated cities in the Muslim world in the thirteenth century, the *entire* population was massacred by the Mongols, bar four hundred craftsmen. No-one was spared, not even babies or old folk. While towns like Samarkand and Bukhara were gradually rebuilt, Merv never recovered. All that is left of this former gem are fragments of walls and buildings, and the bare outlines of what were once famous palaces and libraries.

The Mongols were now unstoppable. While Genghis Khan continued his crusade south, towards the Himalayas and India, the generals Jebe and Subotai led about twenty thousand men further west. They plundered and killed in the foothills of the Caucasus and then carried on to the steppes of Kievan Rus, the precursor of modern Russia. The Mongolian and Slav armies met by the Kalka River in what is now East Ukraine in 1223. The battle turned into a full-scale massacre of the Slavs, even though they outnumbered the Mongols. Prince Mstislav III eventually surrendered, on the assurance that there would be no more bloodshed. The Mongols kept their promise: Mstislav was bound and stuffed under a heavy wooden platform together with the other princes who had been captured in battle. The Slav princes were slowly suffocated as Jebe, Subotai and the other Mongol officers ate, drank and danced on the platform.

Four years later, in 1227, Genghis Khan died. His son Ögedei

---

* According to one account, he only killed the leader and sent the other two back with disfigured faces.

took over as "great leader", and the Mongol Empire continued to expand under his rule.

But what was it that drove the Mongols? Was there no limit to how many countries and peoples they wanted to rule? Apparently not. In 1236, an army of more than a hundred thousand horsemen, led by Genghis Khan's grandson Batu, invaded the Caucasus and Europe again. They conquered town after town with brutal efficiency: Moscow, Vladimir, Tver, Yaroslavl . . . Everywhere they went, they left behind burnt-out towns and rivers of blood. In 1240, the feared army stood outside the gates of Kiev, and soon the city was in flames. This proved to be a death blow for Kievan Rus, or the Kievan Empire, as it was also called. Moscow and the other duchies were able to recover, but Kievan Rus never regained its former glory.

The Mongols continued to push west, invincible. Lublin, Kraków and Liegnitz fell; Vienna was next in line. Europe was quaking. Then, in spring 1242, the Mongols miraculously withdrew. Ögedei, the great khan, had died.

The selection of the new khan took place in Karakorum, the town that Genghis Khan had decided should be the Mongols' capital. He himself never saw the capital. It was not until 1235, eight years after his death, that the Mongols built a city by the Orkhon River, roughly in the middle of modern-day Mongolia. As they had no experience of town planning, the city was designed and built by Chinese architects and construction workers. Descendants of Genghis Khan and leaders from all over the vast empire travelled to the Mongolian steppes to choose the new khan. Two thousand tents were erected on the edges of the town, and there was dancing, drinking and celebrations.

Ögedei's son, Güyuk, was crowned Great Khan. Batu went back to the Russian steppes and territories he had conquered. At its biggest, the Mongolian Empire stretched from Korea in the east to Poland in the west and as far south as Vietnam. The vast empire was divided up into four khanates that were ruled by the Great Khan. In the years that followed, the relationship between the khanates and Karakorum became increasingly distant and the four khans spent more and more time dealing with internal conflicts. Batu's khanate was the one that survived longest, and is perhaps better known as the Golden Horde. The Golden Horde governed the various Russian duchies for 240 years. The period is known as the Tatar Yoke in Russian history.

But how great was the impact on these Russian duchies? They had to pay tax to the Mongols, and new princes had to be approved by the khan, who had the last word in all matters of importance, but the Mongols' cultural influence was minimal. The Mongols were pragmatic: although they subjugated people, plundered their towns and cities, and collected tax from them, they did little to interfere in the daily lives of their subjects. The Mongols were skilled warriors and became efficient tax collectors, but it was never their desire that the conquered populations should be like them or believe in the same god. On the contrary, they were tolerant of other cultures and religions, and often assimilated into the local culture themselves.

Relations between the Russians and the Mongols were, however, reserved. Most of the Mongols continued to live in their yurts on the Russian steppes and maintained their nomadic lifestyle through the centuries. Batu's brother and successor, Berke, converted to Islam and the Horde followed. A few did convert to Orthodox Christianity, but the majority preferred to submit to Islam's strict rules rather than Christianity's emphasis on suffer-ing and forgiveness. Sarai, the capital of the Golden Horde, which lay to the north of the Caucasus, not far from what is today Astrakhan, became a typical Muslim town, similar to many others in the Muslim world. Religious freedom prevailed throughout the empire. As long as the Russians paid their taxes and recognised Mongol supremacy, they were free to live as they wished.

In 1476, the Grand Duchy of Moscow stopped paying tax to the Mongols. Moscow had become stronger under Ivan III, and had started to gain ascendency over other Russian duchies. The Golden Horde was weak at the time, owing to internal strife. It was not until 1480, four years after the Muscovites had stopped paying tax, that Akhmat Khan had the time and energy to deal with his disloyal subjects. He allied himself with Casimir IV Jagiellon, the Grand Duke of Lithuania and King of Poland, and marched on Moscow. The Mongols were stopped by Ivan III's army at the Ugra River, south of Moscow. The promised Polish reinforcements did not come, and on the other side of the river the Russian army grew stronger and bigger by the day. It was freezing cold, and as the weeks passed, the Mongols started to succumb to the cold and epidemics. On November 11, having waited for reinforcements for more than a month, the Mongols retreated to their tents in Sarai.

A year later, on January 6, 1481, Akhmat Khan was killed fighting the Siberian Khanate. The Golden Horde started to fall apart and was eventually absorbed into the Grand Duchy of Moscow. Ivan III also conquered the Republic of Novograd and duchies of Yaroslavl and Tver.

The Tatar Yoke was a thing of the past. Modern Russia was born.

The remains of Karakorum, the Mongols' ancient capital, lie a few hours' drive south-west from Ulan Bator. The scant archaeological finds from the empire's capital have been gathered and displayed in the museum there: shards of pottery, a few glued plates, coins, Genghis Khan's seal (which was found by accident in Rome), a stone tablet, a half-buried oven. The most interesting exhibit in the museum is a model of what archaeologists believe Karakorum looked like. The different parts of the town are separated by wide, straight roads, and contained within square, mud walls. The Mongols lived in their yurts beyond these, although still within the city walls. The model is based on descriptions given by the Flemish Franciscan friar, William of Rubruck, who visited Karakorum in 1254. The monk was not particularly impressed by what he saw: "Of the city of Caracarum you must know that, exclusive of the palace of the Chan, it is not as big as the village of Saint Denis, and the monastery of Saint Denis is ten times larger than the palace."[10]

Much like the American naturalist Andrews seven hundred years later, Rubruck remarked on the Mongols' poor hygiene: "They never wash clothes, for they say that God would be angered thereat . . . When they want to wash their hands or head, they fill their mouths with water, which they let trickle on to their hands, and in this way they also wet their hair and wash their heads." He was more impressed by the Mongols' religious and cultural tolerance. According to Rubruck, there were twelve different temples, as well as two mosques and a church. The Flemish monk's personal mission was to convert to Catholicism Möngke Khan, Great Khan from 1251 to 1259, but after several audiences, he acknowledged that he had failed. "If it had been within my power to perform miracles, like Moses, he might perhaps have been persuaded," he remarked, laconically.

Before sending Rubruck home, his mission unaccomplished, Möngke Khan dictated a long and threatening letter to King Louis IX:

The commandment of the eternal God is, in Heaven there is only one eternal God, and on Earth there is only one lord, Chingis Chan. This is the word of the Son of God, Demugin, (or) Chingis "sound of iron". [...] This, through the virtue of the eternal God, through the great world of the Mo'al, is the word of Mangu Chan to the lord of the French, King Louis, and to all the other lords and priests and to all the great realm of the French, that they may understand our words. For the word of the eternal God to Chingis Chan has not reached unto you, either through Chingis Chan or others who have come after him. [. . .]

The commandments of the eternal God are what we impart to you. And when you shall have heard and believed, if you will obey us, send your ambassadors to us; and so we shall have proof whether you want peace or war with us. When, by the virtue of the eternal God, from the rising of the Sun to the setting, all the world shall be in universal joy and peace, then shall be manifested what we are to be. But if you hear the commandment of the eternal God, and understand it, and shall not give heed to it, nor believe it, saying to yourselves: "Our country is far off, our mountains are strong, our sea is wide," and in this belief you make war against us, you shall find out what we can do. He who makes easy what is difficult, and brings close what is far off, the eternal God He knows.

In the letter to King Louis IX, which Rubruck never personally delivered, it is clear that the Mongols perceived themselves to be chosen by the eternal God to rule over the entire world, and that they believed that Genghis Khan was God's son. Perhaps this belief was why their thirst for ever more conquests was never quenched. They firmly believed their mission was to rule all other people on the earth, from "the rising of the sun to the setting". Their many conquests must have strengthened this belief and made them even more certain that the eternal God was on their side.

But everything is transitory, even empires. Allegiances shift, God changes sides, new rulers appear, external borders disintegrate, and internal conflict eats the empire from within. In 1388, Karakorum was attacked by Chinese Ming forces, led by General Xu Da, and the city was laid waste. Only a few stone sculptures of turtles have survived. Today, cows and goats graze on the slopes that for a short period were home to the capital of the world.

In the Ruins of a Thousand Treasures

"My grandfather was a monk in the temple," Batbayar said in a quiet voice, almost a whisper. He had a shaved head and was dressed in saffron robes and a red cape, as is the tradition for Mongolian monks. "When Grandfather came of age, he had to do his military service, like all other young men. And then when he came back, nearly all the temples had been destroyed and the monks had disappeared. Only the youngest had been spared."

At the other end of the yurt, four monks rocked from side to side as they recited the mantras. Their voices rose and fell. The air was thick with incense.

"As he could no longer be a monk, my grandfather got married and lived a normal life," Batbayar said. "He got a job as a security guard for shops and offices, so that no-one would guess that he had been a monk. No-one would suspect that a man who carried a gun had been a monk!"

The young man smiled and looked down. When he smiled, his whole face lit up.

"My grandfather always hid his prayer beads inside the sleeves of his sweater," he said. "When he meditated, or recited mantras and songs, he always closed all the doors and windows. Even though the killings stopped when Stalin died, Buddhists still risked imprisonment and losing the opportunity to work for the rest of their lives. Grandfather's Buddhist statues were kept hidden in boxes. Talking about the past was dangerous, but sometimes he told us about his teachers and the friends he had lost. He mourned them for the rest of his life."

Batbayar grew up with his grandparents, which is quite usual in Mongolia. Parents are often young and busy with their studies and work, whereas grandparents have all the time in the world.

"I have wanted to be a monk, like my grandfather, for as long as I can remember," Batbayar said. "In 1992, as soon as it was legal to be a Buddhist again, and as soon as I was old enough to be a monk, I joined a monastery."

I looked at his smooth, open face. He could not be much older than me.

"How old were you?" I asked.

"Thirteen. I have never regretted it."

"Your grandfather must have been very proud of you."

Batbayar smiled, abashed, and looked down again.

"Very. He died only a few years ago. He lived to be a hundred. He spent his last years here, with me." He nodded at an older monk, who was sitting on a stool a few metres away, draped in yellow silk. "You should talk to him instead. He knows the history of the monastery much better than I do."

The old monk proved to be both talkative and curious. He had scars on his face and a thin, wispy beard. I forgot to ask his name.

"Erdene Zuu, as the monastery was called – you may already know that that means 'a thousand treasures' – was established in 1586, when Tibetan Buddhism was introduced as the state religion in Mongolia, and it is now the oldest monastery we have," the monk said. "At its peak, there were nearly a hundred temples here, and more than a thousand monks, of whom at least three hundred were learned. Erdene Zuu was an important centre of learning, you see, for Buddhist philosophy and astronomy in particular. There were of course monks who knew medicine too. At the time, there were no doctors in Mongolia, only monks, but perhaps you knew that? Now there are only fifty monks here, nearly everything is gone. Many of us have had to go to Tibet to study our own religion! The only thing we managed to keep is our tradition of recitation. We recite and sing the mantras for five hours a day. Erdene Zuu has always been known for that."

As we spoke, the benches behind me filled up with believers, prayer beads in hand. The monk was not distracted by the crush, and carried on speaking. "Things started to deteriorate before the Great Repression began in 1937. Circumstances were not the best for Buddhism under the communists, they were sad times. Many monks left the monastery and became herdsmen. It was Stalin's idea to kill the monks. Those who were most learned, the oldest, the ones who knew most, were killed first, without trial. Those who were not so old or learned were sentenced to ten and twenty years in prison. The youngest were given the chance to lead normal lives, but had to leave the order. After the terror, there were per-haps only a hundred monks left in the whole of Mongolia."

A young monk, who was probably no more than fifteen or sixteen, came over with a bowl of fermented mare's milk for each of us. The milk smelled of yeast and had a sour taste. The old monk slurped up the warm milk, then continued.

"The ninth Jebtsundamba Khutuktu, the reincarnation of Bogd Khan, died in 2012. He was born in 1933 in Tibet, but we only found out about him in 1993. He spent most of his life in exile in India. Towards the end of his life, his greatest wish was to die in Mongolia. He came here in 2011 and died in March the following year as a Mongolian citizen. Just before he died, he said that the next Jebtsundamba Khutuktu would be born in Mongolia. We are waiting for him to be born now. Buddhism in Mongolia has faced many crises throughout history. But the one in 1937 was the worst, in my opinion, and the last. There are no more crises left. From now on, everything will be fine."

"How did you become a monk yourself?" I asked. "Was it something you had always wanted to do, like Batbayar?"

"No, my ambition was to be a great communist!" The old monk burst out laughing. "My father joined a monastery as a boy. And then as an adult he kept his prayer beads well hidden under his clothes. If anyone had discovered, he would have lost his job. My father had six children, and I am the only one who has become a monk. In 1990, we came here together, my father and I. He wanted to become a monk again, and I got work looking after the monastery's finances. It was sad for my father to come back, because he could remember how it was before. I, on the other hand, had no links to the place and had never even thought of becoming a monk. People used to say in the Seventies that Buddhism would become great again, but I did not believe them. What rubbish, I thought. But then, in the 1990s, when we once again had religious freedom and I moved here with my father, I discovered to my surprise that I had deep faith in Buddhism. So I was ordained as a monk as well."

I had drunk my fermented mare's milk. The benches behind me were now full; people sat squeezed together, obviously impatient. I thanked the monk for his time and left the dimly lit, incense-filled yurt temple. I heard the monks' voices rise and fall behind me.

A low wall, with 108 whitewashed stupas, shaped like white, pointed towers, enclosed the otherwise bare temple area. A century ago, there were several hundred temples and even more yurts within these walls. Erdene Zuu was built on the ruins of the Great Khan's palace in Karakorum, reusing the original stones, perhaps to symbolise that the religious surpasses the secular, or perhaps simply because it was practical to use the building mater-ials that were available. The monastery was pretty much a ruin itself, though a few fresh shoots were starting to appear from the ravages of communism. Only three of the original temples remain; it is assumed that they survived because Stalin wanted to have something to show international guests. After the fall of commun-ism in 1990, a few new, low buildings were constructed to house the new monks. But the rest of the site is empty. Grass. Wilderness.

Before the communists came to power in the 1920s, Mongolia was a deeply religious society, almost a theocracy, like Tibet. Monks were the only people with an education, the only ones who could read and write, and the only ones who knew anything about medicine, literature and astronomy. It is estimated that at least a third of men were monks, which in part helps to explain the negative population growth. The monasteries owned pretty much everything: land, animals, knowledge.

Initially the communists and the monks lived together in relative peace, even though there was some friction. Then in the 1930s, the communist government, led by the revolutionary hero Khorloogiin Choibalsan (in reality, Moscow), started to take a more active role. Hundreds of monasteries were closed and, in the hasty collectivisation process, more than a third of nomads were forced to give their livestock to the state. The nomads slaughtered several mil-lion animals in protest – rather that than give them to the communists. Chaos reigned, famine loomed, and Soviet tanks rolled across the border to keep the anti-communist rebellion in check.

The situation went from bad to worse. In the mid-1930s, Stalin ordered a great purge in Mongolia, similar to the one being carried out in the Soviet Union, ostensibly to weed out Japanese spies and sympathisers. Choibalsan was called to Moscow for instruction. In autumn 1937, the arrests and executions started. More than ten thousand lamas were killed in the following eighteen months. Intellectuals and high-ranking members of the military and central committee, as well as Kazakhs and Buryats, were defined as "ene-mies of the revolution" and persecuted. Thousands were im-prisoned or killed on Choibalsan's orders, as instructed by Moscow. Concentration camps, based on the Soviet model, were built in the villages for the "enemies of the revolution". Executions took place in secret. Even post-1990, there is little openness about what actually happened during Choibalsan's Stalinist terror campaign, and there are no exact figures for how many people were killed. The authorities estimate approximately thirty thousand, but some historians believe that it was many more. Even the lowest estimates suggest that at least three per cent of the Mongolian population were killed within eighteen months.

At the end of the 1940s, when Choibalsan understood that the Soviet Union would never support the unification of the People's Republic of Mongolia and Inner Mongolia (which is now in China), he withdrew his support. He refused to participate in Stalin's seventieth birthday celebrations in 1949, and stubbornly withstood demands that Mongolia follow the example of the Republic of Tuva and formally join the Soviet Union. In 1952, Choibalsan died at a hospital in Moscow where he was being treated for kidney cancer. He was fifty-six. His body was embalmed by the same Russian doctors as embalmed Lenin, and a mausoleum, remarkably like Lenin's, was built for him in front of the parliament in Ulan Bator. The remains of the *pater patriae*, Sükhbaatar, who died in 1923, were exhumed and placed in the mausoleum as well.

Soviet influence on the Mongolian economy and domestic policy continued. It was not until 1990, shortly before the fall of the communist government, that the statue of Stalin outside the National Library in Ulan Bator was removed. The statue of Choibalsan still stands in front of the university, and the town, the fourth largest in Mongolia, still bears his name, but his body is no longer on display in the capital. The mausoleum was closed in 2005, and the two revolutionary heroes literally went up in smoke.

Around fifty per cent of Mongolians today count themselves as Buddhists, and the monasteries are slowly being revived. A month after my meeting with the monks in Erdene Zuu, the Dalai Lama visited Mongolia. At a press conference there, he announced that the tenth incarnation of Jebtsundamba Khutuktu had probably already been born – in Mongolia, as predicted.

Hermits of the Taiga

After spending several days in a row on the back seat of a Russian minibus, I started to hate it. The UAZ-452 was originally built as an ambulance, but proved to be so durable and functional, particularly in the Arctic, that it is still in production, fifty years after the first model rolled out of the Soviet car factory. The driver of a UAZ-452 must also be a qualified mechanic, however, as they break down regularly and need daily maintenance. They guzzle fuel like an alcoholic who has fallen off the wagon, and always smell of petrol, both inside and out.

This one was dirty as well, and cold and draughty. Even when I was wearing a hat, three woollen sweaters and a thick jacket, I was so cold that my teeth chattered. Enkh-Oyun, my guide, had back problems so was in the front, chatting and laughing with the driver while I sat in the back seat. The minibus bumped and jumped and I had to hold tight in order not to bang my head on the ceiling. There were no seat belts. The driver followed faint tracks in the grass, and we crossed semi-frozen rivers both with and without bridges – I would not like to say which was worse. The landscape was beautiful, but monotonous: dry yellow plains and hills, and, in the distance, bare, brown mountains. Every so often we passed flocks of hairy, hardy yaks. The hair under their stomachs was long enough to almost touch the ground. There were yurts here and there, horses, goats.

In the afternoon we came across a family wrapped in so many clothes they could scarcely move. They were in a Russian minibus like us, but clearly lacked the necessary mechanics and had been stranded since the vehicle broke down the day before. My driver got out and had a look at the uncooperative engine. Ten minutes later it was working again. Relieved, they climbed back into the metal box and drove off; they had feared they might have to wait for days before anyone came by.

The sky was streaked violet when we reached the army barracks. As we were so close to the Russian border, we had to register and show our border passes before we could drive on.

"The soldiers say it is too dangerous to carry on in the dark," Enkh-Oyun said when she came back to the minibus. "They have offered us beds for the night. What do you think, should we accept?" She looked at me with a silent plea in her eyes.

We installed ourselves in the very basic building with its dirty kitchenette and four bare beds, and crawled into our sleeping bags, exhausted. Forty seconds later, the driver's open mouth started to emit a loud, rhythmic snore. I woke up a couple of times during the night when one of the soldiers came in to put more wood in the burner. Then I slipped back into a bumpy, shivering sleep.

The following morning, the soldiers came in one by one on some errand or another, to put wood on the fire, make tea, drink tea, make more tea, or simply to talk.

"Is it very boring being a soldier out here in the wilds?" I asked one of them. "There doesn't seem to be much going on here."

"Boring?" He looked at me, thunderstruck. "Oh no, it can be a bit too exciting round here! Only this summer we had major problems with the Tuva from Russia. They ride over the border in groups of five or six to steal horses, which they take back to Russia. If they see any soldiers, they shoot them. This summer a Tuvan cowboy was shot by one of our soldiers, when they opened fire on us. They have also kidnapped Mongols and forced them to take part in their horse raids. So you see, it's the Wild West here."

He pointed out of the window at some simple houses close to the barracks.

"In the 1960s, the Mongolian authorities tried to get the Tuvan refugees from Russia who came here in the Forties and Fifties to settle down. They let them move into the houses you see over there, but it didn't work. These people had herded reindeer all their lives and had never lived in houses before. They left the doors and windows open, took up the floorboards and made fires inside. In the end, the authorities gave up and let them move back into their tents."

We rolled up our sleeping bags and got into the bus. The temperature had fallen overnight. One of the soldiers had followed us out.

"Be careful," he warned Enkh-Oyun and me. "Don't accept anything unless you know what it is, and, whatever you do, don't eat anything that looks suspect. The reindeer people cast spells and have their own way of making girls fall in love with them. You don't believe me? It's the truth, I have seen it myself! One summer a girl came here from Ulan Bator, then she came back again and again, and ended up staying here. Now she is married to a reindeer man and has two children. Her family have come from Ulan Bator to take her back, but she refuses. And a Japanese woman has been here three times to try and convince one of the reindeer nomads to go back to Japan with her. She was here again last summer."

"If they are not back within three days, I personally will ride up to the taiga and bring them back," the driver promised. "By force, if necessary," he added, with machismo.

And off we set. Bump, bump. I held on as tightly as I could. One hour, two hours, three. The landscape opened up around us, and a mountain range with blue, snow-covered peaks came into sight. Deciduous forests with autumn leaves replaced the open steppes. When the forest got too dense, we had to leave the car and travel the final stretch on horseback. The small, energetic woman who rented out her horses to us looked at my clothes with some scepticism.

"Not good," she said, and went to get a long, traditional Mongolian coat which she ordered me to put on, on top of my other clothes. I could hardly move in all my layers, and it was not that cold, so I took off one of my woollen sweaters.

"Why did you do that?" she said, sternly. "You will freeze."

"No," I said. "I am Norwegian, I am used to the cold."

Never have I been so cold. The first stage between the hills was sheltered, but as soon as we reached the top, the Siberian wind hit us. It was unrelenting and cut through all the layers of wool until I could no longer feel my legs. But the view was spectacular. The autumn colours of the western taiga stretched out in front of us, kilometre after kilometre of forest and gentle slopes. On the horizon, the Mongolian landscape spilled over into the Russian; if we had carried on riding through the night, we would have reached the Russian border before daybreak.

A young, lean horseman had accompanied us to show us the way and tend to the horses. He rode in front and happily hummed a lullaby to himself. After a while we crossed a frozen river and carried on into a larch forest. Every time we knocked a branch, yellow needles showered down on us. We heard the herding song before we saw the animals. Coaxing trills and enticing tones. Only when we had gone some way further into the forest did we see the reindeer herd. Pure white fur, long bent antlers. A tiny old fellow ran with a light step in among the reindeer. He bounded over to us, quickly explained the way to the camp, then continued to coax and cajole the animals. We followed his directions and a few minutes later came to the encampment.

This consisted of two lavvu tents and a small wooden enclosure. There was a pole hanging between two trees, to which he had tied all his belongings, so they could be moved easily at short notice. Enkh-Oyun and I installed ourselves in the largest lavvu, each taking a cup of salted tea from the thermos that stood there, then we sat down to wait for our host. Unlike the Mongolian nomads, the reindeer herders live in small lavvus, like the Sami. They are are easier to move than yurts and light enough to be transported by reindeer.

It was spartan inside, even for a lavvu. There was a small bed at one end, a wood burner in the middle, a reindeer skin to sit on, some pots and utensils hanging on pieces of string and a small food store. The little man came back with his animals when we had finished our tea. His face was weathered and wrinkled, and I reckoned he was at least seventy. He had a small frame and was about the same height as the reindeer, so a good head smaller than me. We drank more tea and then were shown to the guest lavvu, which was even more basic, dark and cramped, with no burner or rugs. When the old man had finished with the reindeer for the night, he invited us for more tea. With great concentration, he poured water into a big kettle on the wood burner. He used a small sieve to remove any twigs and dirt, then put in the salt and four teabags. It tasted delicious.

His name was Aragalan Tsagaach and he had been born in 1964, he told Enkh-Oyun. So I had guessed wrong: he was actually only in his fifties. Even though he had lived in Mongolia all his life, he spoke Mongolian with such a strong accent that Enkh-Oyan had problems understanding him. The horseman had to translate for her.

"I'm sorry, I'm not very good at Mongolian," he apologised. "I didn't know a word before I started school, I only spoke Tuvan. As I did not understand very much, I stopped after one year. I learnt Mongolian much later, in the army." He laughed. "Even though I'm married to a Mongolian woman, and my children speak Mongolian, I still find it hard to make myself understood in their language."

Aragalan was Dukha, or a *tsaatan*, which means "those who own reindeer" in Mongolian. When the Tuva Republic was incorporated into the Soviet Union in 1944, hundreds of reindeer nomads fled over the border to Mongolia. In 1956, the refugees from Tuva were given permanent residency by the Mongolian government. There are some three hundred reindeer nomads left in Mongolia. On the Russian side of the border, in Tuva, there are about a quarter of a million Tuvans. Like so many other indigenous people I had met in former communist states, Aragalan did not see himself as an exotic minority, but rather as a Mongolian.

"After all, I was born in Mongolia," he said, with a shrug. "My wife is Mongolian, my children are Mongolian. The only thing that distinguishes me from other Mongolians is that I live in a lavvu and herd reindeer. And I don't speak Mongolian very well."

"Do you not get lonely, living like this?" I asked.

"No, I have lived like this for so long, since I was young. I am used to living alone." He looked at me, ready for the next question.

"Do you miss your family?"

"My children come here with their families in spring, when the cows are calving. They stay with me until it gets too cold for them." He laughed, revealing his toothless gums. "I sometimes find it hard to have so many people around. It drives me nuts. Whenever someone asks if we should be neighbours through the winter, I always say no. I want to be alone. Free." He started to fidget. "Any more questions?"

"How often do you visit your wife in Tsagaanuur?" The horseman had told us that his wife had moved to the village a few years ago, when she started to have problems with her blood pressure.

"Not very often, I don't like it in town," Aragalan said. "Too

many cars, motorbikes and children. It is too much for me." He
sipped his hot tea. "Anything else you want to know?"

"What is a normal day for you?"

"I get up in the morning, let the reindeer out and move around
with them. In the afternoon I come back and chop wood. Then I
go back to look after the reindeer. In the evening I come back to my
tent and make food. I do everything myself, except sew clothes –
men of my generation do everything themselves," he said with
pride. "I eat only once a day. I've always been like that. Never managed to eat more. More questions?"

"Is it not very cold living here in winter?" It was already well
below zero outside. The horseman threw another log on the fire
to keep us warm.

"No, it is cosy out here. The only time I freeze is when I go into
the village, to Tsagaanuur. The trip sometimes takes five days
through the snow. We ride the reindeer when we go to town. They
are faster than horses in winter, never slip, never stumble."

"What is it that you like about reindeer?"

He looked at me, baffled.

"What do I like about reindeer? I don't know. They are my life.
I grew up with them."

"Do you give them names?"

"Some of them." He was quiet for a while before he continued. "Not all of them. I don't need to mark my animals, because
I always recognise them. These days, young people mark their
reindeer with small number tags. They are not smart enough to
recognise them."

"Was being a reindeer herder different under communism?"

"Under communism, the reindeer belonged to the state, now
they are mine, but everything else is the same." He shrugged. "It
doesn't really matter if the reindeer belong to me or the state, I
never really thought about it. The work was still the same. I follow

the reindeer through the year, go where they go, move whenever it is necessary. This autumn, I have moved three times already."

"Do you have a religion?"

"No, I don't need one. My daughter is a shaman, but I am not interested in things like that. More questions?"

"No, I have asked everything I wanted to know," I said.

Aragalan jumped up, visibly relieved. "Good, because I have told you everything I know," he said. He pushed the door to one side, slipped out of the lavvu and went over to the enclosure to check on the reindeer. It was already dark outside. The reindeer stood huddled together and were snoring when I crept into the guest lavvu. The temperature dropped to minus twenty Celsius during the night. The horseman got up a few times to put wood on the fire. As soon as it died down, it was freezing cold again in the lavvu. I was so cold that my muscles ached. When we got up at the crack of dawn, the water and my wet wipes were frozen. The trees and ground were covered in hoar frost. Aragalan and the reindeer were already long gone.

"I knew you were coming," Khalzan said with a broad smile. His lavvu was far cosier than Aragalan's. A small solar panel had been rigged up outside, and there was a big, old-fashioned mobile phone just inside the door. Which started to ring all of a sudden. Two mounds of bread dough had been left to rise beside the wood burner.

"As I was coming home with the reindeer, I met two birds," Khalzan said. "They started to talk together, and from their voices I understood that I would have a visit from two chatty people. Birds would never warn of a man coming, so I knew that you were women before I even saw you. This is a good day." His smile revealed a row of brown-stained teeth. "I love women!"

Khalzan was by far the liveliest bachelor we met in the taiga. He was forty-three years old with handsome, regular features and smooth skin, but his eyes were watery and dead.

"I communicate with my reindeer," he said. "They talk to me with their eyes. Reindeer tell you *everything* with their eyes. In the middle of every month, I perform a ceremony at night that binds me to the earth. Other than that, I follow my reindeer, hunt, and think about the past and the future, and what my grandfather and father taught me. I have a lot of time to think, but I never feel lonely. But tell me, what brings you two girls here in this cold weather? I guess it is cold for you, even though I don't find it cold. Cold is when it is minus forty, if you ask me. By the way, I do not live here in winter, I stay even closer to the Russian border, which is only fifty kilometres away." He laughed. "Sometimes my reindeer cross the border, and then I have no choice but to cross the border illegally and bring them back. What else can I do? *Give* them to the Russians?"

Like Aragalan, Khalzan was born in Mongolia. His family fled there in the 1950s, after Stalin's death, when the control and surveillance of the Tuvan people eased.

"The Russians tried to force the Tuvans to settle, like they had," Khalzan said. "During the Second World War all young Tuvan men were called up, generally to the front. When the war was over, they were called up to the navy, where they were not happy. After Stalin's death, about twenty families from our village fled over the border to Mongolia. My father was just a child, but he remembered a lot from their escape and told me about it on many occasions. It was dramatic. They had to cross a river that was about to burst its banks, and they swam and floated on bits of ice. They wanted to get away from the Soviet Union, even if it cost them their lives. The taiga here in Mongolia has belonged to the Tuvans for ever, and they have always lived in this area. As they were being pursued by Russian soldiers, they could only travel at night. About half of them were caught and sent back to Russia."

Through the opening in the lavvu, we had a view of the white reindeer as they wandered around outside. Some of them looked in at us with curiosity.

"I grew up with reindeer," Khalzan said. "My father started herding reindeer after he had done his military service. I like this life. I cannot imagine a life without reindeer."

A large drum was leaning against the side of the tent. But other than that, there was not much to indicate that Khalzan was a shaman, and famous well beyond his country's borders.

"Winter is quiet, but in summer lots of people come here, foreigners in particular," he said. "People ask me about all kinds of things. Young people often ask where they should live. They want to know if they should live in Europe or Asia, or maybe Australia?" He laughed and shook his head. "The country they come from is obviously not good enough for them. Why can they not just live where they were born? People nowadays move around too much. Instead of moving around, they should live where their parents and grandparents lived. *That* is their land. *That* is where they belong."

Khalzan's maternal grandfather was also a shaman.

"Shamanism follows the bloodline," he said. "As a child, I was often sick. In order to save my life, my mother sent me to my grandfather in the taiga. The shamans saved me. I got better and was given a new name and stayed with my grandfather and the other shamans. It was a good life. Then, when I was seven or eight, the soldiers came. They burned everything they could find that had to do with shamanism. The women cried. In a matter of minutes, a centuries-old culture was destroyed. Everyone had to be the same in the Soviet Union, no-one could be superior to anyone else. No-one could be a shaman. My grandfather was arrested and put in prison for four years, from 1981 to 1984, just for practising shamanism. He was an old man by then, over sixty. The other prisoners soon found out that he was a shaman and used to go to him for help and advice, so he was kept busy in prison. Grandfather used to joke that he had been sent to prison because they needed his help there."

The smell of freshly baked bread filled the lavvu. With a well-practised hand, Khalzan took the bread out of the tin and broke it into piping hot hunks for us to eat.

"Isn't the bread good?" He smiled. "In 1990, when the communists lost power, my grandfather predicted better times. That was when I became a shaman. I only do good things; for example, I help people with health issues. I am on the white side, the peaceful side, I cultivate our connection with the earth and former lives. As a shaman, you have to love the earth. People are starving today because we treat the earth so badly – people are blinded by money. Everything is changing. If we continue to empty the earth of coal and gold, what will be left? If we destroy our earth, where will we live?"

The sun was high in the sky when we saddled up and rode away from the shaman's tent. Khalzan gave us a cheerful wave.

"Hope you include my story in your book!" he called, just before we were out of hearing.

We had not been riding for more than fifteen minutes when we met three tourists: a young woman from Colombia, a woman in her forties from Belgium, and a tall young man with a long beard, who was also from Belgium. The Colombian woman stared straight ahead, her face grey and pale, wrapped in layers of clothes. They had come all this way to stay the night with Khalzan, the famous shaman from the west taiga.

"Did it take long?" the young Belgian asked.

"It's not far now. About fifteen minutes," I said.

"No, no, how long did *it* take?"

I had no idea what he was talking about.

"*The ceremony*, how long did it take?"

"Oh, we didn't ask for a ceremony," I said.

He looked at me, astounded.

"Why not?"

I shrugged.

"We just came to talk."

"But do you not want to *know*?"

On the way back to Aragalan I pondered what I could have asked Khalzan. How many children I would have? If I would get divorced? How long I would live? If there were any great tragedies awaiting me?

I realised that I actually did not want to know the answer to any of those things.

When we got back to Aragalan's camp, Enkh-Oyun, the guide, insisted that we should pack up and go back to the village. She wanted to sleep in a warm bed, she said, she could not face the thought of another night in a lavvu in the taiga, when the temperature was minus twenty. The lad who came with the horses thought it was too late in the afternoon, it would be dark before we got there, and that was irresponsible.

We stayed another night. And with the dark, came the snow. Aragalan had not come back yet, but a friend of his, Duujii, had come to visit. Duujii had been to see his family in Tsagaanuur, where his children went to school, and was on his way back to his tent in the taiga. Like Aragalan, he was in his early fifties but looked closer to seventy.

"Reindeer are special, they are not like goats or sheep, they call for different techniques," Duujii said.

He was also happy with his hermit's existence in the taiga.

"I cannot think of a single thing I do not like about my life," he said. "If there was anything I did not like, it has now become habit, so I don't think about it anymore."

It was snowing heavily outside. A thick, white blanket already covered the ground.

"The only problem is these new, restricted areas where the reindeer are not allowed to graze, and no-one can live," Duujii said. "The areas are guarded by soldiers day and night because apparently they have found gold and precious stones there. If it gets any worse, I may have to go back to Russia."

"Cross the border, just like that?" I said.

"That is how we came here in the first place, so why not?" He looked at his watch with some concern. "What is taking him so long? I hope nothing has happened to him. He should be here by now."

We had made and eaten supper before Aragalan finally came back with his reindeer. He was smiling from ear to ear and could not thank us enough.

"You brought the snow with you, finally we have snow! Thank you, thank you for bringing the snow, I owe you all my thanks."

When we woke the next morning, the landscape was totally white. Before we left, we gave Aragalan some money to thank him for his hospitality. He rolled up the banknotes and put them in a small hand-sewn bag that he had hanging in the lavvu.

"I keep things that are good here – a couple of cigarettes, money, some food, bits of cloth," he said. "Gifts for the spirits. They bring blessings and good fortune."

"I didn't think you were religious," I said.

"I'm not," he said, and ran out into to the snow on light feet, because the reindeer were waiting.

Ninja Miners

The thin, oblong stones stood in a small clutch, without any obvious cohesion. Some of them were two or three metres high, others no more than half a metre. The patterns on the stones had been more or less worn away by the centuries, the wind and the weather, but some of the images were surprisingly clear, all the same. Nearly all were of highly stylised deer and reindeer, ascending to heaven. The remains of colour pigment were still visible.

"A long, long time ago, the Mongols believed that the dead were taken to heaven on the back of a deer," explained Esee, who was going to take me right across Mongolia to the Chinese border. Esee was in his early thirties and had taught himself English with the help of a cassette. If he had not told me that, I would have assumed that he had either studied English at university or spent several years in the U.S.A.

Similar clusters of oblong stones with deer drawings are to be found all over Mongolia, particularly in the north. The deer stones are about three thousand years old, from the Bronze Age. Noone knows why they are there.

"See that one?" Esee said, and pointed at a tall, thin stone. There was a face carved at the top. "This is the only stone with a human face on it. A woman's face. According to legend, the chieftain of a tribe from around here fell in love with a woman from the neighbouring tribe, and wanted to marry her. But the tribe refused his proposal, so a battle ensued. The beautiful woman disguised herself as a warrior and joined the fighting. No-one recognised her and she was killed. Everyone was very sad when they discovered that she had been killed, and this standing stone was erected by her grave, or so they say."

No trace of human remains has been found by the deer stones, however, only animal remains. But more than fourteen hundred larger and smaller graves have been found in the surrounding valley. Many of these are marked with small cairns, whereas others are only visible as low mounds. Was there a connection between the graves and the deer stones? Was it a sacrifice site, a place where shamanistic rituals were performed? So little is known about prehistoric people. Who were they? What did they believe? No matter how much research is undertaken, we can only make guesses and assumptions based on the physical evidence they have left behind. Such as these thin, oblong stones with flying deer and a single human face.

Esee's car, a Land Cruiser, was pure heaven compared with the Russian ambulance. When I think back to Mongolia, it is the endless landscapes, full of sky and colour, that I remember. The view from the windscreen went on and on. The landscape was monotonous, yet ever-changing. The grass colour varied from green to yellow, the mountains in the distance might be brown, blue, red or green. One moment we were driving through a silvery moonscape, hills rolling like waves in every direction, in the next we were by an ice-blue river where camels stood drinking. In this part of Mongolia there are practically no roads. We kept a steady course south-west, following the sun and a chaotic network of tyre tracks. Every so often we passed a nomadic family on the move, with heavily laden camels and flocks of sheep, goats, cows and horses.

In the afternoon of the second day we came across another broken-down car. The group included a woman and four men, and they had set up camp by the car. They had been stranded since the day before. They looked cold. Esee gave them some food and then we drove on.

"In Mongolia, you must always stop when you see someone in need," Esee said. "It may be a long time before anyone else passes. But they needed a mechanic, so there was not much we could do to help them."

When we stopped to eat lunch a little later, we were joined by five men in a Russian UAZ-452. Esee offered them tea and food, and they did not need to be asked twice. The youngest was in his early twenties, but was tall and sturdy, with a round face. The oldest was in his fifties, and was a hydrogeologist, he said. He had excavated many wells in the area.

"And are you here to dig more wells?" I asked.

"No, we are here to dig for gold." The look on my face made him laugh. "There is a lot of gold around here," he said. "All the herders in the area have metal detectors. They take the opportunity when they are out with their animals to look for gold. I have looked for gold whenever I've had free time over the past ten years."

"And have you found any?"

"Oh yes, I once found gold worth twenty thousand dollars in just one day! It was quite a day, let me tell you."

While Esee and I poured more tea and chatted with the others, the geologist wandered around and studied the stones. He looked as though he knew what he was doing, and broke a couple in two.

"Nothing of any value here," he concluded. "But not far from here, there is an eighty-kilometre vein of gold. The last time we were here, we each found gold worth five hundred dollars. Come with us, we'll show you."

We drove behind them for a short while. After a couple of kilometres, they left the criss-crossing tyre tracks and headed towards a low, brown hill. When we got there, the prospectors were getting their metal detectors ready. The small hill was full of pits, most of them about a metre deep and two to three metres in diameter. In some places, there was a greater density, and they were much deeper, up to five or six metres. Channels had been dug out between the holes. The men set to examining excavations, the mounds and the stones. The youngest went over the area with the metal detector. He scanned every inch of the excavated holes, and sometimes he stopped and listened for a long time before moving on.

We were there for about half an hour. The wind was bitterly cold, but the men did not seem to mind. They were utterly focused. In work mode. Their gold fever kept them warm.

"This is usually the best place," the geologist said. "But obviously there is nothing left. Too many people know about it."

When Esee and I left, so did the gold diggers. They carried on to the next hills, and we headed south-west again, towards the sun and the Chinese border.

About a hundred thousand Mongols make their living, either wholly or partially, as "ninja miners", or illegal gold diggers. According to the Mongolian authorities, these unauthorised gold miners dig up as much as five tons of gold a year. Many thousand Mongols also mine illegally for coal in disused or self-made mines, and that is far more dangerous. No-one knows how many people are killed every year in their search for the black gold.

Mongolia is unusually rich in minerals. During the communist era, the Russians developed the copper-mining town, Erdenet, in the north. The Russians owned half of the mine, and in the 1980s it accounted for eighty per cent of Mongolia's G.D.P. The Erdenet mine will soon be surpassed by the Oyu Tolgoi mine in the Gobi Desert, which is expected to be ten times the size. When Oyu Tolgoi is in full operation in a few years' time, it will be one of the largest copper and gold mines in the world, and is likely to triple Mongolia's G.D.P., even though two thirds of the mine is owned by the infamous multinational mining company Rio Tinto and the Canadian Ivanhoe Mines. Whereas Mongolia has traditionally been dominated by its neighbours, first China, then the Soviet Union, it is now cynical multinationals who rule the steppes. Mongolia has very definitely cut its ties with communism and embraced capitalism, neo-liberalism and market forces.

Our journey west continued. Large birds of prey glided on the air streams; a herd of gazelle might suddenly leap across the tracks in front of us. A couple of times we caught a glimpse of voles and small, silvery foxes. Esee spent the time practising throat singing. Simple, guttural sounds with high, shrill overtones from a half-open mouth. He coughed and put a hand to his throat.

"What do you think? Am I any good?" he said, as he massaged his throat. I nodded. He smiled proudly and produced a few more guttural sounds. The same evening we came to a poor, weather-beaten village that was famous for its throat singers. We hoped to meet Dashdorj Tserendavaa, the most famous of them all. We were told that he was in the village and would be happy to meet us, but was in the middle of a card game. While we waited for Tserendavaa to finish playing cards, we installed ourselves in the only guesthouse in the village, which was actually a small shed with three bare beds.

We had almost given up on meeting Tserendavaa when, close to midnight, we were given the message that he was ready to see us now. He came to get us himself. He was a giant of a man, tall and broad, with a bloated face. His enormous belly was kept in place by a wide, tight belt. His voice was deep, definitely bass, and hoarse from years of smoking. His wife, who served us noodles and milky tea, was almost as rotund as her husband.

"My father, who was a herdsman, taught me to throat sing when I was five years old," Tserendavaa said. He wiped the sweat from his face with a cloth, then lit a cigarette. "It is a very difficult technique. You have to practise and practise so you don't cough, and your throat has to be completely relaxed, so the air can pass freely through the vocal cords. Then you make the overtones with your tongue and mouth. I gave my first concert when I was sixteen. It took more than ten years before I was good enough to perform on stage. You have to be very patient and train your lungs. A throat singer has to have good lungs, he has to be able to hold his breath for a long time."

His wife poured more milky tea into our bowls. Tserendavaa disappeared for a long time and then came back with a folder of press clippings and interviews. He waited patiently while I looked through them. Then he invited us into his yurt.

"Here is better for photographs than in the house," he said, and made himself comfortable on the bed. Esee and I sat down on two low stools. "The tradition goes all the way back to the Huns," the master said, as he put on his costume: a wide, blue robe with capacious fur sleeves that was decorated with golden dragons, a large blue hat, and leather shoes with pointed toes. His wife came in to help him put on the shoes.

"Throat singing is how we Mongols express ourselves, it is our feelings and our offering to nature," Tserendavaa explained when he was fully dressed. "Throat singing makes my life meaningful, and I feel good when I sing. I won my first gold medal in a music competition in Ulan Bator in 1981. I was on television and in the papers and everything. My father was very proud of me. Personally, what I am most proud of is that I have managed to teach throat singing to everyone who has wanted to learn, regardless of gender or age. I have taught women and men, children and adults, Mongols and foreigners. Over the years, I have been offered work by all the music theatres in Ulan Bator, but I belong here, in this small village. And yet my voice is famous throughout Mongolia and around the world. So why should I move anywhere else?"

He lit another cigarette, the fifth or sixth.

Esee told him that he could throat sing a little. Tserendavaa nodded.

"Nearly all Mongolians know the basic sounds," he said. "It is part of our culture. Let me hear."

Esee cleared his throat and started. The master listened carefully.

"I could teach you to sing properly within ten days," was his verdict. He lit a cigarette and got out an old, traditional instrument, a *morin Khuur* or "horsehead fiddle". "My father bought this for me when I was five," Tserendavaa said. "It cost seventy-five tugruk, which was a lot of money at the time."

He started to play. The bow ran across the strings, his fingers danced skilfully up and down the wooden neck. When he had finished the first song, a classic apparently, he played a song about the different gaits of a horse. The music was so vibrant that we could see the horses galloping, cantering, trotting and galloping again. Tserendavaa looked us straight in the eye as he played, watching for our response. His stage presence was electric, even if he was not on stage and we were the only audience members.

"There are two main styles of throat singing," Tserdavaa told us. "The deep style, which is called *kharkhiraa khöömii*, and the finer style, which is sub-divided into a further seven categories." He listed the seven sub-categories, and I attempted unsuccessfully to note down the complicated Mongolian names. We were then given a demonstration of one of the seven, accompanied by the fiddle.

The high note that was pressed out through his pursed lips, over the underlying, deep base, produced an unfamiliar but strangely beautiful resonance. When he finished, he took a deep breath, lit another cigarette and wiped the sweat from his face.

"Would you like to see a video of me singing at my first music festival in 1983?" he said. He had already put a tiny television out on a stool. The recording was black and white and the quality was pretty poor. Tserendavaa was the youngest musician in the small group: in his late twenties, charming and handsome, with a twinkle in his eye. Esee was fascinated by the young man in the film and the fact that he was now the fat man sitting in front of us. I tried to shush him when he expressed his delight, but Tserendavaa just laughed. By the time he drove us back to our shed, he had sold us both a C.D. and charged an extortionate amount for the private concert. Show business is show business, wherever you are.

Mid-morning the following day we reached a brand-new, asphalt road. We had it all to ourselves, and it felt like driving on velvet. An overwhelming number of signs had been put up at the side of the road. One displayed the speed limit that was seen as merely a guideline, another reminded us that overtaking was not permitted, but there was no-one to overtake anyway. Every swing and bend, no matter how gentle, was marked "Dangerous Bend".

The asphalt road led to the Chinese border. Mongolia is completely surrounded by its two powerful neighbours: to the north, it borders Russia, and China cups the country to the south, east and west. In order to get to Kazakhstan, I had to cross Xinjiang, China's most westerly and troubled region.

During the communist era, more than ninety-five per cent of Mongolia's trade was with the Soviet Union. Since Mongolia became a democracy in 1990, the pendulum has swung the other way. Now, where once it was the enemy, China is Mongolia's single most important trading partner. More than eighty per cent of the total export goes to the Chinese, something that is underlined by the luxurious stretch of road to the border. The new asphalted road was – not surprisingly – financed by the Chinese government.

Tserendavaa's C.D. was on repeat. Esee practised assiduously to the master's songs, and by the time we reached the Chinese border early the next morning, there was a marked improvement in his singing.

No Foreigners

Only a small batch of travellers was let out of Mongolia at a time. The rest of us had to stand and wait outside the border gate until the guard decided it was time to let another three or four through. There was a chill in the morning air and I jumped up and down to keep myself warm. A man in his forties lost his temper and started to shake the fence and shout at the guard, who got so annoyed that he opened the gate, came through and grabbed the man in a stranglehold. Inside the border station, there was absolute chaos. A young soldier tried to order the queues in front of passport control without much success. All luggage should in theory be scanned, but only the odd traveller threw a bag or two on the conveyor belt. So many people pushed and squeezed through the metal detector at a time that the plastic panels creaked. And then, in the middle of it all, two of the passport control officers disappeared into a back room for a cup of tea. When it was finally my turn, the passport officer got a visit from her little daughter and completely forgot about the queue. Only once her daughter had left did she take my passport and leaf through it slowly, as though it were a riveting read.

"Do you know Chinese?" she said in the end.

"Not a single word," I replied.

She sent me a sympathetic look and stamped me out of Mongolia.

The Chinese side of the border, on the other hand, was a

bureaucratic dream. The border guards were smiling and friendly, and the queues had miraculously vanished.

"Which places are you going to visit?" the young passport officer asked me.

"Urumqi and somewhere I can't remember the name of," I said.

"You cannot remember the name?" She looked at me in surprise, then started to laugh. "And what is the purpose of your visit to China?"

"Tourism," I lied.

The comforting sound of stamps followed.

When you have just crossed a border, you are easy prey. You are confused, overwhelmed and do not know how things work. It is thus not a smart move to go with the most eager and brazen taxi driver, but all too often that is what happens. No sooner had I left the safe and friendly confines of the Chinese border station than I was accosted by a handful of pushy men. "Urumqi? Urumqi?" they all shouted at the same time, and before I had a chance to protest, one of them got hold of my suitcase and started to walk off. The others politely dispersed. I had been claimed.

The man who had taken my suitcase was called Sultan. He was a Kazakh, it turned out, and could speak a little Russian.

"We wait for two more, then we go," he said. "Eight hours to Urumqi. First stop, short break, eat lunch. There by eight this evening, one hundred per cent guaranteed."

Those last words made me suspicious, but the other drivers had vanished. Fifteen minutes later, all the passengers were there, luckily, and we were ready to leave. We had driven no more than five minutes when the driver stopped and let in a sixth passenger who had to more or less sit on the lap of the man next to me. It was all thighs and elbows. The thought of the next eight hours filled me with dread, but I need not have worried. After only a few more kilometres, we stopped again. The other passengers unfolded themselves out of the car and disappeared. Sultan pointed to a simple cafe.

"Lunch," he said. "I am in the shop beside. I collect you four o'clock."

"Four o'clock? But that is four hours away!" I protested.

He nodded and shrugged.

"Give me my suitcase," I said. "I am going to find another taxi. Or a bus. There must be a bus."

Sultan shook his head. "No buses. No taxis. Not from here, not today."

I marched across the road to a small cluster of men I recognised from the border station.

"Are there any buses from here to Urumqi?" I demanded.

One of them, a young man with crumbs in his moustache, could speak rudimentary Russian. "The buses go from there," he said, pointing to the right.

Sultan had followed me and joined in the conversation in a language I could not understand.

"But no buses now," the breadcrumb man said. "No taxis. You must wait until four."

I resigned myself and went to eat lunch. At regular intervals I went out onto the pavement to check that Sultan's car was still there and that he had not driven off with my things.

Sultan did not run off. When I had eaten my noodles and left the smoke-filled restaurant, he came out onto the pavement and waved me into the shop next door. There were garish chandeliers and lights shaped like teddy bears and airplanes hanging from the ceiling. The walls were covered in a jumble of bedside lamps in various colours and shapes, and bathroom mirrors. Otherwise, there was a mixture of mops, electric plugs, foldable keyboards, rubbish bins and toilets. The shop assistant, a young woman in a miniskirt and flowery hijab, was using one of the toilets as a seat. I was offered a stool and a cup of salty butter tea.

"I have found another passenger, so we only need two more," Sultan told me optimistically. "See you at four!" He disappeared out through the door again and drove off with my suitcase.

I was left there underneath the lampshades. The shop assistant poured more butter tea. A customer came in and exchanged a few words with her. When he left, she poured us yet another cup of tea. We drank in silence, as we had no common language in which to communicate. At one point I needed to go to the toilet. I looked up the Chinese character for toilet in my dictionary app and showed the young woman the screen. She stood up, locked the shop and took me across the street, to a shack at the back of a large house. The shack was so revolting that I was advised to do my business on the grass behind the shed, as many others had clearly done before me.

The hours crept by. It was nearly five o'clock when the driver showed up again.

"Quick, quick, we are leaving now!" he said, and ran back to the car. I put down my cup of butter tea and hurried after him. There was already a young boy sitting in the back seat. Sultan accelerated along the bumpy country road and drove through small, impover-ished villages at an irresponsible speed. It was far dirtier here than in Mongolia. The roadsides were full of bottles, plastic bags and other rubbish. Whenever the driver wanted to get rid of something, be it an empty bottle or a cigarette, he rolled down the window and then it was gone. We picked up another woman in one of the small, dirty villages. And then, finally, we set course for Urumqi.

The journey was an eight-hour nightmare. Sultan sat hunched over the steering wheel and seemed to think it was below his honour even to touch the brakes, except on the sharpest bends. The speedometer did not drop below 120 kilometres an hour. We drove along narrow, winding roads and sometimes took a short cut across a field. Only when it got dark did Sultan turn onto the main road. We whizzed past buses, lorries, motorbikes, cars and cyclists. Headlights came towards us in the dark, then disappeared. Sultan talked on his mobile and chain-smoked, without ever slowing down. A C.D. of Kazakh folk music played on repeat throughout the journey. The woman and young boy lay snoring on the back seat. I kept my eyes firmly on the road. The only time it nearly ended in disaster, it was not even Sultan's fault. Another driver made a rash decision to overtake and came driving towards us in our lane at top speed. Sultan reacted immediately, slamming on the brakes, and pulling over to the side. We escaped with nothing more than a fright.

It was well past midnight when we drove into Urumqi. After weeks of solitude in Mongolia, the meeting with Xinjiang's capital was overwhelming. More people live in Urumqi than in the whole of Mongolia. Black skyscrapers towered up in front of us as in a Batman dystopia. The impression was of asphalt and concrete, depressing housing blocks, and cars everywhere you looked.

I did not leave the hotel for three days. Only on the fourth day did I finally manage to pull myself out of the cocoon I had wrapped myself in; exhausted by new impressions, I had watched Western television series with superhuman patience as I streamed them on the hotel's very poor WiFi. "The Bridge", "Fargo" – fifteen seconds here, three minutes there, then "reload" and start again, only to be rewarded with a further two minutes of badly pixelated escape.

The world outside the hotel was noisy, hostile and dirty; every surface was covered with a thick layer of soot. Urumqi means "beautiful pasture", but the name could not be less appropriate. In winter, Urumqi tops the list of cities with the worst air quality in China. Even though it was only the end of October, I could feel my nostrils stinging. The cars were stuck in queues that barely moved, and released a bluish, foul-smelling exhaust. I could just see a pale sky through the grey veil of smog, high up and barely visible between the tower blocks and scaffolding.

No other city lies further from the sea than Urumqi. The nearest coast was more than two thousand kilometres away.

During the Russian Revolution, so many people fled over the border to Urumqi that a Russian quarter formed in the area around the Russian consulate. According to the Swedish explorer Sven Hedin, who visited the city in 1920, the rubbish-clogged streets in the improvised refugee camp were full of potholes and puddles so big that he had seen two horses drown in one. There is still a Russian Orthodox church in Urumqi, but any other traces of the once considerable Russian influence have been swallowed by a conscious Sinicisation and extraordinary growth in the past few decades. In 1949, the Han Chinese made up only six per cent of the population in Xinjiang, whereas now they account for forty per cent. Despite the increasing footprint of the Han Chinese, Xinjiang is still one of China's most multi-ethnic areas. Not so strange, perhaps, given that Xinjiang is the biggest administrative division and has borders with eight different countries: Mongolia, Russia, Kazakhstan, Kyrgyzstan, Tajikistan, Afghanistan, Pakistan and India. Xinjiang is in many ways a continent in itself. With a ground area of 1.66 million square kilometres, it is bigger than Spain, France, Germany and Great Britain put together. The only thing that is small in Xinjiang is the population: the autonomous region has only about 23 million inhabitants. Much of the vast region is inhospitable. Enormous areas are uninhabitable, such as the Tian Shan mountains and Taklamakan Desert, which is the second largest sand desert in the world.

The Xinjiang Museum in Urumqi reopened ten years ago,

having been given an expensive facelift, with modern glass facades and improved exhibition spaces. The various ethnic groups that make up the patchwork of Xinjiang have all been allocated a space in the ethnographic exhibition. Full-size Kazakh, Kyrgyz and Mongolian yurts are on display. One room is furnished like a typical nineteenth-century Russian living room. The information poster says that Russians like to decorate their homes and that round tables are preferred but square tables are also used. The dummies were dressed as Russians from the latter part of the nineteenth century, in felt, lace, shawls and hats. The German dummies in the next room were dressed in late nineteenth-century, German-farmer fashion. It was only after I had seen the Russian and German exhibitions that I realised that the galleries with other ethnic groups must be as outdated – that not many Kazakhs or Tatars wear their folk costumes every day, either. Perhaps it is easier for the Chinese authorities to deal with other "cultures" in this way, as folkloric artefacts, a colourful accessory that can be worn to celebrations. In reality, the authorities have a strained relationship with the country's more than fifty minority groups, not least the Muslims, who form the largest of these groups.

Slightly less than half the population of Xinjiang are Uighurs, a Turkic people with roots in Mongolia and the area south of Lake Baikal in Russia. Like so many other Central Asian ethnic groups, the Uighurs have a long and complicated history. Central Asia, the area between Russia to the north and Iran and Pakistan to the south, is strategically placed between east and west, and has been invaded from all directions through the centuries. The Uighurs had their heyday in the eighth century, when they had a khanate that included all of Mongolia. After about a century at the top of the power hierarchy, the Uighurs were toppled by the Yenisei Kyrgyz, another Turkic people. Many of the Uighurs fled west and settled in a kingdom known at the time as Dzungaria, more or less where Xinjiang lies today. Here they founded the Kingdom of Qocho, which was also known as Uighuristan. In 1209, the Uighurs submitted voluntarily to the Mongols, thereby avoiding the bloody fate of many of their neighbours. The Uighurs were given great freedom under Mongol rule, as they had something the Mongols did not: a written language. Genghis Khan, who was quick to see how useful it was to be able to communicate in writing, adapted the Uighur alphabet to Mongolian and recruited Uighurs who could write to important positions in the administration. In 1390, large parts of Uighuristan fell to the Chagatai Khanate, founded by Genghis Khan's second son, Chagatai. There was a lot of infighting among the Mongol khanates, and the great empire was starting to fall apart. The Chagatai Khanate was divided into east and west before being succeeded by the Kingdom of Dzungaria, the last nomadic kingdom of the steppes, in the seventeenth century. The Uighurs, who had originally been Manichaeans and Buddhists, were forced to convert to Islam by the various Mongol rulers.

China took control of Xinjiang in 1757; the word simply means "new land". In the centuries that followed, the Uighurs maintained their Turkic language and devotion to Islam, but both the written language and name "Uighur" fell out of use. They were known as the "Muslims with turbans" to the Chinese, and they themselves started to use their own names depending on where they came from. The Muslims from Kashgar called themselves Kashgars, the Muslims from Turpan called themselves Turpans, and so on. It was not until the first half of the twentieth century, when the Soviet government started to divide its neighbours into nations, and Soviet republics such as Kazakhstan and Uzbekistan were born, that the Turkic-speaking Muslims in Xinjiang once again started to think of themselves as Uighurs, descendants of the Kingdom of Uighuristan. Conferences were held in the Uighur language and there were extensive debates as to which alphabet should be used and which writing standards should apply.

An ancient people had been resurrected in Xinjiang. This new self-awareness among the Uighurs has become a real headache for China over time. In recent years, the authorities have introduced severe restrictions on Islamic practices in a bid to control the growth of Uighur nationalism and radical Islam. Civil servants, for example, are forbidden from fasting during Ramadan, and worshippers have to be eighteen to go to the mosque.*

Three-quarters of the people living in Urumqi are now Han Chinese, and the town generally feels like any other polluted, overpopulated Chinese city, apart from the neighbourhood around the Grand Bazaar. Having visited Xinjiang Museum, I took the bus there to experience a genuine Central Asian atmosphere. The bazaar itself was orderly and sterile, with armed guards at every entrance, but the surrounding streets were full of women in colourful headscarves and men with round, flat hats. Meat was being barbecued on every corner, and the air was filled with the smell of fresh bread. The big, round loaves were for sale everywhere. I bought one to stave off my hunger; it was nothing if not dry.

Back in the hotel's safe cocoon of white cotton sheets and WiFi, I settled down to watch the last ten minutes of "The Bridge". The Internet was even slower than usual, and I had to shut down every other window and reboot every three minutes. I eventually gave up and watched China Today, the Chinese channel for foreigners. The topic for the evening was Xinjiang's rich past, a colourful, multicultural melting pot with a bright future. Uighurs who had just been given new, well-equipped houses by the authorities showed the television crew around their brand-new modern flats, full of

---

* Since the writing of this book it has come to light that, as well as restricting movement and conducting mass surveillance, the Chinese government has reportedly detained more than a million Uighurs and members of other Muslim minorities in so-called political re-education camps.

pride, gratitude and praise. An engineer wearing a helmet and over-alls explained how the new high-speed trains worked and boasted that the new Silk Road would soon be a reality, that East and West would once again be linked via Xinjiang. At the time of my visit, the Chinese government had invested one billion dollars in the infrastructure project. The Silk Road was about to reopen with high-speed trains instead of camels and caravans, and carriages filled with cheap cotton clothing and electronic goods rather than silk, paper and porcelain.

But not only the trains were shiny; it seemed that Xinjiang itself was in the process of sloughing its skin. The following day I visited Tuyoq, a Uighur village with a pilgrim site a few hours' drive south of Urumqi. The only people to be seen on the otherwise empty streets were Chinese workers, who were energetically laying cob-bles and building mud houses. Cobblestone by cobblestone, house by house, they were building a brand new, traditional Uighur village, a streamlined open-air museum with handpicked inhabit-ants, perfect for busloads of pilgrims and tourists who wanted to experience "real" Uighur culture.

Six days later it was time to leave Urumqi for good and carry on with my journey west, towards the sea, towards Kazakhstan.

Tahir, the young driver who was going to take me to the station, looked anxiously at his watch. The traffic was gridlocked.

"We should make it," he said.

"It is still an hour until the train leaves," I said. "I am sure it will be fine."

"Maybe," Tahir said. "If the queues at security are not too long."

I have never seen so many police, soldiers and armed guards as I did in Xinjiang. There were police checks when you went into every town and city, just as there had been in North Korea, but in contrast to their neighbour to the east, the Chinese had

I.D. scanners and other high-tech equipment. Every single car and every single person was checked thoroughly.

"I don't know what the terrorists think they are going to achieve," Tahir said, with a sigh. He was himself a Uighur. "The recent attacks have just made everything worse."

Since the 1990s, China has been subject to intermittent terrorist attacks by Uighur nationalists. The frequency of these attacks has increased in recent years, perhaps as a result of the ever-tightening grip that the authorities hold on Xinjiang. It has become a vicious circle: every time there is another terrorist attack, security measures are stepped up. There have been too many terrorist attacks to list them all, but the attack in October 2013 is deemed one of the most spectacular. A car was driven into the crowd in Tiananmen Square in Beijing, the most heavily guarded place in China. Two tourists were killed and forty were injured. The Uighur driver and his wife and mother, who were in the car with him, also died. In March 2014, a group of black-clad women and men armed with knives attacked passengers in Kunming train station, in Yunnan Province. Some thirty people were killed and more than 160 injured. A month later, three terrorists armed with explosives and knives attacked passengers at Urumqi station. One person was killed, in addition to the two attackers, and about eighty were injured. In September 2015, more than fifty people were stabbed and killed in a coal mine in Aksu, in western Xinjiang.

"I *really* don't know what they think they will achieve," Tahir said again. "There are too many Chinese to kill them all. And in any case, it is a good thing that they are here. Well, in my opinion. We have oil and gas, and if the Chinese hadn't come, other foreigners would have instead."

Tahir was a Muslim, but not a very strict one. "I only pray on Fridays." He grinned. "And I drink alcohol. I am not a fanatic."

Unlike many Uighurs, Tahir also spoke reasonable Chinese and had a lot of Chinese friends. But when I asked him if he would ever marry a Chinese woman, if she was the one, he was categorical: "No! Impossible."

"Why is it impossible?" I asked.

"It . . . it would not work!" He searched for words, for arguments, but could not come up with any. "It is just impossible," he said. "A Uighur cannot marry a Chinese person!"

Outside the railway station, the police, in helmets and bullet-proof vests, were all lined up beside a tank. With their black machine guns they waved the crowds on towards the station. Only passengers with valid tickets were allowed into the station itself. My suitcase was picked out at security, but none of the security guards could speak English. They pointed emphatically at a picture of a pair of scissors. As I did not particularly want to lose my first-aid scissors, I pretended not to understand. I opened my suitcase and opened my hand, trying to look as uncomprehending and stupid as possible. I must have succeeded, because the guards eventually gave up and let me through.

I had chosen to take the day train so that I could see the countryside, as I had heard so many favourable things about it. Unfortunately, the Tian Shan, or Heavenly Mountains, were hidden behind low cloud and thick fog that day. All I saw was flat, bare fields and the odd cotton plantation. When he was not asleep, the man beside me watched a protracted action film on his iPhone, without earphones. No-one else seemed to be bothered by the volume, and he was not the only one who passed the time by watching a noisy film. When it finally finished, he started testing the various ring tones on his phone.

I must have fallen asleep at some point, despite the films and ring tones. When I woke, the Heavenly Mountains were all around us. The fog had lifted, and through the grimy windows I could see jagged, black peaks and enormous fields of bluish grey ice. A handful of shivering passengers disembarked onto the platform, then disappeared into the snow storm.

I went back to sleep, awaking only when the train rolled into the station in Yining. I quickly grabbed all my things and stumbled out onto the platform. I found a taxi and handed the driver a piece of paper with the name and address of the hotel I had chosen. When I turned up at reception, everyone got very flustered, and before I knew it I was out on the street again. With the help of the translation app on my mobile, the youngest receptionist, who had come out after me, managed to explain that the hotel unfortunately could not accept foreigners. He hailed another taxi for me, said something to the driver and hurried back into reception again. The taxi stopped outside another hotel, where again I caused a stir. None of the three receptionists could speak English, but after half an hour of gesturing and pointing, I was given a keycard. I was too tired to go looking for food, so took the lift down to the hotel restaurant for supper. One after the other, the waitresses sat down on the chair beside me and took a selfie, then vanished out into the kitchen where I could hear them all giggling.

Yining is one of the very few Chinese towns that has been under both Russian and Soviet rule.

In 1851, Yining, or Kuldja as it was better known then, opened for trade with Russia. Relations flourished and Russian influence in the region increased. This was accompanied by a decline in the Chinese emperor's power, and, in 1864, the Muslims in Xinjiang rebelled against the Chinese. The rebellion attracted opportunists from the surrounding areas, including the warlord Yaqub Beg, who came from the neighbouring khanate of Kokand, in what is now Uzbekistan. Towards the end of the 1860s, Yaqub Beg took control of Xinjiang, from Kashgar to Urumqi. He threw out all the Chinese and introduced Muslim law and high taxes. He was overthrown by the Chinese army in 1877.

Russia had, in the meantime, occupied the Kokand Khanate where Beg originated, as well as Yining and the whole Ili Valley, which lies between modern-day Mongolia and Kazakhstan. Ten years later, in 1881, China demanded that the occupied Ili Valley be returned. Russia submitted to Chinese pressure, but in turn demanded nine million silver roubles as compensation for occupation costs, as well as tax-free trade with Xinjiang and Mongolia. In the years that followed, trade between Xinjiang and Russia increased rapidly, as did the traffic back and forth across the border.

When the Qing dynasty collapsed in 1911, the distant western province of Xinjiang was more or less left to its own devices and various warlords. The financial influence of Russia, and later the Soviet Union, was further strengthened in this period. In 1928, following the murder of his predecessor, the Chinese warlord Jin Shuren came to power, not least thanks to a secret agreement with the Soviet government to supply weapons. Shuren confiscated land as he saw fit and introduced travel restrictions for the Muslim population. Many Muslims were also summarily executed, on suspicion of espionage. Understandably, Shuren was very unpopular, and the locals revolted at the start of the 1930s. When in 1933 the Chinese government found out about the secret agreement with the Soviet Union, Shuren was driven out of Xinjiang and forced to seek refuge in the Soviet Union.

In the subsequent power struggle, a new warlord took charge, amply aided by Soviet troops and bombers: Sheng Shicai, who was Chinese. In return for military assistance, Sheng entered into so many trade and defence agreements with the Soviet Union that Xinjiang became a Soviet colony in all but name. Soon the Russians controlled everything from oil wells and tin mines to culture; Russian was the most common foreign language in schools and colleges, and, in the spirit of communism, many of the mosques were converted into social clubs and theatres. Sheng could not make any important decisions without first having them approved by the Soviet consulate in Urumqi.

Sheng had a propensity for brutality, like his puppet master in the Kremlin. During his rule, tens of thousands of "enemies of the people" were killed; mass executions were an everyday event in many towns. When some groups started to rebel against the tyrant in 1937, Moscow took over and five thousand Soviet soldiers moved into Xinjiang. The rebellion was swiftly quelled and Sheng's position secured.

In 1942, in the middle of the Second World War, the perfidious Sheng switched sides and asked the Kuomintang government, which then controlled the greater part of China, for support. The border with the Soviet Union was closed and all Soviet advisers expelled. Sheng also ensured that a number of Chinese communists were executed, including Mao Zemin, Mao Zedong's brother. Following the Battle of Stalingrad, when Sheng understood that Germany was not likely to win the war, he tried to ingratiate himself with Stalin again and sent him a flattering letter. Stalin forwarded his letter to the leader of the Kuomintang, Chiang Kaishek. Shortly thereafter, the Kuomintang took power in Xinjiang, and Sheng was ousted from his position. It is said that he needed fifty lorries to remove all the spoils he had acquired as a warlord.

More social unrest followed in Xinjiang in the wake of the Kuomintang's takeover, in the Ili Valley to the north, in particular. The Soviet Union exploited the situation and established the East Turkestan Republic in Yining and the Ili Valley in 1944, but the following year, at the Yalta Conference, it traded control of the Ili Valley for greater influence in Outer Mongolia. For its inhabitants, however, there was little change. The East Turkestan Republic continued to be a de facto autonomous pro-Soviet state, with its own currency and army. It was not until 1949, when Mao came to power, that the Soviet Union withdrew from Xinjiang for good.

Today, Yining is best known for the 2014 mass trial against fifty-five Uighurs suspected of terrorism, held in the city's stadium. The fifty-five were accused of masterminding in the same year the bomb attack on the vegetable market in Urumqi, which had killed more than thirty people. All fifty-five were sentenced for terror charges, and three were given death sentences. More than seven thousand people turned up to watch the trial.

Because Yining lies so close to the border with Kazakhstan, and because of its history, I had expected many people here to speak Russian, but none of those I met understood a word, nor did they understand English. After breakfast the next day, I hailed a taxi to take me to the old town. The driver did not understand where I wanted to go, but was so excited about having a foreigner in his car that he rang a friend. I then realised that with every minute that passed we were driving further and further away from the old town, and I promptly got out of the taxi. We were right down by the Ili River. The northerly wind stung my cheeks. I pulled my hat down over my ears and started to walk in what I hoped was the right direction, towards the centre.

Yining has a little more than half a million inhabitants, and by Chinese standards is really nothing more than an oversized town, but the air was surprisingly polluted. The soot and exhaust particles that snagged at my throat were in stark contrast to the snow-covered mountains that surround the city. The drivers were unusually aggressive, so it was harder to cross the road than normal.

I eventually found the old town. It was obvious that it had been given a facelift relatively recently, as all the shops had nice, uniform signs which said in Chinese, Uighur and English what they sold. So I could see that the shop with all the leather shoes sold handmade shoes, and the shop with all the carpets sold carpets. I ended up in what must have been Dried Fruit Street. Every shop sold dates, prunes and raisins in a range of colours. It was teeming with people, and everyone, absolutely everyone, stared at me. Presumably I was the only foreigner in the entire city. A flock of young lads laughed maliciously, and everywhere I went I heard voices whisper, *"Rusik, rusik,"* – "Russian, Russian." I have seldom felt so excluded and different.

Back in the U.S.S.R.

Crossing a border is deeply fascinating. In terms of geography, the switch is minimal, almost microscopic. You move no more than a few metres, but find yourself in another universe. Sometimes everything is different – the alphabet, currency, faces, colours, tastes, significant dates and the names that prompt people to nod in recognition.

The no-man's-land between China and Kazakhstan was so wide that there were minibuses waiting at the border stations. I was pushed to the back, squashed between bags, suitcases and women. But at least I got a seat; not many were as lucky. I was immediately adopted by my neighbour, a shapely, young businesswoman from Almaty who had been on a shopping trip to Urumqi. She asked me the usual questions about age, nationality, marriage and children. She was many years younger than me and had three children, aged four, two and one.

"How do you keep in such good shape?" I said, without thinking. "Life must be hectic with so many children."

She looked at me, bewildered.

"I have a nanny, of course," she said.

The bus jolted forward and we drove towards the Kazakh border, *granitsa*, as it is called in Russian. *Granitsa* is derived from the ur-Slavic root *gran'*, which can be traced back to the Indo-European root for "sharp edge" or "end". In most cases this is not a fitting description of modern national borders, which are a line on a map, but it does give an image of what crossing a national border often entails. You step out of one reality and into another.

My new friend made sure that I got to Almaty safely and that I was not ripped off by the taxi driver.

"Four thousand tenge, Erika," she reminded me as she said goodbye. "Under no circumstances must you pay any more, do you understand? Under no circumstances!"

Going back to Almaty was like coming home. I felt a great affection for the grey Khrushchev blocks that were so familiar, almost welcoming. At first, I found myself staring at all the fair people on the street, but no-one was staring at me. I blended in with the crowds; people probably assumed I was Russian. In fact, they even asked me for directions to the nearest pharmacy or super-market. Of course, I had no idea and could not help, but I was so pleased to be asked that I was tempted to make up an answer. All around me, people spoke Russian. Suddenly I was able to under-stand again, and I delighted in eavesdropping on all the conversations.

In the evening I went to eat at the Georgian restaurant where I had had my last meal in Kazakhstan two and a half years before, when I was doing the research for my book *Sovietistan*. Back then I had sworn that I would never return to Kazakhstan. I would go to any of the other Stans, if absolutely necessary, but not to Kazakh-stan. I found the people there colder and less approachable than in the other Central Asian republics. The peculiarities of the dic-tatorship paled into insignificance compared with Turkmenistan, and the few historical remains were nothing when you had seen the magnificent Silk Road cities of Uzbekistan. The Kazakh landscape had nothing on the mountains of Kyrgyzstan and Tajikistan. Kazakhstan is more or less flat as a pancake – Denmark is positively dramatic in comparison. The only two things that made Kazakh-stan special were its size – it is the ninth largest country in the world – and its dark Soviet past.

None of the other Stans had experienced as much suffering and catastrophe during the seventy years of Soviet rule. In the 1930s, more than a million Kazakhs, a quarter of the population, died of starvation as a result of the communists' forced collectivisation. The second largest concentration camp in the Soviet Union, KarLag, was in Karaganda, south of the capital Astana. More than eight hundred thousand people from all over the U.S.S.R., mainly political prisoners, were detained in the camp from 1929 until Stalin's death in 1953. And outside Semipalatinsk, in the northeast, is Polygon, the site where the Soviet government carried out the majority of its nuclear tests during the Cold War, 456 in total. The site itself is as big as Kuwait. The radioactive fallout covered an even greater area and more than two million people suffered as a result.

I certainly had had no plans to go back to Kazakhstan, and yet here I was again, and loving it! The Georgian food was every bit as good as I remembered, but I did not recall the staff being so friendly and caring. No sooner had I finished my red wine than a smiling waiter came to the table and asked if I would like more. If I was wanting for anything, I had only to look around and they were immediately there. "How can I help you?" I took a bite of the delicious Georgian cheese bread and walnut mixture, and the waiter rushed over. "Do you like it? Is everything alright?" After two months in North Korea, China and Mongolia, I found all the polite attention rather overwhelming.

Full and slightly tipsy, I staggered through the doors of the Arasan Baths, the largest and best spa in Central Asia. The baths occupy almost an entire city block in the centre of Almaty, and are a surprisingly successful combination of Soviet and Turkish architecture. The buildings were completed in 1982 as part of the grandiose plans of Dimukhamed Kunayev, the First Secretary of the Communist Party of Kazakhstan, to transform Almaty into a model Soviet city. He was removed from office by Gorbachev in 1986, following accusations of corruption. Just before everything unravelled, Gorbachev made enormous efforts to clean up his party. However, he was insensitive enough to appoint Gennady Kolbin, a Russian, to replace Kunayev. Thousands of furious demonstrators filled the streets of Almaty in protest. They wanted an ethnic Kazakh as head of the Communist Party of Kazakhstan. No-one knows how many people were killed or injured in the course of the two freezing December days that the protest lasted. The number of dead varies from two (the official count) to a thousand, but most likely was somewhere between 150 and 200. The revolt was brutally stamped out and more than a thousand demonstrators were imprisoned. Three years later, in 1989, they got what they had demanded when Nursultan Nazarbayev, a Kazakh, was appointed First Secretary. When Kazakhstan declared its independence from the Soviet Union on December 16, 1991, the last of the five Soviet republics to do so, Nazarbayev became the country's first (and, until now, only) president.

Since taking power, Nazarbayev, a qualified engineer, has run the country as an enlightened autocracy. That Kazakhstan is one of the countries in Central Asia that has best managed the change from Soviet republic to independent state says more about its neighbours than Kazakhstan itself. Thanks to the country's nat-ural resources of oil, gas and valuable minerals, annual economic growth in Kazakhstan has been between five and ten per cent since the turn of the century. Nazarbayev has never tried to disguise the fact that economic growth is his main priority and that democracy and human rights must come second – or even lower down the list. This trend in economic growth has flattened out in recent years, owing to low oil prices; at the same time, Nazarbayev has become increasingly authoritarian. In 2007, the parliament exempted him from the rule that presidents could sit for only two terms, and three years later a motion was passed to give him the honorary title of *Elbasy*, "Leader of the Nation", which in practice gives Nazarbayev the opportunity to decide national policy even after he has stepped down. But for the moment there is little to indicate that he has any plans to do so. In the 2015 election, the seventy-four year old was re-elected with a very comfortable 97.7 per cent of the vote.

"If I were the only person taking part in a race, I would win even if it took me an hour to run a hundred metres," the political scientist Aidos Sarym had remarked drily when I met him earlier that day. "I would be number one because there was no number two. Just like Nazarbayev. His popularity is not real, because he will not tolerate competition. Our main problem is that we have never really been *de*-colonised, or *de*-Sovietised. We have not come to terms with our past. The culture of corruption has only got worse and more systemic. When I ask my students what they want to be, they all say they want to work for the government, because that is where the money is . . . But Kazakhstan has also been affected by the financial crisis. The value of the tenge has fallen almost forty per cent in one year. Instead of opening the country up and trusting the people, the authorities have simply tightened their grip. Only recently, they closed more Internet sites and newspapers. Nazarbayev does not listen to advice, he wants to find all the solutions himself."

My main concern that evening was to ease my stiff muscles. I allowed myself to sink into the bliss of a warm pool. On land, naked women of all shapes and sizes in pointed felt hats went from sauna to sauna. Men and women bathed separately in the Arasan Baths, so there were two of everything: two hamams, two restaurants, two spas and two pools. I had ordered an hour's massage, for a full pampering. As soon as I lay down on the treatment table, I regretted it. The masseur looked mercifully small, but appearances can be deceptive. "Problems, big problems," she said, when she had finished. She ordered me to finish the treatment with a stint in the Russian sauna. Obediently I trundled over to the sauna and sat on the lowest bench, surrounded by felt hats, flabby stomachs and large breasts. It was so hot in there that my skin stung. I lasted little more than a minute before I ran out.

The human rights activist Galym Ageleuov was just as thin and energetic as I had remembered him from two years earlier. His thick, unruly hair was just as moppish, and he was wearing jeans and an oversized T-shirt, as he had done then. Once again, we met in "the old square", as it was known, the place where the demonstrators had protested against the appointment of Kolbin in 1986. The first time had been in spring, and the trees were bursting with chlorophyll. Now the trees were bare, and the town was November-grey and colourless, but Galym seemed to be happier than I remembered. He laughed more and was lighter somehow, perhaps because he was due to become a father again in a couple of weeks.

As he had the time before, Galym immediately started to talk about the situation in his country, changes in the economy and corruption, which according to him was worse than ever.

"Nazarbayev has not managed to take control of the elite," he said, as we wandered along the wide empty paths, surrounded by statues of Soviet heroes. "The problem is that Nazarbayev himself is corrupt, as is his whole family. I think his daughter, Dariga Nazarbayeva, will take over as president after him. All the pieces are in place. She was appointed vice-president earlier this autumn," he said. "As I predicted, the economy is not doing well. Kazakhstan is still heavily dependent on oil and gas, so the economy is sensitive to fluctuations in the oil price. When it falls, there is a downturn, which is effectively what has happened now. And to cover its losses, the government has devalued the tenge and transferred money from the pensions fund to the banks. So, a lot of people have lost their savings and their future pension."

He paused for breath, and I took the opportunity to interject. "*Sovietistan* is going to be translated into Russian," I said. "Do you want me to change your name in the Russian version? You were very critical of the government in our interview, and I don't want you to get into trouble because of me."

"Not at all, just leave my name. I stand for what I say!" He gave a lopsided smile. "I am a human rights activist, after all."

Galym must be one of the most courageous and outspoken men in Kazakhstan. And he pays for it. In 2012, he was arrested and sentenced to fifteen days in prison for taking part in a demonstration. He was held in an eighteen-square-metre cell together with fourteen other prisoners, and not allowed to telephone anyone, certainly not a lawyer. As it was summer, it was unbearably hot in the cell, and the inmates were only allowed to wash once a week. They were let out into the prison yard for an hour a day, but otherwise were kept locked up in the overfull cell. And yet Galym was one of the lucky ones: a number of Kyrgyz and Uzbeks did not even get a cell and had to sleep on the cold concrete floor outside in the corridor, sometimes without a roof over their heads. And he was also lucky to be released when his allotted fifteen days were up.

Since his arrest, Galym has been more careful about what he says in public. Instead, he posts speeches and appeals on YouTube. Even though he is more restrained than he was, his wife, who teaches at the university, was recently given a verbal warning by the rector: he told her that her husband's dubious activities would do her no favours.

"The authorities are clamping down everywhere, on the Internet as well," Galym said. "The situation is worse now than when we last spoke together. Not long ago, two activists were arrested for having started a party on Facebook; they both got two months in prison. A new law has been introduced that makes the Internet moderator liable. And the authorities closed down several Internet sites and newspapers ahead of the presidential election. There is a parliamentary election next year, and they will no doubt close down even more. Soon there will not be any independent media left. I reckon about seventy per cent of the population only watch the state channels anyway and swallow wholesale the government's version of things, for example, that American agents were behind the revolt on Maidan Square in Kiev."

"Who did you vote for in the presidential election?" I asked.

Galym's smile was fleeting.

"I don't vote any more. I used to hand out leaflets during an election, but when the ban on distributing material like that was introduced, I stopped voting. And I am not the only one. I'm not sure that I know anyone who votes these days. People who work in public administration and the civil service, obviously, it is expected of them."

Voter turnout in the presidential election in April 2015 was officially a staggering ninety-five per cent.

In the Realm of the Bears

"Are you scared?" the driver asked me. I cannot remember what he was called. I think I forgot to ask. He was about forty, and had a big brown moustache and a heavy build. Kazakh.

"No, I'm not scared," I lied. "Why should be I be scared?" My throat was dry and my voice sounded croaky and unfamiliar.

"Have you not noticed that we are all alone here? There are no other cars on the road."

Minutes later, we passed a car that had broken down and was parked next to a bank of snow by the side of the road. Winter had come early up here. A man in unsuitably thin clothes was standing with his head under the bonnet. We drove by without stopping. It was already getting dark and the wheels were slipping on the fresh snow. The narrow road was lined by spruces that were weighed down with snow. We crossed a mountain pass that was so high my ears popped, and then started on the descent.

No-one knew that I was sitting in this particular car, with this particular driver, forty kilometres from the Russian border, high up in the Altai Mountains, alone and without coverage on my mobile.

"It can't be that far now," I said, with forced cheer.

"I have no idea, I don't know the road!" The driver laughed. "I have only been to Poporechnoye once before, and that was in summer." He turned and looked at me. "Are you married?"

"Yes," I said. "Happily married. Very happily married. And you?" He did not answer.

"Do you have children?" he said, instead.

"No, no children, not yet. And you, do you have children?"

Again, there was no answer. Instead he let out a crude guffaw. "What do you get up to at night then?"

I pretended not to understand, but he persisted.

"What do you do at night then, you and your husband? Is there no chemistry? You can't do it?" He illustrated with his hands to avoid any misunderstanding.

I kept my eyes on the road. It was almost completely dark now. A pale sickle moon appeared over the treetops.

"And what about you, do you have children?" I asked once again.

He gave a deep sigh.

"Three. Two girls and a boy. Five, eight and twelve."

Around the next corner, there was a sign to Poporechnoye. Three kilometres to go. The driver grinned. "Found it in the end!"

The small village of Poporechnoye lay on the flat steppe, surrounded by high, snow-capped mountains and three narrow rivers. It looked like it had come straight off a Christmas card. Even though there are no more than a couple of hundred people living there, the village has two streets, Central Street and New Street, both marked with large signs. The driver found the right house without any difficulty, and, before I had even got out, a man in slippers came loping over to the car.

"Erika, here you are at last. Welcome! You must be hungry. I *hope* you are hungry, because I have made lots of food!" He took my luggage and ran back into the house. Only once he was back in the hall, did he realise that he had forgotten to introduce himself. "I am Roman Fyodorov. Everyone just calls me Roma. Welcome to our home. It is not very big and not very modern – I am afraid we only have an outside toilet, for which I really do apologise. We do not have mains water in Poporechnoye, but I hope that you will like it here all the same! Are you hungry? As I said, I have made heaps of food, you will want for nothing here!"

Roma spoke with his entire body – his hands, his face, his torso – loud and clear, and always with a friendly smile, eager to please. His fair hair was fading to grey, but it was still thick and healthy, cut like a pageboy's. His face glowed when he spoke, which he did non-stop. He took me by the arm and showed me to my room.

"I hope you will like it. We have just redecorated!" The room was sparse, but tidy and clean: two single beds, a wardrobe and a small mirror.

"Would you like to eat straightaway?" Roma called from the kitchen. He had already set the table. I sat down by the window and let him serve me.

"I am a chef, so you will not go hungry," Roma assured me, as he put butter and jam out on the table. "Mother!" he shouted. "Food is on the table."

A woman came shuffling out of the kitchen. She had a heavy bosom, short, dyed hair and was wearing a long, flowery dress. A tiny, neurotic dog stood behind her, barking.

"Welcome," she said, with a friendly smile, and sat down on the empty chair. "We have more than enough food, so please, help yourself, eat, my dear."

I could choose between pancakes, three kinds of home-made jam, French toast, fresh butter, apples and chocolate. The small table was groaning with food.

"Would you like some more coffee?" Roma laughed with delight. "I am teaching myself English with the Rosetta Stone programme. I am improving all the time. This is my mother, by the way." He gallantly gave her a bow. "My mother. She is called Nina. Her name is Nina." He giggled, and poured me another cup of coffee. "This is Jacobs instant coffee, so German quality. We just put it in a different tin, a Russian tin. But it is actually German coffee," he said, then changed the subject. "I am also studying psychology, by the way. And even though we have not known each other for very long, I can already see that you, with your big eyes, are a good observer. You see people as they really are. You pick up on about ninety-five per cent of what is going on around you. You should write children's books."

When I had eaten more than I should, Roma showed me his room. It was an everything room: an office, workshop, craft room, sitting room and bedroom, full of papers, books and plants. The walls were covered in icons.

"I made them myself," he said. "It is my hobby. I made all the icons in the house, apart from the old one in the kitchen. We are going to donate that one to the new church when it's finished."

After the extravagant welcoming meal, Roma took me on a guided tour of the village. Poporechnoye was blanketed by about a metre of snow, and the flakes were still falling. Our boots creaked on the dry snow with every step we took. Fortunately, the main street had recently been cleared. It even had streetlights. The houses were made from solid, brown timbers, in good old-fashioned Russian style, which meant that it felt very Russian.

"In Soviet times, four thousand people lived here," Roma said. "No-one knows exactly how many people live here now. I would guess somewhere between one and two hundred. Most people have moved into town, and only use their houses here in Popo-rechnoye at the weekends and for holidays."

The mountains were cloaked in the blue light of dusk and the first stars were already visible in the sky. The air was clean and sharp. Roma talked and talked. When we got to the end of Central Street, I knew the whole history of the village.

"In the mid-seventeenth century, Patriarch Nikon introduced many reforms in the Orthodox Church," Roma said. "Among other things, he decided that one should make the sign of the cross with three fingers, not two, as had previously been done. Those who refused to obey the new rules were excommunicated. Many Russians fled to Poland, where they could continue to practise in the old way. We call them the Old Believers. Catherine the Great allowed the Old Believers in Poland to come here, to Altay, or maybe they were forced to come here, I don't know, but a lot of them came. Altay was part of the Russian Empire at the time, not Kazakhstan, as it is now. Poporechnoye was founded by the Old Believers, and at one point there were four churches here. Now there is only one Old Believer left in the village, an old woman."

"Could I meet her?" I asked.

Roma shook his head. "Very bad idea! She does not like talking to people, especially foreigners. She keeps herself to herself." He pointed to a dark, timber house. The shutters were closed, but there was smoke rising up from the chimney. "She almost never goes out," Roma whispered.

When we got back, Nina had set the table for supper. The small table was so full of food that she had had to use the windowsill as well.

"Help yourself, my dear," she said. "We can't have you going to bed hungry."

At about nine o'clock, Nina and Roma started to yawn, and turned in shortly afterwards. It was not long before I heard snores from both their rooms.

Roma was already preparing lunch when I got up. For breakfast, he offered bread, two kinds of porridge, fried eggs, two salads, home-made jam, fresh raw-milk cheese and German-quality instant coffee.

"*Bon appétit!*" he chirped. "Another egg?"

I shook my head, as my mouth was full of food.

"You can look forward to lunch," Roma said. "I am outdoing myself today!"

When I had eaten, Roma invited me out to see the barn. He and his mother ran a smallholding, using old-fashioned methods. All the buildings were wooden, and unpainted. The tools could have been in a folk museum.

"We have two bulls, three cows and six sheep," Roma said. "There is no need for more. Oh, and a calf was born a couple of days ago. Come and say hello to him."

The calf licked my hand with his coarse tongue. A grey puppy dodged in and out between my legs, barking with all his might.

"He's going to be our new guard dog," Roma said. "Everyone here has guard dogs. We live high up in the mountains, so we have to watch out for wolves and bears."

"Have you ever met a bear?"

"Many times! Earlier this year I was almost eaten by one! I was out walking, just beyond the village, when suddenly I saw an enormous bear about twenty metres in front of me. It was already standing up on its hind legs and glaring at me. What should I do now, I thought, frantically. I said a silent prayer, raised my arms and roared as loudly as I could. Then it dropped down on all fours and ran off. I couldn't stop crying."

Roma lifted the cowpats from the straw with a spade and threw them to the side.

"Why are you not married?" I asked. I had spent enough time in Asia for it to seem like a perfectly normal question.

"The short version is that I have never wanted to get married," Roma said. He lifted another cowpat with the spade. "I have never desired a woman. I love my cats, I love cuddling with them, but I have never yearned to touch a woman's skin. The desire is just not there. To me, you are like a sister. Do you think I am strange now?"

"No, not at all," I assured him.

"The long version is that I got sick on my twenty-ninth birthday, in 2004. I was very ill for three months, so ill that I nearly died. I had a raging temperature and was in hospital. Before I got ill, I had thought a lot about what I was going to do with my life. Everything felt bleak. Then one day, a friend came to visit me in hospital with some medicine. I later wondered if it was perhaps L.S.D., because suddenly I saw everything so clearly: my mission in life was to be here in the village. I should be happy for all that I had, open myself up to life, be curious about life again, and, if I did that, people from all over the world would come to visit me." He threw open his arms in delight. "And now people from all over the world come here! We got money from the E.U. to build the guest room and set up in eco-tourism. The first guests who came last summer were from Slovakia. Both Mother and I cried when they left."

It started to snow again. Roma got ready to take the cows down to the river, so they could have a drink.

"And when my mother dies, I want to become a monk," he said, and slipped a rope around the neck of the smallest cow. "I've given it great thought. The fact is that I live like a monk already. I strive to live as piously as possible. Unfortunately, I have not managed to give up smoking yet, but I am working on it! My sisters are both married and live in Ridder. I am the only one who looks after Mother. When she dies, I will join a monastery. There are several monasteries close to Ust-Kamenogorsk, but I would prefer it if the monks came to me, because I do not want to leave Popo-rechnoye. We could have a small monastery here. The world will come to me."

He hummed as he walked down to the river with the three cows behind him. The little puppy followed, barking all the way.

Lunch was extravagant, as promised. When Roma had finished his afternoon tasks in the barn, we went to visit a neighbour, Boris.

"I don't actually like Boris," Roma confided to me on the way over. "I don't know why. I have never had a good feeling about him. But there are some financial things that I need to discuss with him, and you wanted to meet people."

Boris turned out to be a tall man with broad shoulders, a hefty torso and enormous hands; he reminded me of a bear. His face, on the other hand, was boyish, round and immature, and he was already showing signs of a paunch, despite being in his late twenties. His friend Sasha, a man in his forties with small eyes and a scarred face that was both ugly and handsome at the same time, was visiting from the neighbouring town and going to stay the night.

"Mum is in Almaty, so I haven't got much to offer, I'm afraid," Boris said. "Would you like some tea, perhaps? I think I can manage to make tea. All you need to do is boil the water and put the teabags in, right?" He started to fumble around with the kettle. Roma had had the foresight to take a home-made apple cake with him. Boris and Sasha ate with gusto.

"How far are we from the Russian border?" I asked.

"Thirty-eight kilometres!" Boris shouted.

"Would you rather that Poporechnoye was a part of Russia?"

"Of course!" Boris said, with passion. "We are Russians, after all. Of course we would like our village to be a part of Russia! Until the Revolution, this area was an administrative part of Russia. There were no Kazakhs living here before the Russians came, so historically it is not Kazakh territory at all."

"Yes, yes, she knows all that," Roma said, to stop him. "We have already talked about it. Erika, you will get yourself into trouble if you go around asking questions like that."

"Relax, there's no telephone connection here," Sasha said. "No-one can tap us. We can talk openly."

"Are you often in Russia?" I asked.

"I go there as often as I can," Boris said. "I feel more at home in

Russia than here. The police there do not have slanty eyes, all the signs are in Russian and everyone around you is Russian. Whenever I see a Kazakh there, I think, why don't you go home?" He roared with laughter. "Here all the signs are in Russian and Kazakh, and the Kazakh name always comes first! We have to learn Kazakh at school, and if we want a job in the civil service, we have to speak fluent Kazakh. But why should I learn Kazakh? There are only Russians living here."

Even though the Republic of Kazakhstan has only existed since 1991, it celebrated its 550th anniversary in 2015. In 1465, when the Golden Horde started to fall apart, a Kazakh khanate was born in the area that corresponds more or less to modern Kazakhstan. Altay was not actually part of it, but was under a number of other khanates, such as the Naiman and Dzungar khanates. At their most powerful, the Kazakhs also ruled over nearly all of modern-day Uzebekistan, and areas that are now in Iran. At the start of the eighteenth century, the Kazakh Khanate entered into a long and bloody war with the Mongolian Dzungars. As a consequence of the war, and internal strife, the Kazakhs divided into three smaller tribes. At the same time, expansionist Russia started to show an interest in the Kazakh steppes, and, over the course of the following hundred years, Russia took over more and more of Kazakhstan, largely without bloodshed.

In the nineteenth century, when the Russian colonisation of Kazakhstan was completed, hundreds of thousands of Russians streamed into the garrison towns on the Kazakh steppes. The steady flow of migrants did not really accelerate until the 1950s, however, when Nikita Khrushchev started a major campaign to cultivate the so-called Virgin Lands of northern Kazakhstan. By the end of the 1950s, Russians were in the majority in Kazakhstan and accounted for more than forty per cent of the population. The Kazakhs' share was only thirty per cent. The Virgin Lands campaign that had started so successfully soon tailed off when it became apparent that the dry, saline soil of the steppes was not suitable for intensive maize farming.

Today, Kazakhs are once again dominant, making up two thirds of the total population, whereas Russians now only account for roughly twenty per cent. And with every year that passes, the number of Russians falls by about 1.5 per cent. The median age for Russians in Kazakhstan is currently fifty, whereas for Kazakhs in 2019 it was thirty. And Kazakhs generally have more children than Russians. In other words, the ethnic composition of Kazakhstan is changing fast – the Ukrainians have already been ousted from third to fourth place by the Uzbeks, who dominate in the south, and the Uzbek population is growing. Kakazhstan is rapidly becoming a more homogeneous country, dominated by Turkic Muslims. In order to highlight the change in this ethnic balance, and as a marker of the direction in which President Nazarbayev wants modern Kazakhstan to move, it has been decided that the Cyrillic alphabet will be replaced by the Roman in 2025.

The geography, however, remains the same. No other country has a longer border with Russia: the Russian–Kazakh border is 6,467 kilometres long – the second longest in the world, beaten only by that between Canada and the U.S.A. In recent years, the Kazakh authorities have done their utmost to get Kazakhs to settle in the border area, but the most northern parts are still very sparsely populated. More than half of the country's population lives in the three southern municipalities, with only one million people in the northern municipality, most of whom are Russians.

"Do you worry that Russia might do the same in Kazakhstan as they have in Ukraine?" I asked.

"Why on earth would we worry about that?" Boris said. "What happened in Ukraine is the Americans' fault. They sent firebrands and provocateurs into Kiev and Crimea. I don't think Russia could have done anything else."

"Lots of people in the West are worried about what Putin might do next," I said. "The Latvians and Estonians, for example, are very concerned, and with reason."

"Are they?" Boris straightened his back and grinned. "Are they really frightened? We're not scared. Putin has been smart. Everyone knew that he was corrupt and putting money to the side, but then it turned out that he had been using the money to build up the best army in the world! And now we are helping to sort things out in Syria. But the sanctions," he said, with a frown, "they are not good. They are ruining relations between our countries."

"The sanctions are against Russia," Roma said. "Kazakhstan has a good relationship with Europe."

"What kind of news do you get?" I asked.

"Russian!" Boris bellowed. "Mostly on the Internet."

"But you can't get the Internet here."

"No, we can't. We can take a break from all that. But I read the news when I am in town. And by the way, when we *really* want to relax, we go even closer to the borders, where there are only trees and bears. That is where we are happiest."

The conversation then turned to bears. Roma told the others his story about suddenly finding himself twenty metres from an aggressive bear. Boris and Sasha had their own stories. And then there were all the bear stories from the past: all the times that a bear had come into the village, or people had been surprised by a bear on their way to the loo; the resourceful men who had killed bears with a single shot from more than a hundred metres away, or had dispatched them with their bare hands.

A calm descended. The men listened intently to each other's bear stories as they chewed on Roma's fresh apple cake, grunting their approval every now and then.

*

"The end is nigh," Roma said as we wandered back to the farm in the pitch dark. "The earth is burning. Nature is taking her revenge on humankind."

It was so cold that it hurt to breathe.

"We could turn it around, naturally, nothing is written in stone," Roma said, undaunted. "But the way things are at the moment, we are heading the wrong way."

It took no more than five minutes to walk from Boris' house to the farm, but when we stamped the snow off our shoes in the porch, I was freezing and shivering with cold. Nina was waiting for us in the kitchen with some hot tea.

"I just said to Erika that the end is nigh," Roma told his mother. She agreed with a grave nod.

"The earth is punishing mankind," she said, and poured some more tea. "We live in terrible times." She shook her head sadly.

"Altay is the only place in the world that will remain untouched by natural catastrophes and the earth's revenge," Roma said, sipping his hot tea.

"Yes," Nina chimed in, with a glance at the old icon on the wall. "This is a very special place. Altay is Paradise on earth."

City of the Future

On the plane, I passed the time reading the *Astana Times*. One of the main stories was that Kazakhstan had landed at number fifty-nine in a list of sixty-four countries where expats like to live. Ecuador, Mexico and Malta were higher up the list, but Nigeria, Greece and Kuwait were even less popular than Kazakhstan. The journalist made light of this; it was positive that Kazakhstan was on the list at all, she wrote, and they could only hope that their country would do even better next time! A few pages later there was an article about the standard of service in the restaurants in Astana. There was general agreement that the service was poor, that the staff were often unprofessional and, at times, plain rude. But once again the journalist chose a positive angle: "How Astana restaurants are seeking to improve the service sector" was the headline.

Many of those visiting for the first time are impressed by the capital's ambitious, modern buildings and obvious wealth, but I personally had found it irritating and depressing the last time I was there. The sterile architecture and busy, impersonal business centre had left me cold. The distances in Astana are considerable, the roads wide, and the quarters seemingly endless. There is no tram system, or metro, no cycle paths to speak of, only intermin-able queues of traffic. There may be only 800,000 inhabitants in Astana, but the queues are comparable with Beijing, or Ulan Bator, for that matter. And Ulan Bator is the only capital in the world that is colder than Astana. In the taxi on my way to a reasonably priced hotel that I had managed to find, I noticed that the traffic jams were even worse than on my previous visit. The number of inhabitants in the capital had increased by several hundred thousand in line with government plans, but nothing had been done to improve the infrastructure.

However, for anyone who wants to understand modern Kazakhstan, a visit to Astana is a must. The city was originally called Tselinograd and was a small, insignificant, provincial town. Following the dissolution of the Soviet Union, President Nazarbayev decided that the capital would be moved to here from Almaty, which lies almost a thousand kilometres further south. The move was made in 1997, and the new capital was renamed Astana the following year. Astana simply means "capital". It is expected that at some point in the future it will be named after Nazarbayev, leader of the nation and the city's father, but for now he can be happy that the university and airport have been named after him.*

Why did Nazarbayev choose to move the capital from pleasant Almaty in the south to the harsh climate of the north? The official explanation is that Almaty was too small. The city had grown as much as it could; there was no room for expansion or monumental buildings. Almaty is also more peripheral, close to the Kyrgyz and Chinese borders. Nazarbayev felt that a capital should have a more central location. Even though it has never been officially acknowledged, the government may well have wanted to mark their presence and power in the sparsely populated Russian-dominated areas in the north. In terms of area, Kazakhstan is enormous, but the population is small, the armed forces are weak, and not only is the border with Russia long, a fifth of the population is ethnically Russian. In other words, the Kazakh authorities need to maintain good relations with their northern neighbour, and avoid any signs of weakness – a balance that can be hard to achieve.

*   In 2019 the capital was renamed Nur-Sultan, in honour of Nursultan Nazarbayev who resigned from the presidency on 20 March of that year.

In 1994, Nazarbayev initiated talks on the the Eurasian Economic Union, which is sometimes also called the customs union – or the "Anti-European Union" by its critics. The union officially came into force on 1 January 2015 and, in theory, is open to all former Soviet republics. In addition to Kazakhstan and Russia, the other members of the club to date are Belarus, Armenia and Kyrgyzstan. Tajikistan is also expected to join soon. The form and extent of any primary economic cooperation is still unclear. There has been talk of a common currency, but, as yet, the only concrete agreements are on free trade and the free movement of labour across borders. Towards the end of 2013, the dispute as to whether Ukraine should seek to strengthen its bonds with the E.U. or with Russia through the E.E.U. led to big demonstrations in Kiev. As a result of the protests, President Jankovych had to step down, and, in the tumult that followed, Russia annexed the Crimean Peninsula and dispatched provocateurs, weapons and soldiers to East Ukraine.

These events in Ukraine no doubt amplified the Kazakh government's worst fears. How should they react? To begin with, Kazakhstan abstained from voting on the fate of the Crimean Peninsula in the U.N., but in 2016 it was one of the countries that voted against the resolution to recognise Russia as an occupier in Crimea. The year before, following protests in Ukraine, the Kazakh authorities had been forced to withdraw thousands of high school textbooks because one of the maps showed the Crimean Peninsula as Russian territory.

The relocation of the capital could also be seen as a kind of Peter the Great complex: an autocrat's desire to design and build a monumental and impressive city from scratch. The centre of Astana is almost exclusively composed of signature buildings, and several of the most famous were designed by the stellar British architect Sir Norman Foster. These include the Khan Shatyr shopping mall, which is shaped like a glass tent and is the largest structure of its kind in the world, and the Palace of Peace and Reconciliation, a 77-metre-high glass pyramid that houses an opera house with fifteen hundred seats. When Astana Opera opened its doors in 2013, it was the third largest opera house in the world, and was apparently designed in part by Nazarbayev himself.

I had managed to get a ticket to see "La Traviata" and I put on my finest travelling clothes. But compared to the other ladies in the audience, who tottered around on skyscraper heels, and were so styled and made-up that they could have been on stage, I still looked as though I was about to set off on a hike in the wilderness.

The architect had not spared the pennies here either. According to the website, the glitzy chandelier that hung in the foyer weighed 1.6 metric tons. Everything about the opera house was shiny, new and expensive, but unlike the shopping mall, the futuristic national library and even more futuristic national archives, the style of Astana Opera was classical and remarkably similar to the Bolshoi Theatre in Moscow – only bigger.

The performance was not so impressive. The singers' Italian left room for improvement and the set design, the main components of which were a mirror and a large carpet, smacked of budget constraints. The former artistic director had recently been sacked for spending the annual budget on one production.

When I got back to the hotel, my phone rang.

"Good evening, Erika. Are you in Astana now?"

"Er, yes," I said, bewildered.

"How long are you staying in Astana?"

"Um, I am flying back to Almaty on Wednesday," I said, even more confused.

"When is your flight on Wednesday?"

"Quite early in the morning."

"How early is quite early?"

"About eight, I think."

"That is a shame. We have only two days then. In other words, no time to waste. I will make a few phone calls, see what I can do, and get back to you."

I found out that the woman who had called was head of the Assembly of People of Kazakhstan in Astana. Aidos Sarym, the political scientist I had interviewed in Almaty, had contacted her. I had mentioned to him in passing that I could do with some contacts in Astana. Now I suddenly had my own research assistant. Half an hour later, she called me back.

"Erika, you have a meeting with the M.P. Akhmet Muradov tomorrow morning at nine o'clock. He is a Chechen and can tell you about the situation for Chechens here and anything else you might want to know. Then you have a meeting with the chair of the Ukrainian Association. I've also spoken to the head of the KarLag Museum in Karaganda. She can meet you at three tomorrow. Would you like a driver and an interpreter?"

Early the next morning, the woman called me again, with even more interviews and meetings. Suddenly I had a full itinerary and was rushing from one place to the next. I did not have the heart to tell her that I actually needed no more information on the Ukrainians in Kazakhstan, or that I had already been to Karaganda, and obediently went to all the appointments that this stranger had been kind enough to set up for me. Most of the interviews were either about things that had very little to do with having Russia as a neighbour or were with people who had such prominent and offi-cial roles that they just trotted out the same old patter and platitudes, but it was thanks to Akhmet Muradov, that I met Salman Saida-rovych Geroyev.

Salman Saidarovych Geroyev met me at the Vainakh Centre in Astana, the Chechen and Ingush cultural centre of which he was director. He wore a dark suit, white shirt and tie, was polite, engaged and articulate, and came across as far younger than his age. He was somewhere around seventy, but did not know exactly how old he was.

"I think I am seventy-six. Or maybe I am only seventy-three. During the war I lied about my age to get a slice of bread. Officially my date of birth is February 20, 1939, but it is not my real birthday, I know that much."

According to his official age, Salman had just turned five when his family were deported from Ingushetia in the North Caucasus region.

"The police came early in the morning of February 23, 1944. They took everyone. All they could see was nationality, no matter whether someone was a good communist or not. Or even if he or she was a party member. The only thing that mattered was if they were Ingush or Chechen. People were given between thirty and ninety minutes to gather their belongings. All the men who were fit to fight were already at war, so there were really only women, children and old people left. Traditionally it was the men who made the important decisions, so the women had a hard time knowing what to take. Those who refused to leave were simply shot on the spot. Cats and dogs were killed. It was still dark when they came. When it was light, the policemen forced us onto packed freight trains."

As Soviet soldiers were dying by the score on the front and people were suffering and starving, Stalin used enormous resources to empty all Ingush and Chechen homes in North Caucasus of women, children and old people.

"Stalin constructed the lie that we supported the Germans," Salman said. "But the Germans never set foot in either Chechnya or Ingushetia. And our men were all fighting on the front alongside the others."

He took a piece of paper from his pocket where he had noted

down all the relevant numbers and names of the various battalions, and reeled them off: "The Chechens and Ingush had their own infantry, brigades and battalions. Sixty thousand Chechen and Ingush men served on the front!"

The conditions on the trains were indescribable. There were no toilets and nowhere to wash, and people were given next to nothing to eat or drink. Many people died en route. The bodies were just thrown out of the train, as it moved, to prevent more smell and contamination. The journey east took eighteen days.

"My grandmother looked after my brother and me, as our mother was already dead. Our father just disappeared. We have no idea what happened to him, we never managed to find out." Salman wiped the corner of his eye. "I still cry whenever I talk about it."

Nearly half a million people, primarily women and children, were deported from Chechnya and Ingushetia. Various other Turkic groups from the Caucasus, Tatars from Crimea, Germans from the colonies on the Black Sea and the Volga, Kalmyks, Balts and Poles were also defined as enemies of the people and transported east. More than six million people were forcibly moved in the 1930s and '40s, as Stalin became increasingly paranoid. More than a quarter of those deported, sometimes as many as half, died along the way or during the early days of exile. The deportees were dumped in the taiga in the far east, in Siberia and Kazakhstan, where there was so much space and so few people. They often had nothing more than the clothes they were wearing and the few belongings they had managed to gather together before they were chased from their homes. They had to build new lives from scratch.

"We got to Kazakhstan on the sixth or seventh of March," Salman said. "They left us at Akkol, which is 180 kilometres from here. An uncle took responsibility for us and we moved in with him. There were a lot of people in his family, so we were all squashed together. We had to report to the commander, an educated but boorish man. My memories of the first year are like a bad dream. It had been warm in the Caucasus, so our clothes and shoes were not suited to the cold. We were freezing all the time. The Kazakhs were friendly and gave us milk and kurt, a kind of hard, salted cheese. I remember that the Kazakhs smelled different from us and that I thought it was dirty here. The first winter was hard. We had practically no food until spring. I have no idea where they came from, but when spring arrived, we got potatoes to eat. The Kazakhs taught us to make warm clothes, but in those early days we had nothing to make them from. I remember I wore a pair of trousers made from a stolen car cover. There were a lot of funerals in that first year. People died from disease and starvation. There were funerals every day."

Salman was sent to a Russian school, but could not speak Russian.

"The only thing I could say in Russian was 'come here'! I remember I met a Russian boy and said it to him. He came over and talked to me, but I had no idea what he was saying, so I threw snow at him." Salman laughed. "I was a good student and was quick to learn Russian, but, morally, being an 'enemy of the people' was tough. Other children accused us of having helped the Germans, but I argued back. Always. And if that did not help, I hit them. Before we were rehabilitated, we could not join the Party. We were never mentioned in the newspapers, because it was forbidden to use the words 'Chechen' or 'Ingush'. No matter how skilled you were, you would not get a job if your nationality was given as Chechen or Ingush in your passport. Whenever the adults got together, they always talked about the Caucasus. They missed the climate, the vegetables, the fruit, the colours and the smells. As it was dangerous to criticise Stalin by name, they called him the Moustache. 'When the Moustache dies, they will let us back,' they would say."

The Ingush and the Chechens were not rehabilitated until 1956, three years after Stalin's death. Many went back to the Caucasus, but Salman stayed in Kazakhstan. He became the first secretary of the local Komsomol, the Communist Party's youth organisation, and married a woman who was originally from Ingushetia, like himself.

"Even though we had been rehabilitated, we could not gather and discuss the deportations," Salman said. "It was not until 1991, when Kazakhstan became an independent country, that we could meet and talk openly about our history, culture and language. This centre, Vainakh, was established in 1990. I have been the director for twenty-five years now. Following the dissolution of the Soviet Union, many of my friends went back to Ingushetia, but I am from Prigorodny, so there is nothing to go back to. After the deportations, Prigorodny was occupied by our neighbours, the Ossetians, and has never been given back. If Prigorodny were to become Ingush again, I would probably go back. It is warm there and I am an old man. But the truth is that we have a good life here in Kazakhstan, we have everything we need."

Although the majority went back to the Caucasus after Stalin's death, there are still some fifty thousand Ingush and Chechens in Kazakhstan. The country is also home to thousands of Germans, Tatars, Koreans, Poles, Armenians, Greeks and Bulgarians, as well as a number of other nationalities and ethnicities – a legacy of Stalin's brutal regime.

"Only Stalin could have thought of deporting entire nations, and only he could have actually done it," Salman said. "I have read up on it and tried to find other examples, but nothing on that scale has happened before or since."

After the last batch of interviews, Gyulnur asked me out for lunch. She had sorted out all the practical aspects of the interviews: booked meeting rooms, given us water, fruit and tea, and kept an eye on the time. She was in her twenties, and worked as an interpreter and assistant for the government.

We went to a nearby shopping mall. The centre of Astana consists largely of offices, impressive buildings and shopping malls, presumably because it is so cold here in winter. People do not go from shop to shop when it is minus forty; they want everything in one place. Despite my protests, Gyulnur insisted on paying for my lunch, all part of the unwritten rules of Central Asian hospitality. Like so many other young, educated people in the cities of Kazakhstan, Gyulnur was positive about life and the future.

"I am very happy to live in Kazakhstan," she said. She spoke English more or less without an accent, even though she had never been out of Asia. "We are still a young nation, and we are not perfect, but we have achieved so much in such a short time. One thing I appreciate in particular is our multi-ethnic society. I have friends who are Chechen, Russian, Kazakh and Tatar, and I learn so much from being with them."

"But it is not really a democracy when there are laws that forbid any criticism of the president," I argued at one point.

"I have never heard of such a law," Gyulnur said. "And as I have not heard of it, it is hard for me to say anything about it."

"Lots of the people I have met are worried about what will happen when Nazarbayev is no longer with us," I said. "Who do you think will take over from him?"

"I am certain we will find the best successor when the time comes," Gyulnur said. "The older generation are more anxious because they are used to having him as their leader and are scared of change. But I am sure everything will be fine. Together we can build a tolerant, inclusive and modern state. We are nearly there."

The good thing about Astana is that no matter how recently you visited the city, you can guarantee that something new has been built in the meantime. The new National Museum, an extravagant glass building with carefully curated exhibitions filling 74,000 square metres, had opened its doors since I was last there. Having learnt what was worth knowing about Kazakhstan's rich history, Nazarbayev's achievements as president and the nation's recent sporting successes, I visited the Palace of Independence. The palace was in fact opened in 2008, but the last time I was in Astana I had thought the rectangular glass structure was a stadium of some kind and had not gone in. The building is primarily used for conferences and meetings, but is well worth a visit for the model of Astana on the top floor, if nothing else. The Kazakh capital was planned by the famous Japanese architect, Kisho Kurokawa, and is a comprehensive, long-term project. The capital will not be ready until 2030.

"We have completed only thirty-five per cent so far, and mainly here in the centre, in the area surrounding the presidential palace," the guide told me. "The planned residential areas have not been built yet. At the turn of the century, there were about three hundred thousand people living in Astana. The city has now grown to about eight hundred thousand. The plan is that by 2030 there will be two million people living here, so we need lots of homes."

And roads, I argued silently. And bridges. And tunnels. And cycle paths. And a metro system! But the Japanese model does not seem to include such mundane considerations.

"Here, behind the Khan Shatyr shopping mall, we will build the Green Quarter," the guide said, and pressed a button. A large area that is currently full of cranes lit up. "This residential area will have its own renewable energy and water supply. We also plan to build a replica of Venice, but the location has not yet been decided. We have many plans that are constantly being developed and improved. Astana is a city of the future, polyphonic and modern, designed for the twenty-first century."

Bowling in Baikonur

About twenty-four hours after leaving Almaty, the train rolled into the station in Toretam, on time. The other passengers promptly disappeared into waiting cars, and the train departed again. Soon I was alone on the platform.

Baikonur lies well off the beaten track, even by Kazakh standards: far out on the steppe, about 200 kilometres east of the ever-shrinking Aral Sea, and 320 kilometres south-west of the mining town of Baikonur. The Soviet authorities gave the space launch facility the same name as the mining town, in order to confuse the Americans. The cosmodrome and town were built in all haste at the end of the 1950s to accommodate the Soviet Union's ambitious space programme.* During the Soviet era, Baikonur was a state secret and did not appear on any maps. Visiting the space launch complex is still complicated; it remains under Russian jurisdiction, and Russia now has an agreement to lease both the base and town from Kazakhstan for 115 million dollars a year, until 2050. Foreigners who want to visit Baikonur have to apply for a permit from Roscosmos, the state corporation for space activities, Russia's answer to N.A.S.A. Roscosmos also decides the prices, which are astronomical compared with the other attractions in the

---

* The cosmodrome itself, the Russian term used for space launch facilities, has always been called Baikonur, whereas the city around the base was called Leninsk in the Soviet era. Then, in 1995, the name was changed to Baikonur, so both the city and cosmodrome now have the same name.

region. An overnight stay in Baikonur mounts up to well over a thousand dollars, excluding travel.

"Apologies for the delay, I'm very sorry!" A fat Kazakh in his late twenties, dressed in a suit and full-length black, woollen coat, hurried along the platform towards me.

"Not to worry," I said happily, unaware that this was just the start.

There was an armed guard by the entrance to the town. Marat, as my guide was called, held up an emblem and we were allowed to enter without further ado. Once inside the Russian space launch complex, we were met with decay. The paint was peeling off in great strips from the 1950s blocks of flats, many of the windows were broken, and others had been bricked up. The streets were dirty and deserted.

Marat stopped outside a block of flats and explained that he had to go in and get my papers.

"Under no circumstances must you get out of the car," he ordered. "If you get out, you could be arrested for being on your own, without a guide. Do you understand?"

I nodded. Marat was away for more than half an hour, so I had plenty of time to study the building into which he had disappeared. It looked like a very ordinary block with small shops at street level.

When he appeared again, Marat seemed stressed.

"There are some problems," he said. "The town is without electricity, gas and water because of an accident, so we can't take you to the hotel as planned. But don't worry, I have organised to take you instead to a flat, where you can relax."

"I don't need to relax," I protested. "I have been sitting on a train for the past twenty-four hours with nothing else to do but relax. Can we not just get on with the itinerary? There is so much to see and I am only here for one day."

"First I will take you to the flat so you can rest," Marat said firmly.

"But I . . ."

"Then we will eat breakfast. And after that we will visit the museum. Then we will eat lunch, and then we will look around the town. Afterwards, I thought we could visit a monument in honour of a famous Kazakh folk musician about sixty kilometres outside town. That way you will also see the surrounding countryside!"

I did not remember anything about a folk musician in the itinerary I had been given by the travel agent in Almaty.

"Are we not going to see the cosmodrome?" I asked.

"Yes, of course." Marat coughed. "Of course, we are going to see it. It is in the itinerary, isn't it?"

He drove me to a tired-looking block of flats just outside the centre. The entrance was as sad as only Soviet entrances can be. The iron door was covered in rust and the smell of mould and damp was prevalent. A handful of people were hanging around outside. They scarcely glanced at us.

"I am sure the electricity will come back on soon," Marat said optimistically, as he unlocked the door to one of the flats on the first floor. He put my suitcase down in the hallway and made ready to leave.

"But what on earth am I going to do here?" I asked in desperation.

"You can unpack your things," Marat suggested. "And relax."

"But am I not going to stay in the hotel?"

"Yes," Marat said immediately. "Of course you are going to stay in the hotel. That is what it says in the itinerary."

"So why—"

Marat cut me off. "You can watch T.V. I will be back in forty minutes."

"But there's no electricity here, how can I—"

"It will come back soon, I'm sure."

"But why on earth do I have to stay here?"

"I will be back in forty minutes, I said!"

The door slammed behind him, and I was alone. There was no toilet paper in the bathroom, and the kitchen looked like it had not been cleaned in weeks. There was an open can of beer and half a packet of biscuits on the table. I sat down on the sofa in the living room and stared at the black television screen. I eventually decided to ring the travel agent in Almaty. This was simply unacceptable! I got my mobile phone out of my bag, only to discover there was no reception. The Kazakh SIM card clearly did not work in Baikonur.

I went out and tried the front door. It was locked from the outside.

Three-quarters of an hour later, Marat opened the door to the dark flat and took me to a cafe in the centre of town for breakfast. It was obvious that the electricity and water had come back on here; they behaved, in fact, as if neither the electricity nor the water had ever been off.

"The town is starting to come to life," Marat said.

"But it's well past eleven o'clock," I objected.

"Baikonur is a late riser," Marat said. "Did you not notice when you arrived that there was no-one on the street? Everyone was asleep. Everything was closed."

I looked out of the window. There were still no people on the street. In its heyday in the 1960s, there had been more than a hundred thousand inhabitants. Then, in the period after the dissolution of the Soviet Union, Baikonur was abandoned to criminal gangs and became a dangerous and lawless place. Problems abounded for the new Kazakh state, and the old space launch complex was not a priority. The people who lived there started to leave in droves, and many of the Russians went home. In 1995, Boris Yeltsin signed a lease agreement with the Kazakh authorities, and the Russians have poured millions into the town since, without any obvious results. Today, the town has a population of approximately seventy thousand.

"I don't want to go and see a monument sixty kilometres out of town," I said.

"Are you not interested in Kazakh folk music?" Marat asked, astounded.

"I would rather spend the time here in Baikonur. The day is getting on!"

Marat looked at his watch and mumbled that the museum was probably open now.

"The thing is, you see, we didn't know you were coming today," he admitted in the car, on the way to the museum. "When the space launch was postponed from November 21 to December 15, we presumed you would rather come then. So you are on the list of visitors for December."

"But I said several weeks ago that I would come to Baikonur as planned," I said.

"Why don't you come back in December?" Marat suggested. "You could come here and see the launch for free, if you like, you don't need to pay for another permit, you can watch the launch and then go, without staying the night!"

"It's not possible. I will be back in Norway in December."

"Surely there are flights from Norway?"

"This must be one of the most inaccessible places in the world," I protested. "There is no question of my coming back here again. I am here *now*! I have sat on a train for twenty-seven hours and paid a thousand dollars to get here, and I want to see the cosmodrome, now, as I was promised!"

"But no-one is here," Marat said, and swallowed. "Everyone in Roscosmos is at a seminar in Moscow. I'm the only one here."

Natasha, an efficient Russian woman in her forties, showed

me around the space museum in the town's Palace of Culture. The museum cannot have changed much since it was opened in the 1970s.

"Baikonur Cosmodrome was the first in the world and is still the largest functioning rocket launch base in the world. It has been of major significance to global space travel," Natasha reeled off by heart. "The first artificial satellite, Sputnik 1, was launched into space from here in October 1957. In November of the same year, we launched Sputnik 2 with the dog, Laika, on board, the first living creature to be sent into orbit. Then, in January 1959, we launched Luna 1, the first spacecraft to reach the vicinity of the moon, and on April 12, 1961, Yury Gagarin was the first person to be sent into space, a major triumph for the Soviet Union. Two years later, Valentina Tereshkova became the first female astronaut in the world, and her spacecraft was launched from here. This was also a major triumph for the Soviet Union."

By the time we had finished the tour, it was one o'clock. Natasha offered to move on straightaway to a tour of the town, the next item on my itinerary, but Marat insisted that she take a lunch break first. Those were the rules, he said.

"Shall we go and eat lunch too?" he asked.

"We've only just had breakfast," I said, annoyed.

While we waited for Natasha to finish her obligatory lunch break, Marat and I passed the time driving around Baikonur. Marat did not know what to show me, because everything we drove past, we would see later, during the tour of the town. In the end, he drove to the edge of the town, to the river.

"The Kazakh authorities are building a holiday resort over there," he told me, and pointed to the other side of the river. The barren, monotonous steppe stretched endlessly west. As yet, there was not even a crane to be seen.

"It doesn't look like they have got very far," I said.

"No, the funding is not in place yet. But next time you come, it will be finished!"

"There will not be a next time," I said.

We climbed back into the car and Marat drove me to the orthodox church. I got out to take some pictures. As the church door was open, I wanted to have a look inside, but was stopped by Marat.

"Wait, turn around, come back!" he shouted anxiously. "The church is closed, you can't go in there!"

"But the door is open!"

"They are on a break."

I obediently returned to the car. We drove on in silence. After a few hundred metres, we passed a house that had been partially destroyed by a gas explosion. Some boys were playing football in the mud outside.

"Can I take a photograph?" I asked.

"Of course," Marat said, and stopped the car.

I opened the door to get out.

"Can you not take a photograph from the car?" Marat asked. "I can open the window for you."

"No, I want to get out of the car."

"Why?"

"Because the photographs will be better."

Marat sighed.

"O.K., but be quick. Someone might see you and ask questions."

"But I have permission to be here."

"Of course," Marat assured me. "All the papers are in order. Just be quick."

Marat decided that the tour of the town should also be done by car. It was by far the most practical way, he argued, as then we would not need to walk. Natasha pointed and explained from the passenger seat as we drove slowly through the muddy, empty streets. She had something to say about almost everything.

"Here we have a typical residential area from the 1960s," she said, and pointed to a row of grey blocks. "And here," she said, pointing to the buildings on a parallel road, "we have flats that are typical of the 1950s. You may notice that they are not as high, they are a little lower. Can you see?"

In the park, she pointed to the site where the cinema had been. The building had been made of wood and had burned down decades ago. The building behind the Lenin statue, which had originally been a theatre, had also been gutted by the fire and had been empty for years now. And only a few weeks ago, the town's biggest shopping centre had gone up in flames. Natasha knew the history of all the fires in town.

"And this is the Kazakh police station," Natasha said, pointing to a building with a light blue flag flying over the roof. "And there, just beside it, is the Russian station. We have two, in all, in Baikonur. We are half in Russia and half in Kazakhstan, but our currency is the rouble; after all, there are limits. But it is possible to exchange money everywhere, no problem. Just over half the inhabitants are Kazakh, and the rest of us are Russian, for the time being. But we are building our own space launch base in the far east of Russia: Vostochny Cosmodrome, or the Eastern Cosmodrome. When it's finished in 2018, Baikonur will probably not be so important."

"When are we going to see the cosmodrome?" I asked when Natasha had gone back to the museum. It was already late in the afternoon and all that we had seen until now was residential blocks, monuments and the sites of important fires.

"We are waiting for confirmation from Roscosmos," Marat said, clearly nervous. "Since everyone is in Moscow, there is no-one who can meet us at the cosmodrome. We can't just go there, we have to wait until we have heard from them." He looked at his watch. It was four o'clock. "They are probably having lunch now."

According to Marat's calculations, Roscosmos would be finished with lunch around six, Kazakh time. So we went to eat lunch as well. Five o'clock came and went, then six, and still there was no confirmation from Moscow. Eventually Marat went off to ring his boss. He promised me he would give him a piece of his mind, give him what for. He came back an hour later, his shoulders hunched, having failed to make contact. The sun had set. The wide, deserted streets felt even bleaker in the harsh light of the street lamps.

"What shall we do?" Marat asked. "Shall we go bowling?"

"I did not come here to go bowling," I snapped. "I want to see the cosmodrome. Now."

"I want to cry," Marat said.

"I have not seen the cosmodrome museum or the Buran platform, and I have not seen Yury Gagarin's house or Sergei Korolev's," I said aggressively. "And according to my itinerary, we should have visited them all today."

"You have seen at least seventy per cent of what there is to see here."

"I have seen twenty per cent at most."

"Come back in December!" Marat shouted in desperation. "I will pay for your ticket myself!"

"Don't be stupid!"

To prove that he meant it, Marat started to ring his friends to find out how much a return ticket would cost. When he heard the price, he halved his offer: "I can pay for your ticket to Moscow at least, how is that? Or you could take the train. It only takes two days from Moscow and is much cheaper! I would meet you at the station, I promise!"

We went bowling. On our way there, Marat stopped by a block of flats to pick up a girl in her early twenties. She had long, jet-black hair, big brown eyes, and was wearing a miniskirt with high-heeled boots. When we got to the bowling alley, which was in a shopping mall, Marat ordered a bottle of cheap Russian champagne. He drank most of it himself, and with each glass his cheeks got more flushed and his eyes more shiny. He was truly delighted when I won both rounds.

"I want to have five children," the girl said earnestly as she sipped the orange juice she had ordered. "We have to help our country by having lots of children. We are a young nation."

"Five is a lot," I said.

"Five is nothing!" Marat exclaimed. "Before, when there was no contraception, people had thirteen."

The girl and Marat broke into peals of laughter following this bold statement, and nudged each other.

"But," Marat sighed, "I have a major problem. An enormous, impossible problem. She hates me and will never marry me! You hate me, don't you?" He nudged the girl again. She looked down, blushing, and did not answer.

When the champagne bottle was empty, the girl disappeared into the supermarket to buy something with Marat's credit card. He confided in me that they had only been dating for a week, but wanted to know what I thought. Were they a good couple? Did I think they would last?

When the girl came back, they drove to a hotel outside Baikonur.

"It is best that you stay out of town, so you don't miss your train in the morning," Marat said, which made no sense, as he was driving me to the station, and lived in the town itself.

Marat got out his mobile and punched in a number. "Good evening," I heard him say. "I have a foreign tourist with me. Do you have any vacancies?"

Soon after, we pulled into a courtyard outside a small hotel. There was a strong smell of paint and white spirit. Marat carried my suitcase up to my room, which was large and empty.

"If you knock on the bed frame twice at midnight, a man will crawl out," he guffawed.

I instructed him to be there on time in the morning. The only train west left at 5.04 a.m.

He promised me that he was always punctual, and disappeared down the stairs.

The next morning, Marat did not appear. I called him several times, but he did not answer. The receptionist was asleep in a side room, and the courtyard was empty. I could hear a car in the distance. I started to walk in the direction of the engine and eventually found the road. Fortunately, a car appeared almost straightaway. I hailed it and the driver agreed to take me to the station in return for a few roubles.

"Had you thought of walking to the station alone at this time of morning?" he asked in surprise, once I had got into the back seat.

The train was on time, which was something. I boarded and found my compartment, which was as hot as a sauna. In thirty-eight hours' time, I would arrive in Aktau, my last stop in Kazakhstan. I dozed off and did not wake up again until late in the afternoon. Through the window, I could see the flat, barren landscape.

For a moment it felt as though I had landed on another planet.

CAUCASUS

*"Oh Caucasus, Caucasus! It is no coincidence that
the biggest poets the world has ever known, the great
Russians, have visited you, east of the springs . . ."*
Knut Hamsun

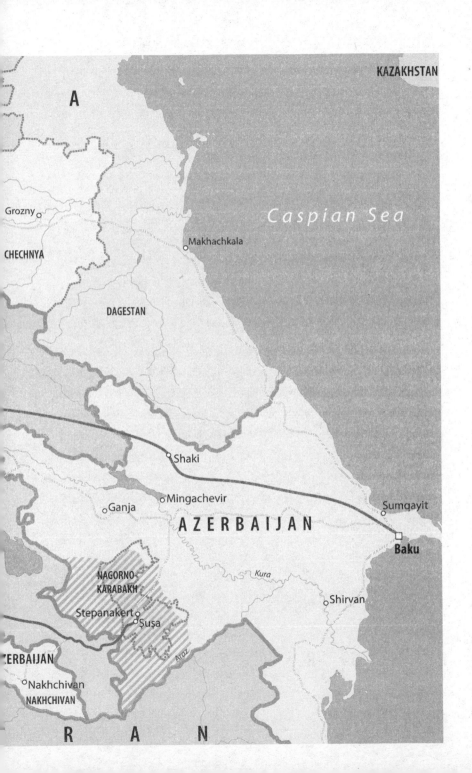

To Wonderland

"The boat to Baku may sail tomorrow," the ticket-seller said. The ferry company offices were hidden away in a residential complex. The premises were so cramped that there was barely space for the woman who worked there. "It normally goes in the morning, around eight or nine, but sometimes does not leave until evening. That will be one hundred and twenty dollars, please."

"How will I know when to be at the port?" I asked, once the payment was sorted.

"The crew will call you two hours before departure."

"Two hours?" I echoed in dismay.

"Don't worry, that will give you plenty of time. If you hear nothing, you can always phone the office, to be on the safe side. They normally don't forget to call, but you never know."

I jotted down the telephone number, thanked her for her help and stood up to leave.

"There is of course a possibility that the boat won't go tomorrow!" the woman called after me. "We never really know when it is going to leave."

I had been looking forward to relaxing in Aktau after three strenuous days. The last time I was there, I had been delighted and overwhelmed by the city's shopping mall, and the Italian-Japanese fusion restaurant on the ground floor in particular. Back then, after three weeks in Turkmenistan, one of the most isolated and authoritarian regimes in the world, the shopping centre in Aktau had seemed liked the epitome of freedom, a modern temple to pleasure and abundance. So as soon as I had got my ferry tickets, I went back there. But now the prized shopping centre in Aktau seemed drab and provincial compared with the luxury malls in Astana and Almaty. No sooner was I inside than I remembered that I do not actually like shopping centres; I find the people and shops stressful. The sushi on the ground floor was swimming in fat, the white wine was tepid and too sweet, and the service was slow and offhand. I left as soon as I could and took a taxi down to the beach instead. I stood there enjoying the gentle, briny sea breeze. It was months since I had smelled the sea and salt water. The Caspian Sea is, of course, not strictly a sea, but rather a saline lake, albeit the largest in the world. And from where I was standing, the horizon was a steely blue ripple.

To what extent can one rely on one's own impressions and memories? Not only are we subjective creatures, we are also capricious. Everything we experience is filtered by our form and mood at the time, our expectations, what we may have just experienced, what we yearn for at that moment. It is often strange to go to the fairground of one's childhood as an adult. What was once big and magical, a wonderland of colours and exotic fragrances, is in fact nothing more than a few rows of tacky stalls and a handful of unremarkable merry-go-rounds. Which prompts the small, but rather unnerving question: is travel literature to be trusted, or any literature that is based on memory, for that matter? The shopping mall that I had stored in my memory as pleasure dome had proved to be really rather ordinary.

But no-one could rob me of the mild, briny breeze from the Caspian Sea.

My mobile rang in the middle of the night. The rather stressed man at the other end spoke to me in a mixture of Russian and English. "Erika, you must come down to the port immediately, now, because there will be a passport control in two hours and the ferry will leave in four hours!"

I checked the time. It was two-thirty in the morning. Half-drunk with sleep, I rolled out of bed and pulled on some clothes. I packed my things as quickly as I could, checked out and caught a taxi to the ferry terminal. There I was shown into a small, miserable waiting room. A slight Asian, possibly Korean, was sleeping propped up against a small rucksack. There was also a young man with long hair and a rucksack full of juggling gear, who sat staring into thin air. And a fat man, who was snoring loudly. Up on the wall, a small television screen informed us that registration had opened and the expected boarding time was 6.30 a.m. Otherwise, there was not much activity to be seen. The customs office was closed, the ticket office was closed, passport control was closed.

I must have fallen asleep. When I woke up there was complete silence in the waiting room. The enormous man was looking down at me. His Russian was sketchy, but I understood that he wanted to know if I was married or not. I told him I was very happily married, but that did not stop him from asking for my telephone number. I explained that my Kazakh number would not work in Azerbaijan. He optimistically passed me a piece of paper with his own number written on it, then wandered back to the metal bench. Soon the small room shuddered with his snores again.

The estimated times proved similarly optimistic. Nothing happened for a long time. Then a handful of staff arrived at dawn. Four or five lorry drivers started to drift in and out with various forms. I lay half-asleep on the metal bench, but caught snippets of conversation: "To travel like that, alone, without a man . . . It's a disgrace . . . How can her husband let her go? . . . If it was my wife . . ." Perhaps it was a dream, because the next time I woke up, the lorry drivers were talking about exchange rates. The hours passed, with no explanation from the crew, only vague promises. "Soon," they said, whenever we asked when the ferry was due to leave. "It won't be long now. Maybe half an hour, max."

Passport control opened at eleven. An hour later, I and the three other passengers were bussed to the ferry and allowed to board. We came straight into a uniformly brown, Seventies lounge where two framed portraits of Heydar Aliyev, the first president of Azerbaijan, and his son, Ilham Aliyev, the current president, were the only things on the walls. A dour lady in uniform checked our tickets and passports.

"Are you travelling together?" She pointed to the long-haired man with the juggling gear. As I had feared that I might have to share a cabin with the overweight Azerbaijani, I quickly said yes. And so Timur and I sailed across the Caspian Sea together. He was in his mid-twenties and worked as a programmer in Almaty. This was his first trip abroad. In addition to his juggling gear, he also had a Japanese wooden sword with him. I never established why. The cabin was dirty but spacious, and pure luxury compared with Kazakh train compartments. There was a dark blue, moth-eaten, woollen blanket on each of the beds. I curled up under mine and fell asleep straightaway. When I woke up several hours later, we were still at the quay. It was not until evening that the ferry finally set sail. Even though there was a brisk wind, the water was so calm that I barely noticed we had cast off. We were lucky, as the Caspian Sea in November is not always as kind.

All was quiet in the ship's corridors too. There were only eight passengers on board. The enormous Azerbaijani popped his head round our door a few times, first to tell us that he was thinking of taking a nap in his cabin, then to tell us that he was going to eat supper. The third time was because he wanted to give us a half-full carton of juice. The restaurant was only open at certain times, and the chef was a parody of what a ship's cook should be: sweaty and unshaven, with a cigarette permanently dangling from the corner of his mouth. The menu was simple: boiled potatoes, strips of meat, borscht, tea and white bread.

We were joined at supper by Chang, who was, as I had guessed, Korean. I had put him at about eighteen or nineteen, but he was in fact twenty-eight and a qualified optician. He had been travelling in Europe and Central Asia for nine months already and now had only a couple of months left before returning home to his spectacle shop and other South Korean duties. The small rucksack he had been leaning against as he slept was all he had with him.

"I don't need very much," he said. "Sunscreen and sunglasses are most important." He giggled. "You have a lot with you."

My suitcase was so heavy that I could barely lift it. We started to talk about our travels and discovered that we had been to many of the same places.

"China was not so good," Chang said. "Too much crime. They look for foreigners like me. My friend was robbed. Europe was even worse! My bag was stolen in Italy. That was when I decided to go to Central Asia. The Central Asian countries are some of the safest in the world, there is practically no crime there. The only problem is the visas." He sighed. "You need a visa for every single country. What kind of visa did you have for Kazakhstan?"

"I didn't have one. They had just relaxed the rules."

"And Azerbaijan?"

"An e-visa," I said. "I applied online and got confirmation by email."

"How much did it cost?" Chang asked with interest.

"I can't remember. I did it all a long time ago."

"You can't remember?" He looked at me in astonishment. "I have a transit visa, so I can only stay in Azerbaijan for five days. I have planned my itinerary and think I will manage to see the most important things. What sort of visa did you have for Uzbekistan?"

When we had finished our meal, I went out onto the deck to watch the sunset. They can be truly spectacular on the Caspian Sea, but that evening the horizon was hidden behind heavy clouds, and all I could see was a weak orange glow in the west. There was a fair breeze, but the air was warm and the sea was still. And there was nothing but grey-blue sea all around. I looked down at the water. It was a long way down. If I fell overboard now, no-one would notice and no-one would find me, ever.

That night, I slept better than I had done for a long time. I simply closed my eyes and sank into darkness.

Early the following afternoon, the Oil Rocks appeared to the starboard side, a small town of oil platforms built during the Soviet era. Chang, who had never seen an oil platform before, was wild with excitement, and dashed here and there, taking hundreds of photographs.

The area that is now Azerbaijan has been known for its oil and gas reserves for a long, long time. The Persians called Azerbaijan *Atropates*, which can be roughly translated as "protected by fire", a name presumably inspired by the many Zoroastrian fire temples in the region. The Zoroastrian priests used oil from natural sources to keep the temples' eternal flame alive. The name Azerbaijan, a modern variant of Atropates, came into use at the start of the twentieth century, and means more or less the same thing; *azar* is Persian for "fire". Prior to this, the Azerbaijanis were often called "Shirvanis", after the Persian dynasty that ruled the region in the Middle Ages, or "Caucasian Tatars", or "Turkics". Like the Iranians, the Azerbaijanis are predominantly Shi'a Muslims, and there are in fact more Azerbaijanis in Iran than there are in Azerbaijan. When the territory that is now Azerbaijan fell to the Russians, following their victories in the Russo-Persian Wars at the start of the nineteenth century, the Azerbaijanis were effectively split in two. In the mid-nineteenth century, oil was discovered outside Baku. When the tsar opened the territory to foreign investors in the 1870s, the Swedish Nobel brothers grasped the opportunity and laid the foundations for what was to become not only their family fortune, but Baku's oil boom. They were joined by the Rothschilds and Rockefeller's Standard Oil Company in the 1880s. By 1900, Baku was the world's largest exporter of oil.

After the Revolution in 1917, Azerbaijan declared its independence from Russia, but this was short-lived. In 1920, the country was brutally reclaimed by the Bolsheviks, who had no intention of letting the valuable oil reserves go. The Bolsheviks chased off the foreign investors, plundered their property, killed those who did not get away in time, and set fire to the oil refineries. Baku's heyday as a cosmopolitan oil metropolis was over.

Azerbaijani oil quickly took on a key role in building a communist utopia. When the Second World War broke out, Baku accounted for eighty per cent of the Soviet Union's total oil production. Germany desperately needed a new supply of crude oil, so put great effort into planning the seizure of Baku. The operation was given the code name Case Blue and was put into action in summer 1942.

The Battle of Stalingrad should in fact be called the Battle of Baku. Stalingrad, which is now called Volgograd, lies just over a thousand kilometres north of Baku, on the other side of the Caucasus mountains. Not only was Stalingrad an important town in terms of industry, it was also strategically positioned on the transport route between the Caspian Sea and the northern part of the Soviet Union. If the Germans had managed to seize Stalingrad, the way south to the Caucasus and Baku would have been open to them. The very name of the city made the outcome a matter of prestige for both Hitler and Stalin. The Battle of Stalingrad was the bloodiest confrontation in the war and is unparalleled in world history. The oil refineries in Baku were evacuated just in case, but thanks to the Red Army's superhuman efforts in Stalingrad, the Germans failed to cross the Caucasus mountains. Had they done that, the history of the world would no doubt have been very different.

When the war was over, Soviet geologists started to map the coastal area around Baku. It was presumed that there were enormous reserves hidden there, and this proved to be true: big oil fields were discovered below the seabed. In 1949, the Soviet authorities started to build the world's first oil platforms here. At its largest, the complex that was given the name Oil Rocks comprised some two thousand drilling platforms and accommodation for more than five thousand workers. In addition to flats and platforms, the complex included a library, a bakery, a laundry, a cinema, vegetable patches and even a park with trees and soil that had been transported out from the mainland. The various constructions were linked by three hundred kilometres of roads and bridges. The communists had built a town out at sea, a well-functioning settlement where the workers could live for weeks at a time, fifty-five kilometres from the mainland.

The golden age is long gone. The platforms have been battered and weathered by the wind and salt water. Most of the rigs are no longer in operation and only around forty-five of the three hundred kilometres of roads and bridges are safe enough to use. There has been talk of transforming Oil Rocks into a tropical holiday centre, but so far these exotic plans have not been realised. And in the meantime, operations are running on one cylinder. There are still more than two thousand people working on the platforms, despite the discovery of bigger and more important oil fields elsewhere in Azerbaijan. It is estimated that the reserves under Oil Rocks will be exhausted within the next twenty years.

Presumably the platforms will then be abandoned and what remains
of this Soviet engineering feat will be left to the sea.*

A few hours later we docked and were escorted ashore. Chang
was agitated. It was already late afternoon and the first of his five
transit days would soon be over. His itinerary was about to be
blown. Fortunately, as there were no more than eight passengers on
board, passport control was relatively swift. I was a little
anxious that my e-visa, which I had bought through a company
on the Internet, would not be valid. The passport officer took his
time studying the print-out. Finally he looked up. "You must
register within ten days," he instructed me.

I promised solemnly to register within ten days.

"Good." He looked at me with curiosity. "What is it actually like
in Norway? It's cold, isn't it? Thor Heyerdahl was Norwegian, wasn't
he? Did he not have a theory that the Norse gods originally came
from Azerbaijan?"

I nodded at everything he said. He beamed and handed back
my passport.

"I hope you enjoy your stay in Azerbaijan!"

The customs officer was not as friendly. Everything from my
toilet bag to my spectacle case was thoroughly inspected. She
pointed suspiciously at a packet of Paracetamol. "What is that?" she
said, aggressively. "And this, what is it?" She held up my contact
lenses case.

If you arrive in a country by airplane, all you have to do is pick
up your suitcase from the luggage carousel and walk through
"Nothing to declare". I have seldom been stopped, and often there
are no customs officers there. If, however, you arrive by land or sea,
there is no end to how thoroughly your luggage can be searched.

* Ten days after we passed Oil Rocks, a fire broke out on one of the platforms, and
at least thirty people lost their lives.

"And what is *this*?" With an air of triumph, the woman held up the Lonely Planet guide to Georgia, Armenia and Azerbaijan.

"It is my guide book for South Caucasus," I said.

"You need it?"

"Yes, as I said, it is a guidebook."

The woman passed the book on to her colleague, who leafed through it doubtfully.

"That is everything, you may board the bus now," the woman said to me, brusquely.

"But what about my guidebook?" I protested. "Are you not going to give it back?"

"Later. We need to check it first. So, please board the bus now."

I did as I was told. The other passengers looked at me with questioning eyes.

"Why did that take so long?" one of the lorry drivers asked. "Did you have any problems?"

"They confiscated my guidebook," I said.

"Why did they do that?!" he said with indignation. "This is a free and democratic country!"

A few minutes later the grim customs officer got onto the bus and sat down at the front. She clutched my guidebook to her chest. When we arrived at the exit from the port, she disappeared into an office with my suspect literature. The other passengers drove off in waiting cars.

"Why are you waiting here?" a curious passport officer asked me. I explained that my guidebook had been confiscated. He shook his head and went into the building. A short while later, he came back.

"They have inspected it and everything is fine," he said, and handed me the book.

Fortunately the editors at Lonely Planet had been wise enough to put the chapter about the breakaway republic Nagorno-

Karabakh, which internationally is recognised as part of Azerbaijan, but in practice is governed by Armenia, in the book's section on Azerbaijan, even though it is only possible to get there from Armenia. Had they done otherwise, I would probably not have seen the book again.

I was collected at the port by Rena, an energetic woman in her forties, with wild, curly hair. This had been arranged through various contacts, and Rena had only been asked to take me to the hotel, but instead she adopted me.

"Have you had a good journey?" she asked in perfect English. "Have you been to Azerbaijan before? What do you like to eat, by the way, and how long are you staying? I will take good care of you."

The road into the city centre was wide and extravagant, edged by solid, well-maintained walls. In the distance we could see an enormous light blue, red and green flag.

"The world's tallest flagpole," Rena told me, with pride.

When it was erected in 2010, it was indeed the world's highest flagpole, at 162 metres – a full 29 metres taller than the flagpole in Ashgabat, the capital of Turkmenistan, which had been the highest in 2008. Tall flagpoles were clearly de rigueur with dictators, and by 2011 the flagpole in Baku had been surpassed by the 165-metre-high flagpole in Dushanbe in Tajikistan. But the tallest flagpole in the world is currently in Jeddah in Saudi Arabia. It is 171 metres high, but not likely to keep the record for long.

Fifteen minutes later we were in the middle of the city, surrounded by elegant buildings that reminded me of Paris. The designer shops could compete with those in Milan. The sea front boulevard and green trees were reminiscent of Nice.

"We held the Eurovision Song Contest there," Rena said, and pointed at a big, brand-new concert hall. "And that is the new carpet museum. We love carpets in Azerbaijan. You must go and have a look."

The museum was designed like a loosely rolled carpet. Rena found an empty parking space and came with me to the lovely boutique hotel that she had booked.

"I will wait in reception while you sort yourself out," she said. "Then we can go for something to eat!"

She took me to a charming little restaurant nearby and ordered everything on the menu that did not contain meat. As my family run a meat-packing business I steer clear of meat products. The waiters came out with qutab (a kind of flat bread) filled with herbs, cheese and pumpkin, as well as soufflés, various cheeses, bread, salmon in pomegranate sauce, salads and fresh vegetables – a veritable feast. When I ordered some water, Rena looked at me, horrified.

"Don't you want alcohol?" she asked.

"Yes, I would love a glass of red wine," I admitted.

Rena lit up and immediately ordered a glass of red wine. She stuck to water herself and only picked at the food.

"This is far too much!" I said, overwhelmed. "And I'm sure you have more than enough to do. You really didn't need to take me out for a meal."

"But that is just normal," Rena said with a shrug and sent my plate a critical look. "Do you not want the salmon? It is very good! I ordered it especially for you."

I quickly helped myself to some salmon.

"Delicious!" I said. "Truly delicious."

Rena beamed and threw open her arms. "This is for you, all of it," she said. "Just for you!"

I ate and ate. It was so good – tasty, fresh and succulent. It was months since I had eaten such good food. While I ate, Rena gave me a crash course in the intricate history of Azerbaijan, from Alexander the Great to Gorbachev, via Christianity in Albania, the

Arabs, the Persians, the Seljuqs, the Ganja Khanate, the Mongols, Timur Lenk, the Shirvanshahs, the Ottomans, the Qajar dynasty, tsarist Russia and the short period of independence after the Revolution. I tried to follow as best I could, but the previous week had been exhausting and I could feel my eyelids drooping.

"You must have some salad too," Rena insisted. I obediently helped myself to some salad. As she continued with the Russians and the Soviet Union, and Stalin and Khrushchev, I looked around at the other guests. Most Kazakhs look like Mongols, with high cheekbones and slanting eyes. Here the people looked more like Turks, with thin faces and darker skin. Many of them had brown, curly hair, like Rena. When they spoke to each other, it sounded like they were singing soft laments.

"We let them come and we gave them our land, and still they were not satisfied. They wanted more!" There was a new resonance to Rena's voice. "And by way of thanks, they killed us and took our country."

I realised she was talking about their neighbours, the Armenians, who had occupied Nagorno-Karabakh.

"I would happily see Gorbachev dead," Rena said. "The bloodbath was his fault. There was a constant flow of refugees from Nagorno-Karabakh to Baku, but what did he do? He did not lift a finger! Only when the Azerbaijanis started to kill the Armenians did he do something, and that was to send in the Red Army. Here, to Baku, in 1990! According to the official figures, 130 people were killed, but the truth is there were many more. I am certain that Gorbachev got money from the Americans. Did you see how his birthday was celebrated in Hollywood just recently? I have told my children that I have nothing against them having Armenian friends, but have also warned them, as they are too young to remember, if an Armenian is asked to kill you, he will do it, even if you think he is your friend."

Once again I was immersed in a new reality. Everything was new: the language, the dates, the alphabet, the history, the stories. The faces and voices. The conversations over restaurant tables.

But the generosity and hospitality were the same. Rena insisted on paying for everything. I tried to dissuade her, but she was adamant: I was her guest and should jolly well behave like one. She also made sure that I got a doggy bag with the leftovers, and then walked me back to the hotel.

"I am already looking forward to taking you out for a meal again!" she said, and kissed me on both cheeks in parting.

Mr President and Mrs Vice-President

When I asked Ivar Dale from the Norwegian Helsinki Committee if he knew any human rights activists or journalists in Baku who were openly critical of the government and might be willing to speak to me, his reply was: "Most of them are either in prison or have left the country." I did, however, manage to track down a few, but one meeting then the next was cancelled at short notice. They suddenly all had so much to do at work and apologised that they would not be able to meet me as agreed. None of them suggested meeting another time.

A knock-on effect of these cancellations was that I had time to visit not just the carpet museum but all the carpet shops in the beautifully maintained old town, as well as many of the other attractions, including the Shirvanshah Palace and the chocolate museum. And beyond the city, I managed to visit Yanar Dag, the burning mountain, where flames of up to three metres burn night and day, thanks to an underground gas reserve. I also saw the mud volcanoes to the south of Baku. The grey, bubbling pools of mud look innocent enough, but every now and then they spew boiling mud metres into the air. No country has as many mud volcanoes as Azerbaijan, tangible proof of the country's enormous oil and gas resources, which are cooking just below the surface.

The Gobustan National Park lies close to the mud volcanoes. There are more than six thousand rock carvings in the area, the oldest of which is forty thousand years old. The cliffs and caves are covered in Stone Age art, quite literally from floor to ceiling. Some of the carvings are so worn that it is difficult to see what they depict, but others very clearly are of a boat, a goat or dancing people. Even though a thousand years might separate one goat from the next, they are carved in exactly the same way, with the same lines and curves. In the 1930s, the site was going to be made into a quarry, but then one bright worker noticed that the cave walls were full of pictures, and the plans were dropped. About half a century later, Thor Heyerdahl visited Gobustan for the first time. He believed that the boats in the rock carvings resembled those he had seen in Finnmark, and he developed a rather wild theory, based on the position of the sun in the carvings, that people from the region had migrated north, with boats and donkeys, and ended up in Norway. This theory then mushroomed into the idea that Odin and the Norse gods originated in Azerbaijan. Heyerdahl believed that Aser, as the gods were collectively called, was literally derived from *Azer*baijan!

After yet another cancellation, I spent an afternoon in the Heydar Aliyev Centre, named after the father of the country. The elegant, white building opened in 2012, and has no straight lines or right angles. The building itself was better and more successful than the exhibition about Heydar Aliyev, which was so modern that it only partially worked. The videos about Aliyev's life started automatically whenever someone came within a given radius, but then stopped as soon as anyone, intentionally or unintentionally, moved beyond this invisible radius.

Heydar Aliyev became chairman of the Azerbaijan K.G.B. in 1967, and two years later was elected First Secretary of the Azerbaijan Communist Party. Here he gained a reputation for giving the party heads extravagant gifts, such as the ring given to Leonid Brezhnev that had a large shiny diamond in the middle, surrounded by fifteen smaller diamonds, symbolising the fifteen Soviet republics. In 1982, Aliyev was promoted to full member of the Politburo, with responsibility for transport and social services. No other Azerbaijani had ever reached such dizzying heights in the Soviet system. He held this position for five years, until in 1987 he was forced to resign by Gorbachev amid allegations of corruption.

In February the following year, a shock decision in the Caucasus sent ripples around the world: the local soviet in Stepanakert, the capital of the autonomous region of Nagorno-Karabakh, had unilaterally voted to leave the Soviet Republic of Azerbaijan in favour of Armenia.

Nagorno-Karabakh became part of the Russian Empire in 1813, following a war with Persia that had lasted many years. Nearly a hundred years later, in 1905, while Russia licked its wounds following its defeat in the Russo-Japanese War, violent clashes broke out between the Armenians and the Azerbaijanis in both Nagorno-Karabakh and Baku. During the civil war that followed in the wake of the Russian Revolution, Nagorno-Karabakh and Baku once again experienced ethnic conflict, and several thousand people on both sides were brutally slain.

In 1923, the Bolsheviks decided that Nagorno-Karabakh should be an autonomous region within the Azerbaijan Soviet Socialist Republic, even though the majority of those living there at the time were Armenian. The conflict continued to seethe under the surface during the Soviet era, only to flare up again in 1988. Workers in Stepanakert, the largest city in Nagorno-Karabakh, went on strike at the start of the year, and the Armenian section of the population marched in the streets in protest that Nagorno-Karabakh was not part of Armenia. These demonstrations spread to Armenia, and on February 25 million people marched in the Armenian capital of Yerevan, to show their anger with the decision-makers in the Kremlin. The supply chain in the planned economy meant that sixty-five radio and television factories throughout the Soviet Union had to stop production as a result of the strike in the electronics factory in Stepanakert.

The tension grew. Tens of thousands of Azerbaijanis fled Armenia, and vice versa. There was a steady increase in violence. On January 13, 1989, more than ninety Armenians were killed in anti-Armenian pogroms in Baku. Hordes of terrified Armenians fled in ferries out to sea. On January 20, Soviet tanks rolled into Baku to prevent any further escalation in the violence, but instead provoked it: more than 130 civilians were killed in the street fights that ensued, the single most bloody incident under Gorbachev's government. The way in which Gorbachev handled the unrest only served to stoke dissatisfaction with Soviet rule. On August 23, 1991 Armenia declared its independence from the Soviet Union, and on August 30 Azerbaijan followed suit. Then, on December 10, there was a referendum in Nagorno-Karabakh as to whether the republic should declare its independence or not. Ninety-nine per cent voted for independence, but the Azerbaijanis boycotted the referendum.

War became a fact in Nagorno-Karabakh in early 1992. Both sides were guilty of war crimes, but the Armenians were responsible for the bloodiest single incident. On the night of February 26, Armenian soldiers took the Azerbaijani town of Khojaly. About three thousand people lived there and they all fled to the neighbouring town, where Armenian soldiers opened fire. Several hundred people died, the majority of whom were civilians.* News of the massacre led to the resignation of the Azerbaijani president, Ayaz Mutallibov, who had governed the country since 1990. He was succeeded by the Soviet dissident Abulfaz Elchibey. Under Elchibey, Azerbaijan managed to regain control over half of Nagorno-Karabakh, but then in June 1993, after only one year in

* The Azerbaijani government claims that 613 people were killed. Human Rights Watch has concluded that the number of dead must have been more than 200.

office, the deeply unpopular Elchibey was overthrown by a military coup and forced to flee. In the vacuum left by his departure, the Azerbaijanis lost most of the territory they had regained. The parliament asked Heydar Aliyev to return to Baku, and, in October the same year, Aliyev was elected president. He started a bloody offensive to win back Nagorno-Karabakh, but failed.

In May 1994, the Russians helped to broker a ceasefire between the two sides. The two-year war had cost between twenty and thirty thousand lives, and more than a million people had been displaced. The population of Nagorno-Karabakh is now about 146,000, of which ninety-nine per cent are Armenian. It still formally belongs to Azerbaijan, but is a de facto part of Armenia. No country has as yet recognised the breakaway republic, not even Armenia. The ceasefire is regularly broken, and, every year, soldiers are killed on the border.

Heydar Aliyev remained in post as president until he died at the age of eighty in 2003. Over the years, he became more and more authoritarian. Not long before he died, he passed on the presidency to his son, Ilham, who has done his utmost to carry on and perfect his father's totalitarian, undemocratic rule. As president, Ilham, who is a qualified historian, has nurtured the personality cult that surrounds his father: there is an enormous portrait of Heydar Aliyev in every city and town. The roads are lined with big posters of him, and entire apartment blocks are adorned with his paternal face.

Aliyev II's tenure appears to be secure. In 2013, he was re-elected for another five-year term, winning eighty-five per cent of the vote, according to the official election result. There is no longer any limit to how many times a president can be re-elected, so, in theory, he can be president for decades to come. Over the past few years, the president's wife, Mehriban Aliyeva, an ophthal-mologist, has been given increasing power, reinforcing the sense of dynasty-building. In 2017, she was appointed the first vice-president of Azerbaijan.

My days in Baku passed quickly. I spent the evenings with Rena, who was generous and kind. One evening she invited me home for a meal. We ate and sang until late in the night, and, even though I was surrounded by strangers, I felt that I was with friends. Every time we met, Rena talked at length, and with great passion, about the crimes perpetrated by the Armenians against the Azerbaijanis. She thought that Ilham Aliyev was a good president, if perhaps not quite as good as his father, and she hoped that he would do as he threatened and go to war for Nagorno-Karabakh. As a leaving present, she gave me a richly illustrated book about the Khojaly Massacre.

Just before I left Baku, I met a young woman who had experienced the war in Nagorno-Karabakh first hand. She was my age, and had long, black hair and an open, friendly face. We met in a noisy cafe in the city centre. She too had considered cancelling the meeting. If anyone found out that she had spoken to me, she risked losing her job in the civil service. So, for her safety, we agreed that I would call her Selcen, which is not her real name.

"In May 1993, they bombed our school," Selcen said. "Lots of the children were killed. I did what my mother had taught me and ran straight home, without taking anything with me. They attacked the hospital where my mother worked, as well. The hospital was full of refugees from other places, where the fighting had been worse."

The family escaped from Nagorno-Karabakh shortly after. Selcen remembers that she touched all the walls of their house in farewell. She was only ten years old, but understood that she would never see her childhood home again.

"We escaped in my uncle's car," she said. "There were ten of us squashed into a tiny car. My cousins, my mother, my grandmother, my little sister . . . My youngest cousins sat on my knee and cried all the way to Baku. There was no room to take much with us. Forty thousand people fled that day in May, and the roads were full of cars and buses. My grandmother could not believe that the Armenians would really take our home for ever. She could not accept it. My father stayed behind to fight, as he thought the situation would change as well. But my mother realised that we would probably never go back, and was very sad."

By the end of the war, half a million Azerbaijanis had left Nagorno-Karabakh and surrounding Azerbaijani areas, which had also been occupied by Armenia to form a buffer zone. Most of the refugees ended up in and around Baku. With a population of approximately ten million, Azerbaijan is one of the countries with the highest number of displaced inhabitants in the world. More than twenty years after the ceasefire was negotiated, many of the displaced people are still struggling to get an education and work. The government has rolled out extensive housing programmes for refugees, but many of them still spend years in temporary accommodation in hospices and schools.

Selcen and her family were relatively lucky and were given a small flat in Baku.

"It was hard to make friends," Selcen recalled. "We moved four times in the first few years, each time to a different part of town. The authorities decided where we would go. And every time I had to make new friends."

A few years after the war ended, both her parents died.

"They died of stress, post-traumatic stress," Selcen said. "My father fought against the Armenians. One time he was in an Armenian woman's house in Nagorno-Karabakh, and she had a small child in her arms. She begged for her life. 'I will not harm you, as I have a wife and children myself at home,' my father told her.

But he killed the others. He said it was not easy, but he had no choice. They were our enemies. Personally, I don't think of Armenians as the enemy. I have never told my daughter that Armenians are bad people, because I don't want her to grow up hating the Armenians. In time, I think we will be able to live together again as friends. We can't fight for ever."

"Would you think of moving back to Nagorno-Karabakh?" I asked.

"Oh yes, I would love to go back!" Her response was heartfelt, without hesitation. "Those of us who have been displaced all want to go back, but, unfortunately, it is not possible. Just the other day, I was looking for my village on Google Earth. I eventually found it, but there is nothing left. My home, the hospital, the school – all gone. It is not even possible to see where our house once stood. The Armenians have put up new buildings everywhere. Even if it were technically possible to go back, I can't imagine starting again from scratch. I have lived in Baku for twenty-three years now, I have work here, my daughter was born here. My home is here now. But it would be lovely to see the places where I played with my cousins and little sister in summer. I remember my first day at school as being really happy. We lived in a small, pretty village. There were hens in the street."

Her smile was sad.

"To be honest, I don't think the conflict will be resolved in my lifetime," she said. "The authorities are not interested in finding solutions. It has already been going on for a quarter of a century."

Selcen is one of those who are doing well. She has a good job in the civil service and a family.

"What are your thoughts on the situation in Azerbaijan?" I asked.

She looked around to make sure no-one was listening.

"There are plenty of problems," she said, hesitantly, in a very quiet voice. "Problems with democracy, human rights, corruption . . . Most post-Soviet countries have similar problems, but they are worse here." She leaned over the table so that only I could hear her. "When it comes to human rights, the situation has got worse in recent years. The people who work for the government all come from the Soviet system. They have no understanding of how democracy works, and they do not accept alternative ideas. If you ask me, all the problems stem from corruption. We have so much oil in Azerbaijan . . ."

"Who do you vote for?" I said.

"I don't vote. I don't like him and I refuse to vote for him. They keep tabs on me, so I can't say his name. As long as we don't mention his name and speak in English, it will be fine." She laughed. "The people who monitor us can't speak English, you see. But, it is probably best if you don't say where I work, or what I am called," she added, to be on the safe side.

"Don't worry, I won't," I assured her. "I will call you Selcen, as we agreed."

"You see, I risk losing my job." She smiled apologetically. "I am ashamed to say it, I wish I was more courageous, but I am not."

When I got back to the hotel, Selcen had already sent me an email. She wanted to make absolutely sure that I would not use her name.

The Black Mountain Garden

"I want to die," the driver said. The Caucasus mountains rose up like a sheer, white wall to our right. "I am going to Syria to die in three days' time."

"What are you talking about?" I exclaimed. "Why do you want to die?"

Amir, as he was called, shrugged.

"My brother, who was a drug addict, died in Iraq. A bomb explosion. His guts spilled out everywhere."

"That is terrible! But you are not your brother, and you are alive," I said.

"I am also a drug addict, just like my brother," Amir said. "I was a wrestler in the Soviet Union. They gave me drugs to make me strong. This is no life, sister." He turned to me, with a wan smile. Half of his front teeth were missing. "In three days, I am going to Syria to die. In five days, you will read about me in the news. Just wait, sister."

I tried to dissuade him. Said that it was crazy to go to Syria. Either he would die there, or end up in prison here.

"I have already been in prison," he said. "For a year."

Dear God, I thought.

"Why were you in prison?" I asked.

"I shot someone."

"So you have killed someone?"

"No, I just shot them."

I got my mobile out of my bag, turned on data roaming and

my G.P.S., and confirmed to my relief that we were actually heading for the Georgian border. We were about halfway.

"Have no fear, sister!" Amir gave a hoarse laugh. "I have already said that you are like a sister to me, so I can say things to you that I cannot say to others. You are good. You want my best. I will drive you to the border, sister."

I put my telephone down in my lap, but did not turn off the G.P.S.

"Do you have a family?" I asked.

"A wife and a ten-year-old son." He sighed. "But they don't understand me."

"What about daughters?" I asked.

"Yes, I have a daughter as well. She is five." He pointed at the snow-covered mountains. "Dagestan is on the other side. Russia. It takes twenty-four hours to get there."

"I'm sorry?"

"I know the way. I have been to Russia many times."

"But are there not border guards everywhere?"

"I know where the soldiers are," he grinned. "They won't find me. I have five passports. If they were ever to catch me, they would not know who I really was."

"What do you do in Dagestan?" I asked. "Why do you go there?"

He shrugged, but gave no answer. We drove on in silence, while I discreetly followed our progress on the map. We were definitely heading for the border with Georgia.

I had met Amir the day before in Shaki, one of the most beautiful towns in Azerbaijan. Once upon a time, Shaki had been one of the biggest towns in the kingdom of Albania, which has nothing to do with modern Albania. It was a kingdom in the eastern part of what is now Azerbaijan from around 300 BCE until the eighth century. A thousand years later, in the mid-1700s, after centuries of Arabic, Mongol, Persian and Turkic rule, the Shaki Khanate enjoyed a brief period of independence, before being engulfed by the Russian Empire, at the request of the khan himself, who needed protection against the Persians. But in that short period of independence, the Shaki khans managed to build a small but beautifully designed summer palace, with stained glass and colourful rooms in which every centimetre of wall is covered with paintings of flowers and animals. The summer palace in Shaki is still one of the most magnificent buildings in Azerbaijan.

When we got close to the border, Amir started to talk about Norway.

"Can you take me with you to Norway, sister?" he asked. "It seems like such a good country. Do you think I could find a job there?"

"I thought you wanted to go to Syria?"

Amir shrugged.

"Yes," he said. "I am going in three days. In five days' time, I will be in the news. Do you promise to follow the news, sister?"

I have seldom been so glad to reach a border.

Even the border check was fast. Within ten minutes I had left Azerbaijan and was in Georgia. And it would have been even faster, had the Georgian customs officer not asked so many questions.

"Do you like Georgian food?" he asked.

"Georgian food is the best in the world!" I answered, enthusiastically. For quite some time I had been looking forward to eating as much as I could of Georgia's delicious cuisine. It is, without a doubt, the best in the former Soviet Union.

The customs officer wanted to know more. "What is your favourite Georgian dish?"

I thought long and hard, but could not remember what any of the typical Georgian dishes were called. With the exception of a couple of other languages spoken in Georgia, Georgian is unlike any other language in the world. The alphabet is beautiful, and

looks a bit like lace. The agglutination and nearly endless con-
tiguous consonants could scare even the keenest linguists; take,
for example, *vprtskvni*, which means "I peel it/them".

"Khachapur," I said, eventually. The delicious round, Georgian
bread was the only thing I could think of.

"There are lots of different kinds of khachapuri," the officer
said, clearly unimpressed. "Which one do you like best?"

"Well . . ." I hesitated. "The one with cheese is really good."

"They all have cheese in them," he said, humouring me. "Which
khachapuri do you like best? Adcharian? Megruli? Guruli? Rachuli?
Imeruli?"

"Er . . . Imeruli," I said. "I definitely like the Imeruli one best."

"Ah, the classic!" The customs officer smiled, and let me
through.

I had a long and complicated journey ahead of me. I would come
back to Georgia, but first I was going to go to Nagorno-
Karabakh. The border between Azerbaijan and Nagorno-Karabakh
has been hermetically sealed since the war, so the only way to
get there is through Armenia. And to get to Armenia, I had to cross
Georgia.

For the first time on my journey, I was in a Christian part of
the world. The driver who took me to Tbilisi crossed himself three
times every time we passed a church. And the closer to the capital
we got, the more churches there were, so he was continually crossing himself. The Caucasus countries lie pretty much in between
everything: between Europe and Asia, between East and West,
between Christianity and Islam, between the Black Sea and the
Caspian Sea, between the Russians, Persians and Turks. The old
Arabs called the Caucasus *djabal al-alsun*: "mountain of languages".
There is no other place in the world where so many languages
are spoken in such a small area, especially if you include those
who live on the north side of the mountains.

There are almost as many enemies and conspiracy theories as there are peoples and languages. During the Soviet era, people could not trust the state news, which was always positive. As a result, Soviet citizens developed a healthy scepticism of official information. And this scepticism remains, long after the collapse of the Soviet Union.

"The way Putin treats us is shameful, particularly given that he grew up in Georgia!" fumed the Tbilisi businessman who was sharing my taxi.

"Sorry, I don't quite follow," I said. "Putin grew up in Leningrad, didn't he?"

"No, he grew up here in Georgia," the driver said. "Everyone knows that. Putin was born in Georgia and grew up in Georgia. It is true that his mother went back to Leningrad, but little Vladimir stayed here with his aunt. His Georgian teacher has even been interviewed on television. The Kremlin of course denies it, but, like Stalin, Putin has roots in Georgia."

"And Putin is dead, by the way," the businessman said.

"Dead?!"

"Yes," the driver said. "Everyone knows that. The real Putin died of cancer many years ago. The person who says he is Putin now is his lookalike."

I was thunderstruck. "Where did you hear that?"

"The real Putin could speak fluent German," the driver explained. "He had lived in the D.D.R. for many years. The lookalike always has to use an interpreter when he is talking to Angela Merkel. See for yourself."

"It's the generals who are in charge, anyway," the businessman said. "Everyone knows that. And Putin is, or rather was, a general in the K.G.B. So everything is as it always has been."

"Nothing has changed," the driver said.

*

I was stamped out of Georgia and into Armenia efficiently and without any fuss. A customs officer popped his head into the minibus and asked if anyone had anything to declare. Everyone shook their head, and we were waved on. The journey to Yerevan continued through a rocky, sparse landscape with patches of snow. We passed lonely stone churches and poor villages where every second house was a half-built, empty shell. Soon the landscape got whiter and more wintry, and after a couple of hours we were completely surrounded by snow. It was early December, and winter had come to the Armenian mountains.

As I wandered around the streets of Yerevan looking for somewhere to eat, I came across a demonstration. To begin with, I thought it was a police parade, but then I saw some elderly demonstrators hiding behind dark uniforms. I asked some passersby what the demonstration was about, but no-one knew.

Once again, I was surrounded by a new language, a new alphabet, another reality. The faces I saw were pale and unfamiliar.

The next day, I got into another minibus that was just as squashed and claustrophobic as the first one, and to a soundtrack of thumping Armenian pop music, we set off for Nagorno-Karabakh. Between four and five hours later, we reached the border. As the only non-Armenian on board, I had to get out and register. A soldier explained that I would have to go the Ministry of Foreign Affairs in Stepanakert to get a visa, and handed me a note with the address.

Then off we set again, into the breakaway republic. The road, which was financed by exiled Armenians, was winding, but in great condition, smooth and well maintained. The landscape was green and mountainous, and the road went up, then down again, then up, then down. In other words, the de facto independent state was deserving of its name: *Nagorno* is derived from the Russian word for "mountain", whereas *kara* is Turkic and means "black". *Bakh* is Persian and means "garden".

Stepanakert, the capital of Nagorno-Karabakh, proved to be a sleepy provincial town with broad streets and little traffic. Only fifty thousand people live there, with barely three times as many in the whole republic. The buildings were largely post-war, functional, unostentatious and – like pretty much everything else there – financed by exiled Armenians.

Sometimes reality is more bizarre than imagination, particularly when visiting former Soviet republics, but not always. I walked the peaceful, empty streets and was almost disappointed by just how ordinary it all seemed. Even getting a visa was straightforward. A friendly bureaucrat listed all the places I was not allowed to go, in practice anywhere near the border with Azerbaijan, and then stuck the visa in my passport.

"I hope you will enjoy your stay with us!" he said, and handed me my passport with a measured but friendly smile.

"It is not possible to create false love – if you don't love each other, you should get divorced," said Davit Babayan, the spokesperson for Nagorno-Karabakh's democratically elected president, Bako Sahakyan. We were sitting in his office in the presidential palace, a building previously used by the communist administration, one of the few that had survived the war.

"Armenia today is only a tenth of Greater Armenia," Babayan said. "For a long time, we were oppressed in our historical territories. Then came the genocide of 1915. Following that terrible event, the Armenians started to suffer from a victim mentality. Nagorno-Karabakh has given us our confidence back! The whole world has seen that we are capable of defeating a country with a bigger army. If you do not have that kind of confidence, you evaporate and disappear, like steam."

"But no-one has formally recognised you, not even Armenia or Russia," I said. "According to international law, Nagorno-

Karakbakh is still part of Azerbaijan."

"What would recognition mean?" It was a rhetorical question. "Of course we would like to be recognised as a country, but it is no longer a fixation. We have resolved our recognition complex. I think that the status quo, frozen conflict, is actually the best alternative for us."

"Yet another soldier was killed at the border yesterday, and lots of people are talking about a possible escalation in the conflict," I said. "Do you think there might be another war?"

"No." There was no hesitation. "War would be a catastrophe for President Aliyev as well. He would not survive losing Nagorno-Karabakh again. And a war would involve Turkey, Iran and Russia, as well as Armenia and Azerbaijan – maybe even Georgia. Another war in Karabakh would escalate into a global conflict."

Later I met the former foreign minister, Masis Mayilyan, who now works as an independent security adviser. He was of a different opinion.

"I think there is a real chance of war," he said. "It could have happened last year. It could happen this year. Azerbaijan is preparing for war. They have invested considerable sums in their armed forces. Last month they used large-calibre artillery by the border. Three days ago they used tanks for the first time since the war in the Nineties. The situation is very grave indeed. It gets closer and closer to all-out war."

Like the president's spokesperson, Mayilyan was convinced that a new war in Nagorno-Karabakh would be catastrophic.

"Another war here would trigger World War Three," he said. "Russia will support Armenia and Turkey will support Azerbaijan. This is not a local conflict. Karabakh is a fault line. And the situation is different now from during the last war. Nowhere in Azerbaijan is safe anymore. We can reach Baku. If Karabakh is destabilised, the region will be devastated."

Mayilyan believed that the way in which the Soviet Union was dissolved was the seed of the conflict.

"The international community only recognised fifteen countries when the Soviet Union collapsed, not eighty. The criterion for recognition was that the country had been a Soviet republic. It was a political decision, not a legal one. Azerbaijan understood that they had carte blanche to attack Nagorno-Karabakh, and so they did. Giving parts of our territory back to Azerbaijan is out of the question. And they would not be satisfied with just Nagorno-Karabakh; they want the *whole* of Armenia."

The Museum of Fallen Soldiers was not easy to find: it was tucked away in a courtyard and I had to go through an apartment block to get there. A security guard saw me and asked where I was going, then showed me the way to the museum. Even though the sign with opening times showed that the museum should be open, the door was locked.

"Come again tomorrow, I am sure it will be open then," the security guard said.

"But it should be open now," I said.

"Yes, it should," he admitted. He took out his mobile and rang the number on the sign. A short while later, two elderly women came and opened the museum.

"I am not very good at Russian," the elder of the two said apologetically. She started to show me around the three small rooms. Her name was Arpik and she had lost both her sons in the war. The walls of the museum were covered with framed black-and-white photographs of serious young men. There were also exhibits from the soldiers' lives, donated by their families. Some had given a carpet, a collection of fish hooks or a bottle of vodka, others had given their Kalashnikovs.

"The parents want the memory of their sons to live for ever,"

Arpik explained. She knew the story of every single fallen soldier and told me in detail, in a firm, unsentimental voice, how this one and that one met their end, in which battle, on what date, with which weapon, and how many others had been killed at the same time. The younger woman, who looked at least seventy, followed silently a few steps behind us. She had lost two sons as well, and kept having to dry her tears.

"We had to defend ourselves, we had no choice," Arpik said. "Otherwise they would have eradicated Armenia. Because that is what they are like, the Azerbaijanis."

She pointed to a piece of shrapnel and explained what kind of grenade it came from. Then, when she had given me a little farewell speech by the door and wished me well in all that I planned to do with my life, I found out that she was ninety-six years old and a qualified physicist.

"Oh my goodness!" I exclaimed. "What is the secret to living to such a great age?"

Arpik shook her head sadly.

"I wish I was dead," she said. "Living so long just feels like a punishment. I should have been underground with my two sons a long time ago. I buried them both only two months apart." Her eyes filled with tears, but her voice remained clear and steady. "My only comfort is this museum. It helps to come here and meet others who have lost their sons, and to hear their stories. I could listen to them for hours."

Tsavag, the driver who took me to Shusha, the old capital of Nagorno-Karabakh, was more interested in love than war. He was a couple of years older than me, nearly two metres tall and had kind eyes and a gentle smile.

"I feel so sad when I talk to you," he said. "You seem so happy. You can do what you want, travel, see the world. I have never been out of Karabakh. And everyone knows everything about everyone here."

When he was twenty-six, Tsavag had fallen in love with a divorced woman who was a year older.

"My parents would not let me marry her as she was not a virgin," he said.

A while later, he fell in love again.

"She was almost as tall as me, slim, with a great figure," he said. "She looked like a model. Every time we met, we turned to look at each other. But I was shy. I did not dare to speak to her. My sight was bad at the time, and I wore glasses. I went to Yerevan that autumn for an eye operation. When I got back, I was told that she had been married off to a rich Armenian and had moved to Moscow. She had not wanted to marry him, and had said no when he proposed. So he kidnapped her and raped her, then took her back to the family, told them what had happened and demanded to marry her. Even though she still did not want to marry him, her mother forced her. The wedding was held two weeks later. When I found out, I cried. Her friends blamed me and said it was my fault. If I had proposed to her, it would never have happened. But I was shy . . . When I saw her again, she was heavily pregnant. We turned and looked at each other, as we always had, but it was too late. The rich Armenian abused her and eventually her father went to Moscow to rescue her. Now she is divorced and lives in Stepanakert with her parents and little daughter. But I am married with two small children . . ."

We parked the car and wandered around the deserted streets. The dirty pavements were full of holes and puddles. More than half the buildings were empty, with gaping holes where once there had been windows.

In the nineteenth century, Shusha was famous for its cobbled streets, churches, mosques and theatres, but it had suffered in the twentieth century. During the riots in 1905, large parts of the town were destroyed by fire. Fifteen years later, during the civil war, Azerbaijani soldiers marched into the Armenian quarter and massacred at least five hundred defenceless Armenians (the figure varies from five hundred to thirty thousand). After that, the inhabitants of Shusha were all Azerbaijani, but in the summer, tourists from all over the Soviet Union used to come to enjoy the mild climate, the clean air and idyllic surroundings.

During the war in the 1990s, the Azerbaijanis bombed Stepanakert from here – from the city walls there is a clear view to the capital. In 1992, the Armenian militia seized Shusha and set fire to most of the city. The Azerbaijanis panicked and fled. The war in Nagorno-Karabakh had in reality been won.

"This was not how I imagined life would be," Tsavag sighed, as we drove back down to Stepanakert. "We live in constant terror that the war will break out again. This is no place to bring up children."

In April 2016, four months after my visit to the breakaway republic, the conflict between Nagorno-Karabakh and Azerbaijan did indeed flare up again. The ceasefire negotiated in 1994 has been broken time and again, but this is the worst single incident. Over the course of four days, also known as the Four Day War, an estimated 350 soldiers were killed. The Azerbaijan government maintains that they regained twenty square kilometres of territory, while the Armenians claim that they lost only eight square kilometres. Both sides blame the other for having started the fighting.*

When the artillery smoke had dissipated and the dead had been carried away from the battleground and exchanged over a

---

* As is often the case, estimates of how many soldiers were killed differ enormously. The U.S. State Department has estimated the number of deaths at 350. According to the Armenian government, 91 Armenian and between 500 and 1,500 Azerbaijani soldiers were killed in the clashes, whereas the Azerbaijani government claims that 320 Armenian and 100 Azerbaijani soldiers were killed.

border that does not actually exist, the situation calmed down again. The only thing we can be reasonably sure of is that it will escalate again at some point and more young men, on both sides, will lose their lives.

Singalong on the Border

Soviet monument builders made up for what they lacked in elegance and grace with location. The Russia–Georgia Friendship Monument was superbly situated on the edge of a mountain plateau, with an open aspect and a steep drop down to a deep and uninhabited valley, surrounded by craggy, snow-capped mountains. The monument itself, on the other hand, in no way reflected the surrounding beauty: a semi-circle of brick and concrete, adorned with happy Russian and Georgian friends, painted in bright colours. The Russians were broad, blond and blue-eyed, the horses white and proud, the Georgians happy and dancing, dressed in traditional costumes. Maintenance had clearly not been a priority.

Georgia is one of my favourite countries. It is a country that has absolutely everything: some of the highest mountains in Europe in the north, you can swim in the Black Sea in the west and in the east you will find world-class vineyards. Add old, almost untouched architecture (everything from medieval villages where stone towers stand side by side, to some of the oldest churches in the world), a cuisine that can compete with Italian, and people who not only are open and hospitable, but always ready to party and have another drink, and you have Georgia. Were it not for their neighbours, the Georgians would probably be the world's happiest people.

In terms of topography, Georgia has been very fortunate, but in terms of geopolitics, not quite so lucky. The small country lies squeezed between the Persians and the Turks to the south, and the Russians to the north, so has forever been forced to walk an impossible tightrope. The gaudy Friendship Monument was built in 1983 to commemorate the 200th anniversary of the Russian–Georgian alliance, an accord which very few Georgians believe deserves to be celebrated.

In 1783, Erekle II, the king who united the greater part of what is now Georgia, signed a bilateral treaty with Catherine the Great, the Treaty of Georgievsk. Russia promised to protect the kingdom of Georgia against invasion by Turkey and Persia in the south if the Georgian monarch and church swore loyalty to the Russian throne. The Russians, however, did not keep their promise and withdrew from Georgia after only a few years. When the Persian shah sacked and plundered Tbilisi in 1795, more or less in retaliation, the inhabitants did not stand a chance. The Persian soldiers destroyed the city. Almost none of the buildings survived and the streets ran with blood. "It is not easy to estimate the number who perished," writes the British historian Sir John Malcolm. "Bigotry inflamed the brutal rage of the soldier. The churches were levelled to the ground; every priest was put to death. Youth and beauty were alone spared for slavery."[11]

Even though they had in fact facilitated the attack by withdrawing from Georgia, the Russians used this as proof that the Georgians were dependent on the tsar's protection. Paul I therefore denounced the Treaty of Georgievsk in 1801 and annexed the entire kingdom of Georgia. This made the Persians angry and triggered the war that broke out between Russia and Persia in 1804. The war ended in a resounding victory for the more modern but smaller Russian army, and the two parties signed the Treaty of Gulistan in 1813. In the treaty, Russia was formally recognised as the ruling power in South Caucasus: what is now Georgia, Dagestan and a substantial part of Azerbaijan, including Nagorno-Karabakh. In practice, the treaty allowed both parties time to nurse their wounds and to mobilise for a new war. Thirteen years later, in 1826, Russia and Persia were fighting once again. This war also ended with a resounding victory for the Russians and the signing of the Turk-menchay Treaty, which gave Russia dominion over the territories that make up modern Armenia and Nakhchivan, which is now an exclave of Azerbaijan. With a few pen strokes, South Caucasus also became part of the Russian Empire, without the people who lived there having any say.

Things were even bloodier to the north of the Caucasus mountains. The Chechens and Circassians, in particular, put up a hard fight against the Russians, and the invasion developed into a protracted and exhausting struggle against local guerrilla soldiers. The Caucasian War lasted from 1817 to 1864, and was led by three successive tsars: Alexander I, Nicholas I and Alexander II.

When the Soviet Union collapsed in 1991, the Chechens once again rebelled against the Russians and demanded independence on a par with Georgia, Armenia and Azerbaijan. President Boris Yeltsin refused, as he feared this might trigger an uncontrollable wave of demands for independence. In 1994, he sent Russian forces into Chechnya to force the rebels to back down. Two years later, having achieved nothing other than the death of tens of thousands of people, Yeltsin ordered their retreat. In 1999, Russia once again mounted an offensive against Chechnya, this time under Vladimir Putin. The fighting in North Caucasus has cost hundreds of thousands of civilian lives, and displaced hundreds of thousands more. Chechnya is currently ruled by the brutal Ramzan Kadyrov, who in 2007 was selected by Putin to lead the republic. In return, Kadyrov ensured that Putin gained 99.76 per cent of the vote in Chechnya in 2012.

The Kremlin wanted to keep hold of Chechnya largely because the federal republic, and its neighbour Ingushetia, had been only

Autonomous Soviet Socialist Republics (A.S.S.R.s) in the days of the Soviet Union. There were twenty-three A.S.S.R.s towards the end of the Soviet era, sixteen of which are now part of Russia. None of the A.S.S.R.s was granted independence following the dissolution of the Soviet Union, nor were any of the autonomous oblasts and regions, which were fewer and had even less independence than the A.S.S.R.s. Both Nagorno-Karabakh and South Ossetia, another breakaway republic in South Caucasus, had the status of autonomous oblast within the Union. The thinking behind these intricate administrative divisions was that each ethnic group would have a degree of autonomy.

The republics that had the greatest autonomy were the union republics, or Soviet Socialist Republics as they were also known (S.S.R.s).* There were fifteen: Georgia, Armenia, Azerbaijan, Estonia, Latvia, Lithuania, Belorussia, Ukraine, Moldova, Kazakhstan, Kyrgyzstan, Uzbekistan, Tajikistan, Turkmenistan and Russia. The autonomous Soviet republics and autonomous oblasts were all part of a union republic. For example, South Ossetia was under the control of the Georgian Union Republic. The union republics, with the exception of the Russian Soviet Federative Socialist Republic (R.S.F.S.R.), all had their own Communist Party and, at least in theory, the right to leave the Soviet Union should they wish (in practice, this only really became possible in Gorbachev's final year as president). The autonomous Soviet republics and autonomous oblasts did not. On March 11, 1990, Lithuania was the first of the union republics to declare its independence. Georgia followed on April 9, 1991. The friendship with Russia was very definitely a thing of the past.

No matter what the diplomatic state of play, the Friendship Monument is still a popular attraction for tourists, largely thanks to

---

* To make things even more confusing, the Soviet Socialist Republics, in other words the union republics, were often simply known as Soviet Republics.

the view. In high season, the place is crawling with souvenir vendors, but when I was there in mid-winter, there was no-one to be seen. On the narrow, twisting mountain road, however, there was a queue. The loads on the heavily laden trailer lorries rocked as they took the sharp bends. From their signage, many of them had driven a long way, some even from Lebanon and China.

Slowly but surely, the convoy of lorries wound its way towards the Russian border. They still had days ahead of them on icy, bad roads. Most of them were presumably on their way to the big Russian cities in the north. The route over the Caucasus mountains has existed since before Christ, but was upgraded to a military route, i.e. with room for horse-drawn carriages, when King Erekle II signed the treaty that made Georgia a protectorate in 1783. The road was officially completed in 1817, but the work continued until 1863. The road links Tbilisi with Vladikavkaz in North Ossetia and is two hundred kilometres long. Many famous people have crossed the Caucasus mountains on the Georgian military road, including Pushkin, Tolstoy, Mayakovsky – and Norway's very own Hamsun. "Anyone whose fate it has been, as it has been mine, to wander in lonely mountains, to gaze for long at their outlines, to breathe greedily the life-giving air of the passes; such a man will certainly understand my wish to communicate to others, whether in plain words or by word pictures, the enchanting sight that met our eyes," wrote Mikhail Lermontov in *A Hero of Our Time*.[12]

Because of the conflict in the breakaway republics of South Ossetia and Abkhazia, the narrow, winding mountain road is currently the only road connection from Georgia, and thus also Armenia, to Russia. And the number of articulated lorries goes to prove this. The queues at the border can be kilometres long, and drivers often have to wait for hours, sometimes even days, before they can pass. When the weather is bad, as it often is in winter, the road can be closed for several days, if not weeks, in a row.

The Caucasus mountains were at their best that day. The sun shone on the white snow and the February air was gentle, almost spring-like. We stopped in the small town of Stepantsminda, a few kilometres from the Russian border. Our destination was the Gergeti Monastery, which is perhaps the most famous monastery in Georgia. But first, we were going to eat. Nino, who ran a small family restaurant in Stepantsminda, had already put the first dishes out on the table when we arrived. For next to nothing, she and her three kitchen assistants, all local housewives, served us a banquet for lunch. One dish after another was carried in – steaming khachapuri, walnut and tomato salads, stuffed aubergines and khinkali (a kind of Georgian dumpling stuffed with meat, potato or vegetables) – and as much homemade red wine and chacha, a strong Georgian grape vodka, as we wanted.

"I can easily drink seven or eight litres a night," the driver boasted, with unashamed pride. "All real men in Georgia can!"

Luckily, he did not drink that day. Julia the guide, on the other hand, was knocking it back. Every few minutes she stood up and raised her glass to me, to Georgia, to herself and to the future.

"Traditionally, there should be twenty-one toasts during a celebratory meal," she told me. "And always in the same order. It is not a problem if you don't finish the food, you are not supposed to eat it all, but you do have to drink all the alcohol!" She emptied her glass of chacha, stood up and recited a long poem in Russian that she had written herself. I have met many eccentric guides on my travels, but Julia was the most memorable of them all. She was twenty-eight, blonde and blue-eyed, and not exactly dressed for hiking, in a body-hugging black top and leather miniskirt, with a small grey hat perched on her short bob. She was born and raised in Georgia, but both her mother and husband were Russian.

"I am really a poet," Julia said, and recited another poem with great passion. Again, it was a poem about nature and love. There were tears in her eyes when she sat down.

"I am so unhappy with my husband," she confessed. "We got married in August, he is my third husband. Russian, like the last one, and a guide as well. But I don't like him anymore. He is too uncouth. He rides a motorbike and uses bad language."

Her previous husband, the father of her two-year-old son, lived in Russia.

"My dream is to experience true love," Julia said, and drained another glass of chacha. "Even if I have to marry eight times to find it!"

"Why did you marry the Russian guide if you don't actually like him?" I asked.

"Because I loved him," Julia said, and downed another glass.

Nino took a short break from her kitchen duties and sat down with us.

"*My lovely,*" she said in her heavily accented, self-taught English, and gave me a maternal pat on the head. "Did you like my food?"

"It was absolutely delicious, all of it!" I assured her.

"I am actually a qualified economist, but numbers get boring after a while," Nino said. "I opened the guest house a few years ago, and now beautiful people from all over the world come here."

"What is it like, living so close to Russia?" I asked. I had been travelling along the Russian border for nearly four months, and had asked hundreds of people the same question along the way. I was starting to feel like a monomaniac.

"Oh, it is hard!" She sighed. "When Saakashvili was president, the border was closed for years. I have a house and family in Vladikavkaz, which is less than an hour's drive from here, but could not visit them. The border is open again, but now instead I can't visit my relatives in South Ossetia!"

She shook her head in exasperation and shuffled back to the kitchen. When she came back a few minutes later with more food and a whole jug of wine, Julia became restless.

"We still have to visit the monastery!" she cried. "The walk is at least an hour, and it will be getting dark soon. We should make a move." She filled her glass to the brim with wine, then drank it quickly.

"You said nothing about having to *walk* there," I said. I was wearing jeans and impractical shoes, though not half as impractical as Julia's.

"Yes, yes, of course we do. The road is closed in winter. No-one clears it!"

My body felt heavy after all the food and wine and it was tempting to drop our trip to the monastery, but Julia was keen.

"It really is worth it, I promise. Gergeti is my favourite monastery!"

We finished the jug of wine and set off, me in jeans and Julia in a miniskirt. Julia walked a few metres ahead of me, and we tramped in silence over the flattened snow. We met a group of Chinese tourists in colourful sports clothes as we climbed the steepest slope. They were excited by the snow, and laughing.

"You better hurry, the sun will go down soon," one of them warned as they slid and tumbled past us.

When we eventually reached the top, I understood why Julia had wanted to come. The highest mountain in Georgia, Kazbek, rose up to our right. Kazbek is called Mqinvartsveri in Georgian, which translates more or less as "ice peak", and is 5,033 metres high. Half the mountain is in Georgia, the other half in the republic of North Ossetia-Alania in Russia.

I had visited the Caucasus for the first time nine years earlier, when I was twenty-four, but then I was on the other side of the mountains, in North Ossetia. I was there to do fieldwork for

my Master's dissertation in social anthropology about the consequences of the terrorist attack on School No. 1 in Beslan in 2004.
More than three hundred people, most of them children, lost their
lives in the hostage drama that lasted three days. When I went
to Beslan, three years had passed since the horrific event, and the
small town was still rent asunder with grief, conspiracy theories,
bitterness and conflict. Many of the mothers visited the cemetery
every day, and they blamed the authorities, each other and
themselves for the fact that their children were no longer alive.
I learned that three years is not a long time and that time does
not necessarily heal all wounds and that the Russian authorities
are more interested in paying out compensation to the victims than
in finding out what actually happened. I also learned that
Russia is not only composed of Russians, but includes many other
peoples and cultures, and I was treated to the famous Caucasian
hospitality for the first time.

On the very first day, I made the cardinal mistake of referring
to the people I met as "Russians". After all, they spoke Russian,
dressed like the Russians and lived in Russia. I was immediately
and bluntly corrected: "We are not Russians, we are Ossetians!"

Djabal al-alsun, "a mountain of language" or "language mountain". The Caucasus is the place in the world where most languages
are spoken, which is perhaps not so surprising, as it is also one
of the places with the greatest ethnic diversity. Through the
centuries, many have migrated here, drawn by the lush plains,
the high mountains, and the protection from invading armies
from the north and south. There are so many different peoples
that it is easy to get confused, but the Ossetians stand out in more
than one way.

The Ossetians can be traced back to the third century, but
can still be considered relative newcomers to the Caucasus. They are
descendants of the Alans, a west Scythian tribe, who wandered

west from Central Asia to the Caucasus in the sixth century. Thanks to their close contact with the Byzantine and Georgian cultures – the Georgians were christianised as early as the fourth century – the Ossetians were converted to Christianity very early on. Their language belongs to the Iranian language group and is related to Persian. The Ossetians were also the first ethnic group in the Caucasus to work with the Russians, and the capital of North Ossetia, Vladikavkaz, was built as a fortified city in 1784. It was from here that the Russians conquered the rest of the Caucasus. And just as Vladivostok means "Ruler of the East", Vladikavkaz can be translated as "Ruler of the Caucasus".

However, the people of the Caucasus were far less amenable than those in the east. Many of the mountain people put up a hard fight and continued to rebel against Russian rule after the dissolution of the Soviet Union. When I was in Beslan, the war in Chechnya was formally over, but the entire region was still deemed to be an "anti-terrorist operation zone". There were harsh visa restrictions; for example, any travel outside the main town or in the mountains required a special permit from the F.S.B., the K.G.B.'s successor. And as I was carrying out fieldwork in cooperation with the Russian Red Cross, I also needed armed guards day and night.

Travel to the south of the mountains was far simpler and more comfortable.

"We're lucky," Julia beamed at me. Her sunglasses flashed in the sunlight. "Normally there's mist up here. I have never been here in such good weather before."

The air was clear and we could see for miles in all directions.

"Amirani, our Prometheus, was chained to Kazbek as punishment for his arrogance," Julia said. "Can you see him hanging there, between the two big, dark stones? An eagle pecked out his liver every day. And every night he healed again. In the old days, locals used to destroy any eagle nests they came across on the mountain, to ease Amirani's suffering." She pointed to the white peak. "If you look closely, you can see the tent that Abraham put up to protect the Tree of Life."

On a hilltop a few hundred metres away, we saw a small stone church with a conical tower, built safely on the Georgian side. I immediately recognised it from postcards I had seen in the tourist shops in Tbilisi. We walked the short distance to the monastery, put on the wraparound skirts that were lying outside, covered our heads and went into the church.

"It is usually full of tourists," Julia whispered.

We had the church to ourselves. There were no windows, so the only light was from the candles. A gas heater hissed quietly. A man with a long, grey beard nodded silently in greeting. I walked around the small church, and stopped in front of an icon of a black Mary.

"It was damaged in a fire," Julia whispered. "Lots of people think it has healing powers. Take as much time as you like, I will wait for you by the door." She went and sat down on a bench by the gas heater. After a while, I joined her. I saw that she was crying.

"I don't know why, but I always cry when I am here," she said.

On the way out, I tried to ask the serious man some questions, but he did not understand Russian. Julia dried her tears, then came over to translate for me.

"How long have you lived in the monastery?"

"Thirty-seven years," he said.

"You must have been very young when you came here," I said.

"No, no, I am thirty-seven years old," he said. "I have only been here four months."

His long grey beard made him look closer to sixty.

"What is your name?" I asked.

"Zviad," he said, in a friendly voice.

"Why did you come here?"

"Because God asked me to."

"How long do you intend to stay here?"

"As long as is needed," Zviad said. "I want to change my life. Not to sin anymore. I have found peace here."

"What did you do before you came here?"

"I worked in a casino in Tbilisi . . ."

When we came out of the church, the sun was going down. The sky was red. We walked a little way, then Julia turned round and looked at me uncertainly.

"It was around here that we came up, wasn't it?"

"Can you not find the path?"

"Yes, of course, I know where it is," she mumbled. "I just thought it was here."

A young man came walking towards us. We stood and waited for him. Perhaps he knew where the path was.

"Excuse me, do you speak English?" he asked in Russian, with a strong American accent. His name was Josh, and he could not find the path either.

It would be pitch black in half an hour. We stumbled about in the snow for some time without seeing any trace of the path.

"Here it is!" Julia whooped. "I said I knew where it was!"

She sat down on her backside and slid down the hill in her miniskirt. Josh and I followed. To save time, Julia said we should take a short cut. We waded through snow up to our waists, over open fields. It was totally dark when we finally reached Nino's house, wet and cold.

"Come inside and get warm," Nino insisted. "You can't go back to Tbilisi in that state!"

We gratefully sank into chairs on either side of Nino's fireplace. Nino put our wet shoes in front of the fire to dry and gave us some slippers and a jug of wine. When we had finished it, she brought us another.

"Do you like pancakes?" she asked.

I hesitated. It was late in the evening and we had to get back to Tbilisi. Without waiting for an answer, Nino disappeared back into the kitchen.

"I knew it!" she shouted. "You like pancakes!"

Soon delicious smells were wafting from the stove. When we had dried ourselves and were warm again, Nino came in with a mountain of pancakes, sour cream and home-made blueberry jam. She had also reheated some of the leftovers from lunch, as we had not eaten everything! We ate and ate, and the pancakes and wine were replenished from the kitchen. With shining eyes and flushed cheeks, Julia stood up and sang a sad, Georgian love song for us. She had a beautiful, husky singing voice, full of emotion, and was quite a performer, with dramatic arm movements. We clapped enthusiastically, and she immediately started on another song.

"Before I became a guide, I was a singer in a nightclub," she said. She emptied her wine glass and sang another song.

"Fantastic!" Josh said, when she was finished. "*Magnifique!*"

"Oh, do you speak French?" Julia simpered. "*J'adore le français!* I studied French when I lived in Russia. And a few years ago, I was offered a job at the Sorbonne and nearly moved to Paris."

"What happened? Why didn't you go?" I asked.

"It was in 2008. And shortly after I had received the job offer, war broke out between Russian and Georgia, and I was not able to leave." She smiled sadly and polished off her wine. Then she stood up again and started to sing Joe Dassin's famous song: *A-a-a-aux Champs-Élysées, a-a-a-aux Champs-Élysées!* Josh and I joined in the chorus and any lyrics we could remember. Nino and the driver sang along too, even though they knew none of the words.

It was late in the evening when we finally left. About halfway back to Tbilisi, the driver stopped at a twenty-four hour super-market and went in to get some drinks. When he came back with a carrier bag of Coke and Fanta, Julia said something to him in Georgian, and he disappeared into the shop again. This time he was away for longer, and when he came back he had a bottle of chacha in one hand. I presumed that he was going to enjoy it when he got home – he had not touched a drop all day – but Julia immediately started to mix the fizzy drink with the chacha in a plastic bottle that had been cut in half. As soon as the improvised glass was emptied, she mixed another drink. It did not take long before she was singing at the top of her voice – Russian songs, this time. Soon she dropped her mobile phone on the floor and had to fumble around for a long time before she managed to pick it up, only to drop it again. When we left the mountains and the landscape flattened out, she stopped singing and started to talk to the driver in Georgian. Her voice sounded serious, complaining. She dried a tear, poured herself another drink, lost her mobile on the floor once more, tried to pick it up again, and eventually gave up and poured herself another drink. When we drove into Tbilisi, the bottle was empty. Julia was flopped over the dashboard, snoring loudly.

No-Man

Georgia is a small country, no more than 69,700 square kilometres, which is about the size of Ireland. If one excludes Abkhazia and South Ossetia, the two republics that broke away in the early 1990s, over which the Georgian government has no influence anymore, another twenty per cent can be subtracted. The population is about five million, more or less the same as Norway. And yet, despite its modest size, Georgia has produced three of the most important men in Soviet history: Eduard Shevardnadze, who was foreign minister under Gorbachev, and went on to be the second president of Georgia; Lavrenty Beria, one of the main players in the Terror of the 1930s, for many years leader of the N.K.V.D. and head of the Ministry of Internal Affairs; and last but not least, Josef Dzhugashvili himself, better known as Stalin.

Stalin was born in Gori, a small industrial town nearly ninety kilometres northwest of Tbilisi, in 1878. He was the only surviving child of the shoemaker Besorian Dzhughashvili and Yekaterina Geladze. When Stalin was a boy, his father drank away his family home and workshop, then disappeared to Tbilisi, so Josef grew up alone with his mother. Life as a single mother in Gori in the nineteenth century was hard, and Ekatrine and her son moved from one miserable dwelling to another. The small brick house where Stalin spent the first years of his life is well maintained and now protected by an enormous marble, temple-like building that was raised in the 1930s. The wretched house can barely be seen behind the solid, Greek pillars. And behind that, there is an even larger building, which also has a magnificent entrance, inspired by classical Greek architecture: the Stalin Museum. Work started on the museum while he was still alive, but it was not completed until 1959, six years after the dictator's death and three years after Khrushchev's famous de-Stalinisation speech. The museum is now a museum of Soviet museums. With the exception of one new, more critical exhibition on the ground floor, it remains more or less unchanged. The Stalin Museum is one of the most popular tourist attractions in Georgia, and in the final, dimly lit room, which is red and shrine-like, sits Stalin's death mask. The museum shop sells Stalin wine, Stalin mugs, Stalin T-shirts and other dictator souvenirs that would have been unthinkable if they had been adorned with the portrait of a certain German. The great statue of Stalin in front of Gori town hall was not removed until 2010, and is now stored in a factory building, perhaps in anticipation of better times.

The Gori in which Stalin grew up was a town ravaged by poverty and violence. Street fights were a favoured pastime. All the inhabitants, including the young Stalin, got involved in the fights, which often erupted on public holidays. In addition to being good at fighting, Stalin was also good at school, and thanks to this, and his mother's ability to charm wealthy men, he got a place in the seminary in Tbilisi, despite being unable to pay the fees. It was in the capital that the young Stalin became seriously involved in Georgia's revolutionary communist circles. His grades deteriorated and he eventually dropped out of school, only a few months before the final exams. He dedicated all his time to the Cause and was constantly on the run from the police. Whereas Lenin and Trotsky were great orators, Stalin excelled in "expropriating assets". He organised several daring robberies while still living in Georgia. The largest and best known took place in the centre of Tbilisi in 1907. With the help of bombs and guns, Stalin and his gang ambushed a large delivery of money to a branch of the State Bank and escaped with 341,000 roubles, equivalent to roughly three million pounds today. Forty people were killed in the brutal attack, which made the news throughout Europe. The heist was in itself a success, but the stolen money was of little use to the Bolsheviks, as the police knew the serial numbers on the banknotes.

Even though the statue of Stalin has been removed, it is as though the Soviet era still casts a shadow over Gori. The centre is dominated by dreary concrete buildings and shabby apartment blocks, and from the main road there is an uninterrupted view to the breakaway republic of South Ossetia, which the Bolsheviks, in their day, gave the status of autonomous oblast.

The Bolsheviks, and Stalin in particular, believed that for primitive societies the way to communism was via nationalism. They therefore spent a great deal of time and energy on drawing up the Soviet map to meet the needs of the various nationalities. People should, in theory at least, be able to speak their own language and live by their own culture (though preferably not religion). The Red Army seized power in Georgia, supported by the minorities who had been promised a bright future under the new regime. The Bolsheviks were true to their word, to begin with at least. As soon as they came to power, they established the Autonomous Soviet Republic of Adjara and the Autonomous Oblast of South Ossetia, which both enjoyed a certain amount of devolution within the Union Republic of Georgia. Abkhazia was first given the status of union republic, but then, in 1931, Stalin changed this to autonomous Soviet republic so it was once again ruled by Georgia.

When the Soviet Union collapsed, both Abkhazia and South Ossetia demanded independence from Georgia. Then in May 1991, the dissident and nationalist Zviad Gamsakhurdia was elected the first president of Georgia, with a huge majority. And instead of accepting the South Ossetians' demand, he rescinded their status as autonomous oblast. Georgia's new president aspired to a Georgia for Georgians. As it so aptly said in his obituary in the *Independent* in February 1994: "Gamsakhurdia was a tragic figure. A fervent nationalist who was incapable of uniting Georgians, let alone non-Georgians. He was only rational when discussing literature. Politics to him was a blood feud." A blood feud it certainly was.

Ossetians had lived in Georgia for centuries. Most of them were fluent in Georgian and many of them were married to Georgians—for example, Stalin's paternal grandfather was an Ossetian. And in South Ossetia itself, about two thirds of the population were Ossetians and the rest were Georgians, but the majority of Ossetians lived peacefully with their neighbours elsewhere in Georgia. The war could no doubt have been avoided if some diplomacy had been used, but that was not one of Gamsakhurdia's strengths. In January 1991, violent clashes erupted between Ossetian and Georgian forces.

At the end of 1991, Gamsakhurdia was ousted by a military coup. His successor, Eduard Shevardnadze, the former Soviet minister of foreign affairs, had the task of sorting out the chaos. In summer 1992, he managed to negotiate a ceasefire between the parties. In terms of the number of dead, the war in South Ossetia was the least bloody of those fought in the Causcasus in the 1990s. About a thousand people lost their lives, while roughly a hundred thousand Ossetians fled from Georgia over the Caucasus mountains to North Ossetia. And more than twenty thousand Georgians escaped from South Ossetia to Georgian-controlled territory. The population of South Ossetia fell dramatically, but the border between the de facto independent republic and Georgia remained open and people could move freely back and forth.

The situation remained calm until Mikheil Saakashvili, another flamboyant and opinionated politician, came to power in 2004, a year after the so-called Rose Revolution. In March 2003, demonstrators, led by Saakashvili, marched into the national assembly with roses in their hands and forced the sitting president, Shevardnadze, who was in the middle of a speech, to flee. The Georgians were tired of corruption, election fraud and old Soviet politicians – they wanted to look to the future, to the West, to Europe.

Saakashvili was thirty-six when he came to power on a wave of goodwill, optimism and belief in the future. The most important point on his agenda was corruption. In the 1990s, Georgia was one of the most corrupt countries in the world – there was corruption at every level in society, and the police, in particular, were infamous for it. Saakashvili rolled up his sleeves and fired almost the entire police force. To prevent the new officers from falling into the same trap as their predecessors, salaries were increased substantially to three or four hundred dollars a month, an amount it was possible to live on.

The young, energetic president also aspired to reuniting Georgia, South Ossetia and Abkhazia as one country. He was prepared to give them a considerable degree of autonomy, but was determined to bring the two separatist regions back into the fold. As part of his strategy, he closed down the black market on the border with South Ossetia, which was supplied largely with smuggled Russian goods and was an important source of income for the autonomous republic. This closure may have increased revenues to the state coffers, but it also ramped up the conflict.

It was not until 2008 that things got really bad. Like many young Georgians, Saakashvili wanted to strengthen Georgia's relationship with Europe and the West. Geographically, both Georgia and Azerbaijan lie between Europe and Asia and are often included in both parts of the world. The majority of Georgians would like to be a part of Europe, as clearly demonstrated by all the E.U. flags that flutter alongside the Georgian flag throughout the country.

They would also like to be a member of N.A.T.O., and at the N.A.T.O. summit in 2008 possible membership for Georgia and Ukraine was on the agenda. To accept Georgia as a full member was not realistic, but many believed the country could take part in the Membership Action Plan (M.A.P.), a kind of sponsor programme tailored to countries that would like to join N.A.T.O. but are not yet ready. The member states were split regarding Georgia and Ukraine. The president of the U.S.A., George W. Bush, actively championed the M.A.P. programme option, whereas Nicolas Sarkozy of France and Angela Merkel from Germany were sceptical. Vladimir Putin kept a watchful eye in the wings. In 2004, three former Soviet republics, Estonia, Latvia and Lithuania, had joined the alliance, as well as the former Warsaw Pact countries, Bulgaria and Romania. Putin was not happy that N.A.T.O. might now take an even bigger piece of what he considered to be Russia's backyard.

N.A.T.O. faced a dilemma. Should they welcome these two young democracies, or should they give in to pressure from Russia and close the door? In the end, they did neither. Instead of inviting Georgia and Ukraine to join a M.A.P. programme, the member states agreed to release the following statement: "*At the Bucharest Summit, N.A.T.O. Allies welcomed Ukraine's and Georgia's Euro-Atlantic aspirations for membership and agreed that these countries will become members of N.A.T.O.*" The last nine words are key here: it was agreed that Ukraine and Georgia should become members of N.A.T.O., but it was a question of time. As a first step, the countries would be included in a M.A.P. programme. The wording was both binding and without obligation, at the same time designed to placate Putin, but possibly also to provoke him. The only thing that was certain was that Ukraine and Georgia would have to fend for themselves in the meantime.

In summer 2008, after Kosovo had proclaimed its independence, tensions rose in Abkhazia and South Ossetia. Russia also carried out a large-scale military exercise in North Caucasus, while American and Georgian forces carried out a parallel exercise on the Georgian side. When the Russian exercise was completed on August 2, the troops and equipment stayed close to the Georgian border. The same week, the ceasefire between South Ossetia and Georgia was broken on several occasions, and peacekeeping troops on both sides were killed. Ossetian women and children were evacuated to safety in North Ossetia, with the help of the Russian government. Some fifty Russian journalists were also taken into South Ossetia. Something was afoot. On August 8, at seven o'clock in the evening, Saakashvili announced on Georgian television that that he had ordered a unilateral ceasefire with immediate effect in order to prevent a further escalation of violence. But the attacks on Georgian villages did not stop, and the same evening, the intelligence services warned the Georgian government that a Russian offensive was under way. Just before midnight, Saakashvili did a complete turnaround and ordered a Georgian counter-offensive. The following day, while President Putin and other Western leaders gathered in Beijing for the opening ceremony of the Olympic Games, Russian tanks rolled into Georgia.

Saakashvili has since been heavily criticised for his decision to mount an offensive against South Ossetia. It was a war that he could not win, given the Russian advantage in terms of numbers and technology. Many believed that by answering the violence in this way, Saakashvili provoked the Russian response, and that the entire war could have been avoided if the Georgian president had played it cool. However, in light of Russia's annexation of Crimea and the subsequent war with East Ukraine, it is hard to see what else Saakashvili could have done to avoid the war. It is interesting to note that the war in East Ukraine also started following a major Russian military exercise in the border region.

The war in South Ossetia lasted five days. The Russians bombed not only strategic targets in the republic itself, but also towns nearby, such as Gori, and towns near the border with Abkhazia. Many people feared that the Russians would not stop until they reached Tbilisi, and people in the capital stockpiled cash and fuel. The U.S.A. provided indirect help by transporting home Georgian soldiers who were serving in Iraq, but no Western country became involved in the conflict. Potential membership of N.A.T.O. now seemed years away.

France was given the role of negotiator, and President Sarkozy flew to Moscow to broker a ceasefire. Putin did nothing to disguise the fact that he wanted to get rid of the leader of the Rose Revolution.

"I am going to hang Saakashvili by the balls," he told the French president.

"Hang him?" Sarkozy said, taken aback.

"Why not?" Putin retorted. "The Americans hanged Saddam Hussein."[13]

Sarkozy not only managed to persuade Putin that any change in government should be up to the Georgians, but also cobbled together a rather vague ceasefire between the two parties.

The war between Russia and Georgia ended formally on August 12. Over the course of five days, eight hundred people had been killed and close to two hundred thousand displaced. It was a relatively minor war, in terms of the number killed, but what was alarming about it was that there had been a war at all. It was the first time that Russian armed forces had intervened in a former Soviet republic. Putin had broken the rules and shown all his neighbours, as well as the rest of the world, that Russia was prepared to defend its own interests with bombs and tanks, if necessary. Anything could happen.

On August 26, 2008, Russia officially recognised South Ossetia and Abkhazia as independent sovereign states, and referred to

Western governments' recognition of Kosovo's independence earlier the same year. The border to South Ossetia has been closed on the Georgian side ever since. In a recent referendum, it was agreed that "Alania" would be added to the republic's name, in line with its big brother to the north, whose full name is North Ossetia Alania. The South Ossetians were due to vote in 2016 on whether South Ossetia should be reunited with North Ossetia, and thus officially become part of Russia again, but the referendum was cancelled indefinitely as a result of pressure from Moscow. The fact that the South Ossetian government had even planned the referendum speaks volumes about who actually holds the power in the breakaway republic.

A little more than fifty thousand people currently live in South Ossetia. Most Georgians have left and are now settled in more or less permanent refugee housing in Georgia. They are not so much victims of local ethnic tensions as pawns in a great geopolitical game. And the power struggle continues to rumble on in the background. The territory of South Ossetia is expanding silently, metre by metre, under cover of darkness. The phenomenon is called *borderisation*, whereby a territory or country is expanded by moving physical entities, such as fences, barbed wire and signage, without permission. Here and there, the South Ossetian border has been pushed several hundred metres into Georgia, with the Georgian authorities as helpless onlookers. Once again, it is ordinary citizens who are sacrificed on the geopolitical altar.

One such citizen is eighty-two-year-old Dato Vanishvili, who woke up one morning a few years ago to discover he was in a new country.

"I am afraid you cannot go any further." The officer at the roadblock was friendly, but firm.

"But I have been here before and it was fine then," Thoma

protested. He was a friend of a friend who had come along to help me with the day's interviews. "We are going to visit Dato Vanishvili – I am sure you know him?"

"Of course we know him, but if I let you go any further, I will lose my job," the officer said. "It is too dangerous. People who have got too close to the border have been kidnapped by the Russians and then imprisoned for crossing the border illegally."

"We will be careful," Thoma promised. "We will not take any unnecessary risks."

"The Russians watch the border with eagle eyes, they see everything," the officer said. "No matter how careful you are, it is still too dangerous. You need permission from the police in Gori to go any further."

We realised that we were not going to get past him, and drove back to Gori defeated. It was already late in the afternoon, and we did not know if the police station was still open. If it was, we did not hold out much hope that they would bother to help us. We had no appointment and I did not have any papers with me to say that I was a journalist.

The police station in Gori was a big, beautiful and bright building, with glass walls to symbolise the new, open and incorruptible Georgian police force. The Georgian flag flew alongside the E.U. flag. Fortunately, it looked as though everyone was still at work. Thoma explained our situation to the policewoman at the reception desk. The twenty-three-year-old was insistent, convincing and charming, and the policewoman was friendly and helpful, but unfortunately did not know who was responsible for that roadblock, and nor did any of her colleagues. We were asked to wait while they tried to find out.

"We are never going to get permission," I said in a fit of pessimism.

"Well, we certainly won't if we don't try," said Thoma, who

was a refugee from South Ossetia. His father had been the chief of police in Akhalgori, a largely Georgian village that had remained under Georgian jurisdiction after the war in the 1990s. But then, after the 2008 war, Akhalgori fell to the South Ossetians. Thoma and his family were among the first to escape – as his father was the chief of police, they knew what was brewing. When the cease-fire had been signed, they returned, certain that the worst was over for a while. But on August 17, five days after the war had officially ended, Akhalgori was invaded by Russian and Chechen forces, and the family had to flee again. Thoma's parents now live in Tserovani, one of the permanent settlements established to provide shelter for the thousands of people displaced by the five-day war.

"My grandparents still live in South Ossetia," Thoma said. "My grandmother is impressed that I travel so much, but she often reminds me that she has travelled a lot too, as she has lived in three countries: the Soviet Union, Georgia and South Ossetia!"

We had been waiting for thirty minutes when the policewoman came back. She had good news: we had been given permission to visit Dato Vanishvili, but we had to be escorted by soldiers.

Twenty minutes later we were back at the roadblock and this time were allowed to pass. Four armed soldiers followed us in a jeep. We passed rows of identical small houses that were built as housing for the refugees from South Ossetia. When the houses stopped, the road petered out, but we carried on regardless.

"I am actually banned from approaching the South Ossetian border," Thoma said. "After we escaped, some Ossetians tried to kidnap my brother and me, as our father was the chief of police. We got away, but the police have asked me to stay away from the border area."

"And you tell me now?!" I said, alarmed.

He shrugged and smiled.

"I like looking over at the old country," he said. "Being close to home, even though I cannot go there. But please, do not tell my mother where we have been today."

Big, blue signs in Russian, Georgian and English told us we were at the South Ossetian border. In the distance we could see the concrete buildings of Tskhinvali, the capital of South Ossetia. A wide barbed-wire fence marked out the border. On the other side of the fence, a cow was grazing happily, and a few metres away there was a big house. An old man in simple, dirty, work clothes saw us and came over to the fence. The soldiers threw a few packets of biscuits and chocolate bars over to him; the old man picked them up and politely thanked the soldiers. He introduced himself as Dato Vanishvili, then launched straight into his story, without asking where we were from or why we were there.

"You have ten minutes," one of the soldiers informed us. "The Russians will be watching, they already know that we are here. It will take them ten minutes to get here."

As Dato spoke only Georgian, Thoma translated for him.

"One morning, five years ago, I woke up and found the fence here," he said. "The original border was a few hundred metres back, but they moved it, and now my house is in South Ossetia."

He spoke quickly and with emotion, obviously aware that we did not have much time.

"My brother's son died of cancer in Vladikavkaz on Febuary 7 this year. He grew up here and was like a son to us, but I was not given permission to visit him when he was ill, and I was not allowed to go to the funeral. My wife is indoors." He pointed towards the house. "She has problems with her blood pressure and cannot stand up without falling. She needs to get to a hospital, but there is no help. I cannot even go to Tskhinvali, because I have no papers. This is no life. Perhaps suicide is the only solution."

"Five minutes," one of the soldiers shouted. "The Russians will be here soon."

"I was born here in Khurvaleti," Dato continued. "I have lived here for more than eighty years. All my life, I have lived in Georgia, and now suddenly I live in South Ossetia. All our neighbours have left, but I have nowhere else to go. Our daughter lives in a village nearby, but on the Georgian side. She comes to visit regularly. That is to say, she stands on the other side of the fence, where you are now, and cries. She is so upset that she cannot see her mother, who is housebound. The Russians soldiers come by all the time. They do not like me talking to people like you, who come to hear my story. They have threatened to arrest me if I talk to any more foreigners and journalists. But I am a human being. I need to speak."

"Time to go!" one of the soldiers shouted and pointed at his watch.

"I can't even change my money," Dato said. "I only have Georgian lari, and they do not accept my money in the local shop. 'We don't want that kind of money,' they say. The Georgian soldiers give us food and medicine, and sometimes people from the village come as well. Once a month, I sneak over the fence to get my pension on the Georgian side."

We had now had our ten minutes and more, and Thoma was starting to get visibly nervous. We hastily said goodbye to the old man on the other side of the barbed-wire fence and were escorted back to the main road.

Stalin's Paradise

The border between Georgia and Abkhazia is oddly desolate. A long, wide bridge crosses a narrow river that has almost run dry. There is nearly more water on the bridge than under it. And as the bridge is in the no-man's-land that lies between the mother country and the breakaway republic, no-one takes responsibility for its upkeep. With every year that passes, the gaping potholes in the asphalt get deeper.

A clutch of women clothed in black followed behind me, all weighed down with carrier bags laden with Georgian goods. Every now and then, a car emblazoned with the logo of some international aid organisation crept across the bridge. Three thin horses passed us pulling a cartload of people who had paid so as not to have to cross the no-man's-land on foot.

I reached the three or four shacks that made up passport control, and waited in the queue. It is not particularly difficult for foreigners to get an entry visa to Akbhazia, you just have to remember to register on the official government website a few weeks in advance. But something had gone wrong with my online registration, as I did not receive confirmation until my entry visa had almost expired. As a result, I had only two days to visit the breakaway republic.

"As soon as you get to Sukhumi, you must go to the Ministry of Foreign Affairs and get an exit visa," the passport officer told me. "Otherwise we cannot let you out again."

I promised to do as he said, popped my passport back in my bag,

and walked into Akbhazia. The first time I had been there
was with my mother, five years earlier. Back then, the border had
felt ominous and frightening. Highly polished cars had stopped
alongside each other, windows had rolled down and money had
exchanged hands. In general, people had seemed unfriendly, almost
hostile, but we eventually found a driver who could take us to
Sukhumi, the capital. The bumpy, potholed road took us past
bombed ghost towns; the bloated cadavers of cattle lay in the
ditches. The warning from the Norwegian Ministry of Foreign
Affairs kept playing in my head: "The Ministry advises against all
travel to the breakaway republics of Abkhazia and South Ossetia."
I imagined the worst, but did not dare say anything to my mother,
as it was I, after all, who had suggested the rather unorthodox
holiday destination.

To what extent can we rely on our memory? Once again I
asked myself that question when I left passport control and walked
over to the car park. The area which had seemed so dismal the
previous time felt very ordinary now, almost inconsequential, in the
February sunshine. I walked over to the row of minibuses, found
one that was going to Sukhumi, and got myself a seat. The driver
neglected to say that he intended to stop for half an hour
in the nearest town, but he did buy me a coffee. After all, I was a
foreigner and a guest.

The view from the window was just as I remembered it, however.
We drove past burnt-out buildings, abandoned villages
and factories that had not been in operation since the Soviet era.
Everything was overgrown and uncared for, and the roads were
in a terrible state – they had been patched together badly and were
full of potholes.

In terms of area, Abkhazia is twice as big as South Ossetia, and
about the same size as Lebanon, which is not the only thing the
two countries have in common. As in Lebanon, people of many

different ethnicities lived side by side in peace before the killing started and war became the norm. The landscape is also similar; by the coast it is green and fertile, with beaches and hotels, but the snow-capped mountains with their slopes and ski resorts are no more than a short drive away. Before the war, about half a million people lived in Abkhazia, twice as many as there are now.

"Abkhazia was a paradise," Giorgi Jakhaia said, when I met the blogger in Tbilisi before I went to Abkhazia. He had escaped when he was eighteen, in the final weeks of the war in 1993. "Everyone was happy, everyone had a house and job, and no-one needed to worry about tomorrow," Georgi claimed. "All the rich people in the Soviet Union lived in Abkhazia. They lived the high life and drove around in their Suzukis, even though no-one in the Soviet Union was supposed to own such expensive cars. If it had not been for the war, Abkhazia would be like Monaco or Monte Carlo today!"

The ethnic Abkhazians are related to the Kabardians and the Cherkessians of North Caucasus, but have lived alongside the Georgians for more than a thousand years. During the war of independence in the early Nineties, the Russians gave them military support, and Russia is now the breakaway republic's closest ally and partner. But that was not always the case. In the nineteenth century, the Abkhazians put up far more opposition to the Russians than the Georgians did. The Abkhazians sided with the Cherkessians to the north of the mountains, and many took part in the fight against the Russian army. In 1864, when after decades of war the Russians had crushed any resistance in the Caucasus, the collective punishment for the Cherkessians was exile to the Ottoman Empire. Several hundred thousand Cherkessians and Abkhazians were squeezed onto overfull boats and sent across the Black Sea, and another couple of hundred thousand were forced to flee. Many of them died, and the Black Sea coast was left empty and abandoned.

In the years that followed, the Abkhazians who were left rebelled on several occasions against the Russians, which in turn led to new deportations and the introduction of a new law that banned Abkhazians from living on the coast or in the largest cities and towns. This law remained in place until 1907. Georgians, Greeks and Armenians moved into the deserted Abkhazian villages. Then, at the start of the 1930s, the feared Lavrenty Beria was put in charge of the South Caucasus region. Beria, himself a Mingrelian, a minority Georgian people, had been born in Abkhazia and he made it possible for even more Georgians to move there. In 1939, the number of Abkhazian inhabitants was as low as eighteen per cent of the total population, and this figure remained stable until the dissolution of the Soviet Union. Close to half the population, that is to say, forty-five per cent, was Georgian.

Under Gorbachev, the divide between the Abkhazians and the Georgians grew. While the Georgians fantasised about independence, the Abkhazians wanted to remain part of the Soviet Union, preferably as a separate Soviet republic and not as part of Georgia. In spring 1989, several thousand Abkhazians signed a declaration demanding the establishment of a separate Abkhazian Soviet Socialist Republic. This provoked the Georgians, and thousands demonstrated against the proposals. Tensions grew and on April 9 the Soviet army rolled into Tbilisi to calm things down. Twenty-one people were killed and several hundred injured. Nine months later, Soviet soldiers marched into Baku, and only made things worse there, too.

In April 1991, Georgia declared independence from the Soviet Union. The Abkhazians, on the other hand, worked to maintain the union. By granting the Abkhazians a generous proportion of seats in the Abkhazian parliament, at the expense of the Armenians and Georgians, the politicians in Tbilisi managed to quieten things down, for a while at least. In February 1992, the Georgian parliament decided to reintroduce the constitution from 1921, which makes no mention of an autonomous Abkhazia, Ossetia or Adjara. In response, the Abkhazians reintroduced in July that year the 1925 constitution, which did recognise Akbhazia as a union republic. In other words, the Abkhazian parliament declared its independence from Georgia. The response was not long in coming: on August 14, Georgian tanks moved into Sukhumi. The Georgian army, which was made up in part of newly released prisoners, had no discipline, and the soldiers rampaged, raped and plundered. The Abkhazians were supported by the Confederation of Mountain Peoples of the Caucasus, which dreamed of a free Caucasus, and they eventually also got weapons from Russia.

Georgia stood to lose a lot. A quarter of a million ethnic Georgians lived in Abkhazia and the region covered about half of the country's coastline on the Black Sea. The war, which barely made the headlines in the West, was a succession of appalling incidents on both sides, and it lurched in fits and starts, punctuated by fleeting ceasefires that were broken time and again. When the Abkhazian forces took control of Sukhumi in September 1993, the remaining Georgians fled the city in panic, in order to avoid the mayhem.

"We left Sukhumi on a Ukrainian warship on September 27," Giorgi Jakhaia told me. "We heard later that Sukhumi had fallen. It happened that very day. Not everyone was as lucky as we were, and many had to flee over the mountains. The snow came early that year, and hundreds of refugees froze to death on their way through the mountain pass. We were put up in a hotel in Tbilisi, the one which is now the Holiday Inn. Nearly all the hotels in Tbilisi were made into temporary accommodation for refugees from Abkhazia. We lived in that hotel room for ten years."

At least eight thousand people lost their lives. With the exception of a few thousand who lived in the Gali district, close to the

Georgian border, all the Georgians left Abkhazia. About 50,000 Georgians from Gali have since returned to their homes, but more than 200,000 Georgian refugees still live elsewhere. Many of them are in temporary refugee centres, and their lives remain on hold.

"I dream of moving back to Sukhumi one day," says Giorgi, who often posts photographs of the old Abkhazia in his blog. "It is the most beautiful place on earth."

Or was. The Abkhazian capital still bears scars from the war at the start of the 1990s. Many of the houses are empty, gaping shells, bombed, burnt-out or full of bullet holes. The streets were as deserted as they were the last time I was in Abkhazia. Before the war, 110,000 people lived in Sukhumi, whereas now the population is only half that. But outside my hotel window and on every street corner, buildings were being renovated, or constructed. The hotel itself was brand new, high quality, with WiFi and card machines – the works. The receptionist told me with great pride that the A.T.M.s also accepted Visa cards. Adele's latest hit was playing over the sound system. Just around the corner there was a shop that trumpeted Apple, and beside that another boasted a home-made blue and yellow IKEA sign. But both shops stood empty, with nothing but bare shelves.

The global market has reached Abkhazia, even if it is the pirated version. And if you ignore the visible signs of a war that was won years ago, Sukhumi is still, if not an altogether beautiful city, certainly a charming one. The quiet streets are flanked by low, colourful, nineteenth-century buildings, and there are palm trees and green parks everywhere. The air is fresh with a faint tang of the sea, and in the evenings you can join the locals for a stroll along the promenade that looks out over the Black Sea, and enjoy the soothing sound of the waves lapping on the sand.

I went to the Ministry of Foreign Affairs to sort out my visa, and was sent to a bank to pay eleven dollars to the government visa account. Armed with my receipt, I was handed a piece of green paper that was tucked into my passport: my exit visa.

"Where is the press office?" I asked the visa officer. The last time I was there, I had managed to arrange at short notice an interview with a spokesperson from the Ministry of Foreign Affairs, thanks to my press accreditation. The press secretary had been deeply apologetic that the foreign minister himself was not there to answer my questions; he had become a father only hours before.

The visa officer had no idea where the press office was; he was not even aware that they had a press office. And I could not remember from my visit exactly five years earlier where it was. But I was given the address, so set off and found an enormous government building. Everyone I met there was very friendly, but no-one knew where the press office was. It seemed to be the first time they had heard mention of such a place. When I thought about it, the interview with Mr Chirikba, the ministry spokesperson, had not been particularly enriching anyway. He had a rather irritating habit of answering a question with another question. Abkhazia is only a small country with 250,000 inhabitants; was that really enough to fulfil all the functions that a national state should fulfil, I asked. Mr Chirikba retorted that most Chinese people would no doubt think that Norway was too small to call itself a state. Could one alternative be autonomy within Georgia, I suggested, slightly desperate. Would independence for Norway within Sweden be an alternative? Mr Chirikba parried. We have no relationship with Georgia, he added, with satisfaction. We have never signed a peace treaty. Technically, we are therefore still at war.

I put any ambitions as a journalist to one side and decided to use the one day I had to see as much as I could of the breakaway republic.

*

Putin's pallid moon-face filled the television screen in the breakfast room.

Abkhazia may have cut all ties with Georgia, but it has strengthened its bonds with Russia. Without military support from Russia
during the fight for independence, the republic would quite simply
not exist, and without Russia's financial and practical support
after the war, it would not have survived its infancy. Like Nagorno-
Karabakh and South Ossetia, Abkhazia is an international pariah.
Only Russia, Nicaragua and Venezuela have recognised the breakaway republic, and the crisis-stricken Pacific island of Nauru, which
was paid 50 million dollars by Russia for doing so. To the rest of
the world, Abkhazia is still part of Georgia, despite the fact that
the Georgian government has had no control there for more
than twenty years.

This pariah status means that Abkhazia is at the mercy of its
neighbour to the north. An Abkhazian passport, for example,
is worthless, so most Abkhazians have Russian citizenship and
passports. Four thousand Russian soldiers guard the border with
Georgia, and, in terms of the economy, Abkhazia is totally dependent on Russian goodwill. Even though it is a fertile country and
self-sufficient for much of its food, all commerce is based on
Russian imports, as no other country wants to trade with them.
Russian investment accounts on average for half the Abkhazian
government budget, and the Russian rouble is valid currency.
Abkhazia is even in the same time zone as Moscow, one hour
behind Tbilisi. About a million Russian tourists visit the Abkhazian seaside every year and the Russian authorities actively
encourage their citizens to holiday there. In the days of the Soviet
Union, Abkhazia was not only a popular destination for weary
workers, but also for party chiefs. Most general secretaries, including Stalin, had luxurious dachas there.

"Stalin loved Abkhazia," the guide said. She was a mature lady with spectacles and pearls. "He had twelve dachas, and five of them were here in Abkhazia!"

I was the only visitor, other than my driver who had come into the dacha with me, and a young Russian couple. The holiday home was furnished with solid furniture in various shades of brown. We were shown into a large room that was dominated by a long table. With as much expression as a robot, the guide relayed the room's dimensions and inventory.

"The dacha was built by German prisoners of war, after the war had ended. So it is good German craftsmanship. One architect was behind all of Stalin's dachas. The fewer who knew about them, the better."

She accompanied us into the office, bedrooms, bathrooms and balconies, rattling off facts and figures at an alarming speed. I only managed to catch about half of what she said. The Russians also seemed to be struggling to keep up.

"Does anyone have any questions?" the guide said, eventually. "You just need to ask. I am here to answer."

"How many dachas did Stalin have in Abkhazia?" I asked.

"Five, like I said," the woman sighed. "I have already told you that. Any more questions?"

Everyone looked at the floor in silence. When the tour was over, we were allowed to wander round and look for as long as we liked. The guide took up her position by the door and picked up a thick book.

"Stalin also liked to read," she remarked as I was about to leave. "He read three hundred pages every day. Imagine, every day! He read everything, but he was particularly fond of literature."

Anton, my driver for the day, was also fond of reading, Nietzsche, in particular. The car journey became one long lecture on moral philosophy, liberally seasoned with quotes by the German philosopher, and possibly also by himself.

"He who knows history, also knows the future," he said, as we stopped for a red light. A short while later we drove past a group of women out walking, all dressed in black.

"Why do so many of the women here wear black?" I asked.

"You can see our culture in the clothes we wear," Anton said. "But no-one cares about our culture any longer. They all wear Western clothes, and young people know nothing about Abkhazian culture."

"But why do so many of the women wear black?" I said again.

"They wear their sorrow."

The road improved noticeably the closer to the Russian border we got. All the holes and bumps gave way to newly rolled asphalt that ran like a funereal black shiny carpet through the lush green countryside. The climate in Abkhazia is warm and damp, and everything seemed to grow here, from grapes and palms to kiwis and melons.

"I am no ordinary driver, even though that has always been my job," Anton said. "My boss is a slave-driver. She wants me to work all the time, but money is not all there is to life. My mother cannot understand how she got such a lazy son."

An hour later, we arrived at Gagra, one of the Soviet Union's most popular health resorts. We were now so close to the Russian border that we could see on the other side a couple of the new Olympic villages by Sochi.

Gagra's history goes back a long way. The port was established by the Greeks in the second century BCE, and was known as Triglite. The Romans later called it Nitica. The port then fell to the Byzantine Empire and became significant for Genoan and Venetian merchants. In the sixteenth century, the whole of western Georgia was conquered by the Ottoman Empire, and the foreign merchants in Gagra were driven out. When the Russians took control of Georgia in the nineteenth century, Gagra was a shadow of its former self: not many people lived there and the town was surrounded by swamps and forest. Today there is little evidence of its long and rich history; the streets in the centre are dominated by monstrous concrete blocks, many of which are still visibly damaged by the war. One of the bloodiest battles of the Abkhaz-Georgian war was fought in Gagra, in October 1992. The Abkhazian forces were led by the Chechen Shamil Basayev.* The battle lasted only a week, but cost the lives of more than a thousand people, of whom at least four hundred were civilians. It ended when all the Georgians in Gagra were forced to flee.

When I visited, the city had long since settled into peace and quiet, but the traffic police did not rest. No sooner had we driven into the centre before we were waved to the side by two police officers.

"I was not speeding!" Anton protested, and for once did not pipe up with an appropriate Nietzsche quote.

"No, but you were driving the wrong way down a one-way street," one of the policemen said.

"But I have always driven down this street this way!" Anton said.

"Previously, perhaps," the policeman said. "The direction has changed, so now you can only drive down the other way."

"How was I supposed to know?" Anton said, with slightly less confidence. After a long discussion, followed by an even longer round of negotiations, Anton had to shell out a thousand roubles,

---

* Shamil Basayev played an active part in all the wars in South Caucasus in the 1990s, and fought against the Russians in both wars in Chechnya. When Russia formally ended the war there, Basayev made his mark as a terrorist and was for many years the most wanted man in Russia. He was behind the Beslan School Siege in North Ossetia in 2004. Basayev was killed by Russian special forces in 2006. In Abkhazia, he was revered as a hero and was appointed deputy minister of defence after the war. Basayev's depiction as a hero has diminished over the years, as Abkhazia's relationship with Russia has strengthened.

equivalent to about ten pounds, for his offence. He was given no official fine or receipt as proof that he had paid.

"I hate them," he said through gritted teeth when we were finally allowed to drive on, this time in the right direction, according to the changes. "They hide in the bushes and wait for you to make a mistake. But what is the point in stopping at a red light in the middle of the night when there are no cars to be seen?"

Before we drove back to Sukhumi, we went for a walk along the beach. The air was gentle, almost spring-like. A handful of Russian tourists were busy photographing each other out on a pier. Anton looked at them with pessimism.

"I am dreading the summer," he said.

"Why?" I asked.

"Now that Russia is boycotting Turkey and no-one dares to go to Egypt any more, I am assuming that hordes of Russians will come here. My boss will force me to work every single day."

There was a putrid smell of stress and faeces up on the hill. The long rows of cages made up small streets. A young man in dirty, torn clothes sold bags of stale bread, carrots and clementine segments. I bought one and went over to the cages. Long, thin, furry arms stretched out towards me. Some of the monkeys bared their teeth and hissed angrily, while others just looked at me with sad, pleading eyes. The rain got heavier and heavier. Within a few minutes I was soaking wet. I distributed the stale bread and carrots as fast as I could so I could get away. Hungry fingers snatched the food from my hand.

The Institute for Experimental Pathology and Therapy in Sukhumi first opened its doors in 1927. It was the first centre in the world to carry out experiments on primates. For decades it was the world leader in its field. The first trials of vaccines for polio and other major diseases were carried out here, but Ilya Ivanovich

Ivanov also carried out far more controversial tests. Stalin allegedly dreamed of creating a whole new race, a strong and hard-working man-ape hybrid that would help the Soviet Union to beat the West. The experiment was not successful, even though there was no shortage of willing participants of both sexes. A few years after the institute opened, Ivanov fell out of favour with Stalin. He was arrested in 1930, accused of having established a counter-revolutionary organisation of agricultural specialists. He was sentenced to exile in Almaty in Kazakhstan, where he died two years later.

The experiments continued in Sukhumi; at its peak, the institute had a thousand employees and more than seven thousand primates. During the Abkhaz-Georgian war in the 1990s, the director of the institute, Boris Lapin, fled to Russia and built up a new centre there. Many of the primates suffered terribly during the war, even though employees risked their lives to get through firing lines in order to feed them. Some of the primates starved to death, others froze to death, and when the war was over, many of those that were still alive were deeply traumatised. Against all odds, the institute survived and now has just under two hundred employees and about three hundred primates. Current work at the institute includes trials of life-prolonging medicines.

An orang-utan grabbed the last pieces of bread. The rain fell even harder, and the screams from the apes were drowned by the sound it made. I ran back down to the town. The smell of the cages and stressed animals lingered in my nostrils for the rest of the day.

An old man stopped and offered me a lift in the downpour. I gratefully jumped in, and he ended up driving me all the way to the border with Georgia. His name was Set, and he was an Armenian. Like so many other Armenians, his family came to Abkhazia as refugees from Turkey to escape the genocide in 1915. Some fifty thousand Armenians currently live in Abkhazia.

"I fought in the war," Set said.

"Which side did you fight for?"

"The Abkhazians, of course."

We drove past an abandoned industrial park. The factory buildings were in a state of collapse and rows of empty windows stared at us.

"Did you kill anyone?" I asked.

Set looked at me as though I was not right in the head.

"Of course," he said. "What do you think happens in wars?"

I handed over my green exit visa at the border and walked back across the bridge to Georgian territory. It was time to leave the Caucasus. No more than 17 million people live in South Caucasus, an area that is roughly the size of Iceland. But the distance between national borders is not great, and even shorter between breakaway republics.

I made my way to the port of Batumi, which is also a fascinating town, with a long and fragmented history, as is the case for most towns and cities this side of the Caucasus mountains. I was not far from the Turkish border, and the smell of kebabs drifted around every street corner. As part of the drive to draw tourists to Batumi, the reformer Saakashvili had made sure, in his last term as president, that there were plenty of signs pointing out the city's attractions. There were arrows pointing to the synagogue, the mosque, the Catholic church, the Armenian church, the Greek Orthodox church and more. Unfortunately I did not have time to visit these places of worship, as I had to catch the ferry to Odessa, Saakashvili's new home town.

EUROPE

"How many victims, how much blood and suffering, are connected with this business of borders! There is no end to the cemeteries of those who have been killed the world over in the defence of borders."

Ryszard Kapuściński

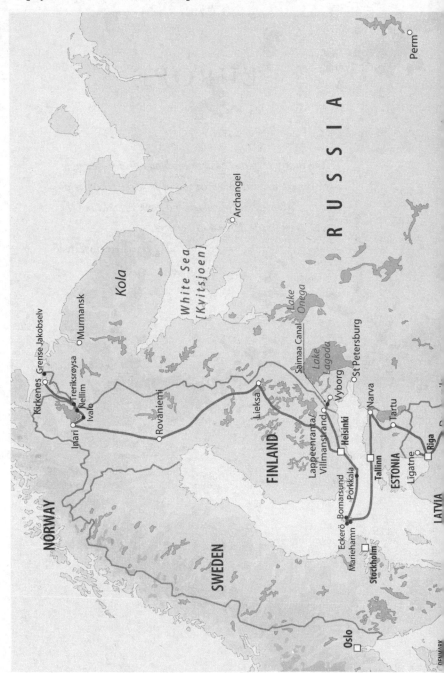

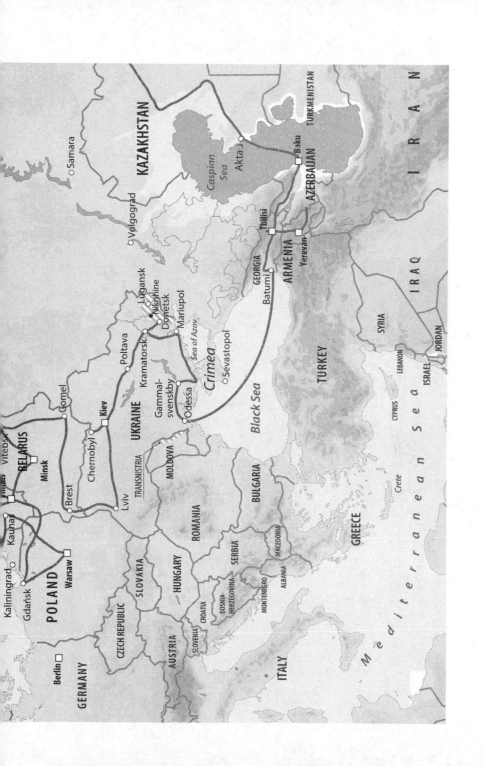

The Inhospitable Sea

Unlike the ferries on the Caspian Sea, those that cross the Black Sea between Batumi and Odessa sail at fixed times. It turned out, however, that the delays and waiting times were of the same order. As I had been sent to the wrong place first, I was half an hour late and came rushing onto the quay.

"Relax." A suntanned Georgian stood smoking beside a truck of fruit. He grinned at me. "Boarding won't start for several hours yet."

He was right. We were not let on board MS *Greifswald*, one of the last ships to be built in the D.D.R., for another five hours. I had a cabin to myself. It was simple, but compared to the cabin I had shared on the Caspian Sea crossing, it was a dream, both light and clean. At dinner, I was put at a table with two other women, Ukrainian Katya and Georgian Zmia. All the other passengers were lorry drivers. Katya, who was tall, slim and blonde, had lived in Tbilisi for many years and was going home to visit her family. The lorry drivers jostled to open doors for her, to pull out her chair, and they let her go straight to the head of the food queue. Zmia was in her fifties; her boss had sent her to work as a chef in his Georgian restaurant in Odessa. She had not wanted to leave Georgia, but given the choice between Odessa and Bangkok, the answer was easy. She was originally from Sukhumi in Abkhazia.

"Oh, that was my favourite place!" she cried, when I showed her a photograph of the promenade in Sukhumi.

Then she started to talk about her life. She told us about her brother who had been an officer in the Georgian army during the

Abkhaz-Georgian War in the 1990s. He and his men were caught in an ambush and realised they would not get out alive, so he let off a grenade he had hidden in the pocket of his army jacket. He was thirty-three years old, and left three children fatherless.

"After my brother died, my family and I escaped to the Georgian side," Zmia said. "My cousin's wife, Lizi, fled too, with her two children, a beautiful fourteen-year-old girl and a ten-year-old boy with learning difficulties. Her husband was fighting in the war. They ran into some Abkhazian soldiers in the forest, right by the border. Lizi offered herself to them; they could do what they liked with her, but she begged them to spare the children. So they shot her thirty times, with the children looking on. They came to live with us, but I never dared asked the girl what they did to her afterwards. She is thirty-eight now and has a family of her own."

Zmia wiped the tears from her cheeks.

"I have so many stories," she said. "You could write a whole book just about me."

In the evening, the restaurant was transformed into a bar, and any sense of propriety evaporated as the alcohol consumption rose. Katya and Zmia retreated to their shared cabin.

"Lock your door," Katya advised me. I did as she said. Every now and then someone knocked on my door and called out my name – the sixty-seven drivers on board had clearly managed to find out who I was – but I did not open. The voices in the corridor got more aggressive as the evening wore on. "That is what they are like, the Georgians!" one man shouted. His colleagues tried to calm him down, without much success. On the back of the door was a detailed list of what everything in the cabin cost, from the pillow-case to the shower head, in case of any damage. The drivers finally quietened down around midnight, when the bar closed. I lay there for a while, listening to the steady throb of the engine, and was rocked to sleep by the Black Sea's gentle waves.

The Black Sea is deep; at its deepest, it is 2,200 metres to the seabed. Herring, sturgeon, sharks, whiting, dolphins, flounders and hundreds of other kinds of fish swim around in the top layers of water, about one to two hundred metres below the surface, as saline levels are low and oxygen levels are high, but at the bottom it is dead. Ninety per cent of the water in the Black Sea contains no oxygen or life, making the Black Sea the largest body of dead water in the world. Dead plants and animals that flow into the Black Sea with the Danube, Dniester, Dnieper and Don sink to the bottom to become part of the wet, organic blanket that covers the seabed, along with tens of thousands of mummified shipwrecks. Wood does not disintegrate and iron does not rust, so even wrecks that have been there for thousands of years are perfectly preserved, caught in a time capsule of lifeless water. The considerable amount of organic matter, combined with a complete absence of oxygen, means that bacteria on the seabed produce record amounts of hydrogen sulphide. Hydrogen sulphide, H_2S, is one of the world's most poisonous gases. One inhalation of the malodorous gas is enough to kill a person. The Black Sea holds the world's largest reserve of hydrogen sulphide.

The Black Sea was once a big freshwater lake, far smaller and shallower than today's sea. According to recent studies, large volumes of water from the Sea of Marmara and the Mediterranean spilled into the Black Sea about eleven thousand years ago. As the glaciers from the last ice age melted, the water level in the Mediterranean rose over time, until it breached a thin spit of land in the Bosporus Strait and flowed into the Black Sea. The water level may have risen by as much as a hundred metres in ten years, transforming the lake into a sea. And the sea may have encroached on the land at a rate of about one and a half kilometres a day, swallowing Stone Age villages with ruthless efficiency. The marine life also changed swiftly. Eighty per cent of the fish that live in the

Black Sea originate in the Mediterranean. Some people believe that the deluge of the Black Sea could be the basis of the Noah's flood story in the Old Testament.[14]

The Ancient Greeks originally called the Black Sea Pontos Axeinos, "the inhospitable sea", but then changed it to the more alluring Pontos Euxeinos, "the hospitable sea". The Greeks established colonies along its shores as early as seven hundred years BCE, and lived alongside the Caucasian and Turkic people who were already there. In the Middle Ages, it was known as Mare Maggiore, "great sea". When Marco Polo crossed the Black Sea on his way to China in the thirteenth century, it had already become an important link in the trade route between east and west, and the crossing was so commonplace that he did not bother to write about the experience.

"We have not spoken to you of the Black Sea and the provinces that lie around it, although we ourselves have explored it thoroughly. I refrain from telling you this, because it seems to me that it would be tedious to recount what is neither needful nor useful and what is daily recounted by others. For there are so many who explore these waters and who sail upon them every day – Venetians, Genoese, Pisans and many others who are constantly making this voyage – that everybody knows what is to be found there. Therefore I say nothing on this topic."[15]

The sea is now known as the Black Sea in most languages, even though the water is no blacker than any other. Perhaps the name stems from the mist that often lies dark and heavy over the water, or the winter storms that can be dramatic, hence all the shipwrecks on the dead seabed. I was fortunate. I had been warned that it was risky crossing the Black Sea at the end of February, but the sea behaved impeccably. Carried on pleasant, gentle waves, we sailed into the Ukrainian time zone and territorial waters. Forty hours after leaving Batumi, the captain switched off the engine. We had arrived.

Three Ukrainian passport officers came on board and occupied a table each in the restaurant. When it was my turn, they stamped my passport without a moment's hesitation, and asked no questions. I was free to enter Ukraine. Katya was in the queue behind me, and the officer kept her talking for a long time.

"He said that he recognised you from the last time you were in Odessa," she said, when she had finished.

"But that was nine years ago!" I exclaimed.

"He said he had a very good memory."

Odessa was my first meeting with Ukraine and second extended stay in a former Soviet country. My first stay in Russia had not left me wanting more. In summer 2006, when I was twenty-two, I attended a Russian summer school in Pushkin, a suburb of St Petersburg. I was given lodgings with an old woman in a dilapidated concrete apartment block. The stairwell stank of urine and rubbish, and because all the blocks were identical, I often got lost. There was a heatwave in St Petersburg that summer; the old lady walked around the flat naked and encouraged me to do the same. I slept in her bed, and she snored on the sofa in the living room. We were separated by nothing more than an orange curtain. She served whole heads of garlic for breakfast, and, if I was lucky, macaroni and ketchup for supper. I counted the days until the end of the course, and cursed myself for choosing Russia as my specialist subject. It dawned on me that perhaps there was a reason why there was so little socio-anthropological research on the former Soviet Union.

Odessa was a far more pleasant experience. I had chosen the city as it was cheaper than St Petersburg and Moscow, and, as a bonus, the people in Odessa were reputedly the friendliest in the Russian-speaking world. While I struggled with verbs of motion and aspects, the snow melted and spring came to Odessa.

It had all started with the language. The people and the city were a by-product. My aim was to read *Crime and Punishment* in the original language. Natalia, my teacher in Odessa, thought this was a great goal, even if it was somewhat out of my reach at the time.

"But you can't just decide to sit down and read Dostoevsky," she warned. "You have to be in the right frame of mind. You have to be alone, in a quiet place. And you have to be open and receptive. But above all, you need plenty of time."

One of the things that I loved most about the Russians and Ukrainians was their deep respect for literature. The two countries share so much history that it does not always make sense to differentiate them. I could, however, have done without all the conspiracy theories. Like so many other Russian-speaking Ukrainians, Natalia believed that the Americans were behind the Orange Revolution in 2004.

"It was all planned by the C.I.A.," she said. "They paid the protesters to come and demonstrate. The goal was to destroy our country and to drive a wedge between us and Russia."

Natalia's opinion, which was in no way original, gave some indication of how divided Ukraine was, and of the split between the Russian-speaking majority in the east and the Ukrainian-speaking majority in the west. And yet, in 2007, the future looked bright. As a result of the demonstrations in Maidan Square, there was a third general election, and Viktor Yushchenko was elected president of Ukraine. Viktor Yanukovych, who had cheated his way to victory in the second general election, had been forced to stand down.

Nine years later I came back to a country in crisis.

The war in Donbass has so far cost the lives of more than ten thousand people, but, fortunately, Odessa is a long way from the front line.* The city was rocked by a couple of serious incidents in 2014, but these have had no further consequences. The worst happened on May 2, when pro-Russian and pro-Ukrainian groups clashed in major demonstrations in the city centre. The pro-Russian faction gathered in Trade Unions House, and from there some of them started to shoot at the pro-Ukrainian demonstrators. At some point, a fire broke out on the second and third floors. Despite the building's central location, it took the fire brigade an hour to get there. Forty-two pro-Russian demonstrators perished in the fire, and six pro-Ukrainian demonstrators died from bullet wounds.

Odessa is one of the most attractive cities in Ukraine, and it was even more beautiful than I remembered, despite the fact that the trees were still bare. In summer, Odessa is an extremely verdant city; avenues of leafy chestnut and plane trees provide tourists with much appreciated shade. Painted in light pastel colours, the buildings in the centre are inspired by Mediterranean architecture, with a fair portion of neoclassicism and baroque. The city felt more modern and relaxed than when I was there last. All the main fashion brands were there, one shop next to the other: Benetton, Adidas and Max Mara – but there were also more strip clubs than I remembered.

Odessa was conquered by the Russians during Catherine the Great's second war with the Ottoman Empire, which lasted from 1787 to 1792. The Turks were fighting to regain the Crimean Peninsula, which had been annexed by Russia six years earlier. But instead they lost more territory and the Russian border moved south to the Dniester River, where the small Moldovan breakaway state of Transnistria now lies.

In gaining the Crimean Peninsula, the Russians had secured a

---

* As of February 2020, more than 13,000 people have died in the conflict.

port on the Black Sea, but transporting goods over the mountains to Sevastopol was laborious, and they were keen to establish a new port. Their choice fell on the small, dusty Tatar village of Khadjibey, just north of the Dniester River. It was conquered in 1789, in just under half an hour, by José de Ribas, a Spanish-Neapolitan admiral who served in the tsar's army. De Ribas was given the task of building the new town, which was named after the Ancient Greek colony of Odessos, which had lain some distance further south. The admiral died eleven years later, in December 1800, in St Petersburg, while helping to plan the assassination of the historically unpopular, and quite probably mad, Tsar Paul I. The assassination was delayed, owing to de Ribas' death, but the tsar was eventually killed in his own bed on March 23, 1802.

During the reign of Alexander I, Tsar Paul I's son, Odessa flourished. In the wake of the French Revolution, prominent refugees made their homes in the Russian port, including Armand Emmanuel de Plessis, better known as the Duke of Richelieu, who was a close friend of Tsar Alexander I. Richelieu was appointed governor general of Odessa and the other newly conquered territories, and during his time as governor, Odessa blossomed into a cosmopolitan city with 35,000 inhabitants. The city architects were mostly Italian, which explains in part why Odessa is unlike any other Ukrainian town and is more reminiscent of a Mediterranean St Petersburg, which was also designed by Italians. The corn merchants were Italian, too, so initially Italian was the most important language of trade. And as most of the sailors and ship owners were Greek, Greek was the language spoken in the port. Flour, Odessa's most important commodity, was supplied by the Poles, who no longer had a homeland after the third partition of Poland in 1795, and Richelieu welcomed Jews from the newly occupied Polish territories, so there was a significant Jewish presence in Odessa. He also built theatres, an opera house, schools and libraries. He returned to France in 1814, the same year that his friend Alexander I rode up the Champs-Élysées in triumph with the other allies, and, following Napoleon's defeat at Waterloo the year after, he was appointed prime minister of France.

In 1828, Richelieu was honoured with a statue in Odessa, the city's first public monument. Dressed in a Roman toga with a laurel wreath on his head, he looks out over the port and the famous Potemkin Stairs, which were built some ten years later. In 1889, Richelieu was joined by Alexander Pushkin, who had also lived in Odessa for thirteen months. Pushkin was exiled from St Petersburg in 1820, and after three years in Chişinău, which had recently been acquired by the Russians, and in the Caucasus, he was transferred to Odessa, at his own request. Odessa's governor general, Mikhail Vorontsov, had taken pity on the poet and personally ensured that he was transferred to the city – something he would come to regret, as the twenty-four-year-old poet immediately fell in love with Vorontsov's wife, Elizabeth, who was seven years older than Pushkin, and the two started a passionate and not particularly discreet affair. Voronstov despaired and eventually begged to be rid of the poet: "Free me from Pushkin," he wrote to the Russian foreign minister in spring 1824.

That summer, the Odessa region was struck by swarms of locusts. Vorontsov sent Pushkin out into the country to report on the extent of the damage. Pushkin was shocked. Never in his four-year career in the civil service had he been asked to write anything official. He reluctantly obeyed and set off for the country to study the plague. A few weeks later he returned with his terse report, written as a poem:

> *The locust flew and flew*
> *and landed late*
> *in the day and ate*

everything in sight
before taking flight
anew.[16]

Shortly after, Pushkin handed in his notice, and Vorontsov was finally rid of the bothersome poet. Pushkin was sent to his mother's property, Mikhailovskoye, near Pskov, where he spent the next two years in productive boredom, writing some of his best poems there.

Given the city's cosmopolitan history, it is fitting that Georgia's former president, Mikheil Saakashvili, was appointed governor of Odessa in 2015. Armed with a shiny new Ukrainian passport, he set to work with great enthusiasm and promised to make the fight against corruption his priority. He had already tidied up in Georgia and now wanted to test the same drastic approach in Odessa. Corruption is an enormous problem in Ukraine – the country has a shared ranking (with Russia) of 131 out of the 167 countries in the Transparency International Corruption Index. Georgia, which also had one of the lowest rankings at the start of this century, now stands in 44th place.

"I hope he manages to tidy up," said Alexandra, a business-woman in her thirties who gave me a lift out of town. "He has promised to fix our roads. As you may have noticed, it is sorely needed."

But as it turned out, not even Saakashvili managed to break Odessa's culture of corruption. In November 2016, after one and a half years as governor, he stepped down.

"I can't stand this, I've had enough," he told the press, when he bowed out. "The reality is, in the Odessa region, the president personally supports two clans. I have decided to tender my resigna-tion and start a new stage of the fight. I am not giving up."[17]

Saakashvili then formed a new party, Movement of New Forces. The plan was that the party would field candidates for the Ukrainian parliamentary election in 2019, but President Poroshenko put a spanner in the works when he stripped the outspoken Georgian of his Ukrainian citizenship in summer 2017. Saakashvili automatically lost his Georgian citizenship when he became a Ukrainian, as Georgia does not allow dual nationality, so the former president and governor is currently stateless.* He probably has no particular wish to return to Georgia, as he was charged by the public prosecutor with abuse of power in 2014, during his time in office as president, a charge he disputed. Several other members of Saakashvili's government were charged with similar offences.

Not even Saakashvili with his sweeping ambition was able to tidy up the unholy chaos of Ukrainian and Georgian politics. He currently has more than enough to do tidying up his own mess.

---

* Saakashvili's Ukrainian citizenship was restored by the newly elected president, Volodymyr Zelensky, and he returned to Ukraine on May 29, 2019.

Quality Swedish Tea

A grey-haired lady with a stoop opened the door.

"Come in, come in!" she said, with a warm smile. "Are you hungry? Would you like something to eat?"

Even though I knew there were descendants of the Swedes in Gammalsvenskby who still spoke Swedish, I was taken aback to actually meet one. No sooner had I entered her simple home, than I was invited to sit down at the table. Maria followed behind me with tiny, tiny steps. With slow, careful movements, she put home-made borscht and stewed apples on the table. She was helped by her son, Alexander, who also spoke Swedish. There was a small Swedish flag on the table, and a calendar with photographs of the Swedish royal family on the wall. Alexander poured me a cup of tea.

"This is quality Swedish tea, not horrible Ukrainian tea," he assured me. He held out a chair. "Mother, why don't you sit down? I can help."

Maria sat down heavily, with a gentle sigh.

"My maternal grandfather was born in 1872, nearly a hundred years after the first Swedes came here," she said. "He and his wife had eight children. My mother had five. Only Johannes and I survived. Our three sisters died."

The history of the Swedes in Gammalsvenskby in Ukraine goes all the way back to Catherine the Great. They originally lived on the island of Dagö, which is now part of Estonia. Between 1561 and 1710, Estonia was ruled by Sweden, and from 1710 until the end of the First World War it was part of the Russian Empire. In 1781, Catherine the Great helped about twelve hundred Swedes from Dagö to move to the newly conquered territories in Crimea, the so-called New Russia. According to some sources, the Swedes were forced to move, whereas others say that the poor farmers were tempted by promises of free homes and land. Whatever the case, the result was catastrophic: more than half of them died on the long journey south. Only 535 people reached Ukraine, and there they had to build a new life with their own two hands, from nothing. According to the church records, only 135 Swedes from Dagö were still alive two years later, in March 1783.

After the Russian Revolution, the Swedes in Gammalsvenskby asked for permission to leave the Soviet Union and go back to Sweden. On August 1, 1929, the year of the Wall Street Crash, which triggered a worldwide recession, 881 of the villagers arrived on Gotland, a Swedish island in the middle of the Baltic, where most of them then settled. Only a handful chose to stay in Ukraine. But life in Sweden was hard, and, at the start of the 1930s, 243 people chose to return to Gammalsvenskby – only a matter of years before Stalin's reign of terror.

"All Swedes were declared enemies of the people by Stalin," Maria said. "Both my grandfathers were taken away. Herman Kristian Andersson and Petter Simonsson Malmas. They shot them in Odessa. I was only two months old."

Maria spoke a very peculiar form of Swedish: the Swedish that was spoken on the Estonian island of Dagö at the end of the eighteenth century, with the odd Russian and Ukrainian word thrown in. She sometimes slipped into Russian without even noticing, then back into her peculiar, melodic Swedish. Even though I understood what she said when she spoke Russian, it was as though the same words had greater impact when I heard them in Swedish, a language closer to my own.

"I was born in 1937," Maria said. "And then the war broke out. The Germans came here and we had to learn German at school. Johannes was only six weeks old when the Germans chased us west in 1943. We were five children then. We had no water, no food. Initially we went to West Ukraine in a horse and cart. My sister died along the way. They left us by the station, and for three weeks we sat there and waited for the train. One of the families put their child, a baby, in a suitcase, then someone stole the suitcase on the train. We were sent to Poland. There we had to wait again. I saw tanks run over people right in front of us. Everything all mashed together . . . blood, brains, everything . . . images one can never forget. There are so many images . . . and now there is a war again, over there in Donetsk. When the war started, I just cried and cried. Everything came back. I could not watch the television. Alexander had to turn it off. I was so upset. They destroyed houses . . . I had seen bombed houses before, I had seen war before. When I see those ruins and the women crying, it all comes back. My whole childhood comes back."

"Mother," Alexander said gently. "Let's not talk about the war. It only upsets you."

Maria put a hand on his shoulder and gave him an affectionate smile. She took a couple of deep breaths, then drank some tea.

"Thank you, Alexander. But I have to finish," she said. "From Poland, we were sent to Germany. Johannes learned to walk in Germany. My mother made a skirt for him. He looked like a ballerina. In Germany, my mother worked as a farmer. She sowed carrots. Things were not so bad for us in Germany. But then the war ended and we had to go home. They sent us back on the train. It got colder and colder and when we arrived, we were not home at all, but in Siberia. We had no clothes, no shoes, and we lived in draughty barracks. They were like a prison. Every family got one bunk. My sisters Elsa and Anna died in Siberia. Anna was only six.

If they had lived, I would have sisters. Johannes is dead now too, he was only fifty-six."

Her eyes glistened. Her voice broke.

"We were in Siberia for two years. Sometimes the temperature dropped to minus fifty. We would throw a bucket of water up in the air and if it froze, we did not need to go to school that day. The other children threw stones at us and called us fascists. When we finally returned from Siberia, there was nothing left of our house. We lived in my grandmother's house with four other families. In 1947, there was famine. People died on the street. Aunt Maria collapsed and died on the street. We buried her. We ate mice, until, eventually, there were no mice left in the village. We ate dogs. We boiled grass. We ate anything that could be eaten."

"Mother," Alexander said again. "Please don't get yourself all worked up."

"Have you ever been to Sweden?" I asked, to change the subject.

"I was allowed to go, yes, but my mother was not, not to begin with," Maria said. "In 1957, my aunt Alvina sent a letter to my mother inviting her to come to Sweden. The Soviet police put my mother in a cellar and kept her there for three days, with only a bit of bread and very little water, until she gave in and signed a document to say she would not go to Sweden. In 1975, Alvina sent another invitation. I was married by then, and had two children, Alexander and Anna, and a job in a nursery. I worked there for thirty-nine years and eight months. But I actually worked for longer than that. As children, we were sent out to pick cotton."

On September 2, 1975, having patiently sent in all the necessary papers and applications, Maria and Johannes travelled to Sweden, as the first visitors from Gammalsvenskby since 1929. They had to leave their children behind as guarantee that they would return.

"I was scared of airplanes and did not want to fly," Maria said. "During the war, we always lay down flat whenever the airplanes came. It was instinctive. So we took the boat. But the voyage was so awful that on the return journey we flew." She chuckled. "When we came back from our three weeks in Sweden, lots of journalists came to ask about our trip to Sweden. 'They have good roads,' Joahnnes said. 'Go there and learn how to make good roads. When you drive on them, there is no sound, it is as if you are hovering above the ground.'"

She laughed so much that her small frame shook.

"In 2004, seventeen years after her permit came through, my mother finally visited Sweden for the first time, and I went with her. We met all our relatives. They were all rich. They all had good lives. They had dishwashers. Washing machines. Leather furniture. We also have a washing machine now. But I was so angry with Alexander when he bought it! Why use all that money, I thought. Now, every day, I am grateful to Alexander for buying it. I don't know what I would do without it. Do you have a washing machine at home in Norway?"

Alexander got out a photograph album of the trip to Sweden. One of the photographs was of Maria's mother, Emma, with her sister, Alvina. Both went to Sweden in 1929, but Emma returned to the Soviet Union after two years. Unlike her sister, Alvina stayed in Sweden and married there. In the photograph, Alvina looks at least ten years younger than Emma, whereas, in fact, Emma was ten years younger than Alvina.

"Alvina was the lucky one," Maria said. "No war, no famine, no persecution. She lived a happy life."

We had been sitting talking in the small living room for so long that it was time for dinner. Maria shuffled into the kitchen to make food. When a stroke a few years earlier had meant she could not live on her own anymore, Alexander had moved back home to help her. Alexander had an ex-wife in Donetsk, and a wife and daughter in the neighbouring town. It was not clear whether they were still together or if they had separated. I found out later that he had had a drinking problem for many years, but with his mother's help he had managed to sort himself out.

The kitchen area was so small that there was barely room for one person. In the corner, behind Maria's stool, was the washing machine that Alexander had bought. While Maria worked in the kitchen, Alexander went out into the garden to collect fresh eggs for breakfast the next day. The house was small and basic, with no luxuries to speak of. In principle they had running water, but there was not always water in the pipe. The toilet was outside, beside the chicken run. With difficulty and patience, and tiny, tiny movements, Maria made a huge portion of mashed potatoes, roast vegetables and cream sauce. She served this with gherkins and home-made fruit juice. Alexander poured some more quality Swedish tea. I ate and I ate, and Maria and Alexander encouraged me to eat more. There was tea and cake afterwards. While I ate, Maria told me more about the war, about her children, about Sweden. I noticed that she had not mentioned her father once, and I asked carefully what had happened to him.

"Oh ..." The tears welled up in Maria's eyes. "Father was arrested by the Germans during the war, before Johannes was born. He never met Johannes. My mother exchanged letters with him while he was in prison, maybe fifty or more. When we were evacuated to Siberia, my mother lost touch with him. Then in 1956 we got a letter from Aunt Alvina telling us that my father was in Sweden. He had been sent there after the war by the Americans. Alvina had written in tiny letters, in old Swedish, so it would not be censored. My mother was only twenty-seven when my father was arrested. She never saw him again."

"Did you ever see him again?" I asked.

"Yes, once, when Johannes and I were on Gotland in 1975. I was thirty-seven and Johannes was thirty-one. They had never met and Father cried when he saw us. He said he remembered me when I was little. Every morning he would come into our bedroom and give us a kiss before he went to work. He had a new wife, a German woman, but no more children. On the day we left to come back to the Soviet Union, his shirt was wet with tears. After we had gone, he got very thin. He died two years later. His new wife took him back to Germany to be buried. We don't know where. It was not until 1987 that Mother was granted permission to visit Sweden. And by then, Father had been dead for ten years," Maria said.

There are now just under two hundred descendants of the Dagö Swedes left in Gammalsvenskby, which has been renamed Zmiyivka, meaning "snake town". Only a handful of them, like Maria and Alexander, have kept up the Swedish language.

"We always spoke only Old Swedish at home," Maria said. "We kept the traditions in my family. I celebrate Christmas on the 24th, like the Swedes. My husband was Ukrainian and celebrated Christmas and Easter two weeks later. When I got married, my mother said that we must celebrate his Christmas and Easter as well, so we have always had two Christmases and two Easters in this house."

"I always rather liked that," Alexander said with a smile, and filled our cups with quality Swedish tea.

The Wart on Russia's Nose

Great big blocks of concrete on the road forced the cars to stop. Every vehicle was checked carefully by armed guards before it could drive on.

I came on foot, and was not going any further.

"Who are you, and what are you doing here?" a guard in a balaclava asked. He had a Kalashnikov hanging down his back. I introduced myself and was led into a tent to meet Shamil, who was the oldest person there that day. The Ukrainian and Crimean Tatar flags were flying side by side outside the green tent.

Shamil was friendly, but guarded. His blue eyes were at once hard and dull, his hair was cropped and his pale face was covered in old scars. Before the occupation, he had run a greengrocer's shop in Yalta. His parents and sisters still lived there.

"If everyone leaves, then who is left?" Shamil asked rhetorically. He himself had moved to Ukraine with his wife and four children just after the Russian annexation.

"I did not want to live somewhere that was occupied by the Russians. They are the cause of huge injustices in Syria, Donetsk and Lugansk. I do not support states that bomb peaceful people. I will soon go back to Donetsk to carry on the fight. My brother too." He waved over a young man in a green combat vest, who was also carrying a Kalashnikov and wearing a balaclava.

"What is your name?" I asked.

The soldier looked at his brother, uncertain what to say.

"You can call him Crimea," Shamil said.

Crimea was twenty-five, twelve years younger than Shamil.

"What is your goal?" I asked Crimea. He looked at his brother again, a bit uncertain, but was given a nod.

"To liberate Crimea," he said. "That is our only goal. To get the Russians to leave. And we will win our battle, even if the whole world is against us."

"We had the idea of a blockade right from the start, but it was only set up last autumn," Shamil said. "We now have blockades on all three main routes into Crimea, and we are stopping the import of all fruit, vegetables, medicine and more. We are not paid, and we do not confiscate the goods, we just send the lorries back. We have also stopped the water and electricity supply on several occasions, but that alone is not enough. We are dependent on greater international sanctions. Why not ban Russians from travelling to Europe and America? Ukraine is a buffer between Russia and Europe. If we do not stop them, they will soon be in Berlin!"

I had visited Crimea nine years before with my sister. We took the sleeper from Odessa and woke up in Simferopol, on the Crimean Peninsula. On our way to the coast, we stopped at Bakhchysarai, the Crimean Tatars' former capital, where we visited the khan's old palace, smoked hookahs and ate baklava. Then we travelled on to Yalta, where Lenin still towers over the main square, his stone face turned towards Lenin Promenade. As it was early spring, the hordes of Ukrainian tourists had not yet hit the beaches, but it was not hard to see why they came. Crimea had everything: exotic Tatar palaces, old stone churches, dramatic cliffs, Latvian beer on tap, Greek ruins, evergreen conifers, long sandy beaches and warm seas.

The Crimean Peninsula was originally part of the Russian Soviet Republic, but in 1954 Nikita Khrushchev transferred the peninsula to the Ukrainian Soviet Republic. To this day, no-one knows why he did it. Khrushchev was born in the village of Kalinovka, not far from the Ukrainian border, in 1894. When he was fourteen, the family moved to Donetsk, on the Ukrainian side. He joined the Communist Party as a young man and had a stellar career. From 1938 to 1949 he was head of the Ukrainian Communist Party and was, by all accounts, genuinely fond of the country. Perhaps the transfer was simply a kind gesture to mark the 300th anniversary of the Cossack leader Bohdan Khmelnitsky's oath of allegiance to the Russian tsar and his signing the Pereyaslav Treaty, which, in Russian eyes, formally reunites Ukraine, as it is today, and Russia.* Khrushchev may also have been feeling guilty: Ukraine was one of the countries that had suffered most during Stalin's regime, and Khrushchev had taken responsibility for the purges there. Or perhaps there were purely practical reasons: Crimea, then as now, was not physically attached to Russia and was dependent on water and energy supplies from Ukraine. There has also been speculation that Khrushchev was in fact drunk.

The transfer had few practical consequences so long as the Soviet Union existed. About a million Russians moved to the Ukrainian Soviet Socialist Republic, but otherwise nothing much changed. Crimea continued to be a spa paradise for weary workers, and the preferred holiday destination for party bigwigs.

* In 1648, the Cossacks rebelled against Polish domination. The word Cossack is derived from the Turkic word *kazak*, which means "free man". They were originally groups of fishermen and hunters – many of them Slav farmers on the run from their lords – who settled on the steppes north of the Black Sea in the fourteenth century. They were then hired as border guards by the Polish governors who ruled Ukraine in the Middle Ages. Over the centuries, the Cossack population grew, and by the end of the sixteenth century, they were a distinct social group. The Khmelnitsky Uprising was successful, and for a short period the Cossacks enjoyed a fragile independence. When it became clear to Khmelnitsky that the Crimean Tatars and Ottomans could not provide sufficient protection against the Polish army, he sought protection from Moscow, and so the Cossacks were taken under Russia's wing. And as the Russians gradually took control over a large part of what is now Ukraine, the Cossacks lost their right to self-determination.

Gorbachev was relaxing in his dacha outside Yalta when the hawks in his party attempted a coup on August 19, 1991, and held him prisoner there for the duration. The coup failed but paved the way for the popular Boris Yeltsin, and Gorbachev returned to Moscow a defeated man. On August 24, he decided to disband the Communist Party and step down as leader. He continued as president of the Soviet Union for a further four months, but in practice had no power and had to watch helplessly as one republic after another declared its independence. By December 25, 1991, the Soviet Union was history.

And Crimea was officially part of Ukraine. For the time being.

Nine years after the Orange Revolution, at the end of November 2013, demonstrators once again streamed into Maidan Square in Kiev. They were protesting against President Viktor Yanukovych, who had failed to sign the long-planned association agreement with the E.U. Instead, he decided to strengthen economic ties with Russia, through membership of the Eurasian Economic Community, also known as the Customs Union. The number of demonstrators swelled, and the protest was no longer just about Yanukovych's pro-Russian position, but also against corruption, abuse of power and human rights violations. On February 18, 2014, the situation got out of hand, and there were violent clashes between the police and demonstrators. The police used rubber bullets to begin with, but soon changed to real ammunition. Over the course of the next few days, more than a hundred people were killed, largely civilians, and more than a thousand demonstrators were injured. On February 22, 2014, Viktor Yanukovych and several of his senior ministers fled Kiev. The same night, Putin called the heads of security in to a meeting, to discuss how they could get Yanukovych out of Ukraine. At seven o'clock in the morning, just as the meeting was about to close, Putin suddenly said: "We must start working to return Crimea to Russia."[18]

The following day, while world leaders watched the extravagant closing ceremony of the Winter Olympics in Sochi, there were pro-Russian demonstrations in Sevastopol in Crimea. On February 27, men dressed in fatigues with no obvious uniform badges stormed the parliament in Simferopol and other places of strategic importance on the peninsula, and military roadblocks were set up on all the main routes into Crimea. Only after the annexation did Putin admit that the men in fatigues were Russian soldiers. On March 16, a referendum was held as to whether or not Crimea should be a part of the Russian Federation. The official result was that ninety-six per cent of the population voted in favour. So, on March 18, 2014, the leaders of Crimea and President Putin signed an agreement that officially transferred Crimea back to Russia.

In a speech given the same day, President Putin said: "In people's hearts and minds, Crimea has always been an inseparable part of Russia. [. . .] Unfortunately, what seemed impossible became a reality. The U.S.S.R. fell apart. Things developed so swiftly that few people realised how truly dramatic those events and their consequences would be. Many people in both Russia and Ukraine, as well as in other republics, hoped that the Commonwealth of Independent States that was created at the time would become the new common form of statehood. They were told that there would be a single currency, a single economic space, joint armed forces; however, all this remained empty promises, while the big country was gone. It was only when Crimea ended up as part of a different country that Russia realised that it was not simply robbed, it was plundered."

By annexing the peninsula, Putin had, in his own view, rectified a historical injustice. Trains no longer run between Simferopol and Odessa, and without a Russian visa I could go no further than the Crimean Tatars' blockade.

"How many are there of you?" I asked Shamil.

He hesitated.

"That is a military secret," he said. "But there are well over three hundred active participants. At least ninety-five per cent of the Crimean Tatars support us. We all boycotted the referendum. The Tatars can no longer speak openly in Crimea. We are their medicine, we are here to help them."

A guard came into the tent and said something to Shamil in Tatar.

"Apologies, but I have to go now," Shamil said. "It is Friday and we have to go to the mosque to pray. You are more than welcome to stay and talk to the women."

I stayed. One woman, who called herself Sara, had long, dark hair and big, brown eyes. She looked like a film star. The other woman was called Miriam, had long, fair hair and blue eyes, and was also a Tatar.

There are various theories about where the Crimean Tatars come from. They appeared as a distinct ethnic group in Crimea in the thirteenth century, in the wake of the Mongol conquests. It is assumed that they were largely descendants of the Turkic tribes who had found their way to the northern shores of the Black Sea a few hundred years before, such as the Cumans and the Kipchaks, as well as the Golden Horde, which included various Mongolian and Turkic peoples. Some historians believe that the Crimean Tatars are also descendants of the other ethnic groups that have lived in Crimea through the centuries, such as the Pontic Greeks, Armenians, Scythians, Italians and Goths. When Crimea became a vassal state of the Ottoman Empire in the latter half of the fifteenth century, the Turkification of the people who lived there accelerated and the different ethnic groups were assimilated by the Tatars. This theory would explain why there is such variation in the physical features of the Crimean Tatars.

Sara was originally from Sevastopol.

"I left six months after the annexation," she said. "I could not bear to see the Russian flag whenever I went out. The Russians basically kicked us out! Lots of people lost their jobs, including me. My brother used to work for a Ukrainian bank, but when it became a Russian bank, he lost his job. I left, but my brother did not want to leave his homeland. He is working in a shop now. Obviously, he is overqualified for that."

Miriam served sweet baklava, made by her grandmother in Crimea, with strong Turkish coffee.

"Everyone knows that the referendum was just playing to the gallery," she said. "We did not acknowledge the referendum and did not want to legitimise it by voting. No-one can speak freely in Crimea any more. The Russians deported us in 1944, now they have come back. I cannot live with people who support Russia. And Russia has major financial problems," she said. "I worked as an anaesthetic nurse before I moved. The Russians promised the world, including free medicine for everyone, but the medicine they give out is poor quality. The doctors at the hospital where I worked refused to use the free Russian drugs in the operating theatre. They gave us their old medicine that they did not need any longer."

There is no exact figure, but some believe that as many as thirty thousand Crimean Tatars, a seventh of the Tatar population, may have left the peninsula after Russia's annexation in 2014. However, many Crimean Tatars were already living elsewhere.

"I was six when we came back," Gyulnara Bekirova told me. She was head of administration for the city council in Genichesk, a port on the Sea of Azov, close to Crimea. "My family went back in 1967, but most people were not allowed back until the end of the 1980s, under Gorbachev. No-one welcomed us, no-one helped us. On the contrary. There were Russians living in my father's childhood home and they refused to give the house back, they said it was theirs now. We did not want to go back to Uzbekistan, so we settled in a small village just outside Crimea. When we came, there were only five families living there. Today, Novo-Alekseyevka is a small town with several thousand inhabitants, mainly Crimean Tatars like us."

Thousands of returning Crimean Tatars had the same experience as Gyulnara. There were Russians living in their houses and they received no compensation from the state, nor were offered anywhere else to live. Many of them therefore ended up settling in the small villages close to Crimea, while others chose to live in Crimea illegally, squatting on land and in houses that did not belong to them. The Ukrainian authorities turned a blind eye and let them live there. The new Russian authorities, however, have not been as generous, and many Crimean Tatars have been evicted from their homes in recent years. There are also alarming reports from Crimea of people disappearing, being killed or being locked up in prisons or psychiatric institutions. Melis, the Crimean Tatars' highest political organ, was branded an extremist organisation and banned by the Russian government in 2016.

The relationship between the Crimean Tatars and Slav people goes back a long way and has been strained more often than not. When the Golden Horde finally crumbled in the fifteenth century, some of the clans gave up their nomadic life and settled on the Crimean Peninsula. These clans were the predecessors of the Crimean Khanate, the longest-surviving khanate of those established in the wake of the Mongol invasions. The khanate became a vassal state of the Ottoman Empire in 1478. The Ottomans chased the Greeks and Genoese away from the Black Sea coast, and in practice closed the Black Sea to European vessels for two hundred years.

The Crimean Khanate and lawless steppes in the south turned out to be a real headache for Russia. One of the khanate's most important sources of income was the slave trade, and tens of thousands of good Christians were taken prisoner on the steppes north of Crimea and either sold as slaves in Muslim countries or released for a ransom. Enormous sums were needed to pay ransom and taxes, and for security measures. One of the main reasons that the Russian tsars were so keen to conquer these regions by the Black Sea was that they wanted to put a stop to the slave trade and raids once and for all.

Another, equally important reason was their dream of making Russia a maritime superpower. In 1689, when Peter the Great came to the throne, Russia, despite its size, still had only one port, in Archangel. This was frozen over for the greater part of the year and was in the far north. Peter the Great managed to secure Russia's access to the Baltic Sea and built a new capital, St Petersburg, there. But all attempts to conquer the Black Sea coast failed. It was only at the end of the eighteenth century, under Catherine the Great, that ships flying the Russian flag finally sailed on the Black Sea. Like her predecessor, Catherine the Great was ambitious. Her big dream was to conquer Istanbul, cradle of orthodox Christianity. She was not successful in that, but in the course of two long wars with the Ottoman Empire, she did manage to ac-quire large parts of what is now South Ukraine, from Odessa in the south to Dnepropetrovsk (now known as Dnipro) in the north, including Crimea.

After the first war against the Turks, which ended in 1774, Crimea was given the status of independent khanate. The freedom was, however, short-lived. In 1783, Catherine the Great announced that the khan in Crimea and his people would henceforth be considered subjects of the Russian tsar. The new territories were called Novorossiya, New Russia. Catherine's lover and secret husband, Field Marshal Grigory Potemkin, who had played an important role in Russia's victory over these areas, was appointed first governor of Novorossiya. He founded many of the most import-ant towns in the region, including Kherson and Dnepropetrovsk. In Crimea, which Potemkin called "the wart on Russia's nose", he established Simferopol and Sevastopol, home to the Russian Black Sea fleet.

Sevastopol holds a unique place in Russian and Ukrainian history, because it was here in Chersonesos, as it was then called, that Vladimir I, Grand Prince of Kievan Rus, was christened in 988.* According to the *Primary Chronicle*, the choice was between Islam and Christianity, and he chose the latter because he could not bear the thought of a life without alcohol. In reality, it was prob-ably more to do with diplomacy: Vladimir I wanted to marry the Byzantine emperor's sister, Anna, in order to strengthen the rela-tionship with the Byzantine Empire, their most powerful neigh-bour to the east. Basil II was sceptical about marrying off his sister to such a barbarian – the Byzantines viewed everyone north of Constantinople as barbarians. Vladimir I was certainly no saint. He claimed the throne having killed both his brothers, and, according to the Chronicle, he had at least five wives and a stagger-ing eight hundred concubines before converting to Christianity and choosing the narrow path.

In order to persuade the Byzantine emperor to agree to the marriage and alliance, Vladimir I took Chersonesos from the Byzantines. He offered to give the city back if he could marry Anna. Basil II consented on condition that Vladimir help him to conquer the Bulgarians, and be baptised. Vladimir agreed to both. After the wedding, he set about Christianising all his subjects. The Christian Byzantine Empire was rich and powerful; perhaps Vladimir hoped that having a shared religion would have the same wondrous effect on his own people.

---

* Vladimir is known as Volodymyr in Ukrainian.

Kievan Rus, the forerunner of modern-day Russia, remained Christian. Following a schism between the Eastern Church and the Western Church in 1054, the grand princes of Kiev were loyal to the Byzantine Empire and eastern Orthodox Christianity, a choice that was upheld after the fall of Constantinople in 1453. By then, Moscow had become a more important centre of power than Kiev, in terms of religion also. Russians believed that Moscow was the third Rome – and that there would never be a fourth. The idea that Moscow is the successor of Rome and Constantinople is the reason why the two-headed eagle, originally a Byzantine symbol, is included in the Russian coat of arms.

In other words, Christian Russia was born in Crimea, in Chersonesos. Sevastopol was built on the ruins of Chersonesos, and since then has been destroyed and rebuilt twice.

The first time Sevastopol was destroyed was during the Crimean War, which raged from 1853 to 1856. The Ottoman Empire, which was often called "the sick man of Europe", was weak, and Russia and the Western powers bided their time, waiting for it to wither away completely so that they could pick up the pieces and share them out among themselves. Tensions in Europe were running high at the time. In France, Napoleon III, nephew of Napoleon Bonaparte, had recently seized power and was keen to make his mark. He demanded that the Ottomans recognise the Roman Catholic Church as the highest religious authority in Palestine. Under considerable pressure, the sultan conceded, which in turn upset Tsar Nicholas I, who felt that the Orthodox Church had been demeaned. In revenge, the Russians attacked the principalities of Moldova and Wallachia, south of Odessa, which were then under Turkish rule. Later the same year, the Russians destroyed the Turkish Black Sea fleet. It was the tenth time that the Russians had gone to war with the Turks, so in many ways it was nothing new, but unusual this time was the fact that the Western powers of France, Great Britain and later Sardinia joined the war on the Ottoman side. They believed that Russia's aggressive expansionism threatened their interests, and feared that the Russians would try to make the Black Sea Russian and thereby gain free access to the Mediterranean.

In September 1854, French and British soldiers landed in Crimea, and a few weeks later there began the siege of Sevastopol, the main base of the Russian Black Sea fleet. In order to prevent the allies from entering the inner harbour, Russian admirals ordered that the greater part of the fleet be sunk. Russian soldiers were protected in their trenches and held out against the bombs for eleven months.

"I do not think that I ever saw such awful injuries as those I was forced to deal with during the final period of the siege," wrote Khristian Giubbenet, a professor of surgery, in his memoirs. By the end of July 1855, 65,000 Russian soldiers had been killed or injured in Sevastopol. Giubbenet recalled that the injured were laid out on the parquet floor of the House of Nobles, "not only side by side but on top of each other. The moans and screams of a thousand dying men filled the gloomy hall, which was only dimly lit by the candles of the orderlies."[19]

The Crimean War was one of the first wars to make such extensive use of trench warfare, and the losses were appalling. It was not firearms or cannons that killed most of the soldiers, however, but epidemics and infections. The British nursing pioneer, Florence Nightingale, served at one of the field hospitals in Istanbul during the war and implemented a number of systematic measures to improve hygiene, including proper latrines, clean kitchens, clean bedclothes, and the regular airing of wards. These simple but effective measures resulted in a dramatic fall in the number of deaths and revolutionised nursing. Unfortunately, the measures did not help the Russian soldiers in Sevastopol, who continued to die at a terrifying rate. Historians estimate that the Russian army lost 450,000 men in the Crimean War.

Sevastopol fell in September 1855. Tsar Alexander II, who had succeeded his father, Nicholas I, the year before, signed a peace treaty with the allies on March 30, 1856. Russia lost Moldova and Wallachia, the areas they had won from the Ottomans three years earlier. But a worse blow for the Russians was the decision that the Black Sea should be neutral, as it meant they also lost their fleet at Sevastopol.

The Crimean War was in many ways the first modern war. War correspondents emerged as an important professional group, thanks to technological innovations such as the railway, tele-graph and camera, and this in turn enabled people at home to follow the brutality of war in a very new and different way. For Russia, the Crimean War was a catastrophe, in both human and economic terms. The empire's position in Europe was greatly weakened and it became obvious to everyone just how back-ward Russia was with regard to its army and industry. One direct consequence of the war was Alexander II's decision to abolish serfdom, despite enormous protest from the nobility. More than a third of the population at the time were serfs. Not only did the system cause considerable human suffering, it hindered military and industrial development as well. The state coffers were empty and Alexander II realised that Russia would not be able to defend Alaska against an attack. Alaska was therefore sold to the U.S.A. in 1867.

Alexander II was a great reformer and one of the most progres-sive tsars that Russia ever had. He was assassinated in 1881, by members of a revolutionary movement called People's Will.

Ninety years after the Crimean War, Sevastopol was at the centre of some of the fiercest and bloodiest battles of the Second World War. The Germans occupied large parts of Crimea as early as 1941, but the Red Army managed to stand against the Nazis in Sevastopol. For the second time in a hundred years, Sevastopol was besieged. By winter 1942, the Germans had gained control of all the surrounding areas and bombarded the city with the railway cannon Schwerer Gustav. The siege lasted 250 days, and by July the city lay in ruins.

The long siege incurred enormous losses for the Germans, although they did finally take the town. In addition to the human and material cost, the fighting had delayed German advances on the Eastern Front and their goal of reaching the oil wells of Baku. On May 9, 1944, after two years of German occupation, Sevastopol was liberated by the Red Army.

Nine days later, Stalin started the deportation of the Crimean Tatars, whom he accused of collaborating with the Germans. There were of course those who had worked for the German occupying forces – some through force and some voluntarily – but there were more who had fought against the Germans as part of the Red Army.

In the course of a couple of hectic days, an entire people was declared responsible, and without trial hounded from their homes and pressed into dirty, overcrowded rail carriages.

"It took no more than two days for all the Crimean Tatars to be deported," Gyulnara Bekirova told me. "More than 230,000 people. They were transported in carriages that were normally used for animals; anyone who resisted was shot. My father, who was twelve years old, was sent to the Urals, while my mother, who was no more than five, was sent to Uzbekistan."

More than a third of those who were deported died en route or during the first few years of exile.

"My parents met in Uzbekistan," Gyulnara said. "And I was born there, but do not remember very much, only that it was dirty. We lived in barracks on a collective farm. We waded through shit.

It was a hard life. When we came back here in 1967, I could only speak Tatar and Russian, not Ukrainian. People here knew nothing about the Tatars anymore, they thought we were gypsies."

She looked out of the window, down at the car park. It was raining heavily. The plinth where once a statue of Lenin had stood was empty.

"On May 18, 1994, fifty years after the deportations, my father talked about it for the first time," she said, without turning her gaze. "He told me that it had been a terrible squash on the train, and hot, with people everywhere. Nine-month-old twins died along the way. As the train rarely stopped, they had to throw them from the moving train. On May 19, the day after he first talked about it, my father died of a heart attack."

Seventy years after the Red Army regained Crimea and the Crimean Tatars were deported, Russian soldiers once again took over the peninsula. The world was shocked by the annexation in 2014. It was only six years since the war in Georgia; Russia had once again broken all written and unwritten rules and encroached on another sovereign state's territory. What was more, it was a European sovereign state. The bear had woken from its slumber and caught the E.U. dozing. The Kremlin had made very clear to the world's politicians who made decisions in Russia's backyard. It was not a place to flirt with N.A.T.O. or discard membership of the E.A.E.U. in favour of agreements of association with the E.U. – or not without consequences.

This bullish foreign policy stance came at a cost. Western countries imposed sanctions on Russia as punishment. A number of Russians were denied entrance to the E.U., the U.S.A., Canada, Norway and Switzerland. In response, to the horror of the middle classes, Russia stopped the import of selected foods from countries that supported the sanctions. In order to enforce the ban on imports, thousands of tons of illegally imported French cheese and Polish apples were destroyed.

In terms of military strategy, one cannot overestimate the significance of Russia's control of the Crimean Peninsula, but, so far, the annexation has been of little benefit to the local population. The number of tourists has fallen by more than two million a year, which is catastrophic for the travel and tourism industry, Crimea's most important source of income. At the time of writing, the Russians are building a bridge over the Kerch Strait, to link the peninsula with mainland Russia. The bridge will be nineteen kilometres long and according to plan will open for cars in 2018, and for trains a year later.* Three thousand labourers are working day and night to get it finished. The cost has been estimated at more than 3.7 billion dollars. Hitler and Stalin tried unsuccessfully to build a bridge over the Kerch Strait. The strait is vulnerable to earthquakes and storms, and often freezes in winter. In other words, the odds are against the bridge, but it is a prestige project for Putin and crucial to the survival of Crimea. If the project is successful, Crimea will be given a sorely needed umbilical cord to Mother Russia, and will no longer be dependent on shipped supplies and goodwill from Kiev, or vulnerable to sabotage by the Crimean Tatars.

Crimea was just the start, it turned out. In the wake of the annexation of the Crimean peninsula, there was a rash of pro-Russian demonstrations in the Donbass region of Eastern Ukraine. The situation escalated quickly, and in May 2014 the Lugansk People's Republic and Donetsk People's Republic declared their independence from Ukraine. Two new breakaway republics were

* The road bridge was inaugurated by Vladimir Putin on May 15, 2018 and opened for cars on May 16 and for trucks on October 1. The rail bridge was inaugurated on December 23, 2019 and the first scheduled passenger train crossed it on December 25. The opening of the bridge for freight trains is scheduled for July 1, 2020.

born. With Russia behind them, the pro-Russian rebels demanded that the entire Donbass region, preferably the whole of Novorossiya, should separate from Ukraine. Important cities such as Slavyansk and Mariupol were regained by Ukrainian troops through the summer and autumn of 2014, but the rebels still control key towns and cities in the Donetsk and Lugansk oblasts. Unlike with the annexation of Crimea, the Russian government vehemently denies sending military aid or regular troops to Eastern Ukraine, but there is a wealth of satellite pictures and witness statements that prove the opposite.

More than two million people have fled from the war, which so far has claimed ten thousand lives. There have been several cease-fire agreements, which in theory were all permanent, but none of them have lasted more than a few days.

I headed north, away from the Crimean Tatars' blockades and the white beaches of the Black Sea. The closer to the front line I came, the shorter the distance between roadblocks. Soon there was more military traffic on the roads than civilian. The war was getting ever closer.

The Youngest Breakaway Republic in the World

A border guard wearing a balaclava, with a Kalashnikov slung over his chest, bent down towards the open car window and took our passports. Gunfire could be heard in the distance. It sounded like firecrackers.

"Stay in the car," Dima, the driver, ordered. "There are mines everywhere. A few weeks ago I witnessed four people being blown to bits while they stood in a toilet queue in the field over there."

There were four of us in the car. My fellow passengers were Chris, a British photographer, and Anya, who was originally from Donetsk. When our passports had been returned, Dima drove us on to the official border station, previously a petrol station. There were bullet holes everywhere: in the walls, in the ceiling, in the petrol pumps, in the signs showing the price per litre. Dima took our documents and ambled over to one of the windows, where presumably they had once sold hot dogs. Before we could drive on, a heavily armed soldier checked the boot. He looked longingly at the bottle of cognac that the photographer had with him.

"It belongs to the foreigners," Dima said.

The soldier waved us on, crestfallen, and we drove into the Donetsk People's Republic, the youngest breakaway republic in the world. It had been a bureaucratic nightmare to get all the necessary papers to travel via the so-called anti-terrorist operation zone on the Ukrainian side and into the self-declared republic. I needed three permits from three different offices in three different towns, all with random opening times. Three permits that must never, under any circumstances, be shown together.

"Hide your Ukrainian press pass now," Dima said as we approached the first roadblock. "If the wrong person sees it here, we could be arrested. You need your Donetsk accreditation here, O.K.?"

The windows in the miserable houses along the roadside were either broken or brand new. Every road sign had been shot through. The road itself was surprisingly good by Ukrainian standards, wide and more or less complete. This luxury lasted only a few kilometres until we were told at another roadblock that we had to take another route to Donetsk. The soldier explained that the situation up ahead was "hot".

The detour took us through the city of Gorlovka. Before the war, a quarter of a million people had lived there. We passed the skeleton of a burnt-out church. One of the corners of an apartment block had been ripped off. Three women in colourful housecoats stood deep in conversation on the grass nearby.

Like many others, Anya had left her job and flat in Donetsk and moved to a provincial town on the Ukrainian side when the war broke out. She had not been back since. In silence, she observed the ravages of war through the car window.

"It must be sad to see all this destruction," I said.

She shrugged.

"Everything was already old and dilapidated, so the war has made very little difference," she said.

I could see from the reflection on the window that she had tears in her eyes.

Before the war, Donetsk was one of the wealthiest and best-maintained cities in Ukraine, and a host city for the 2012 Euros. The city was upgraded for the occasion with the most modern airport in the country and a shiny new football stadium. The same year, *Forbes Magazine* hailed President Viktor Yanukovych's hometown as the best city in Ukraine in which to do business.

Four years after football fever had raged in the streets of Donetsk, it was no longer advisable to visit what little was left of the airport without wearing a helmet and bullet-proof vest. The stadium had been turned into a soup kitchen and warehouse, and the foreign investors had long since fled the city. The wide boulevards were more or less empty of traffic and people. All the bars and restaurants closed at ten in the evening, and there was a curfew from eleven at night until five in the morning. Anyone caught out on the streets then would be arrested and held on remand unless they came to an amicable arrangement with the police, who were not known to be shy of taking bribes.

The following day there was a convergence of people on the otherwise empty streets. March 8 is not a day that goes unnoticed in former Soviet republics. First thing in the morning there were already long queues of men outside the flower shops. Failing to give your wife a gift on International Women's Day is worse than forgetting your wedding anniversary.

I was invited to the home of a Russian soldier.

"I apologise for the mess," thirty-year-old Linar said, with a smile. He was blond and blue-eyed, of stocky build, with a square, scarred face. "We are decorating the baby's room, but it is not quite finished yet."

Vika, his nineteen-year-old wife, served us tea. A vase with a fresh bouquet of flowers stood on the worktop.

"When I heard what was going on in Crimea, I went there to help," Linar said.

"So you were in Crimea when it was annexed?" I said.

"It was not an annexation, there was a referendum," Linar said. "Crimea has always been Russian, since the time of Catherine the

Great. Before I went to Crimea, I served in the Russian army in Chechnya. I was in Beslan as well, I was one of the soldiers who surrounded the school. In 2008, during the war in Georgia, I volunteered in South Ossetia. I was ready to go to Syria, but my wife persuaded me to stay at home. I will go wherever the Russian people are threatened. But I am here as a volunteer, no-one is paying me. That is important. Be sure to say that."

"Is that why you went to Eastern Ukraine, to help the Russians who were under threat?"

"Tell me, what exactly is Ukraine?" It was a rhetorical question. "You see, there is no Ukraine. The people here call themselves Ukrainian, but they are actually Russian. There are Russian dialects that are difficult to understand. Ukrainian is one such dialect."

"President Poroshenko started to take our rights away," Vika said. "We could only get Ukrainian television, everything was taught in Ukrainian at school, but we have always spoken Russian here. In autumn 2014, the Ukrainians started to shoot at people who were living here in peace. Our house was destroyed. I felt that I had to do something, so I came to Donetsk to help the soldiers, make food for them and things like that. That was how I met Linar."

She put her hand on his. He looked affectionately at her round, pregnant stomach, which was very visible in her jogging trousers.

"It was love at first sight," he declared.

"It is a boy," Vika said, with a shy smile. "I am six months pregnant. Would you like to see the wedding video? Linar, why don't we show her the highlights?"

Vika took me over to the computer, which stood in a corner of the bedroom. Scenes from the wedding played on the screen. All the guests were in uniform. Despite the loud music, you could hear grenades and shooting beyond the party. Vika said that her relatives had been there too, but I could not see anyone who was not in uniform other than the bride herself, a few children and a couple of young women in very short skirts. Later in the evening they were seen in passionate embraces with some of the soldiers. Towards the end of the video, some of the soldiers put on women's wigs, acrobats did some tricks, and everything took off. Linar and Vika chortled and pointed.

"That is a soldier's wedding for you," Vika laughed.

Afterwards, Linar showed me his Kalashnikov.

"We are peaceful people," he said. "We are not here to fight, only to defend ourselves. Say that. I came here empty-handed, without any weapons, I could not cross the border with a gun. The guns are my trophies."

"How many people have you killed?" I asked.

For the first time in our conversation, he said nothing. A shadow passed over his clear, blue eyes.

"I . . . I don't know . . . I have never seen anyone . . . It is always dark, I . . ." He stopped and looked straight at me. "You must never ask a soldier that, do you understand? *Never!*"

We went out into the sunshine. It was warm, almost springlike. There were four or five soldiers in the yard roasting meat on skewers over a fire. They offered us beer and meat and insisted that I try their marinated garlic.

"This is how we celebrate Women's Day," one of the soldiers said happily, smacking his lips.

"Where are the women?" I said.

"Well . . ." He looked around. "They must be inside making a salad or something!"

The men roared with laughter and poured more beer into their plastic glasses.

The next day, I was able to visit the institute where the future officers of the People's Republic are cultivated. In a warm, damp classroom, some twenty eighteen year olds were sweating over an English exercise.

"I study at military school," stammered one of the students, red in the face. "I get up at 6.30 in the morning. First we have morning exercise. We study English, Russian, military skills and higher mathematics."

"Very good," said the young teacher, full of praise and enthusiasm. "Please continue."

"Goodness, it is not easy," the teacher told me when we were alone. "I normally teach at the university, but they needed teachers here. We have no textbooks or equipment. All I have is chalk and a blackboard." She gave a brave smile. "Perhaps it will be better next year."

The military academy had reopened in summer 2015. There were still pictures of Ukrainian athletes hanging on the wall, but instead of the Ukrainian flag, the students now had D.N.R., *Donetskaya Narodnaya Respublika*, sewn on their uniforms. When I visited the academy, there were 180 students, of whom ten were girls, including nineteen-year-old twins Zhenya and Sasha.

"I like the discipline here," Zhenya said.

"The days are planned," Sasha added. "Everything is organised, rational. We do not waste any time."

"The Ukrainians never liked us anyway," Zhenya said. "During the demonstrations in Maidan Square in Kiev, they just sat there while we worked in the mines. We kept the whole country going."

"The war is just everyday life now," Sasha said. "It was horrible to begin with, but now we are used to it. The bombs and shooting are becoming tedious. But the Ukrainians kill little children." She was very serious now. "It is worst for the children. I think the best solution would be if we could become part of Russia again. But being independent is alright too. As long as we do not become part of Ukraine again. That is most important of all."

"You are so young," I said. "What are your dreams?"

They thought about this question for a long time.

"Yes, I have a dream," Zhenya said, eventually. "I want to make a small toy car from scratch. One that runs by itself, on electricity. I want to build the whole car, the body, the engine, all of it."

Very early the next morning it was time for shooting practice. There were two a month. The excited students rushed into the barracks to get their Kalashnikovs and ammunition, then squeezed together on the flatbeds of two lorries. A tall man in his forties marched over to me.

"I understand that you are coming with us? Do not move a centimetre to the left or to the right, understood? My name is Vladimir, by the way. Follow me!"

I obediently got into his car, a gleaming white jeep. With pop music playing full blast, we set off behind the lorries. In the east, a blushing sun rose up over Donetsk. The sky turned orange, then milky white.

"Before the war, I was a history professor," Vladimir told me. "Now I'm a tank driver. If you look on YouTube, you will find several videos of me from the front line. I am quite famous!"

The students were dropped in a small village and had to march the final stretch. We drove on, and stopped right by the shooting range. One of the teachers, who was no more than 1.5 metres tall, blond and compact, came over to me.

"So, you are from Norway?"

I nodded.

"I have heard there are a lot of homosexuals there. Here, there are none! We have shot them all!" He grinned. "Tell me, is it normal for a man to fuck another man?"

"A friend of mine has just written an article about how difficult the situation is for gay men in Donetsk," I said.

"What?!" The small man visibly puffed out his chest. "Give me their names, then we will find them and get rid of them!"

The students finally appeared over the ridge of the hill, marching in time. Once they had arrived, they were split into five groups and told to alternate between the various posts, which varied from simple shooting practice to dismantling a Kalashnikov within a set time. I wandered from post to post, catching the odd phrase here and there. "This is not a nursery school!" "Focus, boys and girls!" "The enemy could be anywhere!" In the background was the constant sound of rounds being fired at the shooting range.

Vladimir drove me back into the centre of town when the practice was over.

"The whole of Donbass will be part of Russia again," he declared. "The people of Mariupol and Kramatorsk long to be liberated! The West is contaminated by Muslims and gays, only Russia is strong. Would you like some coffee? There's a drop of cognac in it, Armenian cognac. My wife made it this morning. My *second* wife; she is much younger than me."

When he pulled up outside the hotel, he turned to me. "When are you going home to have children?"

"Excuse me?"

"How old are you? Tick tock, time is passing."

Although there was only a curfew and some discreet transparent tape across my hotel window to remind me that I was in a war zone, I did not need to go far to find evidence of it. In the village of Nikishyne, between seven and eight hundred kilometres north of Donetsk, by the border with the Lugansk People's Republic, there had been heavy fighting until the ceasefire in February 2015. The two parallel streets that made up the village reminded me of scenes from the Balkans in the 1990s: rows of burnt-out, uninhabitable houses. Ninety per cent of the village had been destroyed.

"Before the war, 836 people lived in Nikishyne," Natasha told me. She worked for the village council. "Now there are only 235 people left. When the war was at its worst, from September 2014 until February last year, only a handful of people stayed. Everyone who had somewhere else to go left. Even those who had nowhere to go left."

One of those who never left was Larissa, a large woman in her early sixties, with orange hair and a pink housecoat.

"Come, come," she said, with a hoarse laugh. "I will show you what they did to us and all the destruction."

Larissa showed me around a chaotic backyard and pointed at a big hole in the ground. "A grenade went off here!" She pointed to the ditch on the other side of the road. "A dead solider lay there." She laughed again and insisted that I come into her house. It was big and spartan. There was a large bowl of sugar on the kitchen table.

"I am diabetic myself, so that is only for guests," Larissa said. "Coffee or tea?"

Two cats clamoured around my feet. An old man limped into the kitchen. Ivan Ivanovich was seventy-three. When his house was destroyed, he moved in with Larissa and had been living there ever since.

"There were lots of people here during the war," Larissa said. "Soldiers everywhere, in all the rooms. I have no idea how many there were. They were everywhere!" She lowered her voice. "If you don't give my surname or take any pictures, I will tell you everything. They stole two of my cars, and a tractor, then sold them. It was Russian soldiers who did that, our own! I went to Donetsk to give a statement and show all the documents, but no-one has done anything. Nothing!"

She laughed again, a rasping, melancholy laughter.

"We had no electricity or water, and sometimes we did not

even have food. Sometimes there were so many bombs that we could not even go to the toilet! I cried every day when they were here, and I cried when they left. You see, most of them were good boys. I am from Russia as well, I am a Russian. My sister lives in Moscow, but we have not been on speaking terms since the start of the war. Where would I go? If I had left, my house would no longer be standing, I am certain of that."

I bumped into Lyuvbov Vladimirovna and her husband in the parallel street, which was in an even worse state. They had moved back to Nikishync in February 2015, as soon as the soldiers had left. Over the course of the summer, they had managed to build a small cabin in the ruins of the two buildings where they had lived before. There was just enough room for a stool, two narrow beds and a small television in the room.

"We were here when they came, the fascists, or perhaps I should rather call them the Nazis?" Lyubov said with emotion. "Write that down, and write down my name as well, because I stand by what I say. I was here when they came, the Ukrainian battalions, and they had swastikas, just like the Germans! They wanted to exterminate us. We do not want to be part of Ukraine anymore, and I mean that categorically! They wanted to make concentration camps for us. They saw us as second-class citizens. And this is how we live now!" She gestured wildly with her arms. "We have lost everything. We just want Ukraine to leave us in peace."

Lyubov means love in Russian.

The Donetsk People's Republic declared its independence from Ukraine on May 12, 2014. To begin with, many thought that the territory would become an integrated part of Russia, like Crimea, but now it seems more likely that Donetsk will end up as a break-away republic, like Abkhazia, Nagorno-Karabakh and South Ossetia, not recognised by the rest of the world. To date, no other state has recognised the Donetsk People's Republic, not even Russia.

It takes considerable effort and hard work to build a state from nothing, even one that is not officially recognised. The propaganda machinery seemed to turn day and night. The centre of Donetsk was plastered with colourful posters. Many of them were to encourage young people to join the army, others thanked Russia profusely for its support, and on some the prime minister, Alexander Zakharchenko, congratulated the republic's women on International Women's Day.

The Ministry of Finance blankly refused my request for an interview. I wanted to ask when the Novorossiya rouble, which had been announced as Donetsk's own currency, would be introduced. But I was told that the question was too sensitive. The Russian rouble would, for the time being, continue to be the valid currency of the breakaway republic. Foreign credit cards could not be used.

The ministry for tourism was not very keen to meet me either. But after several attempts, I managed to get a short interview. The ministry, which is officially called the Ministry of Sport, Youth and Tourism, operated from an apartment block, next to a launderette. Irina Kravtsova, "the head specialist", welcomed me rather nervously.

"Our ministry opened in November 2014," she said. "About forty people work here, which makes it the smallest ministry, but I would be bold enough to say that, despite that, we are one of the most active. Sport is our most developed field. One of our women swimmers recently won a competition in Moscow."

"Was she swimming for the Donetsk People's Republic or Ukraine?" I asked.

Irina hesitated.

"I am actually not sure," she said.

"What attractions do you recommend to tourists?"

"The church in Slavyansk and the salt mine in Artemivsk are our most popular attractions."

"But are Slavyansk and Artemivsk not both in Ukraine?" I said.

"Yes, that is true." Irina thought again. "Otherwise, there is the Azov Sea, which has very interesting flora and fauna. There are lots of places of interest in Donetsk. There is a miniature book museum in Gorlovka, for example. And we have a big zoo. Even though we unfortunately are not able to guarantee the safety of tourists at the moment, we have been able to invest in a large amount of sports equipment, thanks to the humanitarian aid from Russia. Our strategy now is to develop the domestic tourist market. We hope that our attractions will become well known and that people throughout the country will hear about them by word of mouth."

I was barely through the doors of School No. 57, when a woman with short red hair came rushing towards me.

"What are you doing here?" she snapped. "I am the head teacher. Why was I not told you were here? You have ruined my day!"

"I have a permit from the Ministry of Education," I said.

"I have not been told about it! What do you want to know? Everything is just fine, thank you very much. The children are suffering, of course. We are living in a war. They miss their friends. There now, I have answered all your questions. Why are you still here?"

I explained that I would like to talk to some of the pupils and other teachers. The angry woman stamped her foot and marched to her office to ring the ministry. When she came back, she sounded much happier and offered me some tea and cake.

School No. 57 is one of the schools in Donetsk that lies closest to the front line. The school had 450 pupils before the war, but only 140 when I visited. On October 1, 2014, a grenade landed by the school building. The biology teacher, who was standing on the steps outside the building when it exploded, was killed.

With the now placated head teacher's blessing, I went into one of the classrooms. Half of the desks stood empty. A girl was called up to the front and asked to read an essay they had been told to write.

"The Donetsk People's Republic was established on April 7, 2014, and the flag of the People's Republic is black, blue and red," she read, in an emotionless voice. "The black represents coal, the blue is the sea and the red is the blood of the soldiers."

"Very good, Sasha," the teacher said. "Is there anyone who knows the names of some famous people from Donetsk?"

A thin girl put up her hand.

"Lenin?"

When the lesson was almost over, the teacher gathered all the children in front of the blackboard and asked them to sing the national anthem. The children obediently warbled their way through a song that had the same tune as the old Soviet national anthem. In the new Donetsk version, the word "miner" was repeated frequently.

Mining was clearly an important part of the Donbass identity. The region's coal mines were its most important source of income in the Soviet era. People had to work hard, but were relatively well paid and their jobs were secure. In the 1990s, many of the mines were closed, which might explain why so many people were negative about the government in Kiev – they blamed the Ukrainian authorities for the closures. More mines have been closed since the war began, and illegal mining is now a major problem. The days when Donbass was the primary motor of the Ukrainian economy are very definitely over. But in truth, it is many years since the end of the coal age.

"Patriotic Education is such a new subject that we don't have

any textbooks yet," the teacher, Violetta Boiko, told me apologetically at the end of the lesson. "It was introduced in January this
year, and is obligatory for all pupils."

How many inhabitants of the Donetsk People's Republic actually
supported the new regime?

It is possible that the empty streets said it all.

In January, two months earlier, the statue of Lenin in Lenin
Square in Donetsk was blown up after several attempts. It was then
ordered that all Lenin statues in the republic be guarded around
the clock by armed police.

On my last evening there, I met Sasha and Sveta, who were
friends of Chris and Anya, the couple with whom I had shared a
car to Donetsk. They had both been born and raised there, but
they supported the Ukrainians in their fight against the separatists.
They were in good humour that evening, almost euphoric. Sasha,
who was fifty-three and already retired, had not been out of her
flat for weeks.

"We can't leave," Sveta said. "Sasha and I are too old to start
again somewhere else."

"Lots of people only support the People's Republic because
they cannot stand Poroshenko and the Ukrainian government,"
Sasha explained. "All the propaganda and arms come from Russia.
But Russia does not need Donetsk. So why are they helping us?
Let me tell you: Russia needs a bleeding arm. They need Ukraine
to bleed."

"Our hope is that one day Donetsk will be a part of Ukraine
again," Sveta said. "But that hope dies a little with every day that
passes."

The queue to leave the People's Republic was a least a kilometre
long. Dima, our driver, waved my press card and we were allowed to

drive past all the waiting cars. A soldier cast a desultory eye over our luggage. No-one smuggles anything *out* of Donetsk.

"Remember to hide your Donetsk press card when you get back over to the Ukrainian side," the soldier told us as he waved us over the border.

The queue was even longer on the Ukrainian side.

"They have been waiting since yesterday," Dima said. "Sometimes the queues are so long that people have to wait three or four days to get through."

People from Donetsk have regularly to cross the border to the Ukrainian side to draw their pension, visit relatives or fill their fridges. Smuggling is widespread. There is a shortage of most goods in the People's Republic.

"How was it to be back after such a long time?" I asked Anya, once we were safely in Ukrainian territory again.

Her eyes filled with tears.

"Things are so different there now," she said. "There are so few people in the streets. Donetsk used to be a lively town. No-one smiles anymore. A lot of my friends are no longer my friends. They have swallowed the propaganda and are now pro-Russian. The war is dividing Donetsk and pulling people apart."

Express Train to Kiev

While the other trains soon fill up, there are always plenty of seats on the Ukrainian Intercity Express trains. The Intercity Express route between Donetsk and Kiev was opened in time for the U.E.F.A. European Championship in 2012 to transport football fans from the capital to the new football stadium in Donetsk within six hours. The same year, a new express train was also introduced between Dnepropetrovsk, Ukraine's fourth largest city, and Simferopol on the Crimean Peninsula. However, all trains to Crimea and the breakaway republic in the east have now ceased; the express train between Donetsk and Kiev still runs, only it now stops at the second last station, Konstantinovka, a sad little industrial town in Ukrainian-controlled territory. A first-class ticket from there to Kiev costs about twenty pounds, which is a not inconsiderable sum in Ukraine, where the average monthly wage is about the same. Many people earn even less.

I leaned back in the soft seat. The Hyundai train slid softly along the rails, passing run-down Ukrainian villages at top speed. A few hours later, about halfway to Kiev, I got off. I wanted to see for myself the place where Charles XII's exhausted troops met Peter the Great's army in 1709. It is strange to think that today's neutral and democratic Sweden was once a military power that killed and plundered its way through Europe with plans of marching on Moscow.

In the sixteenth and seventeenth century, the Swedes conquered the greater part of the Baltic region and Gulf of Finland to become the strongest power in the Baltic. By the mid-seventeenth century, Sweden had the most territory in Europe, second only to Russia. The Swedish Empire stretched from Trøndelag in the middle of Norway to St Petersburg, and included parts of northern Germany as well as Finland and the Baltic provinces. Yet only one and a half million people lived in this large empire. By comparison, the Russian Empire had a population of fourteen million, and France twenty. But Sweden did have the most modern and efficient army in Europe.

In 1682, Peter I, better known as Peter the Great, was crowned tsar at the tender age of ten. He was no more than a child and liked to spend his time building and sailing boats. As he grew up, his ambitions also grew, without his losing interest in boats and sailing: Peter the Great's dream was to make Russia a maritime superpower. He first attempted to conquer the port areas on the Black Sea, but was unsuccessful, so he turned his sights west instead. In 1700, his troops besieged the Swedish-controlled town of Narva, on the current Estonian–Russian border. The clearly inferior Swedish army, led by the then eighteen-year-old Charles XII, were blessed by a snowstorm that blew up behind them and blinded the Russians, who panicked and fled, suffering great losses. Full of confidence, the young Swedish king progressed south to strike a deal with Saxony and Poland and the elector king, August the Strong. In the meantime, Russia took several Swedish territories in the Gulf of Finland, including the Nyenschantz fortress at the mouth of the Neva River. This was where Peter the Great founded St Petersburg in 1703, and thus achieved his goal of having a port on the Baltic. Charles XII was still busy fighting August the Strong, and ordered his troops in the Baltic provinces not to take action. They could always win back Nyenschantz at a later date.

Following a five-year, essentially pointless war, Charles XII finally made peace with Saxony and Poland. The Russians continued to take Swedish fortresses, including Narva. Tsar Peter offered to return the new territories to the Swedes if the Russians were allowed to keep St Petersburg, but Charles XII would not agree. In August 1707, the mighty Swedish army, which at the time comprised 34,000 soldiers, plus servants, cooks, wives, stable hands, prostitutes and whatever or whoever else was needed to keep it running smoothly, turned east.

The Swedish soldiers were far more professional and proficient than most other soldiers in Europe at the time, and in direct combat they were unbeatable. Their weakness, however, was a lack of stamina. A lot of food is needed to feed well over fifty thousand people, and Peter the Great knew how to use this to his advantage. As far as was possible, the Russians avoided direct combat, and burnt all villages, stores and supplies along the way before the Swedes could reach them. Every now and then, there were some confrontations and every time they ensured the enemy suffered great losses. And so, by means of gunfire and exhaustion, the Russians forced the Swedish army further and further back into what is now Ukraine.

The winter of 1708–9 was the coldest there had been in five hundred years. The soldiers suffered terribly, but the king ordered them to keep moving south. "The field-surgeons worked round the clock. Barrels filled with amputated limbs taken from victims of frost-bite," wrote the Swedish historian Peter Englund in his bestseller about the Battle of Poltava. "The soldiers waded through the floodwaters, and often, with no wood-fires to warm them, camped in the field soaked through, under open skies. When the night frost set in, their clothes were transformed into icy armour."[20]

In May 1709, the starving, exhausted and dramatically depleted Swedish army reached Poltava. The king ordered them to lay siege to the town in order to lure the Russians into direct combat.

While the Swedes waited for Peter the Great's army to appear, they built ramparts and prepared for battle. The Russians struck camp on the other side of the city. They also prepared for the fight.

That winter, Charles XII had entered into a defence alliance with the leader of the Cossacks, Ivan Mazepa. Mazepa saw an opportunity for the Cossacks to be free, as they had been for a short period in the mid-seventeenth century. He agreed to provide the Swedes with military support on the basis of bold promises of self-determination and freedom. Mazepa and Charles XII made comprehensive plans for future trade with the Ottomans once victory had been secured. But in the end, only three thousand of Mazepa's men decided to support the Swedes, while the others remained on the side of the Russian tsar.

An ambush was the only way the Swedes might win against the far bigger Russian army. It was decided that this would take place at dawn on June 27.* The Swedes would attack from several positions at once, thus surprising the sleepy Russians. Charles XII could not himself take part in the battle, as he had injured his foot while out on a reconnaissance expedition a few days earlier.

On the night in question, several of the Swedish commanders managed to get lost and were therefore delayed by several hours. In the meantime, the Russians had realised that something was afoot and had readied themselves for an attack. Approximately eighteen thousand Swedish soldiers took part in the battle, of whom roughly seven thousand were killed and a further three thousand were taken prisoner. Charles XII and Ivan Mazepa managed to escape south to Bender, which at that time belonged to

---

* The battle took place on June 27 according to the Julian (O.S.) calendar which the Russians used until the time of the revolution, or July 8 according to the Gregorian (N.S.) calendar, which is used today in Russia, or June 28 according to the Swedish calendar, which was used from 1700 to 1712, as a step in the move from the Julian to the Gregorian calendar.

the Ottoman Empire and is now in the Moldovan breakaway republic of Transnistria. Mazepa died soon after they got there, whereas Charles XII stayed there in exile for five years.

After the defeat at Poltava, Sweden's days as a superpower in the Baltic were over. The following year, Russia conquered the Baltic provinces, including Vyborg and Karelia, and thus managed to become the undisputed superpower in Northern Europe within a decade. Ukraine remained divided between Poland, Russia and the Ottoman Empire, and before long Austria would also get involved in this complex equation.

When Mazepa died, so did the Ukrainian Cossacks' sporadic attempts at independence. In 1714, under some duress from his Turkic host, who was weary of feeding the Swedish king and his large entourage, Charles XII returned to Sweden. In 1716 and 1718, he made two unsuccessful attempts to invade Norway, presumably to compensate for the territories he had lost in the Baltic. He was shot at the Fredriksten Fortress in Halden, not far from the Swedish border, on December 11, 1718.

The Great Northern War ended with the Treaty of Nystad in 1721. The Swedes lost all the territories they had acquired in previous centuries. The former Swedish Baltic provinces and Karelia, including the city of Vyborg, were ceded to Russia.

I wandered around the area where Charles XII and Peter the Great had set up camp more than three hundred years earlier, outside the centre of Poltava. Between the Swedish and Russian ramparts, there is now a road. The decisive battle actually took place some distance from the ramparts on a flat piece of ground that is today covered in trees.

"They ran forward with death before their eyes and were in large part mown down by the thunderous Russian cannon before they could find employment for their muskets," infantry lieutenant Friedrich Christoph von Weihe is quoted as saying in Peter

Englund's book.[21] "In other words the Swedes were mown down before they were close enough to shoot."

On the Swedish memorial outside the city museum, it simply says: *Time heals all wounds.*

The express train carried me on through Northern Ukraine to Kiev, a city which is also closely associated with the Swedes.

Unless one likes Stalinist architecture, the Ukrainian capital is not the sort of city that inspires love at first sight. The main street, Khreshchatyk, was completely destroyed during the Second World War. Prior to their forced retreat, the Red Army planted remote-controlled mines in many of the buildings that lined the avenue. In September 1941, when the Germans had captured the Ukrainian capital and installed themselves in the best buildings in town, the mines were exploded from hundreds of kilometres away. It was the first time that remote-controlled explosives were used in war. Within only a few minutes, three hundred buildings were reduced to rubble in an inferno of smoke, dust and flames. The avenue was widened by almost a hundred metres after the war and lined with monstrous, alienating buildings in classic socialist style.

The only person to describe the origins of Kiev is Nestor the Chronicler in the *Primary Chronicle*, otherwise known as *The Tale of Bygone Years*. If it is to be believed, Kiev was founded by three brothers, Kyi, Shchek and Khoryv, in 482. In Ukrainian, the city is called Kyiv, after the first of the three brothers. The *Primary Chronicle* was written in 1113, in all likelihood by a monk called Nestor, but only later transcriptions by other authors have survived to this day. Despite very limited and vague sources regarding the city's origins, Kiev's 1,500th anniversary was celebrated with great pomp in 1982.

Kiev's golden age was in part thanks to the Swedes. According to the *Primary Chronicle*, the Varangians – a name given to people from the north – were initially driven back across the sea by local tribes, who refused to pay tribute to them. They decided on self-rule instead, but that did not go too well. "... tribe turned against tribe. Disagreements arose between them and they started to fight. They said to one another: 'Let us find a prince who may rule over us, and judge us according to the law!'"[22] In 862, envoys from the Slav tribes sailed across the sea in search of the Varangians, who were also known as "Rus". The word is probably derived from Ruotsi, the Finnish word for Swedes, which in turn is derived from the Norse word *rodr*, to row, the root of which is found in the place name Roslagen in Swedish, but also in the name of Russia itself.

Rurik the Rus accepted the invitation and sailed back over the Baltic to settle in Novgorod for good, and rule over the Slav tribes. In 882, after Rurik's death, his successor, Oleg,* sailed down the Dnieper and established himself in Kiev. Oleg chased away the Khazars, a semi-nomadic Turkic people from Central Asia to whom the Slavs had been forced to pay tribute. Under Oleg and his descendants, the Kiev Empire grew into a power to be reckoned with in Eastern Europe. In the eleventh century, under Prince Vladimir the Great and Yaroslav the Wise, the Kiev Empire, or Kievan Rus as it was otherwise known, stretched from the Gulf of Finland and Moscow in the north, to the Carpathian Mountains and the Black Sea in the south.

Following Yaroslav's death in 1054, the empire was divided between his sons, and Kiev's position as a centre of power for the Slav tribes started to diminish. Then, in 1240, Kiev was invaded by the Mongols, and left in ruins. At the time, the city was home to fifty thousand people, of whom only two thousand survived. The Kiev Empire had very definitely had its heyday, but Rurik's descendants continued to rule over the eastern Slav principalities for

---

*   Helge in Scandinavian languages.

hundreds of years. Vasily IV, tsar of Russia from 1606 to 1610, was the last ruler in the Rurik dynasty. He died a prisoner outside Warsaw in 1612, a year before the first Romanov, Michael I, was chosen as tsar.

Only a few buildings and churches from the time of the Kiev Empire have survived. Pechersk Lavra, the Monastery of the Caves, stands on a small hill just outside the centre of Kiev. The monastery was founded by the monk Anthony and is counted as one of the most important places in the Orthodox Church.

I put on the green wraparound skirt, covered my head, bought a candle and followed the group of pilgrims down the narrow steps. The caves are whitewashed, and vary in size from about one to one and a half metres across and two metres high. The only source of light are the flickering flames of the pilgrims' candles. The mummified bodies of monks who lived here in the eleventh century can be seen in the alcoves, behind protective glass, preserved for posterity by the dry air. The pilgrims stopped by every coffin, crossed themselves and kissed the glass. Slowly the group moved forwards, without skipping a single mummy. Not surprisingly, given all the people and candles, the air was warm and stuffy. In high season, one of the monks is there to make sure that tourists do not follow the same route as pilgrims. But there was no monk on duty the day that I was there, and I followed the pilgrims' slow candlelit journey through the narrow labyrinth of corridors. When I emerged into the daylight, I was dripping with sweat.

Built during the reign of Yaroslav the Wise, St Sophia's Cathedral is even older than the Monastery of the Caves. Archaeologists believe that the foundations were laid as early as 1011, by Yaroslav's father, Vladimir I, the prince who brought Christianity to Kievan Rus. The cathedral was built in the same Byzantine style as Hagia Sophia in Constantinople, after which the Kiev cathedral is also

named. The interior walls are decorated with gold mosaics and frescos from floor to ceiling, many of which are far better preserved
than in its twin in Istanbul. The communists had plans to pull down
the cathedral and make a park in its place, but thanks to the great
efforts of scholars and historians, it was saved. In 1934, it was turned
into a museum. There are plans to open the building for worship
once more, but, as yet, the Orthodox Church and the Ukrainian
Greek Catholic Church have not been able to agree on who will be
able to use it.

St Michael's Monastery with its gold domes is a landmark in
Kiev and stands close to St Sophia's Cathedral. The beautiful
blue church with its bell tower was built only a few decades after
St Sophia's Cathedral, but was not so lucky when the communists
came. In the 1930s, there was some discussion about how much of
the original Byzantine church was left. Not much, the communists
concluded. So first the domes and mosaics were removed, then,
in 1936, the church and its bell tower were blown up. Only the
monks' refectory was preserved. There were several grand schemes
about how to use the monastery grounds, but nothing ever materialised, so in the end some tennis and volleyball courts were
laid there.

After the dissolution of the Soviet Union, the Ukrainian government decided to rebuild the monastery, and St Michael's
reopened its doors in 1991. The work has been done with great care;
the walls are covered in frescos, and, once again, the gold domes
adorn Kiev's skyline, but the sense of history is gone.

Not only the church suffered during Stalin's regime. Outside
the restored monastery is a memorial to the victims of the 1930s
famine. The organisation of agriculture into collective farms resulted
in a terrible famine in the Soviet Republic of the Ukraine, just as it
had in Kazakhstan, where more than a quarter of the
population starved to death. Farms were given strict production

quotas that were decided in the five-year plans, to ensure food supply to the cities. The first five-year plan ended in 1932. As the aim was to make both farming and production more efficient, these quotas were increased for not only the first year, but for each of the following four years. For many reasons, the harvest in 1932 was not as good as in previous years. Farmers were forced to hand over all the food they produced, and still could not meet their quotas. Any theft whatsoever, even if it was a handful of corn, was punishable by death. Armed police went from farm to farm and confiscated every grain of corn, every crumb of bread, every drop of milk, while children and adults starved in front of their eyes. Even though the government in Moscow received reports about the famine, which were stamped "top secret", they chose to interpret the failure to meet quotas as sabotage and to increase the quotas yet again for 1933. The police continued to carry out raids on the collective farms, in zealous pursuit of the grain that they believed the starved farmers were hiding from them.

As every attempt was made to keep the famine secret, there is no precise record of how many people died. Scholars have estimated that somewhere between three and four million people died as a result of the Soviet Union's inhuman agricultural policy in Ukraine. The famine is called "Holodomor" today, a shortening of *moryty holodom*, which means to starve someone to death. The Ukrainian authorities equate the Holodomor with genocide.

The new bell tower is now a museum that tells the history of St Michael's Monastery. As I walked up the stairs, I could read the story of the monastery from its foundation in 1108 by the unpopular Svyatopolk II, to life under the Mongols and the communists, up until the present day. Some helmets and first aid supplies served as reminders of the drama that had played out here only a few years before. During the three months of demonstrations, St Michael's was used as a resting place for the protesters in Maidan

Square. As the situation escalated in the second half of February 2014, many of the injured were taken to the monastery for first aid.

One never has to look far for victims of the revolution in Kiev. The street that leads to Maidan Square has been renamed the Avenue of Pain. All along the street, small niches have been created for the victims of police bullets. A Ukrainian flag, candles and fabric flowers frame the photographs of their often young, pure faces.

Even though the front line was far away, the faces of the war were ever present. At the entrances to metro stations and in the main squares, volunteers were collecting money for the soldiers. To attract people's attention, they had big boards with them displaying photographs of the fallen.

To date, more than ten thousand people have lost their lives in the war in Donbass. And there are nearly always more injured than dead in any war; it is estimated that more than thirty thousand people, perhaps even more, have been injured. Not to mention the psychological damage, which is seldom mentioned or recorded in any statistics.

In Bucha, a small suburb of Kiev, I met Anatoly Kushnirhuk, who administered pastoral care to soldiers on the front line.

"Everyone pays the price of war," Anatoly said. "There are only thirty-five thousand people here in Bucha, but more than three hundred have gone to join the front. Eleven have already come home in coffins. The soldiers' wives pay the highest price. They fight to keep their families together, they fight for their children, and they struggle financially, because not all the soldiers are paid. Eighty-five per cent of marriages end in divorce. The man who comes back from the war is not the same man who left – it is only the same body that comes home. Some drink to forget. Others become angry and violent. Some have to turn the radio up to full volume before they can sleep. Some can hardly wait to go back. *They* are the ones who really need help, the ones who have become addicted to war. There have not been many suicides yet, but believe me, they will come."

The military hospital in Kiev was like a labyrinth. Not a single bed was empty. Young men were rolled down the corridors in wheelchairs, others hobbled along on crutches, with a stump where there should have been a leg. One of the men moving laboriously along the corridor, metre by metre, was twenty-five-year-old Pima. His face was scarred and his mouth and eyes had lost their original shape. The tunnel where he was hiding had been hit by a large bomb. He had spent the past two years in hospital.

"I was one of the first to be mobilised, but I was happy to go," Pima said. "This is Russia's war with us. Putin is like Hitler. How can one country just come and take over another country in the twenty-first century?"

A large man in his forties was sitting in a four-person ward. He did not want to tell me his name, but was happy to talk to me.

"The war has made me sick in the head," he said. "We all are. I went as a volunteer, bought a machine gun with my own money. I had permission to buy a weapon, so it was all legal. I was in Pisky and Marinka. And at the airport . . . Best not to remember what happened there."

His eyes darkened. He stared straight ahead.

"The government does not see us as people," he said. "We are just cannon fodder to them. We were not even given normal food there. Ukraine was not prepared for war. Ukraine was two hundred per cent unprepared! The equipment was old. Look, here are the cartridges we used. They are from the Soviet era. Nothing has improved, all our equipment is from the Soviet era. The separatists, on the other hand, have super-modern equipment, because they get everything from Russia. The majority of soldiers there are from Russia. The propaganda is so powerful that I've almost started to believe it myself."

Thirty-year-old Sergey was lying in the next room, his right leg in plaster. I guessed that he had been injured in the fighting, but he told me that he had in fact been run over while guarding a roadblock. The banalities of war. He had been run over by a drunk driver.

"Peace depends on the politicians, not the soldiers," Sergey said. "We just survive. We decide nothing."

He was going to go home to Odessa as soon as he was released from hospital. He had had enough.

In another room, I met forty-two-year-old Vasily. His right arm was full of scars and the lower arm was in plaster. He was wounded on August 12, 2014, and had been in various hospitals all over Ukraine since then. His arm was shorter as a result of all the operations, but he still had feeling in his fingers.

"At least I can still pray," he said, and demonstrated that he could still fold his hands. "I was in the first group to be mobilised. If they asked me again, I would still go back, I think. God's ways are inscrutable, and war chooses its victims. I am fighting for my people, for my wife, for my children, for the Ukrainian soil, not for the government or M.P.s!"

"What did you do before the war?" I asked.

"I worked in a paper factory," Vasily said. "But now that I am an invalid and cannot work anymore, I will have to get by on my pension. It is just over a hundred dollars a month."

He played with the cross that he had on a chain round his neck, along with his dog tag.

"Nearly all the men in my family have been soldiers," he said. "My grandfather was in Berlin. My father in Cuba. My uncle in Syria during the war between Israel and Egypt. My brother was in Afghanistan. I ended up in Donetsk. But that is enough now. I hope my son never has to go to war."

Time heals all wounds. Independent Ukraine's wounds are still bleeding, and every day more are inflicted. When the Cossack leader Khmelnitsky swore loyalty to the Russian tsar in 1654, the territories that fell under the tsar's protection were called Little Russia. This name was used until the nineteenth century and says a lot about how the Russians saw, and indeed probably still see, Ukraine. The existence of a distinct Ukrainian language was denied for a long time, and until as recently as the 1917 revolution there were severe restrictions in place regarding the use of Ukrainian as a written language. Currently, about seventeen per cent of the population in Ukraine are ethnic Russians, and a third have Russian as their mother tongue; the Russians and Russian-speaking Ukrainians generally live in Eastern Ukraine.

The Orange Revolution in 2004 came as a shock to Putin, who more than anything feared a similar revolt in Russian territory. Unfortunately, Viktor Yushchenko, the father of the Orange Revolution, did not manage to live up to the high expectations that he himself had built up at Maidan Square. His old rival, Viktor Yanukovych, won the presidential election in 2010, whereas Yushchenko only managed to secure 5.45 per cent of the votes. In his inaugural speech, Yanukovych emphasised Ukraine's role as "a bridge between East and West, and an integral part of both Europe and the former Soviet Union".

Yanukovych's failure to build a bridge between East and West was catastrophic. Nine years after the Orange Revolution, the Ukrainians once again filled Maidan Square to express their frustration. Yanukovych is now wanted for mass murder and fraud by the Ukrainian authorities, and rumour has it that he is living in luxury outside Moscow.

Luxury is nothing new for Yanukovych. His former home in Kiev has been renamed the "Museum of Corruption", and is open to curious visitors. Ticket sales are run by a private company, apparently the same company that looked after the property when Yanukovych lived there.

I optimistically set out on foot past the tennis court, swimming pool and heated pond that Yanukovych kept stocked with rare, exotic fish. I soon realised that I would not manage to see more than a fraction of the property if I chose to go under my own steam. Aware of this, the organisers hired out bicycles and scooters. It was also possible to pay for a guided tour in a golf buggy.

I opted for the buggy. We skipped the zoo and barely stopped, and still the guided tour took more than half an hour. An avenue of 150 types of spruce ran from the main gates to the golf course. There were also twenty fountains, a hundred cars and two helicopters on the site, as well as a chemical research institute – the best in the country, no less – where everything Yanukovych ate was tested in advance. The ex-president became increasingly paranoid, and towards the end of his tenure wore a bullet-proof vest and helmet whenever he ventured out. More than a thousand people worked on the estate, of whom four hundred were security.

The person who showed me round the main house, dressed in a red and black cape, was part activist, part guide. In one of the basement rooms, all the vases had been covered in snakeskin, except for one, which was covered in paper with a snakeskin print on it – Yanukovych had clearly been the victim of corruption and deception himself. The draft of a speech was displayed on his desk. The stress for each word was marked, which is normally the reserve of Russian language textbooks. The Russian classics in the bookshelves looked untouched. There were enormous television screens in every room, sometimes several, in heavy gilded frames. The two upstairs bedrooms with ensuite bathrooms were almost identical. One was for Yanukovych, the other for his mistress.

"His mistress originally worked as a maid in the Yanukovych household," the activist guide said. "His wife lived in Donetsk, and never moved to Kiev. They had not lived together for years, and everyone knew that. Apparently they only spoke on the telephone twice a year to say happy birthday."

The lift doors were enhanced with Swarowski crystals. There was a billiard table and a poker table in the games room, as well as several other tables. An intricate, hidden corridor had been built between the walls so that Yanukovych and his mistress need never see the servants. The artwork left on the walls had been declared worthless by the experts, but he had managed to take with him a number of paintings and other valuables when he fled to Moscow.

At the end of May 2014, there was another presidential election in Ukraine. The oligarch and chocolate king Petro Poroshenko was elected the country's new president, the fifth since the fall of the Soviet Union. Poroshenko, who had previously been both foreign minister and minister for trade, had financially supported the Orange Revolution in 2004, and the demonstrations in 2013 and 2014. A few weeks after his inauguration, he signed the economic section of an association agreement with the E.U. and promised to hold a referendum on Ukraine's membership of N.A.T.O. Given the current situation, joining N.A.T.O. is not on the cards for either Ukraine or Georgia, which no doubt was Putin's intention all along. Great Russia has shown the world that it will stop at nothing to put Little Russia in its place.

KAZAKHSTAN

Left and Above: Paradise on earth: Roma hopes that the whole world will one day come to Poporechnoye in the Altai mountains.

Above: After months inland, the briny breeze of the Caspian Sea was almost intoxicating.

Right: My visit to the cosmodrome in Baikonur had been agreed months in advance, but this was as close as I got to seeing a rocket.

CAUCASUS

The flame at Ateshgah Temple outside Baku burns eternally.

The many faces of war, from dismal border crossings to bombed blocks of flats. Dato Vanishvili woke up one morning to find himself in another country.

Gori: the modest dwelling where Stalin spent his early years is now housed inside a somewhat less modest building.

Georgia is still a "wonderland", as it was in Hamsun's day.

The Gergeti Monastery in Stepantsminda on an exceptionally clear and beautiful evening.

UKRAINE

The victims of war are ever-present in Kiev.

Vladimir, a professor of history, retrained as a tank driver when the war broke out. (© Christopher Nunn)

Holodomor: the famine in Ukraine in 1932–3 was devastating. Bare millstones surround this hungry little girl, who clutches a precious ear of corn.

The Chernobyl disaster as a tourist attraction: the physical remains of the catastrophe should not be touched.

BELARUS

Lenin still stands on his pedestal in front of the parliament building in Minsk, but the square has been renamed Independence Square.

Head of state on a minimum pension: Stanislav Shushkevic told me about his role in the dissolution of the Soviet Union.

Maia Levina-Karpina, one of the few survivors of the Germans' grotesque extermination of the Jewish population in the Minsk ghetto.

THE BALTICS

The land around Nida on the Curonian Spit has passed through the hands of many nations.

Narva lies so close to the border that you can see Russia on the other side of the river.

The Līgatne Bunker in Latvia. In the event of a nuclear war, the surviving leaders were expected to talk on a number of different telephones.

The monument to the Singing Revolution in Tallinn.

FINLAND & NORWAY

Above: The symbolic Three-Country Cairn, where Norway, Finland and Russia meet. Walking around the cairn is prohibited.

Right: The Finnish border guards keep an eye on their neighbours to the east from impressive watchtowers.

In summer 1969, Soviet tank guns on the far side of this bridge were aimed at Norwegian border troops for four nerve-racking days, until they disappeared as suddenly as they had appeared.

Group Tour to Chernobyl

Twenty bleary-eyed tourists met at the agreed place on Maidan Square not long after dawn. We were ushered onto the two minibuses, where we were shown an information film that lasted exactly the time it took us to drive the hundred kilometres from Kiev to the Zone, on the bumpy Ukrainian roads.

"A day trip to Chernobyl will expose you to less radiation than a long-haul flight," chirped the smiling lady, as she brandished the Geiger counter. A complicated equation rolled across the screen. Most people slept through the film about how doses of becquerels were calculated, but Roger Molinder from Stockholm was following carefully.

"For a long time I have had a bucket list of things I want to do and places I want to see before I die," he said. "My New Year's resolution is to cross off as many of the things on the list as I can. Life is short. I have wanted to visit Chernobyl since 2008, no, sorry, 2004 in fact, when I discovered it was possible to come here. Originally I thought I should come with someone, but then, well, I thought I might as well come on my own. It is not a long journey. I arrived in Kiev yesterday and I am leaving again tomorrow. It is easy to think that if I am going to be somewhere, I should try to see other things as well, but it never happens."

At the entrance to Chernobyl, we were given five minutes to photograph the city sign. We coincided with another group from another tourist agency. There was quite a squash in front of the Cyrillic concrete letters, then Sergey, our young guide, herded us back to the minibus. The next stop was the abandoned kindergarten.

"You have only fifteen minutes to take pictures," Sergey said. "Don't step on the grass. It is still highly radioactive."

We squeezed out of the minibus and started immediately to document the devastation. It was as though it had been bombed. Mattresses and teddy bears strewn across what had once been the floor, broken windows, a collapsing roof. Cameras clicked and Geiger counters beeped. You could hire them from the tour company for an extra ten dollars. Sergey guided a couple of British tourists over to a stone by the entrance. Their Geiger counter started to beep frantically and flash red.

"Cool," the Brits said. "Really cool."

Fifteen minutes later, Sergey counted us all back onto the bus.

"The authorities allow only ten per cent of a group to be lost. Only joking, hahaha."

Chernobyl was opened to tourism in 2001, and between ten and twenty thousand tourists visit every year.[*] Even though there were no cocktail umbrellas or sombreros or a singalong, it did feel a bit like a package holiday when we drove into Pripyat, where the workers from the nuclear power plant had lived. The city foundations were laid in 1970, the same year that Chernobyl was built, and it was officially proclaimed a city nine years later. In 1986, just under fifty thousand people lived there, of whom seventeen thousand were children. In the afternoon of April 27, one and a half days after the accident, the entire town was evacuated in less than four hours. The inhabitants were told they would be back in three days. As it stands today, Pripyat is a memorial to the Soviet era anno 1986, a radioactive time capsule. The wide streets are deserted, the apartment blocks are silent concrete shells, and

[*] In 2018 some seventy thousand people visited Chernobyl, with even more in 2019 following the success of the television mini-series of the same name.

nature has gradually started to take over the town. Trees and bushes have forced their way up through the asphalt.

"You have twenty minutes to take photographs inside the old school," Sergey said. "It says in the rules that it is not permitted to go into the neighbouring buildings, but obviously no-one pays any attention to that, hahaha."

The feeling of being in a war zone returned inside the derelict building. All the windows were broken. The ceiling panels were hanging from loose wires and the furniture lay higgledy-piggledy everywhere. There were still dusty posters with red slogans and portraits of Lenin hanging on walls.

The speed of decay was visible. Three decades, and everything falls apart.

Sergey guided us through the ghost town; he was clearly well practised. Once he had shown us the abandoned swimming pool, an overgrown football pitch and three basketball courts, it was time for the highlight: the iconic Ferris wheel, which has become the symbol of the Chernobyl disaster.

"There can be up to two hundred tourists here at a time," Sergey said. "Two hundred tourists who have all come to see an abandoned amusement park." His smile was ironic.

The amusement park in Pripyat was due to be opened as part of the Labour Day celebrations in 1986. The park was opened for a few hours in the morning of April 27, to distract the inhabitants before the evacuation. By this stage, most people in Pripyat knew that there had been an accident at the nuclear plant, but only a few understood how dangerous it was, and the local authorities did all they could to play things down.

The Chernobyl nuclear power station was the first to be built on Ukrainian soil, and was an R.B.M.K. type: a water-cooled, graphite-moderated, second-generation reactor. This type of reactor had been developed in the Soviet Union in the 1950s, and was not approved for use in the West, as the construction was deemed to be unstable. There was, among other things, a constant danger that the graphite would ignite, which is precisely what happened in Chernobyl.

In the evening of April 25, 1986, the nuclear physicists at the plant turned off a number of security functions in Reactor No. 4, including the cooling system. They planned to carry out a risky test the following day to establish how long the generators would continue to produce electricity for the cooling pumps in the event of a system shutdown. The test went terribly wrong. At 1.23 a.m. on April 26, the energy level in the reactor rose to 120 times its normal level and the pumps failed. A few seconds later, the reactor exploded. The protective lid, which weighed more than a thousand metric tons, was blown to pieces, releasing large amounts of radioactive dust into the atmosphere, which spread over a vast area. The radiation and fallout were estimated to be two hundred times greater than that released by the atom bombs over Hiroshima and Nagasaki.

Two days later, the alarm went off at the Swedish nuclear power station Forsmark, north of Stockholm. One of the employees' shoes had triggered it during a routine check. It was quickly established that the radioactivity was not from the power plant itself, as had first been feared, and thus the conclusion was drawn that there must have been an accident in the Soviet Union. On April 29, Chernobyl was on the front page of the *New York Times*, but the authorities in Moscow still tried to deny the catastrophe. In Kiev and other surrounding cities, the Labour Day celebrations went ahead as planned, with parades and speeches outdoors. It was not until May 6, ten days after the accident, that schools in Kiev were closed and people in the affected areas were advised to stay indoors as much as possible.

On May 14, Mikhail Gorbachev, leader of the Soviet Union,

officially announced the accident for the first time. "The worst is over," he assured people, before he lambasted foreign governments and media, accusing them of spreading lies and hostile propaganda.

At Chernobyl Hospital in Kiev, doctors still have more than enough to do, thirty years after the accident.

"We have 310 patients in for treatment right now," the senior consultant, Galina Tinkiv, said, when I visited her office after the group tour. "We reckon that we will continue to receive Chernobyl patients for another thirty years. It takes time for the isotopes to break down, and some of the symptoms are slow to develop. The symptoms and illnesses do vary, but generally, the immune system breaks down. A high incidence of thyroid cancer has been recorded in the Chernobyl area."

Anatoly Protsenko was one of the 310 patients. He had been working as a fireman in Chernobyl. He went to work at six in the morning on April 6, to relieve the night shift. He remained at work for four days straight.

"I turned twenty-five on April 27," he said. "I celebrated with tears in my eyes, because my family was evacuated from Pripyat that day. On the fourth day I was really not well. I felt sick and had a headache, and eventually passed out. I was in hospital for forty-five days, but would rather not go into any details, if you don't mind. I kept on passing out. When I was released from hospital, I didn't know where my wife and children were."

He has since been in hospital countless times.

"I am alive today thanks to the doctors here," he said. "They have saved my life, again and again."

Seven of the firemen who were there died of acute radiation sickness soon after. According to the official statistics, thirty-two people died from radiation-related causes in the first few months after the accident, among them helicopter pilots and technicians. Many of those who survived are still plagued by health problems. There is no exact record of how many are still sick or how many have lost their lives as a result of the Chernobyl explosion, but the Ukrainian authorities estimate that there are at least three million Chernobyl victims, and more than four million people still live in areas affected by radioactive fallout in Ukraine and Belarus.

There are countless stories.

Alexander Syrat's is one such.

On April 26, 1986, Alexander Syrat was eight. He got up, ate breakfast and went to school as usual, but what should have been a very ordinary Saturday was anything but. All the teachers were in a meeting so the pupils were left on their own in the classroom. They could hear sirens from the Accident and Emergency unit just down the road. When the bell rang and the teachers had still not returned, Alexander and a friend decided to go down to the hospital to see what was happening. The adults pushed them out of the way, but one did say that there was a fire at the nuclear power plant. The two boys ran to the bridge to have a look, as there was a clear view to the plant from there. It was only a couple of kilometres away, but they were disappointed, as they could not see much – the power plant was hidden behind either smoke or thick fog. A helicopter landed on the riverbank, and then took off again. Alexander and his friend stood there watching as it disappeared. When they could no longer see it, they went down onto the riverbank and started digging in the sand where the helicopter had landed. They stayed there until the end of the school day. His mother wondered why her son was covered in sand when he came home. Alexander lied and said that they had all had to help clean the playground and classroom.

In the evening, a representative from the town council knocked on the door and told them that Pripyat was to be evacuated, temporarily. Alexander and his mother quickly packed their things and went down onto the street, but nothing happened. The adults stood smoking and chatting on the pavement, while the children ran around and played. When they realised they were not going to be evacuated that day, they went in again. Alexander's mother sat up and watched the glow in the sky from the fire.

At two o'clock the following afternoon, the buses arrived to evacuate them. The police sealed the door to their flat and they were allocated seats on a bus and driven away. Because it was a warm day, the windows on the bus were open.

"Pripyat was a very ordinary town," Alexander said. "There is really no reason to glorify it because of what happened. But I spent the best years of my childhood there. After the accident, my childhood was over. I spent twenty-five months in hospital over the next seven years. And I am still sick."

He did not want to talk about his illness or the symptoms. It was too private. But he was more than happy to talk about politics.

"I don't blame anyone, but I hate the Soviet system," he said. "We were not *ready* for nuclear power. They swapped five-year plans for three-year plans. Chernobyl was one of the main factors underlying the collapse of the Soviet Union. Even though the government got help from the international community, the evacuation, damage and clean-up cost an extraordinary amount of money. And everyone knew that the government had been caught in the most devastating lie; they cared nothing about ordinary people."

Before I left, Alexander took me over to an enclosure by his house, where three stocky Przewalski horses were grazing peacefully. The rare wild horses were introduced to the area around Chernobyl at the end of the 1990s, as an experiment. They have since mated so successfully that they have become a pest and a threat to the environment.

"People around here shoot them because they eat all the grass," Alexander said. "I saved these three."

In the absence of people, animal life has thrived in Chernobyl, and to the astonishment of scientists, they do not seem to be particularly affected by the radiation. The exclusion zone covers 2,600 square kilometres, and is home to large wolf packs, bears, foxes and rare birds.

And a few people who have moved back.

Approximately two hundred villages and hamlets were evacuated as a result of the disaster, which amounted to more than 350,000 people. About two thousand of them moved back into the Zone, as the evacuated area is called, in the first few years. The police tried very hard to get them to leave again, but in the end gave up.

There are now fewer than 170 people living in the Zone, as those who returned are dying out.

Eighty-year-old Ivan Semenyuk and his wife Maria, who is seventy-eight, are two of the few who stayed on.

The ground had been covered by a light layer of snow overnight, the Ukrainian winter's final fling, but Ivan and Maria's house was warm. And messy. There were pills, food and clothes everywhere: on the beds, on the floor, on the tables.

"I dropped a pot of hot water on my foot a month ago," Ivan said in a reedy voice, pointing at all the creams cluttering the bedside table, "and it is not healing. The doctors are no help whatsoever. In the days of the Soviet Union, they used to come to your house to treat you. Now, they don't even answer the telephone when you ring."

He offered me and Maxim, the official Chernobyl guide, some moonshine and lukewarm coffee in a mug that looked as though it had not been washed for months. Maria sat on a stool and listened in silence. She nodded off every now and then.

"Four hundred people used to live here!" Ivan shouted. "No-one locked their doors. No-one stole anything!"

"Are you not afraid of the radiation?" I asked.

"No, it is not dangerous," Ivan said. "I can feel the radiation, like heat on the skin. I have a very sensitive face. When we were evacuated after the accident, I was ill. I thought I was going to die. The water there, at the new place, was not clean. Lots of people got tuberculosis and other illnesses from the water. I could not breathe there. They gave us a house, but it had been built in haste and was poorly constructed. The air here is clean. We eat everything, mushrooms, vegetables, herbs, fish. It is all safe. Most of my friends who were evacuated have died."

Ivan had no intention of going anywhere else.

"It is not a particularly nice place to live," he said. "Everything is falling apart, or destroyed. But there is a time for moving and a time for dying. And now is the time to die."

The other houses in the village were like timber skeletons. The windows were broken, the roofs had caved in, and weeds, bushes and trees were taking over the walls.

In one of the houses at the edge of the village the windows were intact, however, and a pale grey smoke was circling up from the chimney. Maxim and I went in. Maria Upurova, who was eighty-one, was sitting on a bed at the far end of the room. She had suffered a stroke three years earlier, and could no longer walk without crutches. An open bible lay by the bed. The room smelt like old, sour milk. A fat cat wove around our feet.

When Maria heard that we had just been to see Ivan, she got very agitated.

"Ivan Ivanovych stole all my things!" she shouted. "The loggers said they saw him carrying my things out. We don't talk to each other anymore. What hurts even more is that they are family. His wife, Maria, is my cousin. They thought I was dead, but I was just in hospital. They took everything. Cushions and curtains. When I came home, the house was empty."

Maria Upurova and her husband moved back to the deserted village in autumn 1986. Every time the police came for an inspection, they hid. Maria eventually told the police: "If you take me away from here, I will go and lie in a graveyard with the dead."

After that, they left her in peace.

In 2012, Maria's husband died and a year later she had her stroke. Her son came and took her to live with him, but in 2015 she moved back to the Zone.

"I did not get on with my daughter-in-law, she doesn't like me," she said. "And anyway, this is my home. I was born here. Living anywhere else is not a good idea. But I cannot forgive Ivan Ivanovych and his wife for coming and taking my things . . ."

In an attempt to find out what actually happened, we went back to Ivan Semenyuk. Maxim was nervous.

"The last time the subject was broached, he got very upset," he said. "I am worried that he might have a turn."

I promised to tread carefully.

"But don't be too careful," Maxim said. "Soviet people are straightforward, they don't understand niceties, they understand plain talk."

Ivan welcomed us back, curious as to why we had returned. We explained as politely as we could, while being direct.

"Maria Ivanovna, right!" Ivan shouted. "I'll tell you what happened. The lock was broken! It was her friends who stole from her. The lock was no good, it was never used. Her friends knew where everything was. I never went there, I gave the key to her friends. It was her friends who took everything after they got drunk with the loggers. I saw them sitting there in the backyard, but didn't want to get involved."

His wife let out a heavy sigh in the bedroom.

"It is worse for her," Ivan said. "Maria Ivanovna is her cousin. Look around, I have so many things, I don't need any more! I am the only man here with four women, and it is not easy, let me tell you. Four grandmothers and me! Personally, I think it was the daughter-in-law who threw away Maria's things. In her eyes, they were worthless, unusable."

He followed us to the door, and past the chicken run, over to the gate that opened onto the deserted street.

"We were all friends here before. No-one locked their doors. Now we don't talk to one another."

Borderland

Coming to Lviv was like coming to another country. Polish tourists and schoolchildren on day trips wandered around the beautiful streets, which are flanked by a mishmash of medieval and baroque buildings, inspired by Italian, German and Eastern European architecture. Lviv was one of the few cities in the region that escaped the relentless bombing of the Second World War, and the historical centre is a U.N.E.S.C.O. World Heritage site.

I went with the flow and wandered up and down narrow cobbled streets and lanes. When I felt tired, I stopped at one of the countless cafes for a cup of strong coffee and the occasional piece of warm apple strudel, before setting off again on my meander through snow-covered streets. It was nearly April, but still snowing lightly, and the bitter northerly wind managed to cut through my layers of clothes. Despite the cold weather, Lviv was a revelation: charming small squares, souvenir shops, Catholic churches and a welcome normality. The war in the east felt very distant. Everything I associated with Ukraine seemed to be distant: the sad Soviet buildings, stray dogs in the street, the dreary restaurant menus, poverty and decay. In contrast to Kiev or Odessa, everyone in Lviv spoke Ukrainian. Everywhere I went, I was surrounded by the melodic, melancholy Ukrainian language, which here in the west, so close to the Polish border, sounded almost Polish. And even though I addressed them in Russian, people more often than not answered in Ukrainian.

Only a hundred years ago, however, it was more usual to hear

Polish, German or Yiddish on the streets of Lviv. Poles were in the majority, but Jews were the most important minority. Ukrainians accounted for only a fifth of the population.

Lviv was founded in 1256 by Daniel of Galicia, a descendant of Rurik.* Daniel was the first king of Galicia, the border region between what is now Poland and Ukraine. On the other hand, he lost Kiev to the Mongols. The town was named after his eldest son and successor, Lev. Over the centuries, Lviv has had many rulers and has belonged to many different empires, and this is reflected in the many variations of the city's name. In German, it is known as Lemberg, while the Poles call it Lwów and the Russians Lvov. In French, it is called Léopol, and in Latin Leopolis: "lion city".

For more than four hundred years, from 1339 to 1772, Lviv was part of the Kingdom of Poland, and from 1772 to 1918, Lviv, or Lemberg, was the capital of the Kingdom of Galicia and Lodomeria, which in turn was part of Austria–Hungary. After the First World War, Galicia and Lodomeria was for a few months part of the independent West Ukrainian People's Republic, before the entire region was integrated into Poland, following fierce fighting. During the Second World War, Lviv was occupied three times: first by the Soviet Union in 1939, then by the Nazis in 1941, then once again by the Soviet Union in 1944. At the end of the war, Lviv and East Galicia were incorporated into the Ukrainian Soviet Socialist Republic, and the Poles were driven out. For a quarter of a century now, since 1991, Lviv has been part of Ukraine. About ninety per cent of its inhabitants are now Ukrainian.

The history of Eastern Europe can make your head spin. Borders have moved back and forth through the centuries; countries have disappeared, only to reappear later. Others have been created. In terms of etymology, the word Ukraine is derived from the

---

* Also known as Daniel of Halych.

preposition *u*, which means "by" or "near", and *kraina*, which means "land", which in turn comes from *kray*, which means "edge", "end" or "border". In other words, the country on the border.* But as the country is so flat, there are few natural borders, so the borders have been fluid and forever changing. The current borders really only came into being with the dissolution of the Soviet Union. And they are moving once again as a result of Putin's aggressive and expansionist foreign policy.

For months, my journey along the Russian border had taken me west, from the Pacific to the Carpathian Mountains.

Now it was time to head north.

It is a little less than three hundred kilometres from Lviv to Brest, but the bus trip took ten hours. The bus driver was in no rush and kept a steady course north, through dense birch forest, along narrow, bumpy roads. The landscape was flat, and the roads were without any twists and turns, but to be fair to the bus driver, there were a lot of extended stops, especially at the border crossings.

The border check on the Ukrainian side started promisingly, but then quickly deteriorated. A border guard gathered in all our passports, and then we had to get out and identify our luggage.

"That suitcase, yes, it is mine."

"Do you have any sausages with you?"

"No."

When everyone had sworn that they had no sausages, we were allowed to board the bus again. Everyone was given back their passports except for me. A border guard I had not seen earlier came onto the bus and waved my passport.

---

* The name Ukraine appears in the *Primary Chronicle* in the twelfth century, but until the end of the nineteenth century, the Russians called it Little Russia, as mentioned before. The name Ukraine started to be used again during the national awakening towards the end of the 1800s.

"Who is the foreigner?" he asked.

I put up my hand.

"Follow me!"

The border station consisted of a barrier and two huts. I was taken into the smaller one.

"Where are you from?" the border guard asked, and peered at my passport. He presumably thought I was trying to read the cover, as he then picked it up so I could not see what it said.

"Well, don't you know where you are from?"

"Yes, of course, I am from—"

"What is your date of birth?" he barked. "And where were you born? Where was the passport issued?"

Following this inquisition, I had to drag all my luggage over to a table for closer inspection. I was told to empty the contents of my suitcase onto the table.

"What is this?" the chief customs officer asked, and held up my earplugs.

"Why do you have so many maps with you?" his colleague said.

He unfolded a couple and inspected them with suspicion. A third colleague began to look through my books, page by page. I started to get seriously worried that the bus would leave without me.

"What is all this?" the chief customs officer asked and held up my contact lens case. I tried to explain, but it was obvious he had no idea what contact lenses were. One of the officers went off with my receipts to study them more closely. A fourth officer appeared and started to check the contents of my toilet bag.

"What is *this*?" screamed the chief customs officer. He held out the sightseeing brochure I had been given by the Ministry of Tourism in Donetsk.

I tried to explain as well as I could, but was constantly interrupted by more prying questions. If they were this strict on the

Ukrainian side, what would they be like on the Belarus side? In a panic, I threw the Donetsk brochure in the nearest bin and started to delete photographs on my camera.

"What are you doing?" the chief customs officer snapped. "Put your camera down immediately!" He snatched it up and started to look through my pictures. His three colleagues stood behind him and looked at the pictures too, full of curiosity. Four hundred photographs later, they let me get back on the bus.

In no-man's-land, on our way towards the Belarus border, I continued to panic and delete photographs from my phone and camera, while I cursed myself for having been so stupid. I was about to enter a dictatorship and had not considered the border crossing.

A Belarusian border guard got on and collected our passports. We then had to get off the bus, pick up our luggage and wait in a queue to have it inspected. The customs officer cast a weary eye over the contents of my suitcase and waved me on. No-one was interested in my camera or my maps, and no-one asked any questions. Quarter of an hour later, our passports were returned to us, complete with all the necessary stamps. The border crossing would have been one of the fastest yet, had the customs officers not then dismantled the bus to look for contraband, presumably sausages. It did not take long to take the minibus apart, but it took longer to put it back together again, even though the driver was clearly used to it. While we waited, I spoke to a Russian couple who had been to Lviv to tell the man's grandmother that they were getting married.

"We drove all the way from Moscow, but left the car in Brest," the young woman said.

"Why did you do that?"

"It has a Russian registration plate, so we didn't want to take it into Western Ukraine," she said. "There are so many stories . . . We were told that they hate the Russians, and warned us not to speak

Russian. But it went well, very well, in fact. I loved Lviv. Everyone was so friendly, weren't they, Sasha?"

The bus was eventually ready to enter Belarus and we arrived in Brest a couple of hours later. I found an A.T.M. and withdrew a couple of a million roubles.* With my wallet bulging with banknotes, I hailed a taxi.

"Everything is so expensive now," the taxi driver complained. "There are no jobs to be had anymore, and no-one has any money because of the crisis. We are living in bad times."

From Ulan Bator to Brest, taxi drivers complained about the same things.

"At least you are in safe hands," the driver said, as we approached the hotel. "The K.G.B. are just over there, on the other side of the fence." He pointed to the big, grey building opposite.

Whereas the modern security service in Russia has changed its acronym to F.S.B., the Belarusian service has kept the old Soviet name.

The next morning I woke up with a bad cough and went out in search of a pharmacy. The streets in Brest were wide, and, as is often the case in dictatorships, immaculately clean. There were no cigarette butts or chewing gum to be seen. The pedestrians were well dressed, but their clothes were conservative: dark and discreet. No-one smiled, but, for the first time since North Korea, the cars did stop politely at every pedestrian crossing. The streets had familiar names such as October Street, Revolution Street, February Street and Karl Marx Street. A straight-backed Lenin stood by Lenin Square and pointed towards a Socialist future.

---

* Future visitors to Belarus are advised not to do this. In summer 2016, there was a currency reform, and the old roubles (B.Y.R.) were exchanged for new ones (B.Y.N.). One B.Y.N. is currently worth about forty pence.

There is much discussion about who the Belarusians actually are. Scholars do not even agree on the origins of the name Belarus, or White Russia. Some believe the name refers to the regions that were not conquered by the Mongols in the thirteenth century. Historically, there has never been a kingdom of White Russia. The independent Duchy of Polotsk, which now lies in the north of Belarus, was established in the ninth century, but soon became part of the Kingdom of Kiev. In the fourteenth century, large parts of what are now Belarus and Ukraine were incorporated into the Grand Duchy of Lithuania, and a couple of centuries later these then became part of the Polish–Lithuanian Commonwealth. When Poland was carved up between Russia, Prussia and Austria at the end of the eighteenth century, the territory that is now Belarus became part of the Russian Empire.

Like so many of the former Soviet republics, the Belarusians enjoyed a brief taste of independence in 1918, but it lasted only a matter of months. On January 1, 1919, the Belorussian Soviet Socialist Republic was established. Seventy-two years later, the state of Belarus was born. The Belarusian language has the same East Slavic roots as Russian and Ukrainian. Belarusian and Russian are both official languages; after two hundred years of targeted Russification, most people speak Russian. No more than fifteen per cent of all books published in Belarus are written in Belarusian.

The history of Brest is, if possible, even more fragmented: the city is first mentioned in the *Primary Chronicle* in 1019 when Kievan Rus took it from the Poles. In 1241, the city was torched by the Mongols, and again in 1500 by the Crimean Tatars. The Swedes conquered Brest and took it from the Poles in 1657 and again in 1706. In 1795, after Poland had been carved up for the third time, the city became part of the Russian Empire. Then, during the First World War, it was occupied by the Germans.

World history was made in Brest on March 3, 1918, when the

new Bolshevik government officially withdrew from the First World War and signed the Brest-Litovsk Treaty. Lenin was put under considerable pressure to accept the tough German demands, which involved giving up the Baltic countries, Belarus and Ukraine, as well as territories in the Caucasus, in order to secure peace. Strictly speaking, he had no choice. The Russian economy was in free fall, and the Russian army was imploding. Tens of thousands of soldiers had deserted. The peace treaty gave the newly established and controversial Bolshevik regime some sorely needed breathing space.

When Germany and the Central Powers capitulated later in the same year, the Brest-Litovsk Treaty was annulled. Not long after, the Bolsheviks regained most of Ukraine and Belarus, while the Baltic countries and Finland maintained their independence. Following a short and intense war between the Soviet Union and Poland, the westernmost third of Belarus, including Brest, fell into Polish hands. Twenty years later, in 1939, the Soviet Union invaded Poland, the Baltic countries and Finland, in line with a secret annex to the Molotov–Ribbentrop Pact, whereby Stalin and Hitler divided Eastern Europe between them. And so Brest became part of the Soviet Union again – for a short while. In 1941, German troops marched into the city and declared Brest a part of Reichskommissariat Ukraine. At the end of the war, Brest was transferred back to the Belorussian Soviet Socialist Republic.

I turned my back on Lenin's keen gaze and found a pharmacy. I gave the pharmacist a brief description of my sorry state, and she gave me an arsenal of cough mixture and throat pastilles, all in very serious-looking brown boxes.

"Do you have any pastilles that taste nice?" I asked hopefully.

"Medicine should not taste nice," was the brusque reply.

"Of course not," I mumbled, and put a 100,000 note down on the counter, then took a taxi to Brest's only tourist attraction of any significance, the Hero Fortress.

There was dramatic music playing in the main entrance, which was formed like an enormous Soviet star. With the exception of the church and the ammunition store, which had been rebuilt, the rest of the brick buildings were badly damaged with visible signs of gunfire and artillery shells.

The fortress was built at the start of the 1800s as part of the Russian Empire's defences to the west. It was of little use in the First World War, but during the Second World War it became a symbol of the Russian people's resistance and courage. In the spring and summer of 1941, the Soviet authorities received intelligence reports that Germany was planning to attack the Soviet Union, but Stalin stuck his head in the sand and refused to believe that Hitler would break the pact they had made. The Soviet Union was therefore woefully unprepared when the Wehrmacht attacked on the night of June 22, 1941. Operation Barbarossa, which involved a total of four million soldiers, the largest invading force in the history of the world, was under way. Brest fell within only a few hours; Minsk fell five days later. But, despite the increasing bombardment, the soldiers in the fortress held strong as their supplies of food, water and ammunition dwindled. It was not until June 29, a week after the initial invasion, that the last soldiers in Hero Fortress surrendered.

Families and couples wandered in and out of the ruins and the gigantic statues of heroes. The Courage Monument, a 32-metre-tall concrete head that is the jewel in the crown, was declared one of the world's ugliest monuments by C.N.N. in 2014. The following day, the television channel had to apologise following a storm of protests from the Russian leader, who felt that it had not shown enough respect for the Soviet Union's bloody history.

During the Second World War, the front moved back and forth across the flat, forested territory of Belarus. More than nine thousand villages were burnt to the ground and two to three million people, almost a third of the population, were killed.

The People who Disappeared

The train chugged steadily east across an unvarying, flat landscape. There were patches of snow here and there, and every so often the forest opened to reveal marshlands or a plain. Thin rays of gold pierced the clouds and the crowns of pine needles and birch leaves. The sunset was peach-coloured and seemed to last for ever. Once in a while we passed through small villages with rows of simple timber houses. I guessed the villages probably looked pretty much the same before the war, before German soldiers burnt them down, often with the inhabitants still inside, caught in an inferno of flames and smoke until they could no longer breathe, and the flames devoured their clothes, hair and flesh. Those who tried to escape were riddled with bullets.

Pine, birch, marshlands, open plains, timber houses, endless skies; the monotonous landscape made me drowsy. I did not wake up until we rolled into the station in Gomel, the easternmost town in Belarus, where I was due to change trains. The journey north to Vitebsk took seven hours, but an ambitious minister of transport could easily have cut the travel time by a couple of hours without much effort. The train stopped all the time, and in Mogilev, where President Alexander Lukashenko had qualified as a history teacher and agricultural economist, we stood in the station for nearly an hour. Just before the train started to move again, a rotund, blond man in his forties plonked himself down in the seat opposite me, even though there were plenty of empty compartments in the carriage. He immediately started to talk about the weather.

"Spring will be here soon," he said. "It is very beautiful here in spring. You are not from these parts, are you? Where are you from? Ah, from Norway? I thought you were Latvian. I have never been to Norway. I have been many places, but never there. What are you writing?" He leaned over towards my Mac as he asked.

"Just a travel diary," I said, and put the laptop away.

"Are you going to write any articles from here and send them home?"

"No," I assured him, suddenly on my guard. "I am a translator," I lied. Was he from the K.G.B.? There was something suspicious about his formal clothes, highly polished shoes, and the way he had come tumbling into the compartment.

"Personally, I sell milk," the fat man said. "I sell milk in Russia and the Baltic as well, so I travel a lot. How much does a litre of milk cost in Norway?"

I calculated in my head.

"About forty thousand," I said.

The fat man burst out laughing and slapped his thighs. "I should start doing business in Norway! Maybe you could help me?"

He told me that his name was Alexander, like the president, but that he had no time for him.

"I didn't vote for Lukashenko in the last election. In my opinion, you have a healthy democracy when the president changes after one or two terms."

Lukashenko has been the president of Belarus since 1994. In the 2015 election, he received 83.5 per cent of the votes.

"No-one I know actually voted for him," Alexander said. "We have a joke here that after the election, the president's closest adviser went to Lukashenko and said: 'Mr President, I have some good news and some bad news.' 'Tell me,' Lukashenko said. 'Well, the bad news is that no-one voted for you. The good news is that you have been re-elected.'"

He roared with laughter.

"Are you sure you are not going to write any articles while you are here?" he said, serious again, all of a sudden.

I assured him that I was only a translator and never wrote anything myself. Alexander nodded and stared out of the window for a long time, even though it was dark and there was nothing to see.

"Hmm, I am not looking forward to this," he said. "I am going to Vitebsk to see an old friend who is dying. He is originally from Gomel. The illness is a result of Chernobyl. There are so many who are ill, especially from the Gomel area. The wind direction just after the explosion meant that we were hit harder than the Ukrainians."

"I am surprised by how open you are about all this," I said. "I thought that people were afraid of saying anything negative about the president and his regime."

"I don't work for the state, so I can say what I want," Alexander said. "There is so much that is wrong with this country. People are still so caught up in the Soviet era. But give it time, give it a generation. Belarus has never been like Russia, we are our own people, we are Europeans, we are not like the Russians at all. The Soviet Union was catastrophic for us."

"Many of the Ukrainians I met said that Belarus was their favourite country because it reminded them of the Soviet Union," I told him. "And lots of the Westerners who come here do so precisely because they want to experience the last Soviet republic."

"Hah! They should have come when we were a Soviet republic!" Alexander shouted. "Everywhere was empty, we had nothing, no goods, only queues! Now you can get whatever you want here. The streets still have Soviet names, and there are Lenin statues everywhere, it's true, but they are superficial things. And with time, they too will disappear. The Ukrainians have already got rid of them, but we obviously need more time. A lot of the older generation miss the Soviet days, they are nostalgic. Give us time." He lowered his voice.

"But we do have one major problem. People drink too much. There are a lot of alcoholics here, especially in the rural areas, which is why life expectancy is so low. The women drink as well. Tomorrow is Friday; go into town in the evening and see for yourself. I personally don't drink, but I do have a vice that I can't seem to give up. I smoke."

He went out into the corridor for a cigarette. When we got to Vitebsk, he carried my suitcase over the bridge and down to the taxi rank.

"If people ask, say you are from Riga," he said, in parting. "Then they will like you straightaway. We are kindred spirits!"

A painter had brought me to Vitebsk. Marc Chagall, or Movsha Khatskelevich Shagalov as he was originally called, grew up here, the eldest of nine children.

Chagall was born in 1887. At the time, Vitebsk had a population of about sixty thousand, more than half of whom were Jewish. The city had thirty synagogues and a thriving Jewish cultural life. Chagall grew up in a deeply religious home and Yiddish was the family language. His father, who worked for a local herring merchant, went to the synagogue every morning before work, and his grandfather was a cantor in the synagogue.

It was not a coincidence that so many Jews lived in Vitebsk. Before the town became part of the Russian Empire in 1772, it had been part of the Polish–Lithuanian Commonwealth. The eastern part of the commonwealth had been a haven for Jews since the Middle Ages, and as a consequence many Jews had moved there over the centuries. When Poland was divided at the end of the eighteenth century, the region became part of Russia. Just short of half a million Jews lived within the empire, giving Russia the highest Jewish population in the world. In 1800, a quarter of the world's Jews lived in Russia. This was a new situation for the

Russian government, as there had been very few Jews in the country before that. Strict regulations were quickly imposed on the Jewish population. Catherine the Great decided that Jews who did not willingly convert to Christianity could only live in the eastern areas that had become part of Russia as a result of the division of Poland, and in parts of New Russia, such as Odessa and Crimea. The area in which Jews were allowed to live was about the size of France, and today encompasses Belarus, Ukraine, Moldova, parts of Poland, Latvia, Lithuania and West Russia. The restrictions on where exactly the Jews could live within these borders were forever changing. For example, they were not allowed to live in Kiev, Sevastopol or Yalta, nor in agricultural areas. Exceptionally wealthy or highly esteemed Jews were granted permission to live in Moscow or St Petersburg.

Jews were also not allowed to attend Russian schools, but Chagall's mother, who had great ambitions for her son, managed to bribe someone to give him a place in one of the town's Russian schools. She thought he could become a clerk or an accountant, but her son had other plans. He had dreamt of becoming an artist from a young age, and when he was nineteen, he left for St Petersburg with nothing more than twenty-seven roubles in his pocket. "Vitebsk, I am deserting you. Stay alone with your herring."[23]

Chagall did not have the necessary permission to live and work in the Russian capital and was dependent on financial support from rich philanthropists. Fortunately there were many who saw the young man's talent and, with their support, he studied at various art schools. In 1910, Chagall headed west to Paris. He did not have much money, yet was freer in Paris than he had ever been as a Jew in Russia. He joined the avant-garde movement, and his poetic, dreamlike, colourful paintings were admired by the poet Guillaume Apollinaire. In 1914, Chagall returned to Vitebsk to marry his fiancée, Bella Rosenfeld. He had only intended to stay for a few months, but the First World War broke out and was followed by the Russian Revolution and civil war between the Reds and the Whites. He was there for eight years. The Jews were liberated by the Bolsheviks, as was art, in principle at least. Chagall quickly became popular with the revolutionaries and was appointed commissioner of the arts in Vitebsk. He arranged a street party in the town, with colourful flags and banners, to mark the first anniversary of the revolution. The new commissioner of the arts was asked why the banners were decorated with green cows and flying horses; what did they have to do with Lenin and Marx? Not long after, Chagall fell out with the leading lights of the Russian avant-garde, who tried to force his art in a more revolutionary direction. Disillusioned, he left his beloved hometown.

After a couple of difficult years in Moscow, Chagall returned to Paris with Bella and discovered, to his surprise, that he was now famous. His reputation continued to grow and Chagall immersed himself in his work. During the Second World War, the Chagalls were forced to flee from the Nazis and were given residency in the U.S.A., where Bella died in 1944. Four years later, Chagall went back to France, where he lived for the rest of his life. Only once, in 1973, did he return to the Soviet Union, for a short visit to Leningrad and Moscow. He never went back to Vitebsk, as he knew that it was no longer the place of his childhood, but he continued to paint dreamlike motifs from there up until his death in 1985.

Before he died, Chagall offered to donate some of his art collection to his home town, but the local authorities politely refused his offer. The Chagall Art Centre in Vitebsk is therefore a disappointment. The museum has none of his original paintings, only a collection of graphic works donated by various collectors from Europe and the U.S.A. When I visited, the first floor was dedicated to the work of a local photographer, and the second floor was closed.

The small museum shop sold postcards and posters of the paintings that can be seen elsewhere.

There was a column in the square next to the Chagall Art Centre, clearly a war memorial. I presumed it was a monument to those who fell during the Second World War, but it turned out to be a memorial in honour of the young men who died in the summer of 1812. At the end of July in that year, Napoleon's army clashed with the tsar's army just outside Vitebsk. The battle was short and the Russians withdrew, pulling back to the east, to Smolensk. Napoleon and his soldiers stayed in Vitebsk to rest for a week before pursuing them. The Russians continued to evade them. On September 14, the French army attacked Moscow, but the triumph soon turned into a nightmare. The city was empty of both people and supplies, and that same day the centre had been set alight. The supply lines failed and the exhausted soldiers had no accommodation or food. Napoleon had no choice other than to order a retreat. Winter came early that year, as it often does when foreign armies try to invade Russia, and it was unusually severe, as it often is when Russia is under attack. Roughly six hundred thousand men took part in the march on Moscow, and only thirty thousand returned to France.

Vitebsk did not suffer too badly during the Napoleonic wars, but was almost wiped from the map by Hitler's army. More than ninety per cent of the buildings were destroyed and all of the city's thirty thousand Jews were killed. The thirty synagogues and many timber buildings that were such an important part of the artist's home town are therefore long gone, but the small one-storey brick house where Moishe Shagal and his eight siblings grew up is still there. Four tiny rooms were all they had. Their mother used one as a shop, from which she sold groceries to boost the family's meagre income. The museum curators have done their best to recreate the poor, nineteenth-century home, but the only thing that is original is a small wall cupboard that was donated by one of Chagall's relatives.

Prior to the First World War, more than half the population of Vitebsk was Jewish. The churches have been rebuilt, but the synagogues are a thing of the past, as are the Jews. A small brick house, a wall cupboard, a memorial to the Napoleonic War and a river where thousands of Jews were drowned in the Nazis' pogroms are all that remain of Chagall's childhood town.

It can be quite overwhelming to think about all that has been lost. There were close to a million Jews living in the Belorussian Soviet Socialist Republic before the Second World War. The Jews accounted for about fifteen per cent of the population and were the third largest minority. Many of them lived in the bigger cities, such as Vitebsk and Minsk, where about a third of the inhabitants were Jewish. After the war, almost all the Jews had gone. An entire people, a whole culture, had disappeared.

With its six hundred thousand Jews, the Minsk ghetto was one of the largest in Europe at the time of the Second World War. Eighty-year-old Maia Levina-Krapina is one of the few survivors.

Maia and her husband Igor welcomed me into their small flat on the edge of central Minsk. Maia had a purplish-red tint to her hair and was wearing a dress with large purple flowers on it and pink slippers. The walls were covered with photographs from Maia and Igor's long career as acrobats in Minsk circus: the two of them flying through the air, her doing a handstand on his outstretched arm, him mid-swing, her posing in the circus ring.

Before we had even started talking, Maia installed me in the kitchen and served me bread, biscuits, cheese and coffee. The fact that I had just eaten lunch was irrelevant. First eat, then talk. Igor, who was five years older than Maia, with barely a wrinkle on his face, danced around me on nimble acrobat's feet, interrupting whenever he could.

"Go away!" Maia said. "You are disturbing us!"

"You talk too quickly, Maia, she won't be able to understand!"

"She is recording it, don't interrupt, get out and close the door behind you!"

Igor chuckled and obediently left, but was soon back again.

"Everything alright? Can she understand what you're saying? Don't be afraid to ask if there's anything that's not clear!"

"Get out, I said!" Maia scolded. "And close the door behind you."

Then she started to tell me her story, without stopping, on the in-breath and the out-breath, the words pouring out of her, stemmed only now and then by Igor who was immediately told to leave again.

"There were five of us, four girls and a boy. I was the youngest, born in 1935. My father was a coachman, and my mother stayed at home and looked after us. We had two horses – at that time, it was the same as having a car. We also had goats, hens and rabbits. In other words, we had everything we needed. We lived together with my grandfather and grandmother, who were very religious. We always got sweets on the Sabbath, so it was my favourite day.

"The adults talked a lot about the war. They were certain that there would soon be a war, but my grandmother always said there was no need to be afraid. Even if the Germans came, they would not harm anyone, she said, and certainly not the Jews. No-one had touched the Jews during the last war.

"The war started so suddenly that the authorities did not have time to organise an evacuation. They started to bomb Minsk straightaway. Everyone who could escaped from the city, but we had just moved into a nice new house, so my grandmother did not want us to go anywhere. She firmly believed that no-one was going to harm us. But the bombs just kept on coming and, in the end, it was impossible to stay. The panic was terrible. Father put us all in a wagon and we left. We did not get very far along the Moscow road, because the bombs were falling all around us. We got nowhere. Father decided that we should go back to Minsk and stay at home. 'Whatever happens will happen,' he said. So we went back to Minsk and continued to live at home.

"Our house survived the bombardment, but then on July 19 orders were issued by the German gendarmerie that all Jews had to live in the same place; the place they had chosen for the ghetto was a small area in the centre of Minsk. It was about one kilometre by one kilometre, and all Jews had to move there before a given deadline. The houses were all wooden, and they were small. Since the house we had lived in before the war was not in the ghetto, we swapped with a Belorussian woman. I lived in Sukhaya Street, just by the Jewish cemetery, for two years and four months. The Germans wanted to build a big wall around the ghetto, but as there was no labour to be had, they decided to put barbed wire around it instead. The gates were guarded by German, Lithuanian and Ukrainian police.

"I was five. I remember everything that happened in the ghetto. I don't always remember the date or year, but I remember everything; I remember whether it happened in winter or spring, I remember everything. At the start of the war, the Germans gave orders that all the men – that is to say, all those who had not already been called up – were to go to a given place by the opera. My father was called up and died within the first few days of the war. Where he died and how, none of us know. Not my brother, nor me, nor my sister, none of us.

"As I said, the houses were small. There were three or maybe four rooms in each one and there might be five or six families in each room. As we had exchanged houses with the woman, we thought that we would have the house to ourselves. But no, we got one room. We had taken an iron-framed bed with us to the ghetto, but there was not room for it, so we had to throw it out and sleep on the floor instead. Then there was another order that everyone in the ghetto had to wear a yellow badge on their chest and back, children and adults alike. Some time passed, then there was an order that we all had to wear a white armband, with our address written on it. If anyone was caught attempting to escape, the police went to their house and killed everyone there and then.

"Work brigades were set up straightaway. Boys could work when they were fourteen, girls when they were sixteen. Because anyone who worked got a little food, all the children lied about their age, said they were a year or two older. My brother got a job as a stoker for the Germans. And my mother worked to begin with, as well. She took our little sister, who was still a baby, with her. But when she saw the fascists pulling babies from their mothers' arms and breaking their backs over their knee or throwing them at house corners so their heads split open, she stopped going to work. My grandfather and my brother worked. The rest of us – my two younger sisters, my mother, my grandmother and I – stayed at home.

"There were no shops in the ghetto, there was nothing to eat there. And as there was no school there either, the children did not go to school. But there was a hospital, an isolation ward and two children's homes. Why two children's homes? Well, the war started in the summer and a lot of the children had been packed off to pioneer camps. And when they came home, their parents had been drafted for the war effort and there was no-one to look after them. If the children in the children's homes got ill, they were sent to the isolation ward, where they died of cold and starvation. There was no heating there, nothing. We were all freezing. In winter, anything that was made of wood, all the cupboards and shelves, were used to make fires.

"The first pogrom took place on November 7, 1941. The Germans always tried to make them coincide with one of their festivals. So the first was some autumn celebration. For each pogrom they would select several streets and kill everyone who lived there. Our street was not chosen for the first pogrom, which lasted two days. Everyone was taken to the Tuchinka clay pits close to Minsk, where they were shot. In the ghetto, you could die any hour, any minute, any second, even when there was no pogrom. The Germans could show up at any time, looking for gold and other valuables; they thought the Jews were rolling in it. They killed, raped . . . did whatever they liked.

"After the first pogrom, people started to think about how to save their lives, and to build hiding places. They dug cellars under the floorboards, real earth cellars. They did it at night and carried the earth as far away from the house as they could so the Germans would not suspect anything. Grandfather made us a hiding place too. When the second pogrom started, there were so many people there that we were all squashed together. We could not move, not even a millimetre. And there we sat, crammed together in the earth cellar, without food or water, almost without air, when the Germans came. We could hear their voices, their footsteps. We did not make a sound, did not move, we were terrified. Our mother had our youngest sister on her lap. She was only nine months old. My mother was still breast-feeding her, and she nursed her when we were down in the hole. But there was no milk, so my little sister started to whimper. Someone put something in her mouth, we don't know what. My mother pressed her hard against her chest and kept her there until the pogrom was over. As we emerged from the cellar, we heard our mother scream. Our little sister was dead.

"One time, when my brother Josef was at work, his German boss whacked him. He stopped going to work after that, then he and a gang of boys started to seek out partisans. Sometimes they went beyond the ghetto, and they eventually found a group of partisans in the village of Porechye. They started to help people leave the ghetto and go to him. That was in 1943. My grandfather was not working anymore either. He had been working at a saw-mill, and one of his fingers was cut off in an accident. A while later, during one of the pogroms, he had helped everyone down into the cellar and was about to come down himself, as the last person, when the Germans burst in. My grandmother was dead by then, so it was just me, my mother, my little sister and my brother.

"One day, the police came to our house and ordered Mother to put on her coat and come with them.

"'I will take Maia,' she said to my brother. 'Perhaps then they will let me go.'

"'No,' my brother said. 'I don't want to be left with Lyuba, she is too small.'

"Lyuba was four, and I was eight.

"'Fine,' my mother said. 'I will take Lyuba. Maybe they will let us go.'

"Mother and Lyuba were taken away. A few days later, a rumour spread through the ghetto that they had hanged a lot of people on Jubilee Square. My brother took me there, and Mother was hanging in the first row. There was a sign round her neck that said: 'For working with the partisans.' Our little sister was not with her. We looked everywhere, but could not find her. We still don't know what happened to her. No doubt they shot her . . .

"My brother and I were now alone. As I said, we lived just by the Jewish cemetery. Four pits appeared. When the first gas tankers came, no-one suspected anything . . . The police decided to test them to see how long it would take before people died. They lured the children by offering them sweets. The children were hungry and easily tempted. The police pushed the children into the tankers, turned on the gas and drove around the ghetto once. When they got to the cemetery, all the children were dead. There were not that many gas tankers, but they got as many people as they could in every one. Then they threw the bodies into the pits in the cemetery and threw calcium hypochlorite over them, as they were afraid of infection. Sometimes the earth moved, people were still alive down there. At night we could hear them screaming. Some managed to get out, but were never quite the same again, having survived something like that.

"My brother continued to guide groups from the ghetto to the partisans. One day, he said he would be gone for a long time and asked one of the women who lived in our house to look after me. 'I will come back and get you out of the ghetto,' he promised. Initially, the woman did look after me and help. But then Josef was away for a week, two weeks. One day the woman did not come back in the evening. It was 1942, and the Germans had started to exterminate the worker brigades that were no longer needed. I was completely alone.

"I was eight years old. I had pains everywhere, a constant headache, and was being eaten alive by lice. There was nothing to eat. My whole body was swollen with malnutrition. My legs were so swollen that I could not walk. 'Dear God, I want to die,' I thought.

"Sometime at the start of October 1943, my brother came back. He was met by a group of youths at the Jewish cemetery, next to the end of the ghetto. The boys had gone underground. They took my brother to the hospital, and told him to wait. The plan was that he would take a group of boys to the partisans, on condition that I would go with them. The boys made sure that I was washed and got some food and clothes. I lived close to the hospital and went there all the time, to my brother's window, to talk to him. He said that we would be leaving soon, and promised that I would not need to suffer anymore.

"When I left the house on October 21, 1943, there were gendarmes and police everywhere by the main gates. The gas tankers were there too. I put two and two together and realised there was going to be another pogrom. I ran to Josef's window. 'Joska, the Germans are planning a pogrom!' I said. He was locked in the hospital, but managed to open the window and shimmy down the pipe. When he reached the ground, he took me by the hand, because walking was difficult for me, and we went to the first house, then the next, but all the hiding places were full.

"'What will happen, will happen,' my brother said. 'Come.'"

"He ran with me in his arms to the station at the end of the cemetery. To our relief, we discovered there was no-one else by the barbed-wire fence. A lot of other children had run with us, fifteen, maybe more, maybe fewer, I am not sure. We tore off our yellow stars.

"'It is light now,' my brother said. 'We have to split up and hide around the station. Let's meet again when it gets dark.'

"Everyone did as he said, and went in different directions. When it got dark, we all gathered where my brother had said we should meet. I was the only girl. All the others were boys. There were some huge pipes behind the station, and we hid there. For three days, we sat silently in the pipes. We ate nothing, drank nothing, and I have no idea where we went to the toilet, because there was nowhere to go. My brother sent some boys to check out the situation in the ghetto. The boys came back and told us the ghetto was gone, it no longer existed. On October 23, 1943, the ghetto in Minsk was liquidated, wiped out. The Germans knew perfectly well that there were people hiding under the floorboards, so they threw explosives into the houses . . . grenades and things like that . . . Everything in the ghetto was destroyed.

"When we heard that the ghetto no longer existed, my brother said: 'We no longer have anywhere to go. If you listen to me, I will take you to the partisans. But only on condition that you take turns to carry my sister.'

"It was early morning when we crept out of the pipes. There was a frost; it was very cold for October. Hungry, dirty and in rags, we walked along the main road. I was still not able to walk by myself, and the boys took turns to carry me. German cars, convoys, motorbikes drove past, but no-one bothered about us. When darkness fell, we went into the forest. There was nothing to eat there, so we chewed on frozen bark and grass. We walked and walked, I don't know how far, but certainly for four days. More than a hundred kilometres. We eventually arrived at the partisan camp. A huddle of Jewish children aged between seven and fourteen. What were they going to do with us? We were taken to a large hut filled with straw and left there. Some of us had scabies, some had lice, it was awful. When I think about it now, I cannot believe it was true. We were given food. They set up a big wooden table, filled a pan with water and a bit of flour, and made us a kind of porridge. Some of us had a spoon, others a cup, we ate with whatever we were given.

"There was a huge boggy area by the village, and people went there to hide whenever the Germans came. The Germans had already taken everything of any value in the village. They had stolen the cows, everything, so the villagers had nothing to eat – they were starving as well – and now they had to feed us in addition to two partisan groups.

"They realised that we would not manage on our own, so spread us around the village. One child per house. I ended up with Anastasia, a good woman who cured me of all my ailments. My brother was with another woman, and she combed out all my nits. Anastasia sent me to the partisan doctor, who had somehow managed to make a cream from pig fat and other remedies. I rubbed the cream in all over, and within a few days the lice and everything else had disappeared. I have no idea where he got the ingredients for the cream.

"When the Germans came, Anastasia managed to take me with her to the bog in time. We hid there for three days. All the children who were found in the village were rounded up and sent to Poland. My brother had not been able to hide and ended up in a concentration camp in Poland. He managed to escape and find his way to a farm, but then someone reported him, and he was sent to another concentration camp, in Germany this time. He did not know if I had survived, but assumed we were all dead, me, our mother and father, grandfather and grandmother, and our older sister, Valya. He thought we were all dead and there was no-one else left. When the Red Army freed the camp, he was therefore adopted by the regiment and stayed with them. One of the colonels adopted him personally and gave him his name, Novikov. It just so happened that the colonel was then sent to Minsk. Around the same time, our village was liberated. I also had presumed that everyone was dead and that I was alone. I wanted to stay with Anastasia, but her father sent me to a children's home so my relatives could find me. I ran away several times, but Anastasia's father sent me back every time.

"It turned out that my uncle, the husband of my mother's sister, who was a colonel and had fought against the Germans, had also survived. He came searching for his family, and found me. So I lived with him for a while. He and my aunt had had four children. The oldest son was lame. During one of the pogroms we had heard screaming. My cousin, who could not walk, was being dragged to the execution spot by his feet and arms. My mother's sister and her four children were killed that day. I told my uncle, and he married again.

"My grandmother, my mother's mother, and one of my aunts also came back. They had both been evacuated when the war broke out. My grandmother could tell us that Valya, my older sister, had lived in a children's home outside the ghetto throughout the war, and that she was still alive. She arranged for me to be sent to the same children's home, so we could be together.

"One of the happiest moments in my life was when I was reunited with Josef. I had long since given up hope of ever seeing him again, when he appeared one day at the children's home where Valya and I lived. Suddenly there was this young man in a uniform standing in front of me, who both looked and did not look like Josef. He had grown, become a man. He said my name over and over: 'Maia, Mayetskya!' Then he hugged me and whispered: 'How small you are . . .'

"Valya finished seventh grade and went on to technical high school. Josef served in the Far East, got married and moved to Riga, and then to the U.S.A. I started dance school in 1948 and trained in choreography and dance. I continued my studies at a sports college, where I met my husband, Igor. We ended up on the Belorussian stage and were acrobats for twenty years.

"And that is that. That is my story. When I think back on it now, I cannot comprehend that I actually experienced it all. You know, we never talked about it, not until the 1980s. Before that, it was still too dangerous. People might take you for a spy if they found out that you had survived the ghetto. People were suspicious if you had survived, so no-one said anything. It is only in the past twenty years that I have been able to tell my story."

A Trip to the Dacha that Changed the World

The destruction of Minsk was such that there was serious discussion as to whether the Belorussian capital should be moved, rather than rebuilt. But a modern city has sprung up from the ruins, with wide streets and impersonal tower blocks. Like the rest of the country, Minsk is totally flat, and it feels like the city spreads and spreads in every direction. The first leader of an independent Belarus, Stanislav Shushkevich, lives with his wife Irina in a very unlovely block of flats.

Irina showed me into the study where her husband was sitting, ready to talk. The former head of state was tall and broad-shouldered, with a round belly, bald head and square jaw. The shelves were full of books about Belarus and physics, and a Wikipedia page about Norway was visible on the computer screen. It was more than two decades since he had been forced to retire, but at eighty-one he showed no signs of slowing down.

"I am going to South Korea tomorrow to take part in a conference," he said. "I was travelling all the time until a few years ago, when we discovered that I had a heart problem. I supplemented my pension by teaching in foreign universities. As you no doubt know, Lukashenko made sure that my pension was not adjusted for inflation. For years, I was not paid more than two dollars a month in pension."

He shot me a canny smile.

"I have not told anyone this before, but my wife managed to have my pension adjusted to my age a couple of years ago. So now

I am paid according to my age, and not the work that I did. About four million a month. Which is O.K. I can manage on that."

Shushkevich had never had any ambitions to be a politician. He is a qualified mathematician and physicist, and has dedicated most of his professional life to science.

"I was never a dissident, I was far too busy with work. I was passionate about research and teaching. My work took up all my time! Like everyone else, I was a communist, even my father, who spent twenty years in a labour camp in Siberia, was a communist, but I eventually came to realise that communism was not the best solution for economic development. In 1990, I was elected a member of the Belarusian parliament."

It was almost by chance that Shushkevich became the Supreme Soviet chairman in early autumn 1991. His predecessor, Nikolay Dementey, was ousted after he supported the unsuccessful coup against Gorbachev in August. The communists did not want a leader who was a member of the Belarus Popular Front, a newly established independence party, so Shushkevich, who was not a member of any party, was catapulted into power. Little did the communists know that the non-partisan physics professor would become one of the key players in the dissolution of the Soviet Union.

"In my opinion, the Soviet Union was already falling apart in August 1991 when the communists tried to take revenge," Shushkevich said. "Fortunately, Yeltsin managed to deal effectively with the mutiny. I am a Yeltsin man, to this day. You Western Europeans have the wrong impression of Yeltsin, just because he sometimes drank a ridiculous amount and did not always behave in the way a politician should. Like every true Russian, he enjoyed his drink, but in my opinion he was an honest and fair man, and an excellent first president for Russia, elected by the people. I am proud to have had him as a friend."

A few months after he had more or less inadvertently become the Supreme Soviet chairman, Shushkevich organised a trip to a dacha that would change the history of the world. The guests included Boris Yeltsin, president of Russia, or the Russian Soviet Federative Socialist Republic as it was then still called, and Leonid Kravchuk, the Ukrainian president, as well as a number of other leading politicians and advisers from both countries. They arrived at the luxury Belarusian dacha on December 7. And by the next day, they had decided to announce the dissolution of the Soviet Union. To this day, Shushkevich maintains that it was never planned.

"We did not meet at the dacha to decide the fate of the Soviet Union, not at all," he said. "We were there to discuss the supply of oil and gas to Belarus. It would soon be midwinter, and the Soviet Union was falling apart. I was concerned that people would freeze and wanted to secure a favourable agreement with Boris Yeltsin and Leonid Kravchuk. So I invited them to a dacha in a very beautiful part of West Belarus. As I said, the plan was that we would discuss gas supplies and do a bit of hunting. I knew that Yeltsin liked to hunt. I have spoken about what then happened many times before. I have even written books about it."

Instead of talking about the export and import of oil and gas, the three leaders started to discuss Gorbachev's weak standing and the future of the Soviet Union. Gorbachev had still not given up hope of saving the Soviet Union through perestroika. He envisaged a federation of all the Soviet republics, bar the Baltic states, which even Gorbachev realised were a lost cause. The federation would have a shared, centralised government, defence policy and president – himself. Neither Shushkevich nor Nazarbayev, the president of Kazakhstan, were against the idea, but Kravchuk, the president of Ukraine, was categorically opposed. On August 24, after the unsuccessful coup, the Ukrainian parliament had voted for independence, with an overwhelming majority. One week before the trip to the dacha, on December 1, a referendum was held to cement this decision. Contrary to what Gorbachev expected, the majority voted for independence from the Soviet Union – even in the Russian-dominated areas of Donbass and Crimea. The Soviet economy was in free fall and people wanted change.

The Ukrainian referendum changed everything. Kravchuk rejected Gorbachev's proposal, relayed by Yeltsin, of what a reformed Soviet Union might look like – the Ukrainian people did not want simply to replace one yoke with another. In the end, Yeltsin declared that he would not sign any agreement if Ukraine was not included. The three leaders started to discuss *alternative* forms of coexistence. Yeltsin was particularly keen to find an alternative and insisted that they should not leave the dacha until they had negotiated an actual agreement. The advisers sat up all night working on a draft. None of them had a typewriter with them, so they wrote it by hand. At dawn, some security guards were sent off in search of a typewriter, so that a clean copy of the historical agreement could be prepared before the leaders got up.

After breakfast, Yeltsin, Shushkevich and Kravchuk gathered in the games room to agree the final details. By early afternoon, once the gentlemen had raised a glass of Russian champagne to each and every paragraph, the fourteen-point agreement was ready: the fifteen Soviet republics would be recognised as independent sovereign states, all nuclear weapons would be transferred to Russia, which would also inherit the Soviet Union's place at the United Nations, and the former Soviet states would be part of the Commonwealth of Independent States (C.I.S.), a loose political, economic and military alliance with no centralised rule and an administrative seat in Minsk. It was no coincidence that Minsk was chosen for this, since Russia's position as the centre of power was now history. Nor was the word "commonwealth" a random choice – Kravchuk had insisted that the word "union" not be used in the agreement under any circumstances.

At two o'clock in the afternoon of December 8, 1991, Shushkevich, Kravchuk and Yeltsin signed the document that has gone down in history as the Belavezha Accords.* Shushkevich was the first person to sign it. In the evening, after George Bush and Mikhail Gorbachev had been informed, in that order, the three gentlemen sent out a press release in which they announced that "the U.S.S.R., as a subject of international law and geopolitical reality, is ceasing its existence."

The Belavezha Accords consigned the Soviet Union to history with three pen strokes. On December 21, Armenia, Azerbaijan, Kazakhstan, Kyrgyzstan, Moldova, Tajikistan and Uzbekistan all became members of the Commonwealth of Independent States. And on December 25, Gorbachev stepped down as president; the Soviet Union formally ceased to exist the following day, on December 26. Russia, the leading country in the union, lost about twenty per cent of its territory and half its population when fifteen independent states were born. Many of them, including Belarus, Azerbaijan and Kazakhstan, had never previously existed on the world map.

"When did you understand that the Soviet Union was history?" I asked Shushkevich.

"The Soviet Union is still not history, it lives on in people's minds," he said. "Throughout the post-Soviet area, the Soviet Union still exists. Only a few republics are leaving it behind, like

---

* The Belavezha Accords are also known in some languages less precisely as the Minsk Agreement (not to be confused with the Minsk Protocol of 2014). "Belavezha" refers to the Białowieża forest, where the dacha was. It is one of the last protected parts of the primeval forest that once stretched across the European plain.

Moldova, Ukraine and the Baltic states. The propaganda machine is still working hard to maintain the Russian Empire."

Autumn 1991 was not Shushkevich's first brush with world history. In 1959, the U.S. Marine Lee Harvey Oswald defected to the Soviet Union. The Soviet authorities had no idea what to do with the bothersome American, so sent him to Minsk, where he was given a flat in the centre of town and a job on the production line at the Gorizont radio factory. Shushkevich had just started working at the same factory, and as he was the only employee who could speak a bit of English, he was given the job of teaching Oswald Russian. The two met, under the beady eyes of the K.G.B., to speak Russian three times a week. Oswald was not a particularly gifted linguist, and the authorities soon decided that he did not, strictly speaking, need to know much Russian to do his work. So the classes were stopped. Two years later, Oswald married the pharmaceutical student Marina Prusakova, and not long after the wedding, the young couple left for the U.S.A. On November 22, 1963, Oswald shot and killed President John F. Kennedy in Dallas, Texas.

"I am absolutely certain that Oswald was not behind it, certainly not alone," Shushkevich said. "To me, he seemed like a rather simple soldier type. The assassination of President Kennedy would have been beyond him. I firmly believe that, if it was him, he must have had help."

Shushkevich was not the leader of Belarus for long. In the same year that he was elected a member of parliament (1990), the thirty-six-year-old director of the Gorodet state farm, Alexander Lukashenko, was also elected. In 1993, Lukashenko was appointed to serve as chairman of the anti-corruption committee. Shortly after, he accused seventy high-standing officials, including Shushkevich, of serious corruption. The accusations of fraud have never been substantiated, but at the start of 1994 there was a vote of no confidence in Shushkevich and he had to step down as head of state.

"Bill Clinton was here on a state visit on January 15, and on January 22 I was out," Shushkevich said.

Later that year, Lukashenko stood as a candidate in the first Belarusian presidential election. To everyone's surprise, he won, taking 45.1 per cent of the vote. Shushkevich took 9.9 per cent. At this point, the young nation was on its knees. There was galloping inflation, agriculture was in ruins as a result of the Chernobyl accident, and the manufacturing industry, which was dependent on oil and gas from Russia and coal from Ukraine, was in deep crisis. Lukashenko was a fresh and uncorrupt alternative to the established politicians. One of his campaign promises was to reunite Russia, Belarus and Ukraine, an idea that found favour with many of those nostalgic for the Soviet Union.

A month after he came to power, Lukashenko took control of the state television channel. A year later, he ensured that he had the authority to disband parliament. Over the next few years he tightened his grip systematically. Any newspapers that criticised him were closed down, the nascent civil movement was crushed, and opposition politicians were jailed or killed, or simply disappeared. The Belarusian K.G.B. is now bigger than it ever was in the days of the Soviet Union, and human rights are being violated all the time. Eighty per cent of farms are still run as state cooperatives and the bulk of business is state-owned.

In 1999, Lukashenko and Yeltsin signed an agreement to reunite Belarus and Russia, and to establish a federation. The federation would have a joint president, a role that Lukashenko had presumably envisaged for himself, rather than the drunken Yeltsin. When Vladimir Putin came to power the following year, the agreement was shelved, though Belarus is still indirectly subsidised by Russia, through cheap oil and gas. Russia has major military bases in

Belarus, and the two countries often carry out joint military exercises.

"How long do you think Lukashenko will hold on to power?" was my final question to Shushkevich.

"Depends on Russia," the former head of state replied. "We have a 1,200-kilometre open border with Russia. Flat, and completely open. Lukashenko may not be that smart, but he is sly. As long as he dances to Putin's tune, he will stay in power."

A couple of weeks later in Warsaw, I met Andrei Sannikov, who came second in the Belarusian presidential election in 2010. Lukashenko won 79.65 per cent of the votes, while Sannikov got only 2.43 per cent.

"Even if you came second, you were nowhere near winning," I said.

"Officially, that is true," Sannikov said, with an ironic smile. He had a full, grey beard, dark rings under his eyes, and spoke fluent English in a deep voice. "In all likelihood, I got closer to thirty per cent of the vote. In Minsk, I got forty-two per cent, whereas Lukashenko got only thirty-three. Which is surprising, because Lukashenko lives in Minsk."

In the evening of December 19, the day of the presidential election, thousands of people gathered in the centre of Minsk in protest against the official result. Sannikov went to join the demonstrators, together with his wife, the well-known journalist Irina Khalip. No sooner had they got there than they were arrested. Six other presidential candidates and several hundred peaceful demonstrators also ended up behind bars.

"Normally they would wait a few days until the election observers and foreign journalists had left," Sannikov said, wryly. "Which says something about how frightened Lukashenko was. The opposition could have won the election, and he knew it."

The arrest marked the start of a nightmare that is not yet over. As both parents were arrested, the authorities threatened to put the couple's three-year-old son, Danik, in foster care. Thanks to the hard work of Khalip's mother and some kind doc-tors who "forgot" to record all her heart problems in her medical record, the boy was allowed to stay with his grandmother instead.

In May 2011, Sannikov was sentenced to five years in prison. His wife was placed under house arrest with severe restrictions.

"Prison was terrible," Andrei said. "They have so many draconian methods for breaking people's spirit. They even manipulate the T.V. We never saw any live television, only recorded, and generally violent documentaries from the war in Chechnya. They also did what they could to break our routines. For people who have never been in prison, it is hard to understand, but routines are really important in prison. It is all about the detail. They confiscated my cup, for example. I was moved from cell to cell, and was constantly being sent to new prisons and labour colonies. They took away what little control I had."

He was also physically mistreated, denied medical help and, in one instance, he claims, poisoned. The temperature in the cells was often no more than eight degrees and the lights were always on. An Afghan prisoner confided to Andrei that he had been treated better by the Taliban in an Afghan prison.

Then, after sixteen months, Sannikov was suddenly released, without warning or explanation.

"It was definitely a reaction to the sanctions," he said. "In March 2012, the international community imposed tougher sanctions. A month later, in April, I was released."

But freedom came at a price. When he was released from prison, he was under constant surveillance and was hounded and threatened. A few months later, he decided to leave Belarus. His wife and son stayed on in Minsk.

"Leaving Belarus and my family was the hardest decision I have ever made," Sannikov said. "I would rather not talk about it, it is too painful. Fortunately, it will soon be summer. The summer holidays are our best times, because that is when we are together."

Sannikov was the most experienced of the nine candidates to challenge Lukashenko in the 2010 election. He is a diplomat and headed the delegation that negotiated the removal of nuclear weapons from Belarus in the early 1990s, in line with the Belavezha Accords. In 1995, he was appointed Deputy Minister of Foreign Affairs by Lukashenko. He resigned a year later and joined the opposition.

"I had been patient for long enough, for *too* long," Sannikov said. "I had hope. Lukashenko won the election in 1994, but it was the only election he actually won. And on the very first day, he started to carve out his career as a dictator. Among other things, he amended the constitution and electoral system so that he had all the power."

In 2015, just before Lukashenko won the election with eighty-five per cent of the vote, a handful of high-profile political prisoners were released, including Nikolai Statkevich, who was also a candidate in the 2010 presidential election. As if by magic, the international sanctions were lifted, and Belarus was once again accepted.

"Lukashenko is wooing the West now, because Russia cannot afford to bail him out like it used to," Sannikov said. "The E.U. has increased its financial support to Belarus. So now it is the E.U. that is saving him, whereas before it was Putin. But nothing has changed, apart from the fact that there are no high-profile political prisoners any more. The situation is worse than in the final years of the Soviet Union. Lukashenko holds all the power, there are no safety valves. The Soviet Union has been resurrected in Belarus like some Latin American banana republic, but with gas pipes instead of bananas."

"What is the relationship between Belarus and Russia, and Lukashenko and Putin?" I asked.

"Putin does not see Belarus as an independent country," Sannikov said. "The Russians want to control the Belarusian military and the transport of oil and gas. Putin watches everything that Lukashenko does, and learns from him. After all, Lukashenko has been in power for six years longer than him. For example, Putin learnt from Lukashenko how to deal with problematic presidential candidates, and that the West soon forgets. Russia is currently more brutal than Belarus, but Lukashenko has tighter control on civilian society. Putin has even started to play ice hockey, like Lukashenko."

Despite everything he had been through, Sannikov was not bitter.

"You cannot think clearly when you are bitter," he said. "I am not looking for revenge. There are no personal feelings involved. My dream is to live in an independent and free Belarus, and I am convinced that one day that dream will come true."

At the time of writing, that day is far away. At the start of 2017, thousands of people once again took to the streets of Minsk to demonstrate against the "parasite law", the popular name given to a new tax law that Lukashenko had introduced, which imposed harsher tax regulations on the unemployed and part-time workers. Having shown unusual restraint for several weeks in a row, Lukashenko hit back with force on March 25: Freedom Day. Several hundred demonstrators were arrested, the biggest mass arrest since the presidential election in 2010.

In winter 2017, when the country was experiencing a financial downturn and rising dissatisfaction, the relationship with Russia reached an all-time low. In February, Lukashenko spun out his annual press conference to a staggering seven hours and twenty minutes, quite probably a world record. The bulk of his monologue was a series of diatribes against their neighbour to the east. Lukashenko's anger was targeted at the very same things that had caused Shushkevich to invite Yeltsin and Kravchuk to the dacha in 1991: oil and gas. Lukashenko believed that the Russians had not reduced gas prices in line with the fall in oil prices. Putin argued that the prices were already well below the market price, which they most certainly were – in the period 2002–15, Russia gave Belarus more than eighty billion dollars in indirect subsidies through stabilisation loans and favourable prices for oil and gas. Furthermore, Belarusian companies have benefited from Russia's import ban on E.U. agricultural products in recent years. E.A.E.U. customs regulations permit Belarus to export E.U. products to Russia if these are further processed or packaged in Belarusian territory. Since the ban came into force, the import of E.U. agricultural produce to Belarus has more than doubled.

When Belarus refused to pay the agreed price for Russian oil and gas, despite all these direct and indirect subsidies, Russia's response was to reduce the supply of tax-free crude oil. They also introduced controls on the Belarusian border. This may equally have been a reaction to the "mobility partnership" that Belarus signed with the E.U. that same winter, which introduced visa-free entry for up to five days for citizens from eighty countries. Towards the end of the marathon press conference, Lukashenko made a threat that he quite possibly did not believe himself. "We can do without Russian oil! It is going to be difficult, but freedom is not measured by money!"

A week after the mass arrests in March, Lukashenko went to Moscow to court the government. He returned with promises of a one billion dollar loan to pay for the gas that had been supplied in 2016 and a further reduction in the gas price for 2018 and 2019. The same autumn, the two countries carried out yet another joint military exercise, Zapad 2017: "West 2017".

Lines in the Sand

The Belarusian border guard studied every passport thoroughly with a magnifying glass. She must have discovered a discrepancy, because a young boy was taken to one side, then thrown off the bus. By way of contrast, it was all quick and easy in Medininkai, on the Lithuanian side. For the first time on this journey, my passport was handed back without a stamp.

As soon as we crossed the border, the roads improved noticeably. The leaves had started to come out on the trees, making them shimmer with a vibrant green. And as the distance between timber houses grew, the shopping centres became more frequent. Half an hour later we pulled into Vilnius bus station. In the cobbled, pedestrian streets of the baroque old town, I heard people speaking Danish, Swedish, Norwegian, German and Finnish, and on the high streets international chains like H&M, Zara and Starbucks stood side by side. There was a Narvesen kiosk on every street corner. In restaurants, I could admire the Lithuanian menu with all its diphthongs and archaic inflection, order in English and pay in euros. And I must say, Lithuanian is a fascinating language. It has retained grammatical elements and features of Proto-Indo-European that otherwise are found only in Sanskrit and Ancient Greek.

These days, Vilnius is a predominantly Lithuanian city. More than sixty per cent of its inhabitants are Lithuanian; the city has never been so homogeneous, certainly not since the early Middle Ages. You rarely hear Russian, unlike in the other Baltic capitals, as Russians now account for only five per cent of the population in Lithuania. The situation prior to the First World War could not have been more different: the majority of inhabitants in Vilnius then were Jews, with the Poles coming second. Some twenty per cent were Russian and only one per cent was Lithuanian. And so it had been for some five hundred years. The city's fragmented and multi-ethnic history is reflected in the many variations of its names: in Polish, it is called Wilno, in Belarusian Vil'nia, in Yiddish Vilne, and in Russian Vil'na.

Vilnius' history stretches back to the Middle Ages when it was the capital of the Grand Duchy of Lithuania. Remarkably, Lithuania was the largest state in Europe in the fourteenth century, and covered the area from the Baltic Sea down to the Black Sea. At the end of the 1300s, the Lithuanian grand duke, Jogaila, who was a pagan, converted to Catholicism so he could marry the Polish princess Jadwiga, who was heir to the Polish throne. The majority of Lithuanians are now Catholic. A continued personal union with Poland eventually became a real union in 1569, with the establishment of the Polish–Lithuanian Commonwealth. The Lithuanian aristocracy gradually started to speak Polish, but the farmers continued to speak Lithuanian. The Commonwealth was eventually swallowed by its expanding neighbours, Prussia, Austria and Russia, towards the end of the eighteenth century. The territory that is now Lithuania fell to Russia, with the exception of a small strip by the coast, which became part of Prussia.

Lithuania and Poland did not emerge again as independent countries until after the First World War. In the chaotic, violent post-war years, Vilnius changed hands six times before it finally became part of Poland. The Lithuanian capital was moved west to Kaunas. In September 1939, Hitler attacked Poland, and the Red Army invaded from the east, as agreed in the Molotov–Ribbentrop Pact. Vilnius was transferred to Lithuania, and therefore to

Russia, in line with the pact, while Germany got a greater share of Poland. In summer the following year, Lithuania, Latvia and Estonia were forced to become part of the Soviet Union. A year later, the Wehrmacht marched into the Baltic Soviet republics, where many greeted them as a liberator.

The three years of German occupation were calamitous for the Jews, however. Close to two hundred thousand Jews, more than ninety per cent of the Jewish population in Lithuania, were murdered during the war.

In 1944, Lithuania rejoined the Soviet Union. The Belorussians wanted Vilnius to be a part of the Soviet Republic of Belorussia, but direct orders were given by Stalin that it should be the capital of the Soviet Republic of Lithuania. The problem was that only Poles lived there. But Stalin knew what to do. He resorted to one of his favourite options: mass deportation. Between 1945 and 1947, seventeen thousand Poles were sent "back" to Poland, largely from Vilnius. For the first time since the Grand Duchy of Lithuania had ruled most of Eastern Europe, Vilnius was a Lithuanian city. Wilno and Vilne were erased from the world map.

Lithuania was not subject to the same aggressive Russification by the Soviet regime as the other Baltic states. There are two likely key reasons for this: first, that the Soviet Republic of Lithuania was not industrialised like the other states; second, that there was no other place in the Union where opposition to the Soviet regime was so tenacious and widespread. Russians quite simply did not want to live there. The armed resistance continued until Stalin's death in 1953. Fifty thousand women and men, known as the Forest Brothers, took part in guerrilla warfare. More than twenty thousand Forest Brothers were killed, and their bodies were often left on display in public places as a warning. The number killed on the Soviet side was about thirteen thousand.

In the years immediately after the war, approximately 130,000

Lithuanians were deported to Central Asia and Siberia – equivalent to five per cent of the population. More than a fifth of them died en route, or soon after they got there. Given this history, it is perhaps not surprising that the Lithuanians were the first to demand independence. On March 11, 1990, the Lithuanian national assembly declared its independence from the Soviet Union. As was to be expected, Gorbachev put his foot down and said that the declaration of independence was illegal. The Soviet government put a great deal of political and financial pressure on Lithuania, and eventually sent in the army. In a desperate attempt by Moscow to gain control of the television tower in Vilnius, fourteen people were either shot or run over by Soviet tanks on January 13, 1991. Naturally, this only strengthened the Lithuanians' desire to be free, and in a referendum in February the same year, more than ninety per cent voted to leave the Soviet Union.

The world was sympathetic to the Baltic states' fight for freedom, so long as there was no violence. The Kremlin therefore tried several times to provoke the Lithuanians to take up arms. The worst incident took place on July 31, 1991, when seven Lithuanian border guards were killed by O.M.O.N. (special Soviet police troops) at the Medininkai border post between Lithuania and Belarus. Twenty-nine-year old Tomas Šernas was the only one to survive.

"I wasn't actually down to do the shift, as I was getting married the next day," Tomas said in broken Russian, the only language we had in common. He was fair, with a pale, moon-shaped face and round glasses. We met in a kindergarten not far from the centre of Vilnius, where he had been to a church meeting. The congregation held their meetings there as there was a wheelchair ramp at the entrance. Surrounded by colourful drawings and small tables and chairs, Tomas told me about that terrible summer night.

"But a friend of mine had to pull out of his shift, so I agreed to cover for him. I reckoned that way I would have more days off for our honeymoon. We planned to go the seaside."

Tomas had signed up as a volunteer that winter, after the television tower massacre.

"My parents were working in Finland at the time. When I went to visit them, I noticed that every single town and village had a cemetery for those who had fallen in the Winter War. And I felt that I had to do something. Doing nothing was embarrassing. Nearly everyone in Lithuania was against the Soviet Union, it was all just a facade. We had a different mentality from the other Soviet republics. We have always looked west, to the Nordic countries. Communism was all well and good in theory, but it didn't work in practice. I am actually a trained vet and I was working at Vilnius Zoo. But then on February 23, 1991, I started to work as a border guard."

O.M.O.N. attacked between four and four-thirty in the morning. Tomas was sitting at a desk in the small border station. A policeman and a guard were outside on the road, and two other policemen were sitting in a car. A fourth policeman and the three other border guards were asleep on the floor. There were only two tables left in the barrack, as the rest of the furniture, including the beds, had gone up in flames during an earlier attack. At the time, the Lithuanian border posts were being attacked on a more or less weekly basis.

"I remember I heard a noise," Tomas said. "I thought it sounded like a shot, though a very faint one. I looked out of the window, and from where I was sitting all I could see was the forest and a stretch of road. Then I saw two men carrying machine guns with silencers on them."

Tomas woke up the sleeping policeman. Moments later, the attackers stormed into the barracks and ordered everyone to lie down on the floor. Tomas did as he was told.

"To begin with, I didn't realise they were shooting," he said. "It was dark and I was not fully aware of what was going on around me, but I did see them shoot one of the policemen. Then they shot me and I must have blacked out. At one point, I regained consciousness and I remember someone speaking Russian. Then it was morning. The birds were singing in the forest. A woman screamed. I thought she was overreacting, that she was too emotional. Then I blacked out again and did not come round until they were carry-ing me out to the ambulance."

Tomas had been shot twice in the head and had to undergo three major operations. For weeks, he hovered between life and death. He was in hospital until the following spring, when he was sent to Germany to recover. As a result of his extensive injuries, he will be in a wheelchair for the rest of his life and is dependent on carers and a driver.

"I did eventually marry Rasa, but I can't remember when." He laughed. "Oh, yes, I remember now. Someone worked out that our wedding was 699 days late, so that means I got married in summer 1993, right?"

Some years later, Tomas started to study theology and was ordained as a pastor in the Evangelical Reformed Church, where he still works.

"There are a lot of things you can no longer do when you can't walk," he said. "I had to find something to keep me busy. I was interested in theology, and when the Soviet Union dissolved, there was a lack of pastors. Another benefit was that the university was in Klaipeda, by the sea. And I wanted to be by the sea."

The O.M.O.N. attackers came from Riga. Only one of them has ever been charged. The other three are Russian citizens, and the Russian authorities refuse to hand them over.

"The orders probably came from Moscow. Who knows?" Tomas said, with a shrug. "Russia has always been undemocratic. They make up their own rules. Even under Yeltsin. He promised to investigate the incident, but nothing happened."

On September 6, 1991, while Tomas was still in a coma, the Soviet Union recognised the Baltic countries as independent states.

"I didn't have an easy time of it after the attack," Tomas said. "I struggled with my guilt and the fact that I had survived. Invalids can be bitter and difficult. I didn't want to be like that. I had survived. You have to think of life as a gift, a gift from God. But what really helped me was the fact that Lithuania was independent. Morally, we had won. We had fought and won."

* * *

In south-west Lithuania, the Curonian Spit runs along the Baltic coast for a hundred kilometres. At its narrowest point, it is only four hundred metres wide. I could happily have wandered for hours through the pine forests, along the wide beaches and over the greyish-brown, desert-like dunes. My feet sank into the warm, soft sand. The dunes rolled on for kilometres, bordered by a grey sea and a pale blue Baltic sky.

"A window to the world" was what Pastor Tomas Šernas had called the Baltic coastline. When he was a child, his family had often gone on holiday there, and he had spent his days with friends, searching for bottles and other items from foreign ships that had washed ashore. For them, the rubbish was a reminder that there was a world out there, on the other side of the Iron Curtain.

The Curonian Spit is five thousand years old. For century after century, sand from the seabed has been carried north-east by the wind and waves and deposited here, along the coast of Lithuania. The pine trees, on the other hand, were planted relatively recently. In the eighteenth century, the green spit was almost destroyed by population growth and over-grazing. In 1757, during the Seven

Years War, the Russian army invaded the area and chopped down what was left of the forest to make boats for the siege of Königsberg, which was one of the most important towns in Prussia at the time. This meant there was no longer enough vegetation to bind the fine sand, and the dunes started to move. Over the course of a few decades, the sand dunes swallowed one village after another. Houses and churches were buried under tons of sand.

In 1825, the Prussian government decided to reforest the spit in order to save it. Hundreds of people were involved in the time-consuming, painstaking project, which took almost a hundred years. First they had to stabilise the ground with various grasses that thrived in sand, then they planted hardy pines and birch trees, metre by metre, tree by tree. About seventy per cent of the sand dunes are now covered in forest, and even though the dunes still move, they are no longer a threat to the picturesque timber villages, which have been rebuilt.

The German author Thomas Mann visited Nida, one of the prettiest villages on the spit, for the first time in 1929. The Nobel Prize laureate was so taken with the place that he immediately built a summer house there. The brown timber house, with blue window frames and a thatched roof, still stands on a small hill, with a view to the lagoon. Mann spent three summers there with his family, until they moved from Munich to Switzerland in 1933, when Hitler came to power.

At the time, the whole Curonian Spit was in East Prussia, an area that had been ruled by Germany since the Teutonic Order crusades in the thirteenth century. In 1945, East Prussia was split between Poland and the Soviet Union, as compensation for the losses and suffering that the Germans had inflicted during the war. Stalin secured Königsberg, the birthplace of Immanuel Kant, and the surrounding area. The town was renamed Kaliningrad after the now forgotten politician Mikhail Kalinin, who was the official head of state of the Soviet Union until 1945, and an important lackey for the real leader, Stalin. Old Königsberg, which was left in ruins by the war, was filled with military bases, concrete tower blocks, and Russian soldiers. Any Germans and Lithuanians were deported.

Back then, Kaliningrad bordered the Soviet Socialist Republic of Lithuania and was a natural southern outpost for the Soviet Union on the Baltic coast. Kaliningrad is now a Russian exclave, surrounded by Poland and Lithuania, which are both N.A.T.O. countries. It is currently the most militarised area in Europe, and an important naval base for Russia, which lost the greater part of the Baltic coast when the Soviet Union fell apart. The exclave is a constant reminder to its neighbours of Russia's military muscle. The Iskander missiles that are positioned there can reach Warsaw within two minutes and twenty-two seconds.

From the top of the highest sand dune, I could see over to Kaliningrad. I wandered on through the pine forest, further and further south, until I came to a sign that said it was strictly forbidden to go any further.

In this corner of the world, borders have moved like shifting sand dunes. The tourist magnet of Gdańsk lies across the bay from Nida, but to get there I had to travel around the Russian exclave, via Kaunas, the old capital of Lithuania, then cross the Polish border and carry on west to the coast.

Over the centuries, Gdańsk has been ruled by Polish kings, the Teutonic Order, Polish-Lithuanian kings, Prussian kings and German chancellors. For a short period, the city was also under Napoleon, who declared it a free city. Known as Danzig in German, it became a free city once again in the inter-war period, but was controlled by the Polish Ministry of Foreign Affairs. More than ninety per cent of the inhabitants were German, and throughout the 1930s there was growing dissatisfaction with the fact that they were part of Poland. *Heim ins Reich* became a powerful slogan.

On the night of September 1, 1939, Hitler started his Polish campaign by attacking the small garrison at Westerplatte, just outside the centre of Gdańsk. The Second World War had begun. Fifty-six people were on duty, and fought heroically against the Germans for hours. But in vain.

Towards the end of the war, Danzig was subjected to intense air raids by the allies. On March 30, 1945, after some fierce fighting, the Red Army invaded the city. Ninety per cent of the historical centre was destroyed in the weeks and days before the city fell. After the war, the city was returned to Poland. The remaining Germans were thrown out, and ethnic Poles moved in and rebuilt the city. In theory, Poland was now independent, but in practice the country was ruled by the Soviet Union as a communist dictatorship.

In the 1970s and 1980s, Gdańsk again became the centre of events that would change the course of history. For a decade, the electrician Lech Wałęsa had organised strikes and social protests at the Lenin Shipyard on the outskirts of the city, and had spent a year in prison as a result. He then became the leader of Solidarność, or Solidarity, Poland's first independent trade union. Solidarity became a significant player in Polish politics through the Eighties. After months of economic crisis and general strikes, Poland became the first country behind the Iron Curtain to announce a free election. Solidarity's supporters won a clear majority and formed a government. The following year, Lech Wałęsa was elected president of Poland.

Cracks were appearing in the Iron Curtain.

There is now a big and lavish museum by the famous shipyard. And there is another ambitious museum in a neighbourhood that was destroyed during the war, just outside the city centre. The museum, which cost a small fortune, is dedicated to the Second

World War and aims to tell the story of the war from the perspective of every country affected. The museum management also wanted to highlight controversial and lesser-known themes, such as the Japanese invasion of Manchuria in 1931, the significance of the Spanish Civil War in the build-up to the Second World War, Poland's role in the Holocaust, the deportation of half a million Poles to camps in 1940, and the Nazis' deliberate starvation of three million Soviet prisoners of war. Only months before the museum was due to open, the conservative Polish government threatened to stop the project as the museum did not show things from a sufficiently Polish perspective. The museum opened its doors in March 2017, all the same, with the tagline: "See it before they close it!" Not long after, the museum director Paweł Machcewicz was fired and replaced by someone loyal to the government, and the expectation is that the exhibitions will be changed to give greater emphasis to what the Poles suffered.

History is a political battlefield in Poland. But there are also many very real battles in Polish history. The greater part of the country is as flat as Belarus, without any natural boundaries, so an easy target for invading armies. In the thirteenth century, the Teutonic Order left their mark, and then the Mongols, and in the seventeenth and eighteenth centuries, the Swedish army destroyed much of the country. But Poland was also a major power in its own right. In the fourteenth and fifteenth centuries, the Polish–Lithuanian Commonwealth was the mightiest power in eastern Central Europe, and from 1610 to 1612 the Poles even occupied Moscow.

Volumes have been written about the complex and difficult relationship between Russia and Poland throughout history. In the eighteenth century, the power balance shifted. Poland–Lithuania was on the wane, largely for domestic reasons. Unlike Russia, Poland was governed by the aristocracy, who also chose the king.

The Polish aristocracy was the largest in Europe and made up about ten per cent of the population. In the mid-1600s, the aristocracy were given further powers and all nobles in the national assembly were given the right to veto any resolution, which in practice made it impossible to pass any laws or measures to secure state income.

Meanwhile, the neighbouring empires were growing in strength. In 1772, Russia, Prussia and Austria each helped themselves to a piece of Poland–Lithuania, in what is known as the First Partition of Poland. Russia secured parts of what is today Belarus. The Polish aristocracy realised that they had to do something to strengthen the country's position, so a number of reforms were passed and a new, liberal constitution was drawn up. Not all the nobles supported the new reforms and some of the most influential looked to Russia for assistance in stopping these developments. As a result, Russia and Prussia took more Polish territory, in the Second Partition of Poland. The Poles revolted, but were thrashed by the Russian and Prussian forces. The Third Partition of Poland took place in 1795, when the remaining territory was divided up between Russia, Prussia and Austria. The Polish–Lithuanian Commonwealth ceased to exist, and about half of the once-so-powerful empire was now controlled by the Russian tsar.

During the Napoleonic Wars, the Poles saw an opportunity to regain some of their territory, and many joined the French army. Napoleon established the Grand Duchy of Warsaw in 1807, but it was short-lived, and reverted to the Russian Empire in 1815, albeit with the status of kingdom. Tsar Alexander I was crowned king of Poland, and was supposed to uphold the Polish constitution. Initially, Poland enjoyed considerable independence, and even had its own government and army. But as the years went by, the Russians tightened their control more and more, until the Poles revolted in 1830. Tsar Nicolas I crushed the rebellion and abolished the Polish parliament, army and currency. The universities in Vilnius and Warsaw were closed, a large section of the Polish intelligentsia emigrated to Paris, and many of the Poles in local administration were replaced by Russians.

In 1863, the Poles revolted again. Alexander II had ascended the throne a few years earlier, and was known to be rather keen on reforms. The Poles had hoped that this might work in their favour, but then conscription was introduced, instead of the longed-for increase in devolution, and it triggered the January Uprising. The Russian response was brutal, and thousands of Poles were executed, imprisoned or deported. In addition, 1,600 estates were confiscated and given to Orthodox Russians. Polish territories were subjected to aggressive Russification: Polish place names were replaced with Russian names, Poles were barred from working in local administration, and Catholic monasteries were closed. Naturally, these measures only fuelled Polish nationalism and resistance to Russian rule.

Like the Baltic states, Poland did not regain its independence until the end of the First World War. But unlike the others, Poland retained its independence after the Second World War, on paper at least. The Polish government was kept on a short leash by Moscow until the end of the 1980s, when the Poles, emboldened by Lech Wałęsa's Solidarity, once again rose up.

* * *

Before I continued my journey north to Latvia, I managed to squeeze in a short visit to the Polish capital.

Warsaw is the complete opposite of picturesque Gdańsk. The streets are wide, the buildings big and tall. It is a city where it would be easy to disappear, to be swallowed up. Like Gdańsk, the old town was rebuilt after the war, something the Poles became very good at in the latter part of the twentieth century.

Fresh roses and bouquets are still left outside the parliament building in memory of the victims of the Smolensk airplane crash in 2010. All ninety-six passengers on board, including the then Polish president, Lech Kaczyński, and eighteen members of parliament, were killed in the crash. The delegation had been on its way to mark the seventieth anniversary of the Katyn Massacre. In March 1940, more than twenty thousand Polish soldiers and officers were shot and killed on Stalin's orders. More than four thousand of the victims were executed and buried in the Katyn Forest outside Smolensk.

And the man who *gave* the orders for the massacre was none other than Mikhail Kalinin, the man after whom Kaliningrad is named, who was the *official* head of state until 1945.

Even though the official investigations carried out by both Polish and Russian commissions concluded that the crash was caused by human error, many Poles still believe that the Russian authorities were involved. On the seventh anniversary of the disaster, Jarosław Kaczyński, the late president Lech Kaczyński's twin brother and leader of the right-wing populist party Law and Justice, which now has a majority in parliament, hinted that the Russian authorities were to blame for the crash: "We know with a very high degree of certainty that there was an explosion, and we will not stop in our search for the truth," he said. "We must be prepared for more opposition to the truth, and more hate."[24]

This long and complicated history of oppression, war and betrayal means that Poland's relationship with Russia can quickly become inflamed, making it easy for populist politicians to stir things up. Even though Poland now has only a short border with the exclave and military base in Kaliningrad, and none with the rest of Russia, the long historical border with the Russian Empire lives on in the Polish psyche.

The Master Race

The border crossing between Lithuania and Latvia was unmanned and desolate, surrounded by small, windswept pine trees. As soon as we had crossed the border, which was marked only by a sign, the road deteriorated. After half an hour on bumpy, potholed roads, we arrived in Daugavpils.

Daugavpils – known as Dvinsk by the Russians and Dünaburg by the Germans – is the second largest city in Latvia, and the largest in Europe where the majority of residents are ethnic Russians. But for all that, it could hardly be called metropolitan. With a popu-lation of a hundred thousand or so, it has only one tall, modern building in the centre: the Park Hotel Latgola.

Everywhere I went, I could hear Russian. In the parks, parents with young children sat drinking cans of beer while their children romped around in the E.U.-approved playgrounds. The mothers were dressed up in cheap clothes, and the men wore leather jackets and tracksuits. Daugavpils had been an important industrial town in the Soviet era, but Soviet heavy industry had not managed the transition to the European market. I got the feeling that everyone who had had the opportunity had left, which is probably not far from the truth. There are fewer inhabitants in Daugavpils now than there were in 1914. And this trend is not unique to Daugavpils – the number of inhabitants in most Latvian towns has fallen dramatically in recent years, and population growth is negative. In 1991, more than 2.6 million people lived in Latvia; by 2016, there were fewer than two million.

Despite the fact that Daugavpils was a poor town, even by Latvian standards, it was far better organised and maintained than any of the Russian towns I have visited. The roads and pavements complied with E.U. standards, the supermarkets were well stocked and characterless. And even though everyone spoke Russian, the signs were in Latvian. Daugavpils was a miniature Russian society stranded in the E.U.

It is no coincidence that so many Russians live there. In the Soviet era, as part of the Kremlin's focused Russification policy, hundreds of thousands of Russians moved to Estonia and Latvia to work in the expanding manufacturing industry. Over the course of fifty years, the Russian population in Latvia tripled. More than a quarter of Latvia's current population, that is to say, more than half a million people, are ethnic Russians. Following independence in 1991, the Latvian authorities refused to provide automatic citizenship for Russians who had moved there during the Soviet era. In order to become Latvian citizens, they first had to pass an exam in Latvian. Consequently, about three hundred thousand Russians in Latvia still do not have a Latvian passport.

Dmitri, the driver who took me to the fortress in Daugavpils, was one of the Russians who do have Latvian citizenship. And yet he could not speak a word of Latvian. "It just goes in one ear and out the other. I have never managed to learn it. That is our mayor," he said, and pointed at a postcard of Vladimir Putin that was hanging above the rear-view mirror. "Daugavpils was originally part of the Vitebsk region in Belarus," he said.

Dmitri was thrilled to have a true Scandinavian in his car, a descendant of the Vikings, and he pointed out the attractions as we passed.

"They are building a new research institute here," he informed me. "There will be an observatory on top, and here we have a school.

There, on the left-hand side, is the waterworks. That is where the water is heated for the city's central heating system."

After that there was nothing more of interest to point out until we entered the fortress area.

Work on the fortress started under Alexander I early in the nineteenth century. At its peak, ten thousand men were involved in its construction, and yet it took more than a hundred years for it to be completed. For a long time, the fortress in Dünaburg was one of the most important defence bases on the western frontier of the empire, and the tsars and tsarinas stopped here to rest on their way from St Petersburg to Europe.

I walked along the ramparts for thirty minutes or so. The fortress area comprised old, dilapidated houses and uncharming Soviet blocks. A couple of thousand people still live within its walls. I had actually come to see the Mark Rothko Art Centre, but it was closed for refurbishment. The iconic Jewish artist was born in Daugavpils in 1903, the year that marked the start of the most serious wave of pogroms in the Russian Empire. The nineteenth century had had its share of pogroms, but they did not compare with what happened in the early twentieth century. The Jews in Odessa, where perhaps as many as 2,500 were killed, suffered most, but no town with a significant Jewish population escaped. So many Russian Jews emigrated west, to countries where life was simpler and there were more opportunities. Mark Rothko was ten when his family abandoned their life in the Russian Empire and emigrated to the U.S.A. He stayed there for the rest of his life.

When Rothko was born, more than half the inhabitants in Daugavpils were Jewish, and the city had forty-eight synagogues. Only one survived the Second World War.

The second and final destination on our sightseeing tour was Church Hill. Both the Catholic and the Protestant churches were closed, but the huge, blue Saints Boris and Gleb Cathedral, the largest Russian Orthodox church in Latvia, was open. Inside the broad doors, it was clear there was extensive restoration work going on. The cathedral was consecrated in 1905, as part of Tsar Nicholas II's Russification policy for the Baltic countries. I could see another church spire a bit further up, so I walked over, and became very excited when I saw the sign: it was the Old Believers' church, which had opened in 1926. I had not managed to meet any Old Believers in Altay, but perhaps I would here in Daugavpils!

The gate was not locked. Nor was the church door. It creaked open, and I went into the dark, sombre interior lit only by a few candles. To the left of the door, there was a corner where visitors could buy candles and other religious effects. An old woman, dressed in black, stood talking to a hunchbacked man. When they saw me, they fell silent. The small, black-clad woman stomped towards me.

"Where are you going?" she snapped. She had a large scarf on her head that was secured under her chin with a safety pin. A couple of wisps of grey hair were still visible. "You obviously think you are at home and can come in as you please!"

"I just wanted to have a look at the church," I stammered.

"You cannot come in here like that!" she hissed, and pointed at me. "In trousers. And that scarf!" She nodded scornfully at the scarf that I had knotted under my chin.

"Oh, I don't understand . . ." I said in Russian, with a thick Norwegian accent.

"Don't understand, don't understand, nonsense! You understand! Now, please, just leave!"

And before I knew it I was outside the church again. The old woman stood glaring at me through the small window in the door.

Crestfallen, I turned away and headed for the panorama restaurant in the Park Hotel Latgola instead. I enjoyed the orange sunset and view of Daugavpils through the dirty window. There were brick houses and low Soviet apartment blocks as far as the eye could see. Later I wandered across the road to the Artillery Cellar Club. I had read in an article in the *Telegraph* that you could not order drinks in Russian there, and was intrigued by this possible Latvian defiance of Russian domination, perhaps even a conflict. The bar was small and dark, populated by a handful of regulars dressed in leather jackets. All men. They looked at me in surprise, but I pretended not to notice, and went and sat down at the bar as if it was the most natural thing in the world. The fair bartender could not hide his curiosity. For the first time in Daugavpils, I was greeted in Latvian.

I cut straight to the chase.

"Is it true that you cannot order a drink in Russian here?" I asked in English.

"Ah," he said, with a dismissive wave of the hand. "That was a bit of a storm in a teacup. An exaggeration to say the least, a mountain out of a molehill." He clearly liked sayings. "People can order whatever they like in whichever language they like," he said.

I ordered a glass of red wine, in English, drank it, then walked back to the spartan hotel where I was staying, by the bus station.

"So, we have a representative of Quisling's people here," Visvaldis Lācis said, when he opened the door. The ninety-two-year-old spoke excellent English. He did not hear very well, but was otherwise in impressively good health, tall and athletic and almost without wrinkles. His wiry, grey hair was cut short and stood straight up. Both his eye teeth were silver. Without wasting any time, he invited me up to his office on the first floor. He climbed the steep ladder with easy grace, and I followed clumsily. From the large windows there was a view to the delightful garden and nearby lake.

Interviewing Visvaldis was a challenge, in part because he found it difficult to hear what I said and was given to long digressions, but also because he generally did not answer my questions, even when he did hear and understand them.

"I have written sixteen books and 405 articles, but I have not worked a single day for the Latvian newspapers," he declared proudly. "I am a free man!"

When he noticed how much I admired the view, he told me: "I built this house with my own two hands in 1964, when we were part of the Soviet Union. There are not many of us still alive who were born in pre-Soviet days, in an independent Latvia. I was lucky enough to grow up in a free country – I went to kindergarten in Latvia. I was sixteen when the Soviet Union invaded. The first year of Soviet occupation was a terrible one in Latvian history. Thousands of Latvians were deported and killed, even babies. It was genocide. My father lost his life in a car accident in 1940, so it was just my mother, my big sister and me. We did not suffer, but many people we knew did."

He stood up and went over to the bookshelf.

"I have five or six hundred books about the Second World War in different languages. Look. Foreign observers wrote that the Latvians welcomed the Germans as liberators, but we did so on the understanding that our country was threatened by two total-itarian systems. The Germans were the better of the two. We had lived under Sweden, Poland, Germany and Russia, and the Russians were by far the worst. We could actually compare! We knew that the Germans were a danger to the world, but to us they represented Western civilisation."

The Latvians and Estonians had special status in the eyes of the Nazis. Ever since the Teutonic Order invaded the region in the twelfth century, the Balts and Germans have lived side by side. For example, Riga was primarily a German town for hundreds of years. The Latvian capital was founded in the middle of the twelfth century by German merchants and became a member of the Hanseatic League in 1282. And even though Riga was ruled by Russia from 1710, following Sweden's defeat at the Battle of Poltava, German was the only official language until 1891. When the First World War broke out, about sixteen per cent of the inhabitants of Riga were Baltic Germans. Most of those who remained were then evacuated in 1939 as part of the Molotov–Ribbentrop Pact: *Heim ins Reich*. Racial hygienists believed, however, that Latvian and Estonian genes had been sufficiently watered down as a result of living with the Germans for so long that they should be given special status among the Eastern European peoples. After the Battle of Stalingrad, the Germans needed more soldiers and ordered full mobilisation in Latvia. In 1943, eighty thousand Latvians were enrolled in the Latvian Legion of the Waffen-SS. Visvaldis Lācis is the only one still alive.

"I was happy to enlist," he said. "I was nineteen and did a lot of sport. I played basketball, and in summer I played football. I was in good shape and I was also well educated for my age – I had finished middle school and learnt Latin, Greek and German. I became an *Unterführer* in the army – a non-commissioned officer – and enjoyed it. After four months' training, I was made a corporal, and then a sergeant."

Before the war, about seventy thousand Jews lived in Latvia. Practically none of the Latvian Jews, except those who were deported by the Soviet authorities before the war, survived the German occupation.

"We were not behind the Holocaust," Visvaldis said. "That was an entirely Nazi project. There was nothing we could do to save the Jews. Our goal was to become independent. I remember we walked the streets singing: 'First we will beat the Reds, then the Greys.' Our goal was to get rid of the Germans as well."

When the Red Army pushed the Germans back in 1944, Visvaldis was leader of a small group of thirty-five infantry soldiers in Courland on the Baltic coast. The soldiers in Courland were some of the last German army troops to capitulate. They did not surrender until May 12, 1945, four days after Germany's unconditional capitulation.

"We knew very well that Hitler had killed himself," Visvaldis said, "it was no secret. I continued to fight in the forest because I wanted to be a partisan, but I had been wounded in the hip and I partially lost my sight. Fortunately my leg could be saved, but I was certified as permanently visually impaired. My mother came to collect me. She had managed to get false documents for me, because at the time you could not get a passport until you were twenty-one. I went to work on a state farm, but soon after was sent to prison in Riga. The K.G.B. officers beat me and asked lots of questions, though I would not call it torture. I should actually have been in prison for longer, but it was soon after the war and there were not enough young men. Stalin decided that three thousand of us should be released. And so I started a new phase, and even though I was a free man, I was treated badly. We former legionnaires were Latvia's white Negroes! I was expelled several times from higher education institutions. And even though I got the best marks possible in Marxism–Leninism, I was not allowed to take a doctorate."

Visvaldis suddenly picked up a handwritten notebook and started to read out loud: "Yesterday I walked twenty-one kilometres and six hundred metres!"

He handed me the notebook, which gave a detailed account of every single walk he had done in recent years. He generally walked five or six kilometres a day. He also calculated the average speed and added comments in English, such as "now feel tired" or "feel good".

"I am an athlete," he said. "When I check in this book I see that I am just as fast now as I was seven years ago. Then I know that I am not exaggerating."

He got up and opened a drawer, then took out a list of marathons. He had underlined all the ones he wanted to run, including the Copenhagen Marathon on May 22, the Amsterdam Marathon on October 16, and the Athens Classic Marathon on November 13. Oslo was not on the list, but he wanted to take part in that as well.

"It is in September, isn't it?"

I nodded.

"Perhaps you could help me to find a cheap hotel? I am no longer a rich man. On July 15 last year, I took part in a marathon here in Latvia. Forty-two kilometres and one hundred and ninety-five metres! It was a walking marathon, and I did it in just over seven hours."

"I have heard that you are also politically active," I said, to get him back on track.

"That is correct, I have been a member of the Latvian parliament twice!" he said. "The last term was from 2006 to 2011, first for the Union of Greens and Farmers, and then for Visu Latvijai. I was the oldest M.P. in Latvian history."

Visu Latvijai (All for Latvia) was a neo-fascist party that lobbied for a ban on Russian in schools and the deportation of ethnic Russians. They took part in the annual memorial for legionnaires on March 15, and organised demonstrations against the Latvian ban on the swastika. In 2011, All for Latvia joined the For Fatherland and Freedom party to form the National Alliance. They took close to seventeen per cent of the vote in the 2016 election and are the fourth largest party in Latvia, with seventeen of the hundred seats in the Saeima, the Latvian parliament. They hold three ministerial posts in the coalition government.

"The Russians are a threat to Latvia!" Visvaldis said. "More than

260,000 Russians in Latvia do not have Latvian citizenship. Almost half of them long for the return of the Soviet Union and nearly all of them want Russian to be the official language in Latvia. How would you react if forty per cent of the population in Norway was German and demanded that German be the official language?"

"But lots of the Russian families came to Latvia long before the war," I argued.

"Yes, the Russian occupation started under the tsars," Visvaldis said. "The tsars sent Russians here, and there were special laws that meant that only Russians could buy land, through the Russian banks. Russia is now a greater threat than ever. Crimea has never been a Russian country!"

He was waving his arms around and almost knocked over a glass of water.

"It has never been a Ukrainian country either, it was the country of the Tatars, their history goes back to the 1200s!" he said, with great passion. "Putin always talks about the Russian world. The Russian world is wherever there are Russians, according to Putin. In 1991, Latvians accounted for fifty-two per cent of the population, now it is sixty per cent. But in 1790 eighty-nine per cent of the population was Latvian! All the Russians should have gone back to their own country when the Soviet Union dissolved in 1991. They are occupiers. But in 1993, the German chancellor said we had to sign an agreement with the people who lived in our territory if we wanted to become a member of the E.U."

Visvaldis would rather that Latvia had not become a member of the E.U.

"From the start I said that membership of the E.U. would lead to mass emigration from Latvia to other European countries," he said. "The experts and young people, in particular, would leave, I warned. And that is what happened. I often lie awake at night and wonder if there will still be a Latvian state in a hundred years' time."

Unrest

"A Russian officer showed up here first thing in the morning on March 25, 1949," seventy-nine-year-old Andrei Ierags said. He lived in the middle of nowhere, at the end of a dirt track that was only usable in summer. It was already warm and cosy in the small living room, but Andrei kept putting new logs in the burner.

"We were given two hours to pack our things," he said. "The officer told us we had a long journey ahead and it would not be easy."

In one single day, more than forty-two thousand Latvians were deported to Siberia. About thirty thousand Lithuanians and twenty thousand Estonians shared the same fate. The deportations were part of the forced collectivisation of agriculture in the Baltic states, and those who were deported were accused either of being *kulaks*, that is to say, wealthy farmers, or nationalists. The intent was to remove all "anti-Soviet elements" from the Baltic Soviet republics, and to do away with any remains of the Forest Brothers, the partisan group that continued to fight against the Soviet regime throughout the Baltic region until the 1950s.

"But let's raise a glass," Andrei said. "I will need it if I am going to tell you my whole life story."

Anna, his daughter, who had driven me there from Riga, immediately got out two bottles of vodka. "I bought them for you when I was in Ukraine," she said, happily.

"Ukraine?" Her father burst out laughing. "They sell that in the local shop!"

A buxom woman in her seventies served us salad, meatballs

and tea. She was a widow, Andrei was a widower, and they kept each other company.

"Our father was arrested in 1943," Andrei said. "He had been part of Aizargi, 'the defenders', a paramilitary group that was established in the interwar years to defend Latvian territory. He never shot anyone, but was sentenced to ten years in prison."

"Do you remember anything of the war?" I asked.

"Do I remember anything? I remember everything. The front line was here in 1943, and the Russian Red Cross worked from this house. The injured were treated here in this house. Legs were amputated here."

As his father had been part of Aizargi, all of Andrei's family were branded nationalists after the war.

"We were transported in freight trains," Andrei said. "I was twelve and a half. My sisters were sixteen and eighteen. The carriages were completely dark. The journey took ten days. We lived in the village of Makushino the first year, then we moved on to Staritsa, which is also in Siberia. I could speak a little Russian, but my teacher thought my grammar was not good enough, so I had to take third grade again. Once a week, an officer would come to our home to make sure we were still there."

The family managed to survive those early, difficult years thanks to his mother's pragmatism. She had taken the family heirlooms and some potatoes with her to Siberia. Almost every day, she went to help a woman in another village with her garden and animals, and in the third year the woman gave her a calf to thank her.

"It was black, I remember," Andrei said. "I built a winter house for the calf from straw, which it then ate through the cold months. When it was big, Mother managed to get it to give milk even in winter. No-one understood how she did it. We lived in cramped conditions, in only one room, with straw on the roof, and were permanently cold. The soil in Siberia is rich, it is like a jungle there, but it was not our home. Our life consisted of work, work and more work."

Andrei's father was released from prison in 1956, but he had to live in Siberia for another ten years. The family moved to the industrial city of Krasnoyarsk, where Andrei got a job in a textile factory. And because he was earning, his family could finally get their own house.

"My mother died in 1960, when I was still in the army," Andrei said. "It is a long story, but owing to bureaucracy and a mistake by my sister, I was not able to get there before she fell into a coma. She was buried in Krasnoyarsk, and never saw her beloved Latvia again."

The day after Christmas two years later, Andrei came to Riga for the first time. He was twenty-six. He had finished his military service, and, unlike his father, was free to go where he pleased.

"I came home with my heart full of hope and joy," he said, before taking another shot of the Ukrainian vodka. "My only goal in Siberia had been to get home to Latvia. When I woke up that morning on the train, just before we arrived at the station, I heard people speaking Latvian all around me. They were even playing the national anthem! And if I had not been a man, I would have cried."

But the *dream* of the homeland was one thing, the reality was another, and Andrei had spent most of his life thousands of kilometres away.

"One of the hardest moments was when I realised that I did not know Latvia. I had no idea how to behave at a Latvian funeral, I knew nothing. I struggled to find a job. I could not come back here, to our farm, as it was now a collective. And I was so used to talking Russian after the army that I automatically translated the Latvian I heard into Russian. Before I said anything, I had to translate from Russian into Latvian in my head."

"He became a ski champion in Latvia!" his daughter said, and put an arm around his shoulders.

"Only in Riga, Anna," he corrected her, with a suppressed smile. "I trained as an electrical engineer and worked on the railway for a while. I travelled all over the Soviet Union during those years."

When the country gained its independence again, the state gave the original owners back their property and land. In 1993, Andrei was finally able to move back to the farm where he had spent his early childhood.

"All I wanted to do was to get the property back in order again," he said. "Why do we need houses? Why do we need to get married? We need houses to have something to come back to. A house should be warm, it should be a place where you are not cold. Siberia was cold and draughty, and I was always freezing. I never want to experience that again, I want a *warm* house. And we get married so there is someone waiting, even if you go far, far away, even if you go to prison."

Before we went back to Riga, Andrei showed us around the garden. It was tidy and well looked after, with colourful flower-beds and a big vegetable patch. Everything was just so, all the tools were hanging in the right place, nothing had been left lying around.

Andrei put his arm around his daughter and gave her a hug.

"To live or not to live," he said. "You always have a choice. I learned to survive in Siberia. I learned to find solutions, to be human. If you can't get out through the door, get out through the window!"

* * *

More than five million Soviet citizens were forcibly moved by Stalin. Women, children, old people. Five million were uprooted and dispatched east – almost always east – in dirty, dark, claustrophobic freight trains.

And everywhere in the ruins of the Soviet Empire, there are people who remember those vile, cramped freight trains. All you need to do is scratch the surface.

There are visible remains of the empire everywhere: statues of broad-shouldered heroes, dilapidated blocks of flats constructed in haste, metro stations decorated with paintings of imaginary model citizens, palaces of culture, and draughty, concrete schools built for eternity. Other remnants are more hidden: K.G.B. prisons with torture and execution chambers, surveillance equipment in walls, kilometres of wires and microphones, long-since-closed Gulag camps, inscriptions on graves that have been erased by wind and sand, mile upon mile of rusty barbed wire along borders that no longer exist. And in people's homes, in closed cupboards and drawers, along an axis that stretches from the Baltic Sea to the Pacific Ocean, there are literally tons of faded red stars, heroes' medals and pioneer scarves, covered in a thin film of post-communist dust.

There are also traces underground. The Līgatne Bunker lies seventy-five kilometres from Riga. It was from here, nine metres below the surface, that the Latvian government and communist elite would rule the country in the event of a nuclear attack by the Americans. In 1982, a sanatorium was built over the bunker, in order to conceal its existence. Staff at the sanatorium had no idea about the concrete labyrinth nine metres beneath them.

The bunker was opened to visitors in 2003. The lobby was full of foreigners, including a large group of noisy Italian pensioners. A smiling young woman in a retro-military uniform showed us around. She had to arch her voice over the Italians, who chattered away nonstop.

The bunker was a subterranean, pistachio-coloured universe: two thousand square metres divided into ninety rooms along three narrow corridors. The walls were painted light green, a colour

believed to stimulate feelings of happiness and well-being by the
Soviet psychologists of the day. A loud ventilation system ensured
there was always fresh air. New arrivals would first have to take
a shower in a special decontamination shower system, and then put
on new, non-radioactive clothes. There was a library with a selection
of Lenin's books and volumes of Soviet law to help pass the time.
The store cupboards contained enough tinned food to feed 250
people for three months. The architects had thought of everything.
Secret war maps provided an overview of the strategic infrastructure in Latvia and possible targets. One of the telephones had only
one button – the direct line to Moscow.

The bunker cost a total of three billion dollars – in 1970! And
this was just one of many such shelters on both sides of the Iron
Curtain.

After all the tourists had taken a turn to pose in a gas mask
in front of the Lenin statue, we were served a Soviet lunch in the
canteen. Pelmeni, a kind of ravioli filled with coarse mince, served
on warm metal plates and a sweet fruit compote. Past paranoia
has become present-day entertainment.

There were no buses back to Riga, but I managed to hitch a lift
to the nearest town with Matt and Cassandra, a young American
couple. He had just been in Norway to take part in the Norseman
Xtreme Triathlon, one of the world's toughest. He did not look
particularly sporty, but that may have been because of his long
beard. I had not spoken to anyone for days, so told them all about
my travels and books. When I had satisfied my need to talk, I
politely asked what they did.

"I am a nutritional physiologist," Matt replied.

"And I am a dominatrix," Cassandra said.

"How would you describe your typical customer?" I felt obliged
to ask a few follow-up questions to show that I was open and
tolerant and hard to shock, but I was also curious.

"Oh, there are all sorts," Cassandra said. "Lawyers, doctors, politicians, you know, all the clichés . . . I also have some clients who are pastors from various denominations."

"Interesting," I said.

"Yes, I have actually thought about writing a book, as I don't like the way in which dominatrices are portrayed. You know, as abused children, drug addicts, losers."

We reached the town at this point, and there was no time to find out more. Matt and Cassandra drove on to an exciting spa hotel they had read about, and I stood in the freezing, Baltic rain, waiting for the next bus to Riga.

A Lesson in Liberation

The border between Latvia and Estonia runs through the middle of a town. A bus shelter is all that remains of the old border station, which was closed in 2007 when the Baltic countries became members of Schengen.

The Baltic Germans called the town Walk, and the name first appears in written sources in 1286. During the Estonian and Latvian wars of independence after the First World War, the parties could not agree on which side of the border the town should be. In the end, the British, who supported the Baltic countries' fight for independence from the Germans and the Russians, stepped in: in 1920, Colonel Stephan Tallents decided that the town should be divided in two, so that is what happened. Just under six thousand people currently live on the Latvian side of Valka, and twice as many live on the Estonian side of Valga. This is because many of the people in Valka have in recent years decided to move to the Estonian side, attracted by the salaries and better social conditions there. The only drawback is that, as Estonian citizens, they have to learn Estonian. Unlike Latvian and Russian, Estonian is not an Indo-European language – it belongs to the Uralic family, and is related to Finnish and the Sámi languages. Whereas German has four cases, and Russian and Latin both have six, Estonian boasts fourteen different cases (but the Finns win this particular grammatical contest with a total of fifteen cases).

Thanks to the Estonian language's similarity to Finnish, Estonians managed to maintain a degree of contact with the Western world throughout the Soviet era. The construction of illegal aerials became an art, and the Finnish communist newspaper, *Kansan Uutiset* (*People's News*), sold out every Saturday – because it included the Finnish television listings for the coming week. The Finns built powerful transmitters so as to reach their kin in the south, but the signals got no further than Tallinn and the north coast of Estonia. Those who lived further south had to make do with summaries of the intrigues in *Dallas* from relatives in the capital.

On June 24, 1987, everyone was waiting for something that could not be summarised in a letter. There were unusually long queues into the city from early morning. According to the television listings in *Kansan Uutiset*, that evening the Finnish state channel was going to show *Emmanuelle*, the erotic French film from 1974. The film is about a French diplomat's wife in Thailand. She is bored at home, as her husband is always at work, and to distract herself, she has a number of sexual relationships with both men and women (with the blessing of her tolerant husband). The husband eventually orchestrates a meeting between Emmanuelle and the older, experienced Mario, who takes her under his wing and introduces her to the more advanced mysteries of eroticism.

There was not a parking space to be found in Tallinn that Wednesday evening, and the streets were quiet and deserted. A blue, flickering light emanated from all the apartment windows. In living rooms across the capital, grandparents, aunts, uncles, neighbours and schoolchildren sat glued to their television screens in order not miss this rare insight into the lives of French diplomats' wives. A remarkable number of children were born nine months later in the Soviet Republic of Estonia.

After a short stop at the bus station in Valga, the bus carried on north to the university city of Tartu, Estonia's intellectual and cultural centre.* The German legacy here is substantial. Both the city hall, built in 1789, and the university, which was founded in the reign of King Gustav II Adolphus in 1632 and reopened under Tsar Alexander I in 1802, were designed by German architects.

In the large, empty university auditorium I met Marju Lauristen, who played a very important role in the Estonian independence movement. She was the minister for social affairs in the early Nineties, and then became a professor in social communication at Tartu University.

"This used to be full of people, now there are only administrative staff. It is the same everywhere," Lauristen said. She was elegantly dressed, with short white hair and the air of a determined matriarch. Her command of English was excellent, and her delivery authoritative.

We went over the street to Café Werner, the oldest cafe in Tartu.

"They don't have cakes like these in Brussels, do they now?" a man said, as he passed our table.

"Nowhere has cakes as good as these," Lauristen said with a smile. She has been an M.E.P. for the Social Democrats since 2014, and is a well-known figure not only here in her hometown, but throughout Estonia.

Without wasting any time, she launched into a lecture on the history of Estonia.

"First of all, you never really decide to start a revolution, or even realise that that is what you are doing," she said. "There is still a debate as to whether the Singing Revolution really was a revolution or not. Perhaps it was just evolution. But the fact is that the Baltic independence movement started with the Singing Revolution here in Estonia. But to understand the Singing Revolution, you need to understand the role of song in Estonian history. The Estonian song

---

*   The city was known as Dorpat in German and Swedish.

festivals are an institution. The first was held here in Tartu in 1869."

I scribbled furiously to keep track of all the points the professor made. She observed discreetly, making sure that I left nothing out.

"And to understand the song festivals, we have to go even further back," she said. "It's an outrage, really, that Sweden lost us to Russia in 1710. You're no doubt aware that Latvia and Estonia were treated differently as there were so many Baltic Germans here. The Baltic Germans were landowners and were allowed to keep their land. The Estonians were Christianised relatively early on, so the German priests had to learn Estonian – as you will know, Lutheran children have to be able to read the catechism. Our farmers and serfs were emancipated fifty years before the reforms in Russia, and the children of Estonian farmers could read and write, which was not the case in Russia. The nineteenth century was a century of nation building throughout Europe. Tallinn was still essentially a German town, which is why Tartu became a hub for Estonian nationalism. Are you keeping up?"

I nodded.

"Good. In 1860, Estonian farmers owned most of the land here. In 1869, the first song festival took place here in Tartu. It was a festival to celebrate Estonian identity. At the time, the Germans were our main problem, not the Russians. German was the language of academia, whereas Russian was the language of bureaucracy. All over Tartu there popped up singing associations, where people could sing together and discuss the songs. The singing festivals were held every five years. We were even allowed to hold them during the Soviet era. As long as the songs were socialist in content, they could be nationalist in form. All socialist organisations had their own song festivals. And every five years we all gathered and sang that we wanted to be free." She smiled. "And of course, we did not mean free only in a socialist sense. Thirty to forty thousand people would take part in the biggest festivals, and a hundred thousand more would listen. You can imagine how powerful that was, especially in the 1980s, when things started to happen."

Lauristen glanced at her watch, then carried on.

"Gorbachev was an idealist. He believed that glasnost would make people better communists. But instead people used their freedom of speech to discuss how to get rid of communism! I was teaching at the university here in Tartu when it all started. I was invited to write an article about the planned phosphorite quarry in North Estonia, and I said yes."

The planned development of phosphorite mining in North Estonia provoked huge opposition from the Estonians and was one of the driving forces behind the demand for independence. If the quarry had opened, more than a hundred thousand Russians would have moved into the area to meet the labour needs. And pollution from the quarry would have contaminated the ground water and made half the country uninhabitable.

"A year later, in 1988, I took part in a project where we calculated the cost of economic independence," Lauristen said. "And that is how I became involved in Rahvarinne, the Popular Front movement. The movement was started on the initiative of Edgar Savisaar, our first prime minster, in a live television broadcast on April 13, 1988. The same day, we marched to the Soviet military base just outside Tartu with three different flags, which combined made up the Estonian flag. It was a bold move, because in the Soviet days you could be arrested for carrying the Estonian flag."

After the Second World War, the Soviet Union had built an airbase just outside Tartu that was one of the biggest in Eastern Europe. Tartu was therefore a relatively closed city under Soviet rule: foreigners were not allowed to overnight there, for example.

"It was a wholly grass roots movement," Lauristen recalled. "People phoned the university in Tartu to join up. We became the hub. The atmosphere was always happy and positive, because people were relieved that they no longer had to stay silent."

One of the most important demands that emerged was that Moscow should recognise that the Molotov–Ribbentrop Pact had provided the basis for the Soviet occupation of the Baltic countries. Gorbachev resisted. On August 23, 1989, fifty years to the day since the pact had been signed, two million Balts held hands to make a human chain that stretched from Vilnius to Tallinn, in a silent protest against Moscow.

"The human chain protest was carefully planned, down to the smallest detail," Lauristen said. "We wanted the international media, such as C.N.N., to be here. We wanted to show the world that the Baltic countries were united, that we were well organised and non-violent, and that the majority supported us. The strength of the Singing Revolution was always that it was a non-violent movement, you understand? If we had used violence, Moscow would have had an excuse to intervene and we would have lost all the goodwill from the West. Before the protest, we drove along all the roads to measure the distances and calculate how many people we would need. Everything was organised via radio. I stood at the top of the Pikk Hermann Tower in Tallinn, as the first person in the chain. I held the Estonian flag in my hand and said into the microphone, in Estonian, Latvian and Lithuanian: 'We want freedom!' Two million people repeated those words in Estonian, Latvian and Lithuanian. It was possibly the best moment in my life."

Two years later, on August 20, 1991, while Gorbachev was being held hostage in the Crimean Peninsula by a *coup d'état*, Estonia and Latvia seized the opportunity to break away from the Soviet Union. Lithuania had already declared independence in March 1990.

"My parents, Johannes and Olga, were underground communists in the interwar period, and were imprisoned for fifteen years,"

Lauristen said. "My father died in 1941, so he never experienced communism in practice. But my mother did, and she quickly discovered that it was not the society she had dreamt of and fought for. There are people in Brussels who still fantasise about a radical left-wing society. They want something pure, but I know that dreams like that just end in totalitarianism. I know what it is like to live in a totalitarian state. As a university lecturer I always had to consider carefully what I would say to my students. It was like living in Orwell's *1984*. Social democracy is the only realistic solution, in my opinion."

The transition to social democracy and a market economy was not without problems, and for a short while food rationing was introduced.

"The Nineties were hard for everyone," Lauristen said. "We lost our most important market, Russia, and the country was in crisis. But we pulled through, and the Estonian economy had an annual growth of eight to ten per cent until the financial crisis. We are ranked third of the new member states in the E.U. when it comes to financial growth. Only Slovenia and the Czech Republic have done better. But growth has stagnated as a result of the financial crisis. We have had to take drastic action and have not been able to tackle some of the social issues."

There are a large number of ethnic Russians living in Estonia, as there are in Latvia, and many of them do not have a passport.

"A quarter of the population, 320,000 people, are ethnic Russians, and 90,000 of them do not have citizenship. Half of these do not want Estonian citizenship – the only disadvantages are that they cannot join the police force or vote in general elections, otherwise they have the same rights as before. The other half, however, would like citizenship, but have not passed the Estonian language exam. They are the ones we have to help, but Estonia is a small country, and Estonian is a small language. The Russians in Finland learn Finnish quickly enough, when they are motivated. The language issue is a post-colonial thing. The Russians were the ruling class in the empire and the Soviet Union. They were the master, but now they are the minority. And that is not easy for them."

The Monument War

The River Narva flowed silently by. Half the river lies in Russia, and half in Estonia. A couple of youngsters canoed down the Estonian side. There were a lot of people on the riverbank – families, children, groups of teenagers, couples and pensioners – all enjoying the mild May evening. All of them Russians. The air hummed with sibilants and soft consonants. The promenade, which was brand new and had clearly cost a considerable amount, was called Europa Promenade, as though to underline for the Russians who live here that they are, indeed, in Europe. This was where the E.U. started. N.A.T.O.'s Article 5, which stated that an armed attack on one of the member states would be seen as an attack on them all, applied here. The promenade was lit by twenty-eight street lamps, one for each of the E.U. countries. Telescopes had been set up in various places so Narva's Russians could look over to the Russians on the other side. I stopped by one of the telescopes and zoomed in on a lonely fisherman and a gang of young lads sitting by the river drinking beer.

In the interwar period, when Estonia was independent for the first time, Ivangorod, the twin city on the other side, was part of Estonia. However, the border was redrawn by the Soviet Union. Narva became part of the Soviet Republic of Estonia, whereas Ivangorod, on the other side of the river, ended up in the Russian Soviet Republic. The current border between Russia and Estonia is the same as the Soviet border, but has still not been ratified by either country. Each party blames the other: the Estonians have said they will finalise the work once the Russians have ratified the agreement, and the Russians, for their part, have said that the negotiation process, i.e. the Estonians' rhetoric, has to be less aggressive if they are to progress. In practice, however, this tit-for-tat about the border is of little consequence: in 2004, Estonia, Latvia and Lithuania joined both the E.U. and N.A.T.O., and even though the border with Russia is as yet only a de facto border, the Estonians plan to build a very real fence along parts of it. The work is due to start in 2018.* Latvia and Lithuania have similar plans. The Poles, however, have decided not to build a fence, but have instead invested in technologically advanced observation towers in order to keep an eye on the Russians. So while boundaries are being dismantled within the E.U., barriers are being built to keep the neighbour to the east in check. Following the annexation of Crimea and the war in Eastern Ukraine, N.A.T.O. now has a greater presence in the Baltic. There are multinational battalions of approximately a thousand soldiers in each country, and these rotate on a six-monthly basis. There have also been several major N.A.T.O. exercises in the Baltic region in recent years. The message to Putin is clear: thus far, but no further. The Baltic countries are once again under the wing of the West.

When I had finished with the telescope, I noticed a man in his sixties standing behind me, watching.

"Sorry, do you want to use the telescope?" I asked.

"No, why on earth would I want to do that?" He was genuinely surprised by my question. "There's nothing to see."

"Do you often go over to Russia?" I asked.

He shrugged.

"Once a year, maybe. I can be in Russia for up to ninety days, if I want, but why would I do that? We have more freedom here.

* As of April 2020 it still had not.

And they are so corrupt over there. There is always someone who wants money from you."

"Were you born here?"

"Yes, I was born here, but I don't have citizenship," he said. "To begin with, it was for practical reasons: my wife is Ukrainian and I didn't need to get a visa whenever we went to visit her family. But now you don't need a visa to go there, anyway. I think they should give us citizenship. After all, I have lived here all my life."

I got out my notebook and started to write down what he had said. He watched me silently, then added: "On the other hand, Estonia is a small country. They want to protect themselves and they want everyone to speak Estonian."

"I have heard that Estonian is a very difficult language," I said.

"Difficult, perhaps," he mumbled. "If you want to learn it, you learn it. But everyone here in Narva is Russian. There is no need for Estonian. There is no reason to learn it. And it would be hard to practise here."

"What do you do for a living?"

"That is a secret," he said. "I can't tell you. Oh, O.K., you don't know my name, after all. I am a security guard."

"How old are you?"

"Sixty-three, close to retirement. How old are you?"

"Thirty-two."

"Nearly the same age as Jesus when he was nailed to the cross. But you are a woman." He folded his arms. "I have more questions for you. Is that O.K.?"

I nodded.

"Put your notebook away."

I did as I was told.

"You said you were from Sweden, didn't you?"

"Norway," I corrected him.

"Ah yes, that's right." He looked me in the eye. "What is your view on immigration to Norway? All those Muslim refugees? Be honest. How can it be good? In a few years' time, there won't be any blonde girls like you left."

Estonia is one of the E.U. countries that takes in fewest refugees and asylum seekers from non-Western countries. This is not due to reluctance on the part of the Estonian government, but because not many asylum seekers freely choose Estonia. The government has agreed to accept some five hundred transfer refugees from Greece and Turkey. A quarter of those who have already come to Estonia have since left.

"There is nothing to worry about in Norway," I assured the security guard.

He looked sceptical, but said nothing.

With the exception of the new Europa Promenade, Narva was a pretty boring town. Before the war, it had been one of the most beautiful towns in Estonia, but the old town was destroyed by the Red Army, who bombed the city for days in late winter 1944. The German soldiers then torched what little remained when they withdrew in July later that year. Ninety-eight per cent of the old town disappeared. Only three buildings were left standing.

The old town may no longer be there, but evidence of the Second World War is still present. The following day, I visited the German war graves just outside the centre. Four thousand German soldiers lie buried here. The crosses are painted white, simple and low, with several names carved on each cross to save space. Most of the soldiers were younger than Jesus when they died.

Constructed by the Danes in the mid-thirteenth century, Hermann Castle was sold a hundred years later to the German Brothers of the Sword, along with the rest of North Estonia. After the Second World War the castle was rebuilt, but the Swedish lion statue, a copy of one of the lions at Stockholm Palace, was not returned to its pedestal. The few monuments that had survived the war – all that remained of the two hundred or so that the Estonians had managed to raise in the brief period of independence between the wars – were replaced by statues of Lenin and Marx and other socialist role models. The old town was not rebuilt either, presumably for fear that it might make the Estonians yearn for better days.

In 2000, three hundred years after Charles XII's decisive victory over the Russians, the Swedish lion reappeared in Narva, high on a pedestal, looking out over Estonia, with its tail turned to Russia. There is a plaque on the pedestal that says *Svecia memor*: "Sweden is remembered". Four years after the Swedish victory, Peter the Great regained the town, but there is no memorial in Narva to mark that victory. Peter the Great is not very popular in Estonia. The first thing the Estonians did when they became independent after the First World War was to pull down the statue of Peter the Great in the centre of Tallinn. When they won their independence for the second time in 1991, they promptly replaced the statues of Lenin and Marx with new versions of the national monuments from the interwar period. The Lenin statue in the centre of Narva was the last to be removed in 1993. The Russian-dominated city council did not have the heart to throw out or destroy the creator of the Soviet Union, so they relocated him instead. Lenin now stands by Hermann Castle, near a memorial plaque to the Finnish soldiers who helped to liberate Narva from the Bolsheviks in 1919.

The Estonians' schizophrenic relationship with their own history became apparent in the so-called Monument War at the start of this century. In 2002, a monument in honour of "Estonian men who fought in 1940–1945 against Bolshevism and for the restoration of Estonian independence" was due to be unveiled in the small town of Pärnu in the west of Estonia. The monument is a bronze relief depicting an Estonian soldier in a German SS uniform on a granite slab, and it was removed by the Pärnu town council before it was even unveiled, because of the obvious association with the Nazis. Two years later, the controversial monument re-appeared, this time in a cemetery in the village of Lihula. Estonia had become a member of the E.U. only a few months before, and it did not take long for the international community to respond. The Estonian government ordered the immediate removal of the monument, but the people of Lihula were strongly opposed. When the crane came to remove the monument, it was prevented from accessing the cemetery by furious protesters, and the police had to use tear gas to disperse them. In autumn 2005, the problematic soldier popped up again, in a privately owned resistance museum in Lagedi, outside Tallinn. Meanwhile, another bronze soldier statue had started to become a headache for the Estonian authorities. This time the controversy concerned the two-metre-tall Bronze Soldier that had been raised in 1947 in memory of the soldiers who fell fighting for the Red Army. For nearly sixty years it had stood without causing any bother, but now the Estonians started to grumble. If *their* soldier could not stand where they wanted it to, why should the Russians be allowed to have theirs in the centre of Tallinn?

The Bronze Soldier was vandalised a number of times. For example, on Victory Day in 2005, it was sprayed with red paint. In late 2007, the government decided that the troublesome statue should be moved from Tönismägi in the centre of the capital to the war cemetery on the outskirts of the city. On April 26, 2008, a big crowd of Russian protesters gathered by the statue to prevent its removal. When the police came to disperse them, the demonstrators started to throw bottles and stones at the officers. The rampage went on through the evening and night, and windows were broken, shops looted and cars vandalised. One person was killed, scores were injured, and some three hundred arrests were made on what has become known as Bronze Night.

Metal and stone can arouse great passion. At the heart of the conflict lie two very different views of history: for many Estonians, the Bronze Soldier is a symbol of the sixty-year Soviet occupation of their country, whereas, for the country's Russian minority, it is a symbol of the Red Army's hard-won victory over the Nazis in the Great Patriotic War, a war that cost the Soviet people dear. If one digs down through the layers of emotion, it becomes clear that the Monument War is in fact primarily about the new imbalance between victor and former colonial power, between the majority and the minority. After the dissolution of the Soviet Union, the history of Estonia was rewritten once again. New monuments were given a place in the sun, and the old ones were relegated to the shade.

"What did they tell you in Narva?" said Andrei Hvostov, an outspoken and, in his own words, controversial Russian-Estonian author and journalist, when I met him a few days later in a cafe in Tallinn. I summarised: they complained about unemployment and about bad Estonian teachers, but most of them thought they had a better life here in Estonia than they would have had in Russia.

"They are also pro-Putin, just like they are in Daugavpils, but they have learnt how to answer 'sensitive' questions," Andrei said. "There are not very many Russians here in Estonia with higher education. Anyone with a qualification went to Russia in the 1990s, and now they go to Western Europe. From a sociological perspective, Narva is a town populated by desperados. Narva is like a ghetto. Anyone who is fluent in Estonian moves to Tartu or Tallinn to study, and they do *not* move back to Narva. So the ones with no education are the ones who stay. Narva is Narva. It is a world unto itself. Narva is the land that time forgot."

Andrei was born in 1963, in neighbouring Sillamäe, which at the time was a closed Soviet industrial town.

"My mother is Estonian, and my father is Russian," he said. "I am something in the middle, neither one nor the other. The Russians call me an Estonian fascist."

His novel, *Sillamäe passion*, a novel about growing up in Sillamäe, was published in 2011.

"After Bronze Night, I discovered that no Russian author had ever written about what it was like to be Russian in Estonia," Andrei explained. "I was actually asked to write the novel, but there was another reason for doing it as well. My son wanted to study psychology, but he knew nothing about the experiences of my generation. So I wrote *Sillamäe passion* to fill that gap."

"And what was it like, growing up in Sillamäe?" I asked.

"Sillamäe was close to Narva, but even more closed. It was a Russian enclave. I think the factory there produced parts for nuclear bombs. No foreigners were allowed to visit the town, nor were people from St Petersburg or other parts of the Soviet Union. The town was not a secret, as the main road from Tallinn to Narva ran through it, but stopping was not permitted. Mentally, it is still closed. After all, Narva has a physical border with Russia, so people there are constantly reminded that they are in Estonia. The Russians and Estonians generally live separate lives and don't have much to do with each other, even here in Tallinn. There are about two hundred thousand Russians in Lasnamäe, the Russian part of town."

Andrei was quiet for a long time. He rubbed his temples, trying to find the right words.

"There is a tendency to focus on the material here in Estonia," he said eventually. "Our wages are higher than in Russia. It is easy to forget that spirituality is also very important for many Russians. Estonian culture, literature and history do not appeal to them. How many Estonian authors can you name? Russia has Lermontov, Pushkin, Dostoevsky, world-class ballet, world-class film, a thousand years of history. The Estonians have pain and depression. They were occupied by the Germans for seven hundred years and the Soviet Union for fifty. Their history is full of trauma and paradox; the Estonians are a schizophrenic people. They are *proud* of their SS past – Estonia was the first country to be *judenfrei*! On the islands in the west, all the signs are in Swedish and Estonian, but no Swedes live there anymore. They have gone. That is why we love them."

The Estonians' relationship with the Russians, who show no signs of leaving, is more complicated.

"There was a lot of talk about decolonisation in the 1990s," Andrei said. "People believed that Estonian society would be pure, that only Estonians would live here, that all Estonians would have four or five children and that everything would be wonderful. The fact is, there are still a hundred thousand Estonians living in Finland, and they do not want to come back here. There are not enough people in Estonia, we are one of the E.U. countries with the lowest population density. The Estonians are living in Lalaland. Well, not just the Estonians. My father is a Russian chauvinist. He still dreams of the Russian Empire. He thinks an independent Estonia is something temporary. Schizophrenia rules!"

In the meantime, the Estonians are doing what they can to break away from the Soviet past. The most bizarre manifestations of Soviet paranoia have been turned into entertainment, as they have in Latvia. And there is plenty to choose from: a guided tour of Soviet Tallinn, a visit to the bunkers and secret military installations in the Estonian forests, or a guided tour of the twenty-third floor of Hotel Viru.

Hotel Viru was built by a Finnish construction company in the early Seventies for the hordes of Western tourists who had started to visit Tallinn. More than fifteen thousand foreigners might come in the course of one summer. Hotel Viru was known to be one of the best hotels in the Soviet Union and had more than one thousand staff, each with their own area of expertise. Every year, someone was crowned employee of the year – for example, one year the bread cutter was the winner. Sixty of the hotel rooms were bugged, and there were microphones and transmitters in the sauna, the bar and the restaurant. The employees were under constant surveillance. The management did not want their staff to understand what was said, so anyone who had relatives abroad or could speak a foreign language was not given work. All employees were instructed to give anything that was forgotten or lost to the administration immediately without checking the contents. K.G.B. agents sometimes planted wallets on the floor so they could test the staff's self-discipline. If the wallets were opened, a dye device exploded and you were in trouble.

Even though the hotel had twenty-three floors, the lift stopped on the twenty-second. From there, a staircase led to the top floor, where the K.G.B. had their offices. Neither tourists nor ordinary hotel staff had access to the top floor. Presumably the K.G.B. agents here were involved with espionage and communicated with spies throughout the Nordic countries, but no-one knows for certain what went on behind those closed doors. When Estonia became independent, they disappeared overnight, taking the most import- ant equipment with them.

About two hundred staff now work at Hotel Viru. The tourists still flock to Tallinn – in high season, numbers can reach fifteen thousand in one day alone. In summer, cruise ships are berthed side by side in the harbour. Every morning, the passengers swarm through the narrow medieval streets of the old town, until all the restaurants and souvenir shops and church towers are full. When evening falls, they return to their ships, to the decks and cabins, disappearing as suddenly as they came.

I was also heading for the harbour, not to one of the cruise ships, but to the Silje Line ferry to Mariehamn.

The Outpost

At Eckerö, on the western tip of Åland, in the middle of the Baltic Sea, there is a post and customs house that is so grand it looks as though it were built for a great capital city. Surrounded by sea, stone and forest, the Empire-style building was designed by the Italian Carlo Bessi and the German Carl Ludvig Engel, the architect who designed Senate Square and the cathedral in Helsinki.

According to legend in Åland, Tsar Alexander I stopped at Eckerö in 1819, on his return from visiting the Swedish king. A big and impressive stone customs house had recently been built in Grisslehamn, on the Swedish side, but at Eckerö they had only a small farmhouse that was in such poor condition that the post-master and customs officers preferred to pay from their own pocket to live elsewhere rather than stay there for free. The sight of this rather wretched post house upset the tsar. When he reached Helsinki, he asked Engel to design a new post and customs house for the westernmost border that would be a worthier reflection of Russia. The result was one of the best Empire-style buildings in Finland.

The story may well be true, and there can be no doubt that the post and customs house on Eckerö was built to impress, but the truth is that Alexander I never got closer to Åland than Åbo, on the mainland. His brother and successor, Nicholas I, on the other hand, later visited Åland to inspect the ongoing construction of the Bomarsund Fortress. But by then the post and customs house was up and running after a difficult birth. Then, as now, the state would put all major projects out to tender, and accept the best offer, often the lowest. And the task of building the new post and customs house went to Carl Anton Lignell, a twenty-two-year-old student. In summer 1824, two years after Lignell had won the contract, work had still not started. The bricks had been ordered and delivered, but had sat uncovered through the winter, so were unusable. In 1826, when the building was supposed to be ready, Engel the architect came out to inspect the work. Parts of the building still lacked a roof, the wrong bricks had been used and the windows were boarded up. It did not take long for Lignell to be fired and both he and his father declared bankrupt. The new post and customs house on Eckerö was finally finished in summer 1828, and the postmaster and his family could move into their new home on the western edge of the Russian Empire.

At the time, Finland had been a part of Russia for no more than twenty years, having been ruled by Sweden for the previous seven centuries. And Sweden was a major power in Europe in the eighteenth century. But then, in the early eighteenth century, the young and conceited King Charles XII met his nemesis in Tsar Peter the Great during the Great Northern War. The king had in reality lost in 1709, following the Swedes' catastrophic defeat at Poltava, but both parties refused to lay down arms. In 1713, Russian troops invaded Finland, where they killed and plundered, and soon conquered the whole country, including Åland.

Despite this indisputable defeat, the Swedes continued to postpone the peace talks for as long as possible. In 1719, Peter the Great became impatient and sent 26,000 soldiers to the Swedish coast, where they razed seven towns to the ground and hundreds of farms. More than 20,000 Swedes lost their homes as a result of the Russian raids, but the Swedish privy council still refused to start talks. Two years later, Russian troops attacked the coast again, setting fire to more towns. Finally the Swedes came to their senses and sat down at the negotiating table. In September 1721, the parties signed the Treaty of Nystad, which forced Sweden to cede its Baltic provinces, as well as Vyborg and large parts of Karelia. The border between Finland and Russia was redrawn, and has remained more or less the same ever since.

Russia was now the most powerful country in the Baltic regions, and it would take the Swedes almost a century to accept that the balance of power had changed for good. The Swedish aristocracy mourned the loss of these territories and dreamed of war and revenge against Russia. In 1741, these dreams became reality when Peter the Great's daughter, Elizabeth, made the Swedes a tempting offer: if the Swedes declared war on Russia, thus helping her to wrest power from Tsar Ivan VI, who was still only a baby and so had a regent, she would give Sweden back the territories it had lost. The Swedes were more than happy to accept the deal and on July 28, 1741 declared war on Russia. Elizabeth carried out the planned coup in December, but broke her promise to return the former Swedish territories to Sweden. Thus the war continued for another year, and, once again, the Russians occupied the whole of Finland.

The peace talks were hard-fought, but Elizabeth eventually agreed that Åland and the greater part of Finland should be given back to the Swedes on condition that they chose her relative, Adolph Frederick of Holstein Gottorp, as crown prince. The Swedish author Herman Lindquist has described him as "perhaps not the brightest of princes, but at least a good and friendly man who liked to listen to music, who played the cello and composed his own small pieces."[25] As Adolph Frederick was also related to Charles XII and Gustav Vasa, the Swedes agreed to make the German prince heir to the throne. The Russians were happy, but the Danes were furious that their own crown prince Frederick was no longer heir, and prepared for war. The Swedish army was much depleted after the fiasco in Finland, so had no choice but to ask the Russians for help. The tsarina sent a few thousand men across the Baltic Sea, and the Danes were driven back. The dream of revenge ended in total humiliation.

In 1788, Adolph Frederick's son, Gustav III, made another attempt to win back the lost territories from Russia, presumably in the hope of improving his popularity at home, first staging an ambush on some Swedish border guards in order to justify his attack on Russia. A few months later, however, the king had to hurry home to avert another war with Denmark. When the danger had passed, he returned to the east to continue the war with Russia. Despite a couple of victories on the part of Sweden, the border between Russia and Sweden remained unchanged during the subsequent peace talks in 1790. This time, at least, the war had not ended with Russia occupying Finland; it had, however, cost the Swedes dearly. If all the soldiers who died from typhus and other illnesses are included, the Swedish army lost forty thousand men. And the national debt tripled during the three-year war.

In summer 1802, the historical enemies almost went to war again. At the heart of the conflict was a bridge over the Kymi River that at the time marked the border between Sweden and Russia but is now in Finland. The Swedish king, Gustav IV Adolph, had visited the area and discovered that half the bridge was painted in the Russian national colours of red, white and blue, even though the bridge was on the Swedish side of the border. The Russians and Swedes shared the maintenance of the bridge, as both parties thought it was the fairest option. The king, however, was of a different opinion and immediately gave orders for the bridge to be painted in blue and yellow, the Swedish colours. In response, the Russians painted the whole bridge red, white and blue. Gustav IV Adolph did not back down and ordered the bridge to be painted yellow and blue again. An impassioned exchange followed, which culminated in Alexander I mobilising soldiers to the border. This did not frighten Gustav IV Adolph. Sweden was prepared to fight! After long and heated negotiations, the Russians repainted the bridge one night with tar. The danger had been averted, but not for long, the reason being that, three years earlier, Napoleon Bonaparte had seized power in France.

Under Napoleon, the French army conquered one country after another in Europe. And in 1807, it also conquered Russia. On July 7, 1807, Napoleon and Alexander I met to negotiate on a raft on the Neman River, close to Tilset, between the French and Russian zones. The two emperors divided Europe into French and Russian spheres of influence in much the same way that Hitler and Stalin divided Europe into German and Russian areas of interest a hundred and thirty-three years later.

Denmark was included in the French zone, whereas Russia was given free rein when it came to Sweden. And both countries were forced to take part in a continental blockade against British ships and goods. In retaliation, Great Britain launched an attack on Copenhagen harbour. Several thousand Danes were killed in the attack, with the result that Denmark allied itself with France. Meanwhile, Alexander I ordered Sweden to close the Baltic Sea to all foreign warships, which Gustav IV Adolph refused to do. On February 21, 1808, the first Russian soldiers marched into Finland. Less than three months later, the greater part of Finland, including Åland, was once again in Russian hands.

In the middle of the war, the increasingly unpopular Gustav IV Adolph was forced by his own officers to abdicate. On March 27, 1809, the same day that the Swedish king signed his declaration of abdication, the Finnish estates swore allegiance to the Russian tsar. This time the Russians intended to keep the conquered territories, so Alexander I, who saw himself as a kind and enlightened ruler, gave Finland a special position within the Russian Empire:

the country was given the status of Grand Duchy. And the Grand Duchy of Finland was allowed to keep its two official languages, Swedish and Finnish, as well as its Lutheran faith and Swedish laws.

During the Finnish–Russian border negotiations in September the same year, the Swedish ambassador, Kurt von Stedingk, fell seriously ill. Alexander I, who had known the ambassador for many years, sent his best doctors to treat him and asked for a map of Sweden and Finland in return. Without any further thought or consideration, he drew a red line between Sweden and Finland, and the border still stands today. Thus, with a stroke of a pen, Sweden lost a third of its landmass and a quarter of its population. But it did keep Umeå and Kiruna and all the marble, even though, by that time, Russian troops had pushed far into northern Sweden.

Åland was a great loss. The Swedish negotiators tried in vain to convince the Russians to let them keep the archipelago in the Baltic. Russia had yearned for ice-free ports and dreamed of dominion over the seas since the days of Peter the Great. Not only did Finland provide a good buffer against Sweden, but the Åland Islands sealed their position in the Baltic Sea and their firm hold on the Swedes – it is only 135 kilometres from Mariehamn to Stockholm, as the crow flies. The Swedes were defeated once and for all, and have never tried to exact revenge on their powerful neighbour to the east.

The Russian Empire stretched from the Kamchatka Peninsula on the Pacific Ocean to Åland in the Baltic Sea. With every victory, there was more to look after and more to protect. As a rule, the solution was to take even more land to safeguard previous victories. St Petersburg, which had previously been exposed, given that it was only a few hundred kilometres from Swedish cannons, was now well protected by the newly acquired Finnish territory.

But these new areas had to be defended. In 1832, the Russians started to build an impressive fortress at Bomarsund on the Åland

Islands, which included a hospital, magazines, fortified towers and barracks. A small community developed at Bomarsund while the fortress was being built, comprising soldiers, construction workers and prisoners. They had their own schools, churches, shops and maybe even a synagogue. All that remains from those years of hectic activity are the graves on the small, neighbouring island of Prestö, where Greek Orthodox, Catholics, Protestants, Jews and Muslims – possibly prisoners of war from the Caucasus – lie side by side, each buried according to their customs and traditions. The graves are proof of just how big and multicultural the Russian Empire had become.

When the Crimean War reached the Baltic, work on the fortress came to an abrupt halt, twenty-two years after it had started. In 1854, a large French-English fleet attacked the fortress, which was not even half-finished, and the troops there were forced to capitulate within weeks. Before withdrawing, the British and French blew up the fortress. Today, only fragments of the walls and foundations remain, partially hidden by trees and wild flowers – a discreet reminder of the century when Åland was the western outpost of the Russian Empire.

During the peace talks in Paris in 1856, it was decided that Åland should be demilitarised, much to Sweden's relief. When Finland became independent in 1917, Åland was included in the deal, even though the Ålanders, who are Swedish-speaking, wanted to be part of Sweden again. The Finnish government instead offered the islands a degree of self-rule, and Åland now has its own flag, car registration plates and stamps. The archipelago is still a demilitarised zone, so there are no soldiers or military installations on the islands. And there is no conscription for the islanders.

Unlike the other Baltic countries, Finland, and therefore the Åland Islands, did not become a part of the Soviet Union.

But freedom came at a price.

The Field Marshal

Coming to Helsinki was *truly* like coming home. Engel's grand, white cathedral in Senate Square, goat's cheese and watermelon salad at the nearby Café Engel, hordes of tourists down by the harbour, the excessive selection of reading material in the Akademiske bookshop, the Kinopalatsi cinema with morning screenings, the green trams, the odd mixture of old and new. It was fourteen years since I had lived in Helsinki, but everything was more or less as before.

I moved to Helsinki when I was eighteen, to take my last year of school there. I had already done two years at a lycée in Lyons and felt it was time to move on, to new adventures and other worlds. The Finnish school was a dream compared to the authoritarian French system; it was solution-based, it encouraged independent thought and mutual respect. But Helsinki was a cold city. In January, the chilly, damp air crept into your skin, no matter how many layers of wool you wore. And the people seemed to be equally cold and unapproachable. If a double seat was vacated on the tram or bus, the person beside you would jump up and move. It took a while for me to understand that it was, in fact, a form of politeness. They only let go at the weekend, for a few fleeting hours on Friday and Saturday nights; bottles clinked, things became hazy, and the night reverberated with hoarse screams and shouts before they once again turned inwards and hid behind their stony Nordic stoicism. When the year was over, I took the boat to Stockholm, which felt a bit like arriving in America for the first time. Everyone was so friendly. I was immediately stopped by people asking for directions, or the time. That had not happened even once in the entire year I had lived in Finland.

This time, however, I did not find the Finns cold and unapproachable; on the contrary, they were kind, friendly and polite. I met some of the most talkative people on the whole journey in Finland, of all places. It is, of course, entirely possible that the collective Finnish psyche has undergone a metamorphosis in recent years, but I think it is more likely that it was because I was no longer eighteen. It also helped that it was May, and the sun shone brightly in an azure sky. It was already so warm that the *flâneurs* on Esplanaden were wearing their sandals, shorts and summer dresses.

When I lived in Helsinki, I used to take the local train into Eliel Saarinen's elegant central station every morning, then walk up Mannerheimvägen and take a tram from a stop with the same name. From the tram window, I had a view of Kiasma, the museum of contemporary art, and of the great statue of Mannerheim on his horse to the right. Mannerheim was mentioned quite frequently during history lessons, and everyone nodded, myself included: Mannerheim, yes. But I did not know much about him, unlike my Finnish classmates. Just how little I knew, I discovered when I went to the Mannerheim Museum, a large wooden villa at Brunnsparken in the south of Helsinki, where Gustaf Mannerheim lived from 1924. On the whole, museums of people's homes are very similar and not particularly informative. The interiors are of their time but not original, as with Chagall's childhood home in Vitebsk, and at best provide an impression of what things had been like.

The villa at Brunnsparken was different: the interior was as it had been in Mannerheim's day, and the furniture and ornaments on the wall bore witness not only to a developed sense of aesthetics, but also to an unusually interesting life. There were Buddhist thangkas and the unmistakable long, curled horns of Marco Polo goats, a hardy species that is only found in Central Asia. On the living room floor, laid on top of a Persian carpet, was a Bengal tiger skin, shot by Mannerheim himself when he was on a hunting trip in India. The drawing room was furnished for comfort and the bathroom was supermodern, with running water. The bedroom, however, was strikingly spartan. According to the knowledgeable guide, Mannerheim suffered from a bad back and rheumatism as an adult, and therefore preferred to sleep on a simple military camp bed, as he was accustomed to from his army days.

Gustaf Mannerheim, or Baron Carl Gustaf Emil Mannerheim, to give him his full name, was born to a family from the Swedish-speaking nobility on June 4, 1867, the same year that the first volume of *Das Kapital* was published. His great-grandfather, Carl Erik Mannerheim, had played a key role in the negotiations that led to Finland becoming an autonomous grand duchy within Russia in 1809, and was also a member of Finland's first senate. In 1824, he was made a count, which was a hereditary title. The title was of little use, however, to Gustaf's father, Carl Robert. As a young man, Carl Robert joined a group that was critical of the court and fell from favour with the upper echelons of St Petersburg society. The doors to a career in the civil service were slammed in his face. Carl Robert tried his luck in business instead, and founded a paper manufacturing company. In 1879, the company went bankrupt. The count had, in the meantime, run up a considerable gambling debt. Before everything collapsed, he had managed to marry Hélène von Julin, and they had had seven children together. When the bankruptcy became fact, Carl Robert ran off to Paris with his mistress. The family fortune was gone, and what few possessions they had left were sold at auction to cover the debt. Hélène and the children were taken in by her family. One and a half years later, when Gustaf was thirteen years old, Hélène's heart stopped.

Significantly, Gustaf Mannerheim's autobiography begins in

1882, at the start of his military career. He chose a very different path from his siblings, who, like their father, were highly critical of the Russian tsar. His eldest brother, Count Carl, was exiled in 1903 for his leading role in a resistance group that fought against Russian oppression in Finland. As a grand duchy, Finland enjoyed a special position in the Russian Empire and in practice was a state within a state, with its own laws, languages and stamps, its own senate, money and religion. This changed, however, towards the end of the nineteenth century under the reign of Tsar Alexander III, and got worse under his son and successor, Nicholas II. An intense Russification process was instituted across the empire, first in Poland and the Baltic countries, and then in Finland. The Finnish military was to be integrated with the Russian army; Russian would be the main language in the senate, public offices and schools, and Russian law would apply. The aim was to unite the different peoples who made up the enormous Russian Empire, but all it did was strengthen everywhere the opposition to tsarism.

Shortly after his brother had been exiled, Gustaf signed up to fight for the Russians in the Russo-Japanese War. The brothers lost all contact. Carl settled in Sweden and never returned to Finland, even though his exile was revoked a couple of years later. He died in 1915 without knowing that his pro-Russian younger brother would become the very symbol of an independent Finland.

Gustaf Mannerheim's military career ended more gloriously than it began. In 1879, the same year that his father disappeared to Paris, he was expelled from Helsingfors Lyceum after rampaging through town with a group of friends, breaking windows. Three years later, when he was fifteen, and basically an orphan, he enrolled in the Finnish military academy, but was once again expelled after a few years, this time for repeatedly breaking the rules, including sneaking out to get drunk. In 1887, his luck turned: he was accepted into the Tsar Nicholas Cavalry School in St Petersburg.

Mannerheim, who had a profound love of horses and riding throughout his life, flourished. Thanks to his family's connections, he was received into the prestigious Chevalier Guard Regiment three years later, the tsar's own life guard.

At one of the many balls in the capital, the tall, handsome Finn was presented to the twenty-year-old Anastasia Arapova, a wealthy Russian general's daughter. They got married in spring 1892, and soon had two daughters. They had little in common, however, and Mannerheim had at least one long-term extramarital relationship. After eight years, Anastasia had had enough, and left without warning for the Far East to work as a nurse in a Red Cross hospital that treated soldiers who had been wounded in the Boxer Rebellion. One year later, she returned with a broken leg. As soon as her leg had healed, she moved to France with their two daughters. The couple did not meet again until 1936, the same year that Anastasia died. Neither of them remarried.

His complicated personal life, which also affected his purse after the divorce, is probably one of the reasons that he volunteered for active service in the Russo-Japanese War in 1904. In a letter to his brother Carl sent before they lost contact, he wrote: "I often feel so saddened and discouraged that I must harm myself in order to continue this life."[26] In late winter, Mannerheim took part in the Battle of Mukden, one of the largest battles ever fought up to that point. Mannerheim proved to be well suited to fighting. He kept a cool head and had the necessary authority. He was promoted to colonel as a result.

When he came back to St Petersburg, Mannerheim was asked, to his surprise, if he would lead a two-year expedition through Turkestan to Beijing, as an intelligence officer. The purpose was to establish how well prepared China was for a potential conflict with Russia along its shared border. Even with strikes, revolt and protests at home and the defeat in the Russo-Japanese war fresh in people's minds, Nicholas II had clearly not yet given up hope of expanding his empire further into Asia. At the time, Russia had recently conquered the greater part of Turkestan, which is now five separate countries, Kazakhstan, Kyrgyzstan, Tajikistan, Turkmenistan and Uzbekistan, but the tsar's ambition was clearly limitless – there was always room for more people and different tribes.

Mannerheim had been fascinated by exploration since he was a child, and he had of course read all the travel books written by his famous uncle, the polar explorer Adolf Erik Nordenskiöld. He said yes immediately. The plan was that he would travel as a civilian with a French archaeology expedition, in order not to arouse suspicion. But it did not take long before he fell out with the French archaeologist, so Mannerheim and his small entourage carried on alone. Over the next two years, the Finnish spy rode back and forth across Central Asia, from Tashkent via Xinjiang and Manchuria to Beijing, often under strenuous conditions. "Only now, having trekked up and down through the mountains for two months, in the cold, wind and rain, without any food other than dry biscuits and mutton, have I learnt truly to appreciate civilisation and what it has to offer. The eggs that the Dungan woman boiled for me, and her mouldy bread, tasted more delicious than the finest meal. It was a joy to ride through cultivated fields and inhabited parts,"[27] Mannerheim wrote in his diary on July 5, 1907, after crossing the Tian Shan mountains on horseback. As he travelled, he drew a precise map, took hundreds of photo-graphs, carried out some rather half-hearted archaeological digs to reinforce his civilian alibi, and also made military-related, meteorological and ethnographical notes and records. The latter were matter-of-fact, and, at times, crass: "Today was a day of anthropological measurement," he wrote on May 30 the same year. "I came across a respectable number of Kalmyks from the Surgan tribe, thirty-four in all. All of them, apart from the richest, followed my instructions to wash before the measurements began, without protest. It was no pretty sight to see a score of these half-naked, short people adorning the banks of the small river that runs past our camp. There was much merriment when they had to wash off the outer layers of acquired grime, and the bath was all for nothing, as to be effective one would have needed soap, warm water and a stiff brush."

The high point of the expedition was a meeting with the thirteenth Dalai Lama, who was staying in a Buddhist temple south-west of Beijing, following the British invasion of Tibet, under the strict surveillance of the Chinese authorities. As was the tradition, the Dalai Lama gave Mannerheim a *khata*, a traditional, white silk scarf, as a gift for the tsar, which the Finn was then able to give to Nicholas II in person, some months later, during a long and convivial audience.

The most exotic artefacts in the villa at Brunnsparken were from this two-year expedition in Central Asia. Most of the dip-lomas, medals and honours were from later years.

After his successful expedition to the Far East, Mannerheim was posted to Poland, where he was responsible for his own regiment. Those years in Poland were some of the happiest of his life. His career was going well – he was promoted to general major – and he enjoyed socialising with the Polish aristocracy.

But this idyllic life came to an abrupt end in late summer 1914. Close to 18 million people are estimated to have lost their lives in the four years that followed, when the Allies – Russia, France and Great Britain – fought against the Triple Alliance of Germany, Austria-Hungary and Italy. The two alliances had been established towards the end of the nineteenth century, and were in part responsible for increased tensions in Europe. An international crisis loomed ever closer, and on June 28, 1914, when the

Austro-Hungarian heir to the throne, Franz Ferdinand, was shot and killed in Sarajevo together with his wife, it became reality. The assassin was a Bosnian Serb with links to the Black Hand, a Serbian terrorist organisation. Austria-Hungary accused the Serbian government of being behind the assassination and declared war on Serbia on July 28. Russia stood by Serbia, even though Serbia was not one of the Allies, and Tsar Nicholas II gave orders for full mobilisation. On August 1, Germany, a member of the Triple Alliance, declared war on Russia, and so the alliance system triggered a world war.

Mannerheim's cavalry brigade suffered heavy losses on the front line in the first weeks of the war. These losses took their toll on Mannerheim and he changed his tactics – foolhardy bravery and self-sacrifice had no place in this new, modern warfare. In December, only four months after the outbreak of war, Mannerheim was awarded the Order of St George, fourth class, one of the highest military decorations in tsarist Russia, for his leadership on the front. The Finnish general was given more and more responsibility as the war continued, and in autumn 1916 he was transferred to the dangerous Romanian front. After a few tough months, Mannerheim's division was given a month's leave. Mannerheim took the opportunity to visit family at home. He travelled north via St Petersburg, which had changed its name to Petrograd since the outbreak of war. Here he was given a brief audience with the tsar and tsarina. Mannerheim noted that Nicholas II seemed distracted and apathetic, despite the obvious tension in the city. In Helsinki, on the other hand, everything was as before, if not better. Finnish men did not have to fight, and the northern front ran through the southern Baltic region, a safe distance from Finnish territory. And Finnish industry had boomed since the war. These were good times.

When Mannerheim returned to Petrograd at the beginning of

March 1917, the situation was beginning to spiral out of control. The war had resulted in food shortages, which in turn had led to general strikes and protests. In the evening of March 11, Mannerheim went to the ballet. As he walked back to the Hôtel de l'Europe afterwards, the streets were remarkably empty. Earlier in the day, several hundred hungry protesters had been shot and killed by the tsar's soldiers. The following morning, many of the soldiers refused to fire into the crowd again, and one regiment after another switched to the side of the people through the course of the day. The revolution had started, and Mannerheim, who had loyally served in the tsar's army for thirty years, found himself in the midst of it. The hotel doorman warned him that officers were being detained, so Mannerheim sought refuge in a friend's office. The situation calmed down again after a few days, and Mannerheim managed to get a ticket on the night train to Moscow. When he arrived early in the morning of March 15, he was met with the news that the tsar had abdicated.

Mannerheim returned to the front and remained at his post, even though discipline seemed to be a thing of the past, not only on the front line, but everywhere. The death sentence was abolished and war-weary soldiers deserted in droves. In September, Mannerheim fell from a horse and injured his leg. He was given leave to convalesce in Odessa. As soon as he got there, he applied to be released from active service. On September 25, he received a telegram from the new commander-in-chief, who informed him that he had been transferred to the reserves as he had not been able to adjust to the new circumstances. Earlier in the year, Mannerheim had supported the then commander-in-chief's attempted coup against the provisional government, as had many other generals, in the hope that they could re-establish order and discipline in the army. It had not been successful; Kornilov was arrested, and all the generals who had supported him were later dismissed.

Mannerheim stayed in the respectable Hôtel de Londres on the promenade in Odessa while he considered his options. He was fifty years old and had served in the Russian army for his entire adult life. A few lines in a telegram and his career was now over.

It took him a few weeks to decide that he should go back to Helsinki. He realised that he should get himself some civilian clothes, as it would be dangerous to travel in a general's uniform. This was easier said than done, because all the cobblers and tailors in Odessa were on strike. While Mannerheim waited for the tailors to return to their sewing machines, the Bolsheviks seized power in Petrograd. On November 7,* the Red Guard took over key posts such as bridges, strategic crossroads, military camps and command centres, police stations and telegraph stations. It all happened quietly and calmly, and almost without bloodshed. When night fell, the Bolsheviks invaded the Winter Palace and arrested the ministers in the provisional government that had ruled since the tsar's abdication.

Time was running out for Mannerheim. On December 3, he boarded the train in full uniform, and two weeks later, against the odds, arrived at the train station in Helsinki unscathed. In the meantime, the Finnish senate had on December 6 declared Finland's independence from Russia. Then, on December 31, just before midnight, Lenin and the Bolshevik government in Petrograd recognised Finland's independence, and allowed Finland to reinstate the border from 1812, which was based on the "old" borders from the time when Sweden had been at its most powerful. This meant that Karelia and the city of Vyborg remained part of Finland.

"You can imagine how lovely it is to have Gustaf here," wrote Mannerheim's sister Sophie, in a letter to their aunt on January 9,

---

*   Or October 25, according to the old Russian calendar.

1918. "[...] To have life and health after all he had to go through is already something to to be thankful for, and for a man like him, with his ability and experience, there must be found something to do in a country where everything will now have to be built up from the ground. It is, however, strange to think how little one knows and how little the career one makes and the position one attains have now come to mean. The whole structure has been built on soft sand."[28]

And there was indeed soon use for a man with Mannerheim's abilities and experience. That winter, the unrest in Russia spilled over the border into Finland. Following independence, the Bolsheviks hoped to encourage the Finnish social democrats to seize power and start a revolution in Finland as well. The bourgeois senate was worried, and not without reason. Finland did not have its own army, and there were still more than forty thousand Russian soldiers stationed in the country. In the middle of January 1918, General Lieutenant Gustaf Mannerheim, the most experienced military man in the country, was given the task of building an army that could ensure peace and order in the newly independent state.

On January 27, a red lantern was raised in the tower of Paasitorni, the Workers' House. The revolution had reached Finland. But unlike in Russia, the White Guard, Mannerheim's forces, would beat the Red Guards in the short but harrowing civil war that ensued – thanks, in part, to assistance from Germany. The senate did not heed Mannerheim's advice, and asked Germany for help. At the start of April, thirteen thousand German soldiers arrived on the shores of Finland. Then, on April 14, the Germans occupied Helsinki, where they held a big victory parade, despite the fact that there was still fighting in other parts of the country.

On May 5, 1918, the last Red Guards capitulated after 108 days. Mannerheim organised an extravagant victory parade in Helsinki on May 16, and the Germans were not allowed to participate. Mannerheim headed the parade and was met with cheers from the delighted crowd.

The brief but bloody civil war left deep wounds in Finnish society. Approximately 8,500 people were killed in the fighting, a relatively low figure given the massacre that was going on in the trenches on the Continent. The main problem was the brutality that went on *behind* the front lines. Roughly 8,300 Reds and 1,700 Whites were summarily executed during the war and in the weeks immediately after, and 80,000 Reds were taken prisoner. By the end of 1918, more than 12,000 prisoners of war had died from starvation and disease. Many working-class people held Mannerheim responsible for the ruthless treatment of the Reds.

"We have had long discussions about what to call the war," said Professor Henrik Meinander, one of Finland's leading scholars on Mannerheim. I met him shortly before I left Helsinki. Meinander has written a four-volume history of Finland, and at the time was writing a biography of Mannerheim. "Civil war?" It was a rhetorical question. "War of independence? Which, by the way, was Mannerheim's preference, but I personally think the correct name is the First World War. The war in Finland was part of a chain reaction to the First World War, as was the Russian Revolution. In many places in Eastern Europe and Russia, the war continued for several years after Germany surrendered in November 1918."

For the first few months after the civil war, Finland was treated more or less like a German vassal state. Mannerheim thought that the senate should cut all ties with Germany and enter negotiations with the other Western powers. When the senate showed no sign of following his advice, Mannerheim applied to be released from his position as commander-in-chief of the Finnish army, and his request was immediately granted.

By October, it was obvious to everyone, even the Finnish

senate, that Germany would lose the war. Mannerheim was sent to London and Paris to convince the Allies to recognise Finland's independence. He was therefore surprised to meet a delegation on the boat to Stockholm that had been dispatched by the senate to inform the German Prince Frederick Charles of Hesse that he had been chosen to be king of Finland. Germany capitulated before Frederick Charles could ascend the throne, however, and the senate withdrew their offer.

On December 10, 1918, in a volte-face, the senate chose Gustaf Mannerheim as Finland's head of state. The general attacked the many difficult and urgent problems with energy and verve: a split country had to be united, and the war-weary and hungry population needed food. The Western powers also needed to recognise Finland's sovereignty. Even though he already had more than enough to do, Mannerheim, who probably at this point saw Finland's independence as temporary, tried to get the government to make an anti-Bolshevik intervention in Russia. But there was no appetite for that, and in July 1919, in the first ever presidential election in Finland, which, exceptionally, was an internal election in the national assembly, Mannerheim lost.

For the next twelve years, Mannerheim had no official position in the Finnish state and enjoyed a comfortable life in Helsinki. In 1922, he was appointed chairman of the Finnish Red Cross, and gave his all to the role. Otherwise, he dined out in restaurants, invited guests to lavish meals at his home, bought expensive clothes, and surrounded himself with celebrities. He also travelled and hunted throughout Europe, his other great passion besides riding.

In 1931, Finland elected a new, conservative government, and Mannerheim was asked to be chairman of the defence council. Since the revolution, Mannerheim had been convinced that, sooner or later, Finland would face armed conflict with the Soviet Union, and he therefore invested in a sorely needed upgrade of the Finnish defence forces.* In 1933, he was awarded the rank of field marshal – the first and only in Finland. As there were no instructions as to how a Finnish field marshal should dress, Mannerheim had the symbols sewn onto the sleeves of his Burberry trench coat.

On September 1, 1939, one week after the Molotov–Ribbentrop Pact had been signed, Germany attacked Poland. The Second World War had started. The Red Army marched into east Poland on September 17. Not long after, the Baltic states were forced to allow Soviet military bases on their territory. In Helsinki, people realised that Finland was next in line, and true enough: on October 5, the Finnish government was invited to Moscow. The Soviet Union offered Finland a bilateral defence agreement, but the Russians also wanted the Hanko Peninsula, to the west of Helsinki, to be made into a Soviet military base and demanded that the Finns cede some of the islands in the Gulf of Finland, in return for some land further north. Finland refused all the Soviet proposals outright, unlike the Baltic countries, despite repeated and increasingly aggressive demands from Moscow. Mannerheim believed that this was a mistake, and that the Finns should show greater understanding of the Russians' need to protect Leningrad. He was also convinced that the Finnish army would not be able to hold the Red Army back.

On November 30, the Soviet Union attacked Finland. Stalin mobilised 460,000 soldiers for the campaign that he reckoned would be over in two or three weeks. However, it soon became clear that Stalin, and Mannerheim himself, had underestimated the Finnish army.

"Several factors worked in favour of the Finnish army during the Winter War," Professor Meinander said. "Their strong desire

---

*   Six years were to pass before Mannerheim's prediction came true.

to fight, difficult terrain and poor infrastructure, and an unusually cold winter. The Red Army were also weaker than anticipated, owing to Stalin's recent purge of the officers' corps. The troops that were sent here were made up largely of Ukrainians who had already taken part in the invasion of Poland. They had never been on skis in their life."

During the months that followed, the Red Army increased its strength considerably. As spring approached, the Allies planned an intervention in order to gain control of the iron ore mines in northern Sweden, which was not in the interests of either Finland or Russia. After 105 days of combat, the Finnish government agreed to Stalin's tough conditions for a ceasefire, and the Moscow Peace Treaty came into force on March 13, 1940. Stalin's conditions were considered so harsh that the Finnish flag hung at half-mast throughout the country that day: Finland had been forced to cede Karelia and parts of the Salla region in the north-east, and to lease Hanko to the Russians as a military base for the next thirty years. The Soviet Union was the clear victor, but had gained less than ten per cent of Finland's territory. The Finns lost about 25,000 men, but the Soviet Union had lost at least five times as many.

The war raged on in the rest of Europe. Denmark and Norway were occupied by Germany in April 1940, and, soon after, Hitler commenced a major offensive in Western Europe. In the summer, the Soviet Union occupied the Baltic countries, and made demands on the Finnish nickel mines in Petsamo in the north. Mannerheim, who remained in post as commander-in-chief, believed that it was only a matter of time before Finland would again be at war with the Soviet Union. At the same time, there were signs from Berlin that the Germans were interested in some form of cooperation with Finland. In August, the two parties agreed that the Finns could buy arms from Germany if Germany was allowed to move troops through Finland.

Finland was pulled deeper and deeper into the partnership with Germany. It was imperative, however, for the Finnish government that their entry into a war with the Soviet Union be seen as a separate war. The alliance between the two countries was therefore never officially recognised, and when Germany embarked on Operation Barbarossa and attacked the Soviet Union on June 22, 1943, the Finns sat on the fence and waited for three days, as agreed. On June 25, President Risto Ryti informed the Finnish people that Finland was once again at war with the Soviet Union. He presented the war as defensive and later called it a separate war, but today it is known as the Continuation War.

The Finns took the opportunity to try to win back the territory they had lost and to conquer East Karelia, even though it had not been Finnish (or, more correctly, Swedish), since the Great Northern War at the start of the 1700s. Aided by the timely mobilisation of Finnish troops into Karelia, Mannerheim managed to avoid the involvement of Finnish soldiers in the German siege of Leningrad. The siege lasted 872 days, and cost the lives of more than one million people.

In the summer of 1942, Hitler paid an unexpected visit to Finland, to celebrate Mannerheim's seventy-fifth birthday. It was his only trip abroad during the war, other than his triumphant visit to Paris in June 1940. In order to avoid any hint of officialdom or a state visit – after all, the countries were not *officially* allied – Mannerheim resolved the awkward situation by ensuring that the unexpected summit took place on a train, far from the capital.

Following the Germans' defeat in the Battle of Stalingrad in winter 1943, the Finnish government realised that Germany would also lose this world war. They entered into secret negotiations with the Soviet authorities. Stalin demanded that the border be returned to that of 1940, and that 600 million dollars be paid in war reparations. The Finns thought this was too much, and their troops stayed in Karelia.

In February 1944, the Russians bombed Helsinki for three nights in a row, and in June the same year, they started a major offensive in Karelia. The Finnish government accepted an offer from Ribbentrop, the German foreign minister, for new arms supplies, and in return promised that they would not enter into a separate ceasefire with the Soviet Union. President Ryti then stepped down on August 4, leaving Mannerheim in charge. As he was not part of the government, he was not bound by the promise to Ribbentrop, and could therefore withdraw from the agreement without infuriating Hitler by breaking his word. Mannerheim wrote a polite letter to Hitler and thanked him for a good working relationship, then went on to say that if Finland was to survive as a nation, it had to cut its ties with Germany. Hitler did not answer the letter, but he told a Japanese diplomat a few days later that he did not see it as betrayal, because the Finns had only given up when they were losing bargaining power.

The peace negotiations with the Soviet Union were arduous. In the end, Finland had to cede not only Karelia, but also Petsamo. And they had to agree to lease the Porkkala Peninsula to the west of Helsinki to the Soviet navy for fifty years. Furthermore, the Finnish state had to pay the Soviet Union 300 million dollars in war reparations and drive all German soldiers out of the country immediately.

And so the third and final phase of Finland's world war started in autumn 1944: the Lapland War. To begin with, the Germans withdrew with good grace. The Finns had managed to maintain good working relations with the Germans, who accepted that they had to leave Lapland. However, Stalin was not happy with the pace and demanded that the Finns speed up the German withdrawal. The Finns had no choice but to do as Stalin said. The Germans responded by burning down bridges and other strategic infrastructure in order to delay the Finnish soldiers. Rovaniemi was razed to the ground. The material damages were considerable, but not many lives were lost.

By April 27, 1945, the Winter War, the Continuation War and the Lapland War were all over. Finland had lost twelve per cent of its territory to the Soviet Union. More than four hundred thousand people, primarily from Karelia, had been evacuated to other parts of Finland. Ninety-five thousand soldiers had lost their lives, but civilian deaths were surprisingly low at only two thousand, and, unlike many countries in Central and Eastern Europe, Finland had not been left in ruins. The fighting had largely been along the Eastern Front, some of it in the Soviet Union itself, and far from the cities. But perhaps most important of all: the Finns' willingness to fight had convinced Stalin that another invasion of Finland was more than he could afford. Thus Finland escaped the fate of the Baltic countries, and never became a Czechoslovakia. The Soviet army did not try to cross the Finnish border again.

On March 8, 1946, at the age of seventy-eight, Mannerheim stepped down as president for health reasons, but also because he felt his job was done. Even though he was plagued by rheumatism and the complaints of old age, the field marshal still managed to fit in another romance before he died. On a trip to Paris in 1945, he was introduced to the fifty-one-year-old Countess Gertrud Arco auf Valley, and for the next few years the couple travelled extensively on the Continent. They stayed in luxury hotels and lived the good life, while the countess footed the bills. She encouraged Mannerheim to write his memoirs, which he did with gusto, but the countless rewrites and edits by the man himself meant it was not published until after his death in 1951. When it did come out, the two-volume memoir was an immediate success.

The statue of Mannerheim on horseback was unveiled in

Helsinki in 1960. It is no wonder that the Finns wanted to honour their great field marshal with a suitable monument in the capital. Slightly more surprising, however, was a memorial plaque to Mannerheim that was unveiled at his old school, the Tsar Nicholas Cavalry School, in St Petersburg in 2016. The chief of staff of the Presidential Administration of Russia, Sergei Ivanov, made a speech to mark the occasion, and the Russian minister of culture was also present. When he was a K.G.B. officer, Ivanov had been stationed in Helsinki and perhaps felt it was only right that the famous Finnish general should have a memorial in St Petersburg as well. After all, Mannerheim had served in the tsar's army for thirty years before becoming a champion of independence. The response was immediate, with accusations and protests. How could they endorse a memorial plaque for a Nazi? No more than a few days after it had been unveiled, the plaque was sprayed red, just like the Bronze Soldier in Tallinn. A few months later, the plaque was taken down for good. And Sergei Ivanov was relieved from his position as chief of staff, though it is unlikely that it was because of the unfortunate plaque.

The Finns, on the other hand, cannot get enough of Mannerheim. In the past two years alone, four new biographies of the field marshal have been published.

"As I am sure you understand, Mannerheim aroused passion in his compatriots when he was alive," Meinander said. "He was praised and revered in bourgeois circles, whereas the socialists described him as the White Butcher, as a consequence of the civil war in 1918. But because of his incredible efforts to defend Finland's independence during the Second World War, many socialists came to appreciate him. He continued to be an object of hate for the communists, however, throughout the Cold War. Opinion of him is no longer as polarised, though there are of course still Mannerheim worshippers and Mannerheim haters. Most Finns, though, agree that the alliance with Germany between 1941 and 1944 was the price the country had to pay in order not to be occupied by the Soviet Union."

Some names grow in strength and importance over the years, and as time passes seem to shine even more than when they were alive.

Others become a historical parenthesis remarkably quickly.

Like Porkkala.

A Lesson in the Value of Maintenance

"I was three when Porkkala was evacuated," said seventy-five-year-old Lena Selén, who ran a small museum about the twelve years when Porkkala was a Soviet military base, known as the Porkkala Parenthesis. "My grandparents lived here in Degerby, and I often came to stay with them. Their house was built in 1939, and they only lived there for five years. The order to evacuate was issued on September 19, 1944, the day that Finland and the Soviet Union signed the peace treaty."

The 7,200 people who lived in Porkkala were given ten days to leave their homes.

"After the war, there were nearly half a million displaced people in Finland," Lena said. "Little Porkkala was not the biggest problem at the time."

But for the country's government, little Porkkala was very definitely a problem. Between fifteen and thirty thousand Soviet citizens moved to the Porkkala Peninsula, which officially became part of the Leningrad oblast. The Russians built a large military base just thirty kilometres from Helsinki. The Soviet Union had a stranglehold on Finland.

The military base also gave rise to practical problems. The trainline between Helsinki and Turku, Finland's second largest city, crossed the Porkkala Peninsula. To keep the trains running, the Finnish government had to negotiate a special deal with the Russians.

"I must have taken the train through Soviet-occupied Porkkala more than a hundred times," Lena said. "The Finnish train stopped in Esbo, and everyone had to change onto a Russian train. When we reached Finnish soil again, we had to switch back to a Finnish train. There was an armed guard in every carriage on the Russian train. The windows were blacked out, so we could not see their secret military installations. We called it the Porkkala Tunnel, the longest tunnel in the world. It took a whole hour to cross Porkkala back then, because the trains were slow, slow. In 1952, when the Olympic Games were held in Helsinki, the Porkkala Tunnel was a big attraction. Everyone wanted to take the train through the Soviet Union!"

In 1955, just after he had ordered the withdrawal of Soviet soldiers from Port Arthur and Austria, Khrushchev unexpectedly gave Porkkala back to Finland.

"I don't know why they gave Porkkala back," Lena said. "Perhaps Khrushchev wanted to show the world how nice he was. But the Porkkala base was also expensive for the Soviet Union, and the weapons from the Second World War were outdated. Plus, they had Kaliningrad and the whole Baltic region. The expansion of Porkkala was stopped in July 1955. Before Christmas that year, it was possible to take the train through Porkkala without the windows being covered, so everyone wanted to take the train through Porkkala again!"

On January 6, 1956, the border was officially reopened.

"It was a good thing that it happened when it did," Lena said. "In November 1956, the Soviet army invaded Hungary and the tide turned. It is now sixty years since we got Porkkala back, and to mark the anniversary we are putting on an exhibition about what it was like to come back. The farmers had to do a major clear-up. It is only now, working on the exhibition, that I fully appreciate just how much work was needed! There was barbed wire *every-where*, the fields were full of barbed wire. It was a nightmare for the farmers, and many of them eventually gave up. Most of the houses had been destroyed as well. My grandmother's timber house had been taken apart in 1955. There was a shortage of building materials in the Soviet Union, so I guess they needed the timber. And believe me, I have looked, but I've never managed to find my grandmother's house. It is probably lying in a pile, rotting, outside St Petersburg."

Nothing remains of the Soviet parenthesis. What little was left has now gone.

"The Russians who come here ask where all their buildings have gone," Lena said. "They built so many great things here, they say, schools, hospitals . . . The truth is that we demolished it all – everything. The Soviet buildings were in such a terrible state that they fell down almost without any help."

When I had looked around the small museum, Lena accompanied me to the bus stop. We walked along quiet, country roads, past small farms, surrounded by corn and green fields.

"Just imagine what it would have been like if the Russians had stayed here until 1994," Lena said when we reached the main road. "We would presumably have been in the same situation as the Baltic countries. Thirty thousand Russians who don't want to move. All the Russians I have spoken to who lived here during the Porkkala Parenthesis say that they were better off here."

During the Cold War, Finland had to tread carefully and not provoke its neighbour to the east. At the exhortation of the Soviet authorities, Finland declined help from the Marshall Plan, and instead signed an agreement of friendship, cooperation and mutual assistance with the Soviet Union. This obliged Finland to resist attacks against the Soviet Union from Finnish territory. Unlike Hungary and Romania, however, Finland was not obliged to consult the Kremlin about foreign policy questions or to participate in military operations outside its own territory. The treaty was signed by Juho Kusti Paasikivi, who was president from 1946 to 1956, and was upheld by his successor, Urho Kekkonen, who had been involved with the agreement at the pre-negotiation stage.

Although Finland had a far freer relationship with the U.S.S.R. than the countries to the east of the Iron Curtain, the Soviet authorities did keep a close eye on what was written in the Finnish newspapers, and while there may not have been any direct censorship, Finnish journalists were careful about criticising the Soviet Union. On a couple of occasions, Moscow did intervene in Finnish politics. The most famous was "the Note Crisis".

On October 30, 1961, the Soviet foreign minister handed a note to the Finnish ambassador in Moscow. The note was a request for consultations with the Finnish government on the defence of their two countries, in accordance with the Finno-Soviet Treaty, given the tensions in northern Europe. On the day that the note was delivered, the Soviet Union detonated the 27-ton hydrogen bomb *Tsar Bomba* over Novaya Zemlya in the Arctic Ocean. It was the largest and most powerful nuclear weapon ever to be tested. The flash from the explosion was visible in Vardø in Finnmark, northern Norway. The Cold War was at its very coldest at this point: earlier that year, the C.I.A. had unsuccessfully tried to invade the Bay of Pigs on Cuba, and the Berlin Wall had been built in August.

The news that the Soviet Union wanted to start defence consultations with Finland caused quite a stir internationally. Did this mean the end of Finland's independence and neutrality? Would the Soviet Union station troops on Finnish soil? President Kekkonen was on holiday in Hawaii at the time, and is reported to have received the news with stoical calm. He did eventually cut his holiday short and return home to sort things out, but only after he had been photographed swimming in the Pacific, in red trunks. On his return to Finland, he dissolved the parliament and brought the upcoming presidential election forward to January; his justification for the decision was that the Finnish people had a right to voice their opinion on the country's policy in regard to the Soviet Union. At the end of November, Khrushchev invited Kekkonen to Novosibirsk to discuss the situation face to face. The following day, Kekkonen told his people that the Soviet Union had decided to postpone the consultations and that Khrushchev was confident that Kekkonen, as the country's leader, would steer a steady course in terms of foreign policy. As a result, Kekkonen's opponent in the presidential election, Olavi Honka, who was more West-leaning, withdrew his candidature and Kekkonen was re-elected with a substantial majority, as the Soviet Union had hoped all along.

There has been speculation that Kekkonen had had a hand in the Note Crisis, or at least knew about it from the beginning, but nothing has ever been proved. There is, however, little doubt that the note was a deliberate intervention in the Finnish presidential election: the Kremlin wanted Kekkonen, rather than the West-friendly Honka, to be re-elected. A rather pejorative term, "Finlandisation", was coined in the wake of the crisis. It means "to become like Finland": in other words, when a major power exerts pressure on a smaller country to do its bidding.

Kekkonen remained in post as Finland's president until he stepped down for health reasons in 1981, at the age of eighty-one. He continued the active neutrality policy to the end. The Finno-Soviet Treaty remained a cornerstone of Finnish foreign policy until the dissolution of the Soviet Union. Finland did not become a member of the E.U. until 1995. And though Finland now cooperates extensively with N.A.T.O., just as Sweden does, it has never been asked to join. Thus Finland, which has the longest border with Russia in Europe, will not be drawn into any future war between N.A.T.O. and Russia.

The Cold War was a difficult time for the Finns in terms of

politics, but having the Soviet Union as a neighbour was a financial benefit. Approximately fifteen per cent of Finland's exports went to the Soviet Union, and several Soviet statement buildings, such as Hotel Viru in Tallinn, were designed and built by the Finns. While the Soviet Union was dedicated to socialism and a planned economy, the Finnish market economy was steadily growing. When Finland first gained its independence in 1917, it was one of the poorest countries in Europe. Now it has one of the most developed welfare states in the world. A Finnish pensioner receives on average 1,600 euro a month and can expect to live to about eighty. By way of comparison, most Russian pensioners have to manage on less than 200 euro and statistically can expect to live to only seventy.

The gap in wealth becomes very apparent if one travels through Karelia to Vyborg, which was one of Finland's most attractive towns before the war. It is possible to go there without a visa, as long as one travels by water, and as I happened to be there for the first cruise of the year, I joined a group tour to the city that had been my first encounter with Russia, fourteen years earlier.

Even though we set sail shortly after eight in the morning, there was soon a queue for beer at the bar. Later in the morning, the women started to drink Russian champagne, and their husbands switched to something stronger. The old riverboat was small and the tour was almost fully booked. We sat close at the tables, the pensioners and I. The pensioners could not speak Swedish or English, but nodded in my direction with a friendly smile every now and then and raised their glasses.

The sun was shining and we were surrounded by Karelian forest. At regular intervals, the boat stopped to pass through a lock. The Saimaa Canal, which runs from Lappeenranta on the Finnish side to Vyborg in Russia, is 43.9 kilometres long and was opened on September 7, 1856, the same day as Tsar Alexander II's coronation.

Over the years, the canal has been modernised, widened and shortened; there were originally twenty-eight locks, whereas now there are only eight. Slightly more than half the canal is in Russia, but Finland has permission to use the waterway until 2063. Every year, two million tons of goods are transported on the canal, as are several thousand visa-less passengers. If you go into and out of Russia via the canal as part of an organised group, you can even spend a night or two in Vyborg without a visa.

At some point in the morning, a balding man in his fifties sat down at a keyboard and started to play Finnish songs. It did not take long before everyone was singing along, even me, so, verse after verse, song after song, we sang our way across Karelia and over the Russian border, which is in the middle of a lake.

The Russian side is identical to the Finnish side: forest all around. We moored in Vyborg in the early afternoon, and were channelled through passport control, then sent to our respective hotels. Before we were given our keycards, we were offered a very full glass of vodka. The Finnish pensioners did not need to be asked twice.

I found an A.T.M. and took out about fifty pounds in roubles. When I had last been in Russia, five or six years earlier, that had come to about 2,500 roubles. The Russian economy had suffered in those intervening years, thanks to sanctions, inflation and falling oil prices, and fifty pounds now bought double that. With my wallet stuffed full of roubles, I headed for Vyborg Castle, the primary attraction and symbol of the city. The fort was built in 1283 by the Swedish commander Torgils Knutsson. For centuries, Vyborg constituted Sweden's eastern frontier with Russia, and was therefore an important fort. As it said in the information brochure I was given: "It has been destroyed more than once and resurrected again." In 1710, when the Swedes were defeated by Peter the Great's army, Vyborg was taken by the Russians. Less than a hundred years later, in 1808, the town became part of the Grand Duchy of Finland and was a part of Finland until the Second World War.

The castle now houses a museum. One of the exhibitions was about the period when the city, Viipuri as it is called in Finnish, had a population of close to eighty thousand and was the second largest city in Finland, and the most international one, with a rich cultural life and thriving industry. In the interwar period, the Finns built in Vyborg an art gallery, a summer theatre, a polytechnic and a library designed by the world famous Finnish architect Alvar Aalto. As though to underline the city's cosmopolitan heritage, all the signs and labels in the exhibition were written in Russian, English, Swedish and Finnish. The contrast with the next exhibition about the Second World War, which was not financed by the Finnish state, was stark. The cabinets were full of dusty weapons and all the information was in Russian. Detailed maps of the Red Army's assault positions hung on the wall, alongside photographs to illustrate how good Soviet citizens rebuilt Vyborg from the rubble after the Second World War.

"We will be closing shortly," the attendant at the entrance to the tower said.

"But it is only ten past six," I said.

"We close at half past six."

"But it says here that you close at seven," I said, and pointed to the sign giving opening times.

"Yes, but in order to be fully closed by seven, we have to start locking up at six-thirty," she said. "You had better get a move on, there are lots of steps."

I was out of breath when I reached the top. The young couple who were coming up behind me turned back about halfway – the worn, loose steps had definitely not been built by Finnish engineers. But the view was well worth the effort, if a little monotonous. Forest as far as the eye could see. I stood looking east. All there was to see was the green crowns of trees, millions upon millions of trees – a green belt that stretches from here to North Korea. There was doubtless the odd bear to be found padding around under the trees, some castle ruins, and every now and then an impoverished, alcohol-sodden village, but the trees dominated.

It was strange to be in Russia again. Since I had landed in Pyongyang in September, nine months earlier, I had travelled and travelled along the Russian border, sometimes so close that I could look over to the promised land, other times further away, but never so far that Russia had not left its mark in one way or another. Every day, every waking hour, I had thought about Russia. I had talked about Russia with everyone I met along the way, and asked about their relationship with Russia, what they thought about Russia, what is was like to have Russia as a neighbour. In the process, Russia had taken on almost mythical proportions.

And now, here I was, and it was almost disappointing just how ordinary and undramatic everything was. Couples walked hand in hand along the narrow, potholed pavements; old, bent women struggled with heavy shopping bags, a couple of middle-aged men sat by the river fishing. None of them paid the slightest attention to me.

I found a simple restaurant serving pizza and sushi, and I ordered a pizza. There was only one other family in the place, which was big. From my table, I had a view of Lenin's straight back in the square outside. A couple of faded posters, decorated with black and orange stripes, invited people to celebrate Victory Day on May 9, two weeks earlier.

The last time I had visited Vyborg, when I was eighteen, I had also been with a group of Finnish pensioners, only we had travelled by bus. We had stopped in Vyborg for lunch en route from Helsinki to St Petersburg. Vyborg had made an impression on me, not because of the beauty, but because of the decay: there were enormous potholes in the road, the pavements were full of puddles and dirty snow, the men walked around in dark, mafia-like leather jackets, the waitresses were surly and unfriendly, half the windows were broken and the walls were full of holes. Decay everywhere. A couple of the pensioners burst into tears at the sight of the former Finnish beauty.

Like many cities, Vyborg was more attractive in spring – everything was lighter and greener. There were fewer leather jackets, but there were still not many smiles. Despite their hard faces, I no longer thought the people of Vyborg were frightening and thuggish, just poor. The city had reportedly had a total facelift since I was last there, but everything was just as sad and worn as I remembered. Several of the buildings in the centre were about to give in to gravity, as no-one had bothered to pull them down. Most buildings, even the houses that were obviously inhabited, had at least one broken window. Yet, despite all this, it was not hard to imagine how beautiful Vyborg had once been, with its parks and pastel-coloured nineteenth-century buildings.

If Stalin had got his own way in 1939, the whole of Finland would have been like one enormous Vyborg.

It had been gloriously sunny when we arrived in Russia, and we left in pouring rain. The pensioners were even rowdier on the way back. They had clearly enjoyed their morning in the neighbouring country. Even before we had left the quay, there was a long queue at the bar. The radio was on for the whole journey, but no-one seemed to be listening until the entire boat broke out in a rapturous roar. I realised that it must be something to do with ice hockey, because only brutal skating sports can trigger that kind of emotional response in Finland. True enough, Finland had just scored a goal in the semi-final of the world championship, and was now ahead of Russia. The ritual was repeated twice more and then a third time, when victory was secured. There was no end to the celebrations. The patriotic revellers thronged the bar and some started spontaneously to sing Finnish songs while they waited. Felted Viking helmet hats were produced from the depths of shopping bags and donned in sheer delight.

Lapland

From the train window, I looked out at the forest, small lakes and nearby trees that filtered the milky-white May light. Around midnight, I fell asleep to the soporific sound of the wheels on the track. When I woke, still all I could see was forest and lakes, but they were now bathed in a sharp, golden, morning light. A bitter wind hit me when I got off the train. Rovaniemi was rebuilt in haste after it was burnt down by the Germans during the war, and it was not a particularly attractive town. The new town was designed by Alvar Aalto and from above resembles a reindeer. But at street level, there was nothing about the low, square, concrete buildings that seemed to be planned.

Every year, hundreds of thousands of tourists visit Rovaniemi. Very few, however, come to admire Alvar Aalto's creative town planning or concrete buildings; the high visitor numbers are due to a remarkably successful investment by the Finnish tourist board. Tourism became an increasingly important income for the state after the Second World War, but how on earth have they managed to lure so many people to the harsh climes of the north? In a moment of inspiration in 1984, a member of the tourist board suggested that they market Lapland as Santa Claus's official home.

The idea in itself was nothing new. In the early 1950s, the industrious and long-serving head of tourism in Oslo, Alfhild Hovdan, announced that Santa Claus lived in Oslo, and made sure that all letters addressed to *Santa Claus, Oslo, Norway* ended up on her desk. She answered, in person, thousands of letters, and often sent a book or small gift in return. The intention, of course, was to put Oslo on the map. Alfhild Hovdan died in 1982, and none of her successors had the capacity to deal with all the correspondence. Slowly but surely the letters stopped coming to Santa Claus in Oslo.

Fortunately, other Santa Clauses have appeared in the meantime. In addition to the Santa Claus in Rovaniemi, colleagues in the Christmas House in Drøback, just south of Oslo, and in Santaworld in Dalarna, Sweden, also accept wish lists. In other words, the Nordic countries are well represented when it comes to Santa Claus, but there is no Russian equivalent, despite the fact that Russia recently laid claim to the North Pole itself. There is a reason for the absence of a Russian Santa Claus: even though Nicholas is a very popular saint with Orthodox Christians in Russia, the children there do not believe in Santa Claus, but rather in Ded Moroz: Grandfather Frost. And he does not come with gifts at Christmas, but on New Year's Eve. The communists initially banned Grandfather Frost, and then started to market him as an alternative to the decadent Western Santa Claus. In 1998, Veliky Ustyug, a small town eight hundred kilometres north-east of Moscow, was declared the official home of Grandfather Frost, and has since received millions of letters. A few years ago, the Ukrainian post office decided to compete with Veliky Ustyug and, thanks to sponsors and energetic marketing, has received more than twenty thousand letters. The Ukrainian Grandfather Frost does not have a specific home, but answers letters from seven different post offices around the country.

None of the other Nordic Santa Clauses has been as successful as the Finnish one. Santa Claus Village outside Rovaniemi opened in 1985, with a post office staffed by Santa's helpers, and the highlight: Santa's office, where visitors can be photographed with the man himself for a princely price. Its success has outstripped expectations. Some three hundred thousand people a year visit Santa

Claus in Rovaniemi, of which a growing number are Chinese. Not even Santa Claus is immune to fluctuations in the global economy, however. In 2015, Santa Claus in Rovaniemi was forced to file for bankruptcy as he owed millions in tax – a consequence of the financial crisis in Europe and falling visitor numbers. Fortunately, Santa managed to refinance his debt and open his doors again.

The road north from Rovaniemi was more or less straight. Reindeer stood grazing in the occasional light-filled clearings in the forest.

Four hours later I arrived in Inari. I checked into the hotel and was given a room with an en suite sauna. As soon as it was warm enough, I sat down on the top bench and enjoyed my view of the petrol station. I was almost at the end of my journey. It was no more than a few kilometres to the Finnish–Russian border. And then the final stretch, the 196-kilometre border between Norway and Russia.

For a short period, from 1920 to 1944, Norway bordered only Finland and Sweden. In their border negotiations with the Bolsheviks in 1920, the Finnish delegation did not manage to convince the Russians to return East Karelia, but they were given an area by the Arctic Ocean and the Norwegian border that had never previously been Finnish: Petsamo. Finland had to cede Petsamo in the 1944 peace negotiations, and all the Finns in Petsamo were evacuated, but the Skolt Sámi, who were largely Russian Orthodox, were allowed to choose which country they wanted to live in. Not everyone was given an honest choice.

"It was lovely in Petsamo," said Katuri Jefremoff. The eighty-three-year-old is one of about seven hundred Skolt Sámis who still live in Finland. I visited Katuri in her small, timber house in the tiny village of Nellim, where she had lived all her adult life. Her face was wrinkled, her body fragile and bent, but her voice was strong. She still spoke beautiful Swedish, even though she had not used it for more than sixty years.

"We lived four kilometres away from the Petsamo Monastery, near the Petsamo River," Katuri said. "We had reindeer, everyone had reindeer. My whole family was from Petsamo, my grandparents, my great-grandparents, everyone. In my family, there were six girls and two boys. My brother was the eldest, then Marta and Olga, then me. None of us could speak Finnish, but we had a little Russian; that was our second language. Otherwise we spoke Skolt Sámi. When I started boarding school, I did not know a word of Finnish. I understood nothing, but then I was not able to stay there for very long. Three months after the start of term, the war broke out. The Finnish authorities did not manage to evacuate us in time, so we were all sent to prison. We were put on a boat and taken first to Murmansk and then to Luujärvi. The time in prison was not much fun. It was hard for us as children, but I am sure it was even worse for our parents. There were lots of other Skolt families in the prison. We did get food, just not enough, but luckily we were never cold. We did not have to work, but there was no school either. When the war finished, we were released. We came home to Puska, our village, in spring 1940. And it was so good to be back, but the Russians had taken all our animals, they were gone."

Katuri sighed and rubbed her face.

"I am very sad at the moment. Olga just died. I was at her funeral last Friday. She was everything to me."

She sighed again and dried a tear.

"Now, where were we? Yes, 1940. The following year, 1941, German soldiers came to our village. It was the year that the Continuation War started. My mother died in 1943, so then we were all motherless. We were moved to a children's home in Petsamo, and then sent to Sweden as war children. I went first, then the others followed, I was sent to Gävle, the others to Skellefteå. I had a nice family and a good life in Sweden. I could not speak a word of Swedish, obviously, but you had to go to school, even if you understood nothing. And now I can speak Swedish!"

When she smiled, her face transformed into a web of fine wrinkles.

"I went to a Swedish school for three years," she said. "When the war ended, I was sent back to Finland. Everything here had been destroyed. Ivalo had been burnt to the ground. We lived in the German bunker to begin with. I had forgotten the Sámi language, and I had never learnt Finnish, so it was hard in the beginning. Swedish was the only language I could speak, but no-one else spoke Swedish. I really wanted to stay in Sweden, but was not allowed. After all, my mother was dead and my father was in prison. And why was he in prison? A lot went on in those days, and they accused him of something or other, I don't know what exactly. When I first got back, I lived with my grandmother. We got a government grant and were able to build a small hut not far from here. My son lives there now. I was later sent to live with a family."

"Did you go back to school?" I asked.

"No, I was already fifteen by that time!" Katuri exclaimed. "I had to start earning a living. There was not much I could do, so I looked after children. My father was released from prison in 1945, but did not have a long life. He was killed down south, in Kokkola, the same year. We never found out who was responsible."

She went into the living room and came back with a thick book about the Finnish war children.

"I have only looked at the pictures," she said, and showed me a photograph of herself and her siblings. "I do not want to read it, it would be too hard. I think it is best not to read it. Now, where was I? Oh yes, I got married in 1951. My husband was a Skolt Sámi as well. We fished and kept reindeer to begin with, but we only had two reindeer and that was not enough. Fortunately, my husband got a job. He helped to build the roads up here. We had seven children and no running water!"

She got up again and this time came back with a photograph album. One of the first pictures showed all the children together. "I can tell you, life has not been easy!" She chuckled. "Seven children and no washing machine!" She turned the pages with an arthritic finger. Then she pointed at a photograph of herself in traditional Sámi costume.

"I made it myself," she said, proudly.

As I was leaving and we were saying our goodbyes, she took hold of my hand and started to sing in a strong, clear voice. The first words are all I can remember: "I miss my homeland . . ."

Jouni Männistö was a border guard for his entire working life. A couple of years ago he turned fifty and retired.

"I was lucky," he said, with a smile. "Now they have to work until they are fifty-seven."

I had been lucky to find Jouni. There is no road to the Three-Country Cairn (Treriskrøysa), where the Norwegian, Russian and Finnish borders meet. The only way to get there is to walk those final few kilometres. The poorly marked path is not well maintained, and the distance is big enough to make it difficult to get there and back in a day. There is a quicker route with a far better path, but it passes through the border zone that runs along the entire Finnish–Russian border, which is between five hundred metres and three kilometres wide. There is a similar zone on the Russian side. The Russians made the border zone a requirement and the Finns have chosen to keep it for practical reasons. Entry to the zone is strictly forbidden without permission, but Jouni had organised a special permit for me via his contacts.

The path followed the border through the spruce and birch forest. A high fence marked the actual border; it was designed not to keep immigrants and dissidents out of Finland, but rather to keep reindeer in. The ground on the Russian side was covered in a solid layer of light-green lichen.

"Overgrazing is a big problem in Finland. We have too many reindeer," Jouni said. "And there are none on the Russian side."

The border was delineated by markers – the Finnish markers were blue and white, the Russian red and green – and the boundary itself was an eight- to ten-metre corridor that had been cleared of growth. It is illegal to walk there.

"We can't see them, but they are watching, so it is best to follow the rules," Jouni said.

The terrain was stony and uneven. We were about halfway there when we came to a disused border station.

"I used to work here," Jouani said, sitting down on the steps of the main building. "It must be at least twenty years since I was here last."

The yellow border station had stood empty for almost as long as Pripyat in the Chernobyl zone, but none of the windows were broken. There were no holes in the roof and the floor and walls were intact. The building was clearly derelict; inside it was messy and the dust lay thick. The bushes and grass outside were overgrown and wild, but it did not look like a bomb had dropped there.

Not long after, we came to a border watchtower in which Jouni had spent many a night.

"Can we go up?" I asked.

"No," Jouni said, then started to climb the rusty steps. He indicated that I should follow.

The tower swayed gently with every step he took. I was worried that the whole thing might topple over or collapse, and regretted having asked. It had stood unused for a long time. Jouni was already at the top. I decided to trust his judgement and Finnish engineering, so up I went, holding tightly onto the rail.

From the top, we had a view of the Finnish forest to the west, the Russian forest to the east, and low blue mountains to the north.

"It was exciting to begin with, but sitting up here soon got boring – all alone, all night," Jouni said.

"Did you ever see anything suspicious?"

He shook his head. "No, not once in the twenty years that I worked as a border guard did I experience any drama, or see anything suspicious." He blinked in the bright sunlight. "It was quite exciting being so close to the Russian border, but the Russian side looked exactly the same as here. It was a quiet border, not much happened here. Every now and then a drunk Russian soldier might wander into Finnish territory, but then we just let them know and it was sorted."

We climbed down from the tower and carried on heading north, towards Norway.

"Unlike Norway, where you have conscripts guarding the borders, our border is guarded by professional border guards who are part of the police force," Jouni explained. "A lot of the work now involves cameras, cars and snow scooters, but in my day we were outside much of the time, and we walked a lot. When I had a shift at the border station, I had to walk thirty kilometres to get there. I have always liked being outdoors, so the job suited me well. But obviously, when I had just met my wife and was in love, it was hard to be away for two weeks at a time . . ."

It took us over three hours to reach the Three-Country Cairn, which stands on top of a gentle ridge. For the first time in several months, I planted my feet on Norwegian soil. The cairn marks the border, and on top there is a white triangle, showing the point where the borders actually meet. Two young soldiers sat at a fire nearby, cooking sausages. They greeted us politely with a smile. One of them had a face full of freckles.

"Are you hungry?" he asked, in Norwegian.

The Border

"You can walk right up to the borderline, but if you then lean forward to look at your toes, you will have violated the border. Do not throw anything over the border – that too is a violation and punishable by law. The borderline does not necessarily run down the middle of the river, so keep an eye on the markers, and make sure you don't accidently end up on the wrong side. You are not allowed to talk to the Russian guards on the other side. That also is considered a violation. Is that clear?"

The Norwegian border commissioner, Roger Jakobsen, dressed in a full colonel's uniform, gave us a stern look. My father and I nodded.

For the first time on my journey, I had a companion. When my father heard of my plans to walk and canoe along the Norwegian–Russian border, he immediately volunteered his services as expedition assistant. He was so keen that he even answered the emails I sent – my father has never fully embraced the digital world and I thought he never read my messages. I thanked him for his offer, because when it comes to camping and survival in the wild, I am something of a novice; I can barely light a fire in a wood burner by myself. My father, on the other hand, is the kind of man who worships the great outdoors. So I would now have the opportunity to learn from a master.

"Excellent, then you can sign here," Jakobsen said, and pushed two sheets of paper towards us. Then he handed us a number for each of our kayaks. "You have to take them off again as soon as you leave the border area, is that understood?"

The Norwegian–Russian border is 196 kilometres long and makes up no more than eight per cent of Norway's total border. But while the borders with Sweden and Finland are open and informal, and only discreetly marked with the odd customs station here and there, the border with Russia is guarded by armed patrols. Kirkenes is the only city in Norway with its own border commissioner.

"We are carrying out a comprehensive review of the border at the moment," Jakobsen said. "It is far too long since it was last done, in 1947, no less. The work started in 2009."

"And it is not finished yet?" My father looked at him in astonishment.

"No, but we reckon to be finished fairly soon," Jakobsen said. "It is time-consuming and laborious. The border was fixed in 1826 and in principle has barely changed, but the natural conditions have changed. For example, the border is supposed to be at the deepest point of the Jakobselv river, but that point has moved in many places so the border has to move as well. In the Pasvik River there can be several deep points, so then the borderline has to be adjusted to ensure that both countries have equal rights when it comes to using the river and exploiting its natural resources. There are also technical errors. After all, they did not have G.P.S. and had to stand out in the river with measuring instruments and a pen and paper. If it rained, a number two could quickly bleed into a seven. Once we have mapped out the border again, we need to work out how much Norway has lost and how much Russia has lost. The agreement is that neither country should change size, so if we can't get it to add up, we will have to find places in the wider waterways where we can adjust the borderline accordingly."

We dutifully stuck the numbers on our kayaks as soon as we had

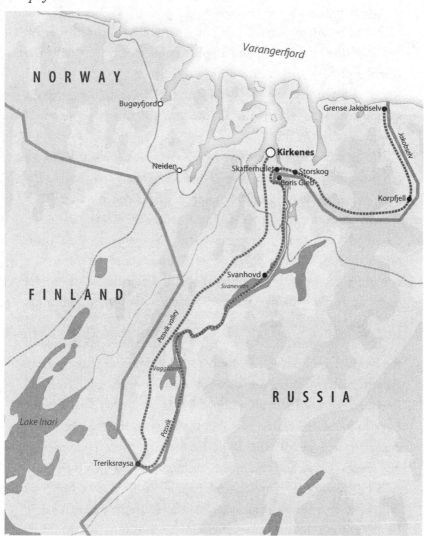

Map of Finnmark

left the border commission. Then we went in search of midge repellent – the people who live in Finnmark do not call the midges there "grey terror" for nothing.

Like Rovaniemi, Kirkenes is not a particularly attractive town, and as is the case throughout Lapland, the reason for this is the Nazis' scorched-earth tactic during the Second World War. The whole of Finnmark was left in ruins after the war, so it was rebuilt as quickly as possible, with all the straight lines and practical materials of the 1950s.

The building work continues to this day. The people of Kirkenes recently got a new, modern primary school, kindergarten and sports hall, and a big new regional hospital is under construction. Even though fewer than four thousand people live there, with about ten thousand in the municipality as a whole, the town boasts two swimming pools, several large shopping centres, a department store and five sports shops. The fact that all the street signs are in both Norwegian and Russian gives some indication of who all this is aimed at.

For a few years, people who live within thirty kilometres of the border have been able to apply for a local border traffic permit. Approximately fifty thousand people now have this and can travel freely in the border zone without a visa. People from Kirkenes flock to Nikel, the closest town on the Russian side, to buy vodka, cigarettes and petrol. The Russians used to come in hordes to buy sports clothes and equipment, instant coffee, which they think is better quality in Norway, and nappies, which are cheaper in Norway than in Russia. This is largely thanks to the national nappy campaigns run by supermarket chains to lure in new customers. Delighted Russians used to bulk-buy nappies before staff even had time to unpack them from the pallets, and there used to be scarcely a parking place to be found in Kirkenes on Saturdays. However, as a result of sanctions and a weak rouble, that is no longer a problem.

In Oslo, 1,400 kilometres further south, any talk of Russia is often crass, coloured by fear, prejudice, international politics and the general mood, but in the north, the relationship between the Norwegians and the Russians is largely one of mutual respect and understanding, precisely because they live as neighbours. After all, Russia is only a shopping trip away.

The northerners' mercantile approach to the Russians is nothing new. In the eighteenth century, Russian merchant ships started to appear in the fjords and at trading posts in northern Norway. The merchants came from the White Sea and Kola Peninsula. The area was called Pomorye, which means "land by the sea" or "coast land", and the people who lived there were called Pomors. The pomor trade, as it became known, was an important source of income and business for both parties. The Pomors' main wares were corn and flour, but they also had salt, meat, peas, iron, tar, timber, soap and other useful products. They traded these for fish, as the Russian church's frequent fasting days meant there was an enormous demand for fish. Bartering was eventually replaced by money and the rouble was valid currency in many places in northern Norway. A pidgin language developed that was used by the Russians and Norwegians, which was called *russenorsk* by the Norwegians and *moya-po-tvoya*, "mine in yours", in Russian. There is a body of about four hundred words, primarily Russian and Norwegian based, but also words that are derived from Sámi, English, German and Dutch.

The pomor trade continued until the First World War, when the danger of being attacked by German submarines made it too risky. It was officially discontinued after the Russian Revolution in 1917. Trade between Finnmark and Russia started to flourish again after the collapse of the Soviet Union, but, as mentioned, the main wares now are nappies, vodka and petrol.

With the exception of a few minor feuds in the Middle Ages,

Norway and Russia have never been at war. Consequently, Norway is the country, among its fourteen neighbours, that has had the most peaceful relationship with Russia. Norway has largely been protected by its geography: the border area lies far to the north and is therefore difficult to reach. Up until the First World War, the quickest and simplest route from St Petersburg to Murmansk was to sail across the Baltic then around the Scandinavia peninsula! The word Murman is in fact a distortion of the word "nordman" (Norwegian) and in the early Middle Ages, Norwegians could collect tribute on the Kola Peninsula. Norwegian fishermen and trappers were far more active along the Arctic coast than the few Russians who lived in the area.

Towards the end of the nineteenth century, a lot of Norwegians settled on the coast of the Kola Peninsula, attracted by the fishing and trading privileges granted by the Russian tsar. Entirely Norwegian communities were established on Fiskerhalvøya, otherwise known as the Rybachy Peninsula, among other places. Most of the Norwegians chose to remain in the Soviet Union after the revolution. The Norwegian fishermen were forced to join the Polar Star work collective in 1930, and suffered terribly during the Great Purge. In 1940, all the Norwegians on the Kola Peninsula were deported to Karelia, and then on to Archangel, where most of them starved to death. After the war, those who survived were not allowed to move back to their homes on the Kola Peninsula, and gradually forgot their Norwegian language and background; they could not speak about this freely until after the dissolution of the Soviet Union.

The situation on the Kola Peninsula changed with the building of the Murman Railway during the Second World War. The railway runs from Petrozavodsk in Karelia to the port of Murmansk, which was founded in 1916. Murmansk finally gave Russia a large, ice-free port in the north. The subsequent changes in the industry, demographics, ideology and geography in the area were swift.

In 1920, the Bolsheviks ceded Petsamo to Finland, so Norway did not have a direct border with the Soviet Union until September 4, 1944, when Finland was forced to accept Stalin's harsh peace negotiations, and Petsamo became part of the Union of Soviet Socialist Republics.

Six weeks later, on October 18, the Red Army crossed the border into Norway and forced the Germans to retreat. Kirkenes was the first town to be liberated by the Russians on October 25, 1944.

"I was only seven, but I remember it well," said Jostein Eliassen, a tall, well-built seventy-nine year old. "One morning, there were four soldiers in uniform outside the cave. They spoke a different language, not German. There was peace. People raised the flag and sang the national anthem. The Russians pulled out a German field kitchen and made soup for us all."

The Germans used Kirkenes as a base for the Murmansk front. About ten thousand soldiers were stationed in and around Kirkenes, and there were Germans in practically all the houses. However, they never got further than the Litsa River, about halfway between the Norwegian border and Murmansk. The front stayed here for four years, until autumn 1944. And during that time, Kirkenes was bombed frequently by the Russians.

"Personally, I thought those war years were exciting, the bombing raids in particular," Jostein said. "It was always a thrill to see the anti-aircraft rockets hit the planes. There were more than three hundred air raids over Kirkenes through the war, and the siren sounded more than a thousand times. As children, we were never allowed to go far from the house in case there was an air raid. When the siren started to wail, there was always a mother there to get you to safety. Our mothers were parents to many."

When the Finns drove the Germans out of Finland in autumn

1944, the German soldiers on the Murmansk front were also pushed back westwards towards Norway. Hitler ordered them to apply the scorched-earth tactic: not even an outhouse should be left standing for the Soviet soldiers. Before they withdrew from Kirkenes, the soldiers therefore set fire to the buildings that had survived the bombing raids. The Red Army were by then so close, however, that the last remaining soldiers had to flee before they had managed to fully destroy the town. They were more successful in the rest of Finnmark. As they withdrew, the Germans burned and destroyed an estimated 12,000 homes, 150 schools, 20 churches, 200 fishing ports, 350 motorboats and many thousands of rowing boats. The local population were ordered to evacuate, but more than twenty thousand people, that is to say more than a third of the population in Finnmark, did not and instead hid in turf huts, caves and burnt-out buildings. Some three thousand people sought refuge in the Bjørnevatn Tunnel by the iron ore mine near Kirkenes, including Jostein and his family. The tunnel has now been closed, but Jostein took us down into the opencast mine and showed us the entrance to the tunnel.

"People started to hide here from the beginning of October," he said. "They took food with them and made bunks from the materials that were lying around outside, three tiers high. I remember lying in the top bunk, looking out over the sea of people below. People sang in the tunnel, argued, got drunk. The light came and went. More than three thousand people living cheek by jowl, with all the uncertainty and tension. There were a lot of scuffles and tiffs. Everyone who could made their way to the tunnel. People made food in huge pots. Some had taken their pets and animals with them; children were even born in the tunnel. They saw daylight for the first time on October 25. We were not in the tunnel for that long, because my father took us to some crags not far away where there was a cave that was forty to fifty metres deep, but not much wider than the aisle on a bus. A stone protected the entrance, and a woollen blanket kept out the smoke; everything was burning. We were not allowed to talk, because the Germans were snooping around looking for fugitives."

Once the Germans had been driven back, people had to rebuild their lives from nothing. All their material possessions were gone.

"Most of them had no house to go home to, so a lot of them stayed on in the tunnel until December," Jostein said. "Everyone rolled up their sleeves, dug down through the ash, and put a roof over their heads. We were lucky, our house was still standing. My parents had buried two metal bathtubs filled with cups and containers, and they survived too. Two families who needed shelter moved in with us. The Russians stayed here until September 1945, so almost a year. Some of them stole pocket watches, but not all of them were thieves. One of the soldiers was a tailor, and he borrowed my mother's sewing machine. He gave it back before he left."

Like so many others from Kirkenes, Jostein worked in the ore mine as an adult. It was the most important employer in the area and the very reason that the town existed.

"I started to work in the mine in 1960. After my first day, I swore I would not stay another day. But then I worked there for thirty-seven years, until 1997. And I would do it all over again. I was responsible for the blasting, and, let me tell you, some of those charges were beasts! Whenever we detonated big charges, we had to warn the power station at Boris Gleb, so they could turn down the turbines. We were always outdoors, summer and winter, so it was a tough job. My brother died in a landslide here in 1949, when we were tidying up after the war. He was only twenty-five."

We drove back up out of the opencast mine, which did not look so big from above. It was only when you were in it that you could understand the true scale.

"In the 1970s, a German came here to buy equipment," Jostein said. "He sat down next to a Norwegian here in the mine, and asked if he could have a light. 'No fucking way!' the Norwegian said, 'the last time your lot were here, they left only seventeen houses standing.'"

A couple of reindeer trotted down the verge into the mine. Jostein observed them.

"Reindeer are the world's best barometer. They come here a day or two before it gets warm, as it's always cooler in the mine. They could be a real pain whenever we wanted to blast!"

The road from Kirkenes to the Three-Country Cairn was reminiscent of the badly maintained Soviet roads in Kazakhstan. It was narrow and bumpy and full of potholes. The kitchen utensils in my father's camper van made a terrible noise. We had at least been warned. Someone had put up a sign at the start of the road which said in Norwegian, English and German that this was the worst road in Norway.

We had the radio on, and the Finnmark news sounded rather exotic to us: there had been an accident the evening before, involving nineteen reindeer. The reindeer police suspected that it was a case of speeding and that the animals had been mown down. The Norwegian Food Safety Authority warned against the consumption of fish and berries from the area around Nikel, because of the dangerously high levels of nickel. I had just eaten perch for lunch.

As was the case in Finland, it was not possible to drive all the way to the Three-Countries Cairn. The last five kilometres had to be done on foot. When we got to the parking place, it began to pour with rain and it did not take long before the ground was mud. Two other vehicles with foreign registration plates were parked there. They looked like they might belong to professional adventurers who had lived in their cars for years. Two border soldiers, a smiling girl and a shy boy, came over to speak to us in the rain. The girl gave us advice and tips on the terrain, and reminded us not to cross the border. She was from the south, like us, and was so enthralled by the far north that she had applied to do an extra six months' service.

I christened my new, light-green tent by pitching it under the awning of the camper van. My mobile was only receiving Russian signals, so I turned it off and lay there listening to the rain. The July night was light grey, like the smoke from a midge coil.

Early the next morning, we set off for the Three-Country Cairn. Even though there were duckboards, the path was still sodden after the rain, and we waded through water up to our knees. There were two soldiers by the cairn, tending a fire. They were not cooking sausages this time – perhaps it was too early in the day. The fire was to keep the midges away, one of them explained.

"And because it is always nice to have a fire," the other said. "We sat up here waiting for you yesterday, but you didn't come."

"You knew we were on our way?" I said.

"Of course, we are here to keep an eye on everything."

When we got back to the parking place, my father began to prepare the kayaks. The valley that the Pasvik River runs through is rocky and uneven, with poorly maintained paths. And the midges can make life hell. So it was best to kayak down the river for the first few days. The border passed through the middle of the river. We could not get any closer. It was only when my father asked which kayak I would like that it dawned on me that I did not know how to paddle. I had never been in a kayak before. So with a lot of fuss, and too much assistance, I lowered myself into one of the kayaks, as it rocked alarmingly.

The truth is, I had never given this stretch of the journey much thought; I had just imagined rather vaguely that everything would be fine, that I would glide along the surface of the water without any problem, in harmony with the elements. It would be one of the more pleasant stages of my journey. But the wind was against us, and the current ran in the opposite direction. It was like paddling in syrup. My arms ached, and my thumbs were soon covered in painful blisters. When we got to the first dam, where we were going to camp for the night, I was soaking. My father, on the other hand, was in top form and suggested that I join the Oslo Kayak Club.

"I don't have a canoe," was my grim reply.

"Oh, that's not a problem," my father said. "You can have one of mine."

He pitched the tents and made a fire and heated up some food. I did nothing, just sat there and watched. As we ate, my father wittered away about how much better life was when you had a kayak.

The next day the sun shone down from a blue sky, and we kayaked downstream with a comfortable wind blowing from behind. The occasional car rattled past on the terrible road, but, other than that, all that could be heard was the splash of the paddles, and the birds. There was no sign of life on the Russian side; all we saw was forest, abandoned observation towers and the odd bird.

Sometimes the border ran close to the shore, especially where the river was at its narrowest. But in other places, where the river was wide as a lake, the border ran through the middle of the water. The borderline was only occasionally marked by buoys, so it was fortunate we had G.P.S. On every little island, every holm, there was either a Russian or a Norwegian boundary marker to show which country it belonged to.

As evening fell, we set up camp on a Norwegian island, two hundred metres from the Russian mainland. We had the deserted island to ourselves, but we were clearly not the first who had gone ashore there: there was even an outside toilet on the island.

On the Russian islands, however, there were no buildings, only red and green boundary markers. The border agreement accords Norway and Russia equal rights to the river, but in practice only Norwegians can access the river, as civilians are not allowed to be near the border on the Russian side. Why on earth do the Russians want all those holms and islands when no-one is allowed to use them?

My father pitched the tents by boundary marker number 55. There are 396 Norwegian markers in all along the Norwegian–Russian border, including cairns and concrete pillars. The markers are positioned so that the next one can always be seen from the shore. Each country's marker stands opposite the other on their respective banks, and each of the 396 border markers has its own specification, setting out to within ten centimetres where the border point is between the two markers. Every detail is precisely regulated. A Norwegian border marker must be two metres tall, measure 22 × 18 centimetres, and be painted yellow (RAL 1018). The coat of arms, which must be eighteen centimetres wide and twenty-three centimetres tall, is to be placed five centimetres below the lower part of the black tip (RAL 9017), facing the national border and the Russian border marker. The black tip is eighteen centimetres in height, of which the pyramid accounts for ten centimetres. All border markers are numbered, and the number must be attached fifteen centimetres from the bottom of the coat of arms, and symetrically positioned in relation to the sides. The number itself must be seven centimetres tall, and in Gill Sans Bold type.

The Russian border markers are not so pedantically regulated. The markers along the Norwegian–Russian border on both sides are fibreglass, as it is lightweight and does not need much maintenance, but in other places along the Russian border, the markers are wooden or concrete. The Russian authorities are currently working to replace all the wooden and concrete markers with fibreglass.

The work is due to be completed in 2020. As I followed the Russian border, I had tried to find out how many markers there were, from North Korea in the east to Finnmark in the west, not forgetting the coastline, which is even longer – but no-one knew. It must be tens of thousands.

My father ran hither and thither taking photographs.

"This is magical!" he shouted. "Magical!"

He was already dreaming about organising tours here.

"I think it would be a huge success," he said eagerly. "People would come from all over the world to experience this, I am sure of it!"

We read in the local online newspaper that there had been snow in Finnmark the night before, but far away from where we were, fortunately. Finnmark is the largest county in Norway, bigger than Estonia, with enormous distances. Now it has been combined with Troms, it is even bigger. Here in Pasvik, the sun was still warm, but the leaves had already started to turn, even though we were not yet in August.

I fell asleep to the sound of gurgling water. During the night, I was woken by the wind. The tent side pressed in against my cheek. It felt like lying in a billowing green sack.

For the past year, I had told anyone who cared to listen that the border between Norway and Russia was not particularly long, *only* 196 kilometres. As I fought against a strong headwind, paddling across Langvann, which was indeed as long as the name indicated, I decided that I would never again say that the Norwegian–Russian border was short.

The following day, we carried on towards Melkefoss. The water-fall remains only in name: in the Sixties and Seventies, the Pasvik River was harnessed, and a huge power plant was built – a rare example of successful cooperation between Norway and the Soviet Union. The current was so strong by the power plant that I almost fell victim to a turbine. My father grabbed the tip of my kayak and pulled me in to the shore.

White smoke from the nickel refinery in Nikel was the first sign of life on the Russian side. The plant was built between the wars, when Petsamo was Finnish. The Soviet Union took over production after the Second World War. Because of its location just next to the Norwegian border, Nikel was one of the Soviet Union's many secret towns – it was not shown on any maps until the 1980s. The nickel refinery is now co-owned by the multi-billionaire Vladimir Potanin, and production has increased many times over, without any measures to reduce poisonous emissions. Annual emissions of sulphur dioxide are five times those of the whole of Norway. The refinery produces, on average, five lorry loads of sulphur dioxide every twenty-four hours, which amounts to hundreds of thousands of metric tons a year.

The area of Russia that borders with Norway is the most polluted place in the world, though not just because of the nickel refinery. Andreev Bay lies on the Kola Peninsula, some fifty-five kilometres from the Norwegian border, and was the Soviet Northern Fleet's service base during the Cold War. Nuclear fuel rods for a hundred nuclear submarines were stored and changed here. There are currently spent rods equivalent to five thousand Hiroshima bombs stored in Andreev Bay. The waste is haphazardly stored, at best, and poorly secured – and this led to an accident in 1982, when 700,000 metric tons of radioactive water leaked out into the Arctic Ocean. After the dissolution of the Soviet Union, maintenance of the base was minimal, and it is reckoned to be one of the largest and most dangerous radioactive sites in the world.

Over the past two decades, several Western countries, led by the U.S.A., U.K., Italy and Norway, have invested enormous amounts in cleaning up the radioactive waste on the Kola Peninsula. During

Putin's current term in office, the Russian military budget has increased considerably – in 2015, Russia spent about 52 billion dollars (taking into account the fall in the value of the rouble) on defence – but the Russian authorities are quite happy to let N.A.T.O. countries pay the lion's share of the cost of cleaning up their nuclear waste. After twenty years of planning and negotiation, the actual work finally started in 2017, and the first shipment of spent fuel rods was loaded on the specially built Italian ship, *Rossita*. The clean-up of Andreev Bay is expected to continue until 2025.

At Svanevatn, the last lake we were going to cross by kayak, the water was rough. The headwind was so strong that the kayak barely moved forwards, and if I rested my arms for so much as a moment, it drifted back. I eventually accepted my father's offer to pull me. He tied my kayak to his with a tow rope and paddled us both over the lake, while the wind blew and the waves rocked our boats.

We pulled the kayaks up onto land. From here, we would continue our journey on foot. But first we were going to spend the night under a roof, and sleep in a proper bed at Svanhovd conference centre, which also houses the centre for Øvre Pasvik National Park and the Norwegian Institute of Bioeconomy Research (N.I.B.I.O.). As all the employees had left for the day, we had the place to ourselves.

Before it became a state research and conference centre, Svanhovd was a demonstration and experimental farm, established in 1934 to help boost settlement in the area. When the Norwegian–Russian border was drawn up in 1826, the Pasvik valley became part of Norway. But there were almost no Norwegians living there, only Russian Orthodox Skolt Sámi and Kvens. The first Norwegian to settle in Svanvik, in the 1850s, was Hans Kirkgaard, a vet who originally came from the south. His fate is described in a 1902

travel book by the district doctor, A.B. Wessel. Under the heading
"A Martyr of Colonisation", Wessel wrote: "What fate had driven
a man in his position to the extraordinary lengths that he would
settle here in the wildest isolation is a mystery; he remained
utterly silent on the matter." Things did not go very well for the vet
from the south, because "a practical man, he was not. [. . .] He was
the kind of idealist who is slow to learn from the hardships of
reality, and, as with so many others like him, in the end buckles
under as a martyr to his cause." Kirkgaard ran out of money, and
was forced to take out a loan and let his servants go, "until he
was all alone in Svanvik, a lonely and impoverished man, who
had to work with his own hands and often suffered great depriv-
ation". The farm was sold after ten years, and the vet moved to a
fishing village on the Jakobselv, where he lived even in winter.
"Months could go by without him seeing a soul. It is said that he
had a loyal dog, and that he would hold forth great monologues
for the dog in order not to lose the power of speech. For years he
lived here, alone, a life of extreme moderation and frugality, until
finally a stroke ended his life at the start of the Eighties. He was
then about seventy years old."

Approximately seven hundred people now live in Pasvik.

It was time to use our legs. We pulled on our heavy rucksacks
and tramped off down the road. After about a kilometre, we passed
the remains of a cinema that had been built in the war. The cinema
itself was long gone, but parts of the projection room, built in stone,
had survived. Some two thousand German soldiers had been stationed in Svanvik during the war, and they had clearly anticipated
that they would be there for a good while.

It was a grey day, but at least it had stopped raining. Later on in
the afternoon, we left the road and followed a military A.T.V. track
into the forest. We made camp by the Boris Gleb dam. It was

our last night by the Pasvik River. From our tents, we could see a yellow border buoy in the middle of the water. Every now and then, the ducks and forest birds would quack and scream and make a fuss. One of the birds sounded like a Jew's harp, and to begin with I really thought there was someone sitting alone on the Russian side, playing to the night. But there was never anyone there.

The next morning we came to a simple cabin that had been painted grey and had a small lookout tower, in other words, an "installation", as the military like to call their buildings. A young soldier appeared and told us that we did not have permission to go any closer to the installation.

"How long are your stints here?" I asked.

"Three weeks," the boy said, with obvious exasperation.

"Do you have long to go then?"

"I try not to think about it," he said, and looked at the ground.

In the distance, on the Russian side, was a similar installation, which was no doubt manned. So there they sat, for three weeks at a time, watching each other. Far below, we could see some gold cupolas between the trees.

The first church in Boris Gleb was built by the Russian monk Trifon in 1565. Trifon was the son of a poor priest in the Novgorod region. He was born in 1495. He was a devout child and spent a lot of time in church. He never went to school, but taught himself to read and write. According to legend, he was out in the forest praying one day, when he had a revelation and Christ told him to go to "the land that was hungry and thirsting" in the north to teach the gospel to the "wild" people who lived there. Trifon came to the Kola Peninsula around 1520, and came into contact with the Sámi people for the first time. He spent many years learning their language and traditions, but any attempt to convert them to Christianity was met with hostility. More than once he had to flee for his life. But Trifon never gave up; he returned to the

Sámi time and again, and eventually they all converted. And that is why most Skolt Sámi are now Orthodox Christians.

In 1532, Trifon established the Holy Trinity Monastery by the mouth of the Petsamo River, and, over time, a settlement grew up around the monastery. He died in 1583, at the ripe old age of eighty-eight, having spent more than sixty years in the north. Shortly after his death, a cult developed around him, and he is now one of the few Orthodox saints who is recognised by the Catholic church. When he was alive, he often helped sailors in need, and Russian seamen still pray to him when they are in danger. The Skolt Sámi revere him as their apostle.

Trifon built many churches, including Boris Gleb, which is named after the sons of the grand prince of Kiev, Vladimir the Great, who brought Christianity to Kievan Rus. Boris and Gleb, who were both Christians, were killed by their brother Sviatopolk, who seized the throne after his father's death. The Skolt Sámi see the Boris Gleb church as their spiritual home and it was the subject of endless negotiations between Norway and Russia when the border was drawn up in the early nineteenth century. How to ensure that the holiest church for Skolt Sámi did not end up on the Norwegian side?

Prior to 1826, there was no border between Norway and Russia. Instead, there was a marchland where the two countries each held the right to tax their people. This pragmatic arrangement was in part due to the peripheral nature of the region, so far to the north and away from the capitals, but also took into consideration the migration of the Sámi with their reindeer herds from East Finnmark to Petsamo throughout the year.

In 1812, Sweden had entered into an agreement with Russia that Norway be transferred from Denmark as compensation for the Swedes losing Finland. Alexander I demanded in return that the Swedes fight with the Allies against Napoleon, to which they agreed. Norway was formally ceded to Sweden in the Treaty of Kiel in 1814. Like Finland, Norway was given devolution within the union, with its own constitution and political institutions, but with its foreign policy controlled by Stockholm. The Swedish government wanted to negotiate an official border. They feared that the Russians might decide to colonise Finnmark and they therefore wanted the border to be formalised as swiftly as possible.

The work started in 1825. Based on the principle of natural borders, it was initially thought that the border would run along the Pasvik River. However, this gave rise to problems for both parties. The Norwegian border commissioner, Johan Henrik Spørck, wanted to secure compensation for the Sámi who would lose grazing grounds on the east side of the river, whereas the Russian commissioner, Valerian Galyamin, was concerned that the Skolt Sámi might lose the Boris Gleb church, which was on the west bank. Spørck suggested that they move the church over to the Russian side of the river, but that was not an option, as it was not only the building that was holy, but also the ground on which it stood. The parties finally agreed that the Russians would keep Boris Gleb on the west side of the Pasvik River, on condition that the border did not follow the Pasvik after the holy church, but rather the next river, the Jakobselv, some thirty kilometres further east. The inhabitants of the marchland would be given three years to decide whether they wanted to be Norwegian or Russian.

Both Tsar Alexander I and King Carl Johan, the Swedish-Norwegian king, who had been selected from Napoleon's army and asked to be the heir to the Swedish throne, were satisfied with the result. On November 19, 1825, only a few weeks after he had agreed to the proposal and a few days before the border treaty was due to come into effect, Alexander I died suddenly, at the age of forty-eight. His widow and court swore allegiance to Alexander's younger brother, Constantine, who at the time was in Warsaw. It took the

messengers six days to get to the new tsar, who then said, to everyone's surprise, that he had relinquished his right to the throne, and
that Nicholas, his younger brother by seventeen years, was in fact
the new tsar. Nicholas had at this point sworn allegiance to his
elder brother, and for several weeks, during which the
missives from Warsaw and St Petersburg crossed paths, there was
much confusion as to who should assume the throne. Nicholas
requested that Constantine come to St Petersburg and relinquish
the throne in person, but Constantine never came. By December
14, Nicholas had accepted the situation and allowed the counsellors
to swear allegiance to him. But senior officers in the army refused
to swear loyalty to Nicholas, and there was a revolt.

This revolt, which has gone down in history as the Decembrist Uprising, led to an indefinite delay in the ratification of the
Norwegian–Russian border. The case was further complicated by
the fact that two officers accused Galyamin, the Russian border
commissioner, of supporting the revolt. The truth was that they
wanted to settle a score in a private love drama in which Galyamin
was involved. Galyamin was put under house arrest while the
accusations were investigated. He was released a few months
later, owing to lack of evidence, but was then sent to Finland, as
a precaution.

Nicholas I used cannons and bullets to suppress the revolt, and
the guilty officers were severely punished. Naturally, the new tsar
was deeply disappointed by the General Staff Corps, and never
entirely trusted those officers again. He was very sceptical of the
border agreement that had been negotiated by Galyamin. Perhaps
there was some truth in the accusations against him even though
no evidence had been found. Nicholas therefore decided that he
wanted the Pasvik River to mark the border after all, even if it
meant Russia losing the Boris Gleb church. The feeling in Stockholm was that they needed to get an agreement in place as soon as

possible, no matter the cost, so on April 22, 1826, the Swedish-Norwegian government also accepted the border proposed by Nicholas I. However, before this message had reached the tsar, he had changed his mind again, preferring to continue his brother's policy of friendship with his neighbours, so the border remained as origin-ally decided: Boris Gleb on the "Norwegian" side was incorporated into Russia, and as compensation for those 3.6 square kilometres, Norway received several hundred square kilometres of land between the Pasvik and Jakobselv rivers.

Many Russians were not happy with the border agreement, and the newspapers started to posit all kinds of conspiracy theories. Galyamin had been bribed with a gold casket set with diamonds; no, he had received a sack full of coins from the Swedish-Norwegian government – but when he opened the sack he discovered that it was only coppers! According to the rumours, Galyamin then realised that he had betrayed his country for nothing, and went and hanged himself. In reality, Galyamin went on to become director of the Imperial Porcelain Factory in St Petersburg and eventually ended up as a cabinet minister, one of the highest civil positions in imperial Russia.

In addition to several hundred square kilometres of land, the small timber church in Boris Gleb also cost Russia several hundred square kilometres of ocean and access to the deepwater port at Kirkenes – which is ironic for a country that has always been obsessed with ports. The original wooden church from Trifon's day burnt down in 1944, but a new, grander church, complete with gold cupolas, had already been built in Boris Gleb at the end of the nineteenth century. This is still in use, but because it is in the border zone, visitors need a special permit to get in, and these are not easily obtained.

We walked around the church, on the right side of the reindeer fence and at a safe distance from the Russian surveillance cameras.

In one place, an elk had clearly got caught in the fencing, and only its skull remained. In a clearing, a memorial had been erected to the Soviet soldiers who died in camps here as German prisoners of war during the war, and were buried in unmarked mass graves.

An estimated 5.7 million Soviet soldiers were held as prisoners of war by the Germans in the Second World War. The Germans saw the Slavs as inferior and treated them appallingly, and more than half of those held in prisoner of war camps died. Approximately 93,000 Soviet prisoners of war and 7,000 civilians, so-called *Ostarbeiter*, were transported to Norway during the war. They were used as labour for the major industrial and infrastructure construction ventures that the Germans initiated with Norwegian companies. For example, 13,000 Soviet prisoners of war helped to build the Norlandsbanen railway for Norwegian State Railways (N.S.B.), which was under Norwegian management throughout the war. The management were happy for prisoners of war to be exploited as labour. In an interview published in *Morgenbladet* in August 1945, the director of N.S.B., Otto Aubert, did not deny the fact that the company had used prisoners of war, adding that their work had not been particularly efficient.

About 13,700 Soviet prisoners of war died in Norway. In comparison, 11,893 Norwegians were killed during the war. Even though the trials of collaborators after the war were relatively harsh, Norwegian companies were never held accountable for their cynical exploitation of Soviet prisoners of war.

After the war, the prisoners were sent back to the Soviet Union, where many of them were treated with suspicion, and suffered reprisals and punishment. Soldiers who had surrendered or allowed themselves to be caught alive were considered traitors – the standing order in such situations was to commit suicide. Prisoners of war were not rehabilitated until after Stalin's death. The Norwegian authorities, for their part, did their utmost to avoid any question of compensation for the treatment of prisoners of war; on the instruction of the Ministry of Foreign Affairs, N.S.B. refused to give any details of their work to the Soviet Union. Instead, with Director Aubert at the helm, N.S.B. insisted that the prisoners of war had been weak and sickly, with a poor work ethic.

The Soviet prisoners were not even granted peace in the grave. In 1951, Soviet representatives raised complaints about the poor maintenance of the prisoners' graves. They wanted to look after the graves themselves. The Norwegians feared that the cemeteries might then be used as meeting places for spies, so decided that all the bodies should be gathered together in one mass grave in Tjøtta, in Nordland. A total of 8,084 bodies were exhumed in the three most northern counties. The Norwegian Public Roads Administration was given responsibility for gathering up the bodies in bags that had previously been used for asphalt. The people who dug up the bodies were given the equivalent of five pounds for every skull; consequently, the rest of the body was often left in the old grave.

* * *

With its wide, recently tarmacked surface, new tunnels and German-built bridge, the E150 was a revelation. Some years ago, it was decided that the road should be upgraded on both sides of the border in order to cope with the increase in border traffic. The work was now almost finished, but the increased border traffic was conspicuous by its absence. Following the introduction of sanctions two years earlier, Russia had stopped importing Norwegian salmon, and, suddenly, all the heavy traffic had ceased. There was scarcely a Russian car to be seen, thanks to the decline of the rouble, and even fewer pedestrians and cyclists, despite the fact that they had Norway's widest pavement and cycle path.

A year before, the cyclists at Storskog had been headline news day after day. The first refugees arrived by bike in September.

Crossing the border on foot is not allowed, but riding a bicycle is seen as driving. Over the next few months, more than 5,500 refugees cycled across the Norwegian border, which is perhaps a small number in the bigger picture, but a huge number in the small Sør-Varanger district. The route via Murmansk to Storskog became known as the "Arctic asylum route", and the word spread quickly on social media. Bicycle sellers in Russia had a heyday. But the bikes piled up into a mountain of metal and rubber on the Norwegian side of the border. At the peak, three tons of bicycles were taken away and destroyed daily. The refugees came from many countries, but mainly from Syria, Afghanistan, Iraq, Pakistan and Egypt. Some had been living in Russia, others had only a short, single-entry visa. At the end of November, the Norwegian parliament decided that it would not process asylum applications from those with Russian residency permits, as they did not have a valid visa for Schengen. The stream of refugees dried up from one day to the next.

Not long after, asylum seekers instead started to flood over the Finnish–Russian border at Salla in Lapland, in old bangers – in Finland, cycling across the border is also prohibited. Nearly eight hundred asylum seekers managed to do this before a law was passed at the start of 2016 that only Finnish and Russian citizens were allowed to cross at the northernmost border stations. The Norwegian government decided the same year to build a 250-metre-long fence at Storskog, to improve control at the border crossing. The barrier cost four million Norwegian kroner (a little more than £300,000). Some weeks before the fence was completed, the border commissioner discovered that about fifty metres of the fence were a few centimetres too close to the Russian border, and therefore had to be moved.

When the Soviet Union collapsed in 1991, geographic and polit-ical borders had to be redrawn. The Iron Curtain that had divided Europe into East and West disintegrated almost overnight. For decades the world's population had lived with two superpowers who stood in opposition to each other, each with a finger on the nuclear button while they fought vicarious wars in other countries. The West against the East, capitalism against socialism, the U.S.A. against the Soviet Union, N.A.T.O. against the Warsaw Pact. Many of the former Warsaw Pact countries are now members of N.A.T.O. Alliances shift quickly and wars are no longer fought only with tanks and nuclear briefcases; Russia's modern warfare takes place both in cyberspace and with the help of little men in green with no uniform markers. Putin, a former K.G.B. officer, stops at nothing to gain power and influence. Rules are only followed if they are in Russia's favour. Perhaps the refugee crisis at Storskog was a tiny part of this new type of warfare, a reminder of the chaos that Russia can cause if it so wishes. In all likelihood, both chance and opportunism played a role, as is so often the case with Russian foreign policy.

The small, yellow border station reminded me of a tourist cabin more than anything. Storskog, a place that had dominated the news for an entire autumn, seemed oddly undramatic in the summer drizzle. A couple of Russian cars were parked outside, but otherwise it was quiet. Not an asylum seeker in sight.

We left the road and kept a steady course east through the forest towards the Jakobselv. Just before midnight, we stopped by a small lake and put up our tents. The shifting sky was reflected in the still water. The next day we came to the plateau: the undulating, reddish-brown landscape stretched out in front of us. The hours passed peacefully as we put one foot in front of the other, then again and again and again. When evening came we set up camp. As we turned in for the night, the mist rolled in over the plateau, and blanketed the landscape. I went to get some water from the closest stream and lost all sense of direction. I wandered around in the

cold, milky-white mist, trying to get my bearings. The next morning, the sun shone down once again from a blue sky, and we carried
on eastwards. Up on a hillside we could see three white, futuristic
domes: one of the military's many intelligence service installations
in Finnmark. There were no paths leading to it.

After the Second World War, Norway had to choose a side. As
had been the case with Finland, Einar Gerhardsen's government
understood that Norway needed a strong partner to survive.
Traditionally, Norway had been neutral, but that had in no way
prevented the Germans from attacking the country in 1940. In an
increasingly polarised world, it was no longer an option to stand
alone. In February 1948, Stalin asked Finland's President Paasikivi
if Finland would like to enter an agreement of friendship with
the Soviet Union, as Hungary and Romania had done. The following month, the Norwegian Ministry of Foreign Affairs received
messages from its embassies in Moscow, Helsinki, Warsaw and
Washington to say that Norway could expect an enquiry similar to
the one Finland had just received. In April that year, as previously
mentioned, Finland and Russia signed the Agreement of Friendship, Cooperation and Mutual Assistance, which severely restricted
the Finnish government's room for manoeuvre. The international
press wrote that it was now Norway's turn.

Norway, and the whole of Europe, was under a lot of pressure.
In spring 1948, Belgium, France, Luxembourg, the Netherlands
and the U.K. signed the Treaty of Brussels, a multilateral Western
European defence alliance which was initially intended as a mutual
defence against Germany. However, the situation in post-war
Europe was one of rapid change: in February the same year, the
communists had seized power in Czechoslovakia. A few months
later, the first major crisis in East–West relations took place.
On June 24, the Soviet Union blocked all the main arteries into
West Berlin, in protest against the currency reform that had been

implemented in West Germany in an effort to stem galloping inflation. Instead of giving in to pressure from the Soviet Union, the Western alliance established air corridors so supplies could be flown into West Berlin. At one point, planes were landing every minute. The Soviet authorities eventually realised that their blockade was not having the desired effect, and on May 12, 1949 it was lifted. Eleven days later, on May 23, the Federal Republic of Germany was established. The German Democratic Republic was established later that year, on October 7. Germany, and Europe, had been split in two.

Earlier the same year, in February 1949, the Norwegian government received the awaited correspondence: the Soviet government suggested that Norway and the Soviet Union should enter into a non-aggression pact. The Norwegian government rejected this with reference to the U.N.'s ban on the use of armed force. It was naturally an attempt by the Soviet Union to prevent Norway from entering into other military alliances, but they were too late, as the U.S.A. was now involved as well. The Americans feared that more European countries would fall victim to communism, and believed that the best way to prevent this from happening was to form a broad defence alliance and thus stand united against the Soviet Union. On April 4, 1949, the parties to the Treaty of Brussels – Belgium, France, Luxembourg, the Netherlands and the U.K. – and Canada, Denmark, Iceland, Italy, Norway, Portugal and the U.S.A. signed the North Atlantic Treaty, and together became known as N.A.T.O. The member states committed to defend each other should one of them be attacked by a foreign power.

As Norway only had a relatively short border with the Soviet Union and had never been a part of the Russian Empire, the country was in a far better position than Finland to choose its allies after the war. And Norway chose the U.S.A. and Western Europe. The border with the Soviet Union, latterly Russia, and membership of N.A.T.O. are without a doubt the two key factors that have had most influence on Norwegian foreign policy since the Second World War, and the many intelligence service installations in Finnmark bear witness to this.

There were no paths up to the futuristic domes, but there was a wide, signed road to Korpfjell, the defence forces' most north-eastern border station. A lieutenant who was there to carry out an inspection caught sight of us and invited us in for coffee and cake. There had been thirty soldiers stationed there until late spring, but they had now been moved to a larger base at Storskog. One small patrol had stayed to keep guard and to man the watchtower. The lieutenant gave us an impromptu tour of the partially abandoned station, which included a gym, a drying room, a large kitchen, a T.V. lounge and even a music room.

My father was shocked that the state would squander such good facilities.

"You should work with the Trekking Association," he said. "It is not right that a place like this should stand more or less empty. I am a hundred per cent sure that tourists would flock here, foreigners as well – there is enormous potential!"

The lieutenant did not think it was a particularly good idea.

"The observation tower is still in use," he said.

"And what observations do you make?" I asked.

"We watch the border," he replied, evasively. "During the Soviet era, things were different. The soldiers were ordered to report everything they observed about daily life in the Soviet border stations. How many people were there, if they kept animals. We knew so little about them that everything was of interest." He laughed. "When the Soviet Union started to fall apart, the border stations on the other side became more like smallholdings than watch posts. Did you know that Norway and the Soviet Union came close to war in the summer of 1968? Come with me, I will show you, it is not far."

We got into his car and he drove us a few kilometres down the bumpy road to the Jakobselv. We stopped by a rusty bridge.

"In the early morning of June 7, 1968, scores of Soviet tanks and hundreds of vehicles appeared here," he said. "The other observation towers reported similar build-ups. The Russians had mobilised an entire infantry division, and had positioned three hundred tanks and more than four thousand other vehicles along the Norwegian border. The Norwegian border troops had orders to set fire to all the border stations in the event of an invasion and to prevent the enemy's advance as best they could. As soon as the enemy crossed the border they should open fire. In practice, the border patrols up here were cannon fodder. Tensions were running high. Soviet guns followed the Norwegian soldiers' every move."

"What happened?" I asked.

"On June 10, the Soviet soldiers withdrew just as suddenly as they had appeared, without having fired a single shot."

This dramatic incident was kept secret for over thirty years.

"There has been a lot of speculation as to what might have prompted this sudden demonstration of power," the lieutenant said. "It might have been a response to the N.A.T.O. "Polar Express" exercise that was happening in Troms. Ten thousand allied soldiers took part, including West Germans for the first time. It could also have been a cover manoeuvre or a practice run for the invasion of Czechoslovakia, which took place two months later. Whatever the case, it was dramatic. And if someone had lost their cool, it could have been even more dramatic."

The lieutenant drove us back to the border station. We continued north. The river was in spate because of all the rain.

"We could have kayaked here as well," my father said, looking at the fast-flowing water with longing.

That evening, our last, we pitched our tents on a rocky headland, only ten metres from the Russian mainland. The river made a bend here, so it was shallow and narrow. We could easily have waded across. Sometimes we heard the throb of a car engine from the Russian side, the first man-made sounds we had heard from the other side on the whole trip. There was a narrow, grey observation tower on the top of the hill, presumably a relic from Soviet days. Perhaps they were sitting up there watching us.

My father put out the fire and we crept into our tents. The river gurgled; every now and then a big fat salmon would leap up. After a long, strenuous journey, it had finally reached its destination.

And I would reach mine too, very soon.

In the past years, I had travelled more than twenty thousand kilometres along the Russian border. With the help of North Korean domestic flights, Chinese express trains, Kazakh slow trains, buses, minibuses, horses, taxis, cargo ships, kayaks and my own two feet, I had travelled through fourteen countries and three break-away republics: North Korea, China, Mongolia, Kazakhstan, Azerbaijan, Nagorno-Karabakh, Georgia, Abkhazia, Ukraine, the People's Republic of Donetsk, Belarus, Lithuania, Poland, Latvia, Estonia, Finland and now, finally, Norway. I had moved slowly from the south-east of Russian to the north-west, country by country.

And none of the countries I had travelled through were without wounds or scars left by their neighbour, Russia. For centuries, the smaller countries and peoples, in particular, had been ground between the millstones of power, torn by wars between the major players, and pulled here and there.

Nations have no collective memory; nations have no healed wounds. It is the individuals, millions of them, who carry the scars.

The borders have changed and multiplied time and again over the centuries, most recently in 2014, when Russia annexed Crimea. Borders are not set in stone; the new fibreglass boundary markers are easy to move. The world's biggest country is low on self-esteem;

the economy is failing and the population shrinking. Thus the need to assert itself is even greater.

After two years of travelling along Russia's border – in real terms, along dusty country roads and across the sea, and in figurative terms, charting its long and complex history – I now have more questions than answers. Which is not unexpected. My main impression is of a lack of direction and of opportunism. The Russian Empire grew to the size it did because tsar after tsar seized any opportunity to expand the empire's borders, using violence, trickery and war if necessary. And one group of people after another, from the nomadic tribes of Siberia to the Muslim khanates of Central Asia and Russia's Slav neighbours, was encompassed by the great empire, willingly and unwillingly. In the borderlands and on the periphery, freedom came and went. History teaches us that those who were once part of the Russian Empire are most at risk of falling under its yoke in the future. Norway is therefore luckier than its neighbours.

There is only one country between Norway and North Korea, but it is so vast that you can say one thing about it, then the opposite, and both will be true. It is not just its neighbours that are disparate; Russia contains within its border myriad disparate histories, terrains and ethnic groups.

Throughout history, the very size of Russia has been its greatest defence. The distances are so vast that no foreign army has ever managed to gain control of the enormous land mass. But its size is also its greatest weakness. The Roman Empire, the Persian Empire, the Umayyad Caliphate and the Mongolian Empire all fell because they had grown too big. The centre could no longer control the periphery or protect it from invading armies.

When the Soviet Union finally collapsed, it was because the people on the periphery revolted, and so, stitch by stitch, republic by republic, from Lithuania to Georgia, the empire was undone.

Russia lost about twenty per cent of its territory and more than half its population.

And yet, it is still a gigantic country – four times as large as the E.U., nearly twice as big as the U.S.A. or China. Russia's border, as it is described here, will no doubt soon be history. Perhaps it will first become longer, only then to become shorter, like the convulsions of a dying snake; because it is hard to imagine how, in the long term, Russia can continue to exist as one country for another generation, another hundred years, another two hundred years, with almost two hundred ethnic groups and nationalities, an area of 17 million square kilometres and a 60,000-kilometre border.

In 1991, Russia gained eight new neighbours. And there may soon be more. One of the reasons that Yeltsin, and then Putin, was so hard on the rebels in Chechnya was the fear of further fragmentation. Chechnya is still ruled with an iron hand by the dictator Ramzan Kadyrov, but iron curtains and irons hands can rust and disintegrate, sometimes overnight.

We walked past an abandoned school, then houses, some inhabited.

When we had walked for a long, long time, we spotted King Oscar II Chapel in the distance. The little chapel was built in 1869, so that Russian fishermen would know where the border was. It was a peaceful alternative to a battleship, which had also been suggested. It was originally whitewashed so the fishermen could see it from the sea, but now the small stone chapel, with its narrow arched windows and light-green copper spire, blended well with its hilly surrounds. Unfortunately it was closed for renovation, so all we could do was peer in through the windows.

"This must be the most beautiful church I have ever seen," my father said, full of emotion.

The landscape opened up in front of us, allowing us to look straight out to the Arctic Ocean. We could feel the salty air on our faces.

I sat down on the damp sand and let the grains run through my fingers. One small handful contains ten thousand grains, each one a tiny world in itself.

© Svein Fatland

ACKNOWLEDGMENTS

This book would never have been possible without the help of many kind and knowledgeable people in Norway and elsewhere.

A massive thank you to all the people I met on my journey, who opened their hearts to me and shared their stories. Wherever I went, I was welcomed with openness, friendliness and generosity. This book is the result of those meetings.

Some of those who told their stories did so in the knowledge that if the wrong people found out that they had spoken to a writer, they would lose their jobs or be in trouble with the authorities. I have therefore changed their names and other information so that they cannot be identified. Others did not even know that I was writing a book, as I deliberately did not tell them, for their safety and my own. This includes all those I met in North Korea. They too have been anonymised.

I had invaluable help from friends and strangers all around the world. Marc Lanteigne shared his knowledge of China and the Northeast Passage, and MiRee Abrahamsen gave me useful contacts in China and Georgia. Jing Wu and her husband Bjørn Theisen made a heroic attempt to teach me survival Chinese before I left. That it was unsuccessful is entirely due to the student's lack of musical sensitivity.

My hostess in Ulan Bator, Zoljargal Naranbaatar, showed me true Mongolian hospitality: she went to enormous efforts to organise interviews and tours for me. Thanks also to Yury Krutskin for the interesting insights into Mongolian history and culture. Aidos

Sarym and Galym Ageleuov in Almaty were enlightening about political and financial trends in modern Kazakhstan and put in me in touch with useful people in other towns and cities. Håkon Vik helped me with the Black Sea and Caspian Sea crossings – a daunting prospect for even the most seasoned globetrotter. In Baku, I was treated to Rena Houseynlis' extraordinary hospitality; she made me feel like an old family friend. Natia Chkhetiani and Thoma Sukashvili were both of enormous help in Georgia, and Helge Blakkisrud generously shared his Nagorno-Karabakh contacts with me, as well as giving me useful advice on the chapters about the Caucasus.

In Ukraine, I owe a big thank you to Morten Jentoft, Per Christian Selmer-Anderssen, Vladimir Subotovsky, Darya Mikhaylova and Christopher Nunn for their practical advice and assistance; to the ever-energetic Natalya Voronkova, who was kind enough to show me around the Military Hospital in Kiev and who helped me to contact patients and doctors; and to Alexandra Gribenko, whose help in the field in Donetsk was invaluable.

Thank you to Berit Nising Lindeman, Ane Tusvik Bonde and Andrey Dynko for their good advice and contacts in Belarus. In Warsaw, Bartosz Kamiński went beyond what I could have expected of him as a publishing contact, and set up a number of interesting interviews with Polish academics and specialists. The same is true of Tauno Vahter in Estonia – he even turned up in Tartu with his family and took me on an outing to Peipus Lake to meet the Old Believers there. My Finnish publisher, Aleksi Siltala, also went out of his way to find the best people for me to interview in Helsinki.

Morten Strøksnes gave me much good advice about Finnmark, and Frode Berg was very helpful during my time in Kirkenes – unfailingly enthusiastic, he took care of everything, from interviews about the Second World War to information about Norwegian border-marker regulations. A big thank you, too, to Jostein

Eliassen, who took me on a tour of Sydvaranger Iron Ore Mine and shared his dramatic story. And special thanks, of course, to my father, who taught me to kayak, saw that we had a fire every night and made sure that our tents were pitched in the best place. The hardest part of the journey to arrange was the Northeast Passage. I would like to thank Felix Tschudi and Ulf Hagen for their patience, good advice and insight. My thanks also to Patrik Mossberg of Marinvest and Mads Boye Petersen of Nordic Bulk Carriers, who were both willing to let me "hitch a ride" had one of their boats been travelling along the most northerly sea route at the relevant time. Unfortunately we did not manage to find a cargo ship, but a small New Zealand expedition company happened to be planning a trip in August 2017. Thank you to Rodney Russ of Heritage Expeditions for letting me join the company's first ever trip through the Northeast Passage, and for giving me "authors' rates". And a big thank you to the crew and my fellow passengers who all helped to make the trip very special indeed.

Thanks also to the Norwegian foundations, associations and unions that have made it financially possible for me to write this book. It has taken me almost three years to complete, and the journey itself took 259 days. Without the three-year stipend I was given by the Norwegian Non-Fiction Writers and Translators Association, which provided security in the otherwise unpredictable life of a freelancer, I would not have been able to dedicate so much time to the project. Nor would the extensive research trip have been possible without the generous support of Free Word, and of the Bergesenstiftelsen for the Northeast Passage leg.

The writing itself was made so much easier by the enthusiastic team at Passa Porta International House of Literature in Brussels, who offered me a two-month residency in their writer's flat in spring 2017. Thank you as well to the Bergman Estate on Fårö for a five-week residency in summer 2017, when I was in the final stages.

Per Egil Hegge and Ivar Dale read the entire manuscript and gave me good suggestions and advice: my thanks to both of you! I am also grateful to Geir Helgesen, Øyvind Rangøy, Snorre Karkkonen Svensson and Henrik Meinander, who all read parts of the manuscripts and caught some errors. The globetrotter Jens A. Riisnæs shared his knowledge and experience with me from the start, and also read the manuscript and made valuable suggestions. A special mention goes to my Polish translator, Maria Gołębiewska-Bijak, who worked hard to check and double check all the facts in the manuscript. I alone am to blame for any mistakes that may remain.

And last, but absolutely not least, thank you to my husband, Erik. His enthusiasm and support buoyed me when I was travelling and when I was at home; he has stood by me throughout. No-one, not even my great editor Tuva Ørbeck Sørheim, has read the manuscript as many times as he has. Thank you, thank you for your sound advice on the language and content, for your steady belief in the project, for all the wonderful meals and the fact that you are always there for me.

Florence, Oslo, La Gomera, Brussels, Berlin,
Fårö and the Arctic Ocean, 2016–17

BRIEF OUTLINE OF THE HISTORY OF RUSSIA

862   Rurik, a Varangian chieftain, settles in Novgorod and establishes the Rurik Dynasty.

882   Oleg, Rurik's successor, moves the capital to Kiev and establishes the Kiev Dynasty, otherwise known as Kievan Rus, the forerunner of modern Russia.

988   Vladimir I, Grand Prince of Kiev, allows himself to be baptised in Chersonesos and then Christianises the empire.

1223   Slav armies meet Genghis Khan's Mongolian horsemen in the Battle of the Kalka River, in what is now Donetsk. It is a decisive victory for the Mongolians. Kievan Rus was by this stage already in decline and had fragmented into smaller principalities.

1237–40 Batu Khan, Genghis Khan's grandson, conquers Kiev and the other Russian principalities, including Moscow, Vladimir, Tver and Yaroslavl, as well as the Republic of Novgorod. As subjects of the Mongol khanate, the Russians had to pay tribute to the Golden Horde for the next 240 years.

1476   The Grand Duchy of Moscow stops paying tribute to the Golden Horde.

1478   Novgorod surrenders to the Grand Duchy of Moscow.

1480   The Mongols lose Moscow following the Great Stand on the Ugra River. The battle never actually happened, as the Mongols retreated following a stand-off that lasted several weeks.

1485   Moscow conquers the Principality of Tver.

1510   The Pskov Republic, the last of the independent Russian republics and grand duchies, falls to Moscow.

1533   Ivan IV, also known as Ivan the Terrible, becomes Grand Prince of Moscow.

1547   Ivan the Terrible is crowned Tsar of Russia.

1552   Moscow conquers the Kazan Khanate in the east and thus subjugates a different people for the first time.

1556   Moscow annexes the Astrakhan Khanate by the Caspian Sea.

1580–1647   The conquest of Siberia and the Far East. Tobolsk is founded in 1587 and serves as the capital of Siberia. Okhotsk on the Pacific Ocean is founded in 1647.

1584   The port of Archangel in north-west Russia, on the White Sea, is founded, and for a long time is the most important port in Russia.

1598   Fyodor I, son of Ivan the Terrible, dies. As he has no heirs, the Rurik Dynasty dies out.

1613   Mikhail Fyodorovich Romanov – Michael I – is chosen by the nobility to be tsar. His descendants remain on the throne until 1917.

1648   The Cossacks in Ukraine rise up against the Polish hegemony.

1648   Semyon Dezhnev sails through the Bering Strait.

1654   The Cossack leader Bohdan Khmelnytsky swears allegiance to the Russian tsar and signs the Treaty of Pereyaslav.

1689   The Treaty of Nerchinsk, the first border agreement between Russia and China, is signed.

1689–1725   Reign of Peter I, better known as Peter the Great.

1700–21   The Great Northern War between Sweden and Holstein-Gottorp on one side, and Russia, Denmark-Norway and Saxony-Poland on the other.

1703   St Petersburg is founded by Peter the Great.

1709   Peter the Great's army wins the battle against Charles XII's Swedish army at Poltava.

1710   Russia conquers Estonia and Livonia.

1721   The Treaty of Nystad ends the Great Northern War. The Swedish Baltic provinces and Karelian Isthmus are formally ceded to Russia.

1728   Vitus Bering sails through the Bering Strait.

1730–1845   The nomads in what is now Kazakhstan are gradually colonised by Russia.

1741   Bering's second expedition, which was part of the Great Northern Expedition, reaches the coast of Alaska.

1762–96   Reign of Catherine II, otherwise known as Catherine the Great.

1768–74 War with Turkey. Russia conquers new territories north of the Black Sea, which become known as New Russia.

1772 First Partition of Poland.

1783 Russia annexes Crimea.

1783 King Erekle II, who had united a great part of what is now Georgia into one kingdom, enters a bilateral agreement with Russia and signs the Treaty of Georgievsk.

1784 Founding of the fortified town of Vladikavkaz in North Caucasus.

1793 Second Partition of Poland.

1795 Third Partition of Poland. The Polish–Lithuanian Commonwealth ceases to exist.

1799 The Russian-American Company is established to run and oversee the fur trade in Alaska.

1801–25 Reign of Alexander I.

1801 Russia annexes the Kingdom of Georgia.

1804–13 Russo-Persian War. The war ends with the signing of the Treaty of Gulistan. Dagestan, Georgia and much of what is now Azerbaijan are formally ceded to Russia.

1808–9 Finland is incorporated into the Russian Empire and given the status of Grand Duchy.

1812 Napoleon's march on Moscow.

1815 Napoleon is finally defeated at the Battle of Waterloo.

1817–64 The Caucasian War.

1825–55 Reign of Nicholas I.

1825 The Decembrist Uprising.

1826 The border between Norway and Russia is defined.

1826–8 Russo-Persian War. Russia wins again and acquires the territories that are now Armenia and the Azerbaijani exclave of Nakhchivan.

1830 Revolt in Poland is quashed. Nicholas I abolishes the Polish parliament and the Polish army.

1853–6 The Crimean War.

1855–81 Reign of Alexander II.

1858 The Treaty of Aigun is signed by Russia and China. China cedes the territories north of the Amur River to Russia.

1860   Russia and China sign the Convention of Peking. China cedes the areas east of the Ussuri River to Russia.

1861   Serfdom is abolished.

1863   The Poles rebel and once again the revolt is quashed.

1864   Any final remnants of resistance to Tsarist Russia in North Caucasus capitulate. Several hundred thousand Circassians are deported to Turkey.

1865–95 Russia conquers the remaining nomadic tribes in Central Asia and the various Muslim khanates in the countries that are now Kazakhstan, Kyrgyzstan, Uzbekistan, Tajikistan and Turkmenistan.

1867   Alaska is sold to the U.S.A.

1878–9 Adolf Erik Nordenskiöld sails the *Vega* through the Northeast Passage.

1881   Alexander II is assassinated. His son, Alexander III, ascends the throne.

1891–1903 The Trans-Siberian Railway is extended.

1894–1917   Reign of Nicholas II.

1898   Russia establishes Harbin as the administrative city for the Chinese Eastern Railway in Manchuria.

1904–5 The Russo-Japanese War. It ends in a crushing defeat for Russia.

1905   On January 22, more than 130 peaceful demonstrators are killed in St Petersburg, in what has gone down in history as "Bloody Sunday". This marks the start of demonstrations and strikes throughout the empire. In order to calm the situation, Nicholas II agrees to introduce the State Duma.

1914   The start of the First World War. Russia sides with the Allies.

1915   Russia loses Lithuania, Courland, Poland and the western part of Belorussia to Germany.

1917   The February Revolution. Nicholas II abdicates on March 15.

1917   The Bolsheviks seize power in St Petersburg on November 7 and 8, in what is known as the October Revolution.

1917   Finland declares its independence on December 6. On December 31, the Bolshevik government recognises Finland's independence.

1917–22 Civil war between the Reds and the Whites.

1918   Ukraine, Lithuania, Estonia, Georgia, Armenia, Azerbaijan, Poland and Latvia declare their independence. Lithuania, Estonia, Poland and Latvia maintain their independence throughout the interwar period. The Reds take power in Ukraine (excluding Galicia and Lodomeria in the west, which are incorporated into Poland) and in the Caucasus during the civil war and the two become union republics in the Soviet Union.

1918   Russia signs the Treaty of Brest-Litovsk and withdraws from the First World War. Germany capitulates on November 11.

1922   The Reds, led by Vladimir Lenin, defeat the Whites. The Soviet Union is established.

1924   Lenin dies and Joseph Stalin becomes leader of the Soviet Union.

1929–33 The first five-year plan. Mass collectivisation.

1932   Otto Schmidt sails through the Northeast Passage in ten weeks, without having to spend the winter there.

1933   Famine. Ukraine and Kazakhstan are hit particularly hard.

1936–8 The Great Terror and the Moscow Trials, a wide-reaching campaign of persecution and repression instigated by Stalin. Includes the purging of the Communist Party, repression of farmers, deportation of ethnic minorities and arbitrary imprisonment and execution of individuals.

1939   The German–Soviet Non-Aggression Pact, otherwise known as the Molotov–Ribbentrop Pact, is signed on August 23. In a secret appendix, Hitler and Stalin carve up Eastern Europe between them. On September 1, Germany invades Poland and the Second World War starts. The Soviet Union annexes East Poland and East Galicia.

1939–40 The Winter War. Finland is forced to cede the Karelian Isthmus, among other places, to the Soviet Union.

1940   The Soviet Union annexes Lithuania, Latvia, Estonia and Bessarabia.

1941–5 Germany invades the Soviet Union on June 22. The war continues until May 8, 1945 (May 9, according to Moscow time) and ends in victory for the Soviet Union and the Allies. More than 20 million Soviet citizens have lost their lives in the war.

1941–4   Many ethnic minorities, including the Kalmyks, the Crimean Tatars, the Chechens and the Ingush are deported on Stalin's orders. Most are sent to Siberia or Central Asia, and are only allowed to return home after Stalin's death.

1944   The Red Army liberates Finnmark in Norway.

1945   The Red Army drives the Japanese out of Manchuria and Korea. Stalin appoints Kim Il-sung leader of North Korea.

1950–53   The Korean War. The Soviet Union aids North Korea with air raids.

1953   Stalin dies. Nikita Khrushchev becomes the General Secretary of the Communist Party.

1954   Crimea is transferred from the Russian Soviet Federative Socialist Republic (R.S.F.S.R.), to the Ukrainian Soviet Socialist Republic.

1955   The Warsaw Pact, a military alliance between the Soviet Union and Albania, Bulgaria, Poland, Romania, Czechoslovakia, Hungary and the D.D.R., enters into force.

1956   The Soviet Union uses military force to quash the Hungarian Revolution.

1961   The Berlin Wall is built.

1968   The Soviet Union and other Warsaw Pact countries invade Czechoslovakia to prevent political reform.

1979–89   The Soviet–Afghan War. More than a million Afghan civilians are killed.

1985   Mikhail Gorbachev becomes General Secretary of the Communist Party and introduces perestroika and glasnost.

1986   The Chernobyl disaster.

1988–94   War between Nagorno-Karabakh and Azerbaijan. Nagorno-Karabakh becomes a de facto independent state.

1989   On August 23, the fiftieth anniversary of the Molotov–Ribbentrop Pact, the Baltic Way takes place in the three Baltic Soviet Republics.

1990   Lithuania declares its independence on March 11.

1991   Unsuccessful coup against Gorbachev in August. The remaining union republics declare their independence, one after the other. On December 8, Boris Yeltsin, Leonid Kravchuk and Stanislav Shushkevich meet in Belarus and announce the establishment of the Commonwealth of Independent States. On December 26, the Soviet Union formally ceases to exist.

1991–2   The war between South Ossetia and Georgia. South Ossetia, with the support of Russia, becomes a de facto independent state.

1991–9   Boris Yeltsin's presidency.

1992–4   The war between Abkhazia and Georgia. Abkhazia, with the support of Russia, becomes a de facto independent state.

1992   The war between Transnistria and Moldova. Transnistria, with the support of Russia, becomes a de facto independent state.

1994–6   The First Chechen War.

1999–2009 The Second Chechen War. The war ends officially in 2000, but the anti-terror operation continues until 2009.

2000   Vladimir Putin is elected president for the first time.

2008   Five-Day War between Georgia and Russia. Shortly after the ceasefire is signed, Russia officially recognises the breakaway republics of South Ossetia and Abkhazia.

2014   Russia formally annexes Crimea on March 21, a few weeks after the pro-Russian president Viktor Yanukovych is removed from office following bloody demonstrations in Kiev. In April, war breaks out in East Ukraine. On April 6, the People's Republic of Donetsk is announced. On April 26, the People's Republic of Lugansk is announced.

2015   The Eurasian Economic Union, also known as the Customs Union, is officially established by its member states: Armenia, Belarus, Kazakhstan, Kyrgyzstan and Russia.

NOTES

1 Quotation from *Where the Sea Breaks Its Back. The Epic Story of Early Naturalist Georg Steller and the Russian Exploration of Alaska* by Corey Ford. Portland: Alaska Northwest Books, 1992 [1996].

2 Ibid.

3 Ibid.

4 Quotations from *The Voyage of the Vega Round Asia and Europe*, Vol. I, by Adolf Erik Nordenskiöld. Kristiania: PT Mallings Boghandels Forlag, 1881.

5 Quotations from Bjørvig's diary in *Paul Bjørvig – Hardhausen. Dagbøkene 32 år etter. Frans Josefs land og Svalbard.* Svalbardminner nr. 1, Skien, Vågemot forlag, 1996. Bjørvig's orthography.

6 Quotation from *Grensekonflikten Kina-Sovjet* by Albert Henrik Mohn. Oslo: Gyldendal Norsk Forlag, 1970.

7 Quotations from Nicholas II and Witte from *The Romanovs: 1613–1918* by Simon Sebag Montefiore. London: Penguin Random House, 2016.

8 Ibid.

9 Quotations from Roy Chapman Andrews' *Across Mongolian Plains. A Naturalist's Account of China's 'Great Northwest'.* Hard-Press, 2015. First published in 1921 by
D. Appleton and Company.

10 Quotations from *The Journal of William de Rubruck. Account of the Mongols.* BookRix GmbH & Co., digitalised in 2002. The edition is based on W.W. Rockhill's translation from Latin from 1900, updated and checked against Peter Jackson's translation from 1990 (Hakluyt Society).

11 Quotation from *The Caucasus. An Introduction* by Thomas de Waal. Oxford: Oxford University Press, 2010.

12 Quotation from *A Hero of Our Time* by Mikhail Lermontov, translated by Reginald Merton. London: Folio Society, 1980.

13 The conversation, which was reported in the French press, is cited in *A Little War that Shook the World* by Ronald D. Asmus. Hampshire & New York: Palgrave Macmillan, 2010.

14 The Black Sea deluge theory was launched in the *New York Times* in 1996. It has been widely criticised, in particular the date, which was estimated as 5500 BCE, but the extent to which the rise in water level was sudden or gradual has

also been questioned. I have based my information here on a study that was published in 2017 in *Marine Geology*, vol. 383: "Compilation of geophysical, geo-chronological, and geochemical evidence indicates a rapid Mediterranean-derived submergence of the Black Sea's shelf and subsequent substantial salinification in the early Holocene" by Anastasia G. Yanchilina, William B.F. Ryan, Jerry F. McManus et al.: http://www.sciencedirect.com/science/article/pii/S0025327216329961

15 Quotation from *The Travels* by Marco Polo.

16 Untitled poem by Alexander Pushkin, translated from the Russian by Sasha Dugdale.

17 Quotations from Reuters, Monday November 7, 2016, from the article "Quitting as Regional Governor, Saakashvili hits out at Ukraine's Poroshenko" by Natalia Zinets and Alexei Kalmykov: https://uk.reuters.com/article/uk-ukraine-crisis-saakashvili/quitting-as-regional-governor-saakashvili-hits-out-at-ukraines-poroshenko-idUKKBN132184

18 Putin himself tells this story in the documentary *Crimea – The Way Home* by Andrey Kondrashev. The film was shown on the television channel Rossiya 1 in 2015.

19 Quotations from *Crimea. The Last Crusade* by Orlando Figes. London: Allen Lane (Penguin), 2010.

20 Quotations from *The Battle That Shook Europe: Poltava and the Birth of the Russian Empire* by Peter Englund. I.B. Tauris, 2013.

21 Ibid.

22 Quotation from *Ukraine. A History* by Orest Subtelny. Fourth edition. Toronto: University of Toronto Press, 2009.

23 Quotations from *Chagall* by Gill Polonsky. New York: Phaidon Press Limited, 1998.

24 Quotation from the article "Poland Says Explosion Behind 2010 Plane Crash in Western Russia" by Marek Strzelecki and Wojchiech Moskwa. Published on April 10, 2017 on www.bloomberg.com

25 Quotation from *När Finland var Sverige* by Herman Lindquist. Stockholm: Albert Bonniers Förlag, 2013.

26 Quotation from Henrik Meinander's biography *Gustaf Mannerheim: from Russian Spy to Finnish Statesman*. Stockholm. Lind & Co., 2017.

27 Quotations regarding the expeditions are taken from *Til Häst genom Asien, Carl Gustaf Mannerheims egne opptegnelser fra reisen*. Stockholm: Natur & Kultur, 1961.

28 Quotation from J.E.O. Screen's biography, *Mannerheim. The Years of Preparation*. London: Hurst & Company, 1970.

EPIGRAPHS

THE OCEAN: Quotation from "Foredrag om Fram-ferden", 1887, in *Nansens røst – Artikler og taler 1897–1915*. Oslo: Jacob Dybwads Forlag, 1945.

ASIA: Quotation from *Secondhand Time: The Last of the Soviets* by Svetlana Alexievich, translated by Bela Shayevich. London: Fitzcarraldo Editions, 2016.

CAUCASUS: Quotation from *In Wonderland* by Knut Hamsun, from an article by Arne Melberg for the Hamsun Centre, translated by Nina Brevik.

EUROPE: Quotation from *Imperium* by Ryszard Kapuściński, translated by Klara Glowczewsk. London: Granta Books, 1994.

BIBLIOGRAPHY

To maintain the flow of the text, I have only given sources when I have used a direct quotation. The following is an overview of the books I found useful when working on my book.

Amundsen, Roald: *Nordøstpassasjen.* Kristiania: Gyldendalske Boghandel, 1921.

Applebaum, Anne: *Iron Curtain. The Crushing of Eastern Europe 1944–56.* London: Penguin Books, 2012.

Asmus, Ronald D.: *A Little War that Shook the World.* Hampshire & New York: Palgrave Macmillan, 2010.

Bjørvig, Paul: *Hardhausen. Dagbøkene 32 år etter. Frans Josefs land og Svalbard.* Skien: Vågemot forlag, 1996.

Brophy, David: *Uyghur Nation. Reform and Revolution on the Russia–China Frontier.* Cambridge, Mass.: Harvard University Press, 2015.

Demick, Barbara: *Nothing to Envy. Real Lives in North Korea.* London: Granta Publications, 2014 [2010].

Englund, Peter: *The Battle that Shook Europe. Poltava and the Birth of the Russian Empire.* New York: I.B. Tauris, 2013.

Figes, Orlando: *Crimea. The Last Crusade.* London: Allen Lane (Penguin), 2010.

Ford, Corey: *Where the Sea Breaks Its Back. The Epic Story of Early Naturalist Georg Steller and the Russian Exploration of Alaska.* Portland: Alaska Northwest Books, 1992.

French, Paul: *North Korea. State of Paranoia.* London: Zed Books, 2014.

Halperin, Charles J.: *Russian and the Golden Horde.* Bloomington & Indianapolis: Indiana University Press, 1985.

Heier, Tormod and Kjølberg, Anders: *Norge og Russland. Sikkerhetspolitiske utfordringer i nordområdene.* Oslo: Universitetsforlaget, 2015.

Holtsmark, Sven G. (ed.): *Naboer i frykt og forventning. Norge og Russland 1917–2014.* Oslo: Pax Forlag, 2016.

Jaklin, Asbjørn: *Brent jord.* Oslo: Gyldendal, 2016.

Jentoft, Morten: *Mennesker ved en grense.* Oslo: Gyldendal, 2005.

Jukes, Geoffrey: *The Russo-Japanese War 1904–1905.* Oxford: Osprey Publishing, 2002.

Kappeler, Andreas: *The Russian Empire.* Translated by Alfred Clayton. New York: Routledge, 2013.

Kasekamp, Andres: *A History of the Baltic States.* Hampshire: Palgrave Macmillan, 2010.

King, Charles: *Odessa. Genius and Death in a City of Dreams.* New York: W. W. Norton & Company, Inc., 2011.

King, Charles: *The Black Sea. A History.* Oxford: Oxford University Press, 2004.

King, Charles: *The Ghost of Freedom. A History of the Caucasus.* Oxford: Oxford University Press, 2008.

Lankov, Andrei: *The Real North Korea. Life and Politics in the Failed Stalinist Utopia.* Oxford: Oxford University Press, 2015.

Lindqvist, Herman: *När Finland var Sverige.* Stockholm: Albert Bonniers Förlag, 2013.

Longworth, Philip: *Russia's Empires. Their Rise and Fall: From Prehistory to Putin.* London: John Murray, 2005.

Lopez, Barry: *Arctic Dreams. Imagination and Desire in a Northern Landscape.* New York: Charles Scribner's Sons, 1986.

Man, John: *The Mongol Empire.* London: Corgi Books, 2014.

Mannerheim, Carl Gustaf: *Til Häst Genom Asien.* Stockholm: Natur & Kulture, 1961. Ebook: 2010.

Marshall, Tim: *Prisoners of Geography. Ten Maps that Tell You Everything You Need to Know about Global Politics.* London: Elliott and Thompson, 2015.

Meinander, Henrik: *Finlands historia 4.* Helsinki: Schildts, 1999.

Meinander, Henrik: *Gustaf Mannerheim. Aristokrat i vadmal.* Stockholm: Lind & Co. 2017.

Meyer, Michael: *In Manchuria: A Village Called Wasteland and the Transformation of Rural China.* New York: Bloomsbury Press, 2015.

Mjør, Kåre Johan: *Russiske imperium.* Oslo: Cappelen Damm Akademisk, 2017.

Mohn, Albert Henrik: *Grensekonflikten Kina–Sovjet.* Oslo: Gyldendal Norsk Forlag, 1970.

Moss, Walter G.: *A History of Russia. Volume I: To 1917.* Second Edition. London: Anthem Press, 2002.

Nielsen, Jens Petter (ed.): *Russland kommer nærmere. Norge og Russland 1814–1917.* Oslo, Pax Forlag, 2014.

Nordenskiöld, Adolf Erik: *The Voyage of the Vega round Asia and Europe.* Cambridge: Cambridge University Press, 2013.

Palmer, James: *The Bloody White Baron.* London: Faber & Faber, 2008.

Payer, Julius: *Die Österreichisch-Ungarische Nordpol-Expedition in den Jahren 1872–1874.* ISBN 978-90-268-4802-2, e.art.now, 2015.

Plokhy, Serhii: *The Last Empire. The Final Days of the Soviet Union.* New York: Basic Books, 2014.

Polonsky, Gill: *Chagall.* New York: Phaidon Press, 1998.

Robbins, Christopher: *In Search of Kazakhstan. The Land that Disappeared.* London: Profile Books, 2007.

Sannikov, Andrei: *My Story.* Translated by Catherine A. Fitzpatrick. Minneapolis: East View Press, 2016.

Screen, J.E.O.: *Mannerheim. The Years of Preparation.* London: Hurst & Company, 1993 [1970].

Screen, J.E.O.: *Mannerheim. The Finnish Years.* London: Hurst & Company, 2014 [2000].

Sebag Montefiore, Simon: *Stalin. The Court of the Red Tsar.* London: Weidenfeld & Nicolson, 2003.

Sebag Montefiore, Simon: *Young Stalin.* London: Weidenfeld & Nicolson, 2007.

Sebag Montefiore, Simon: *The Romanovs: 1613–1918.* London: Penguin Random House, 2016.

Snyder, Timothy. *The Reconstruction of Nations. Poland, Ukraine, Lithuania, Belarus, 1569–1999.* New Haven & London: Yale University Press, 2003.

Subtelny, Orest: *Ukraine. A History.* 4th edition. Toronto: Toronto University Press, 2009 [1988].

Sunderland, Willard: *The Baron's Cloak: A History of the Russian Empire in War and Revolution.* Ithaca & London: Cornell University Press, 2014.

Todal, Per Anders: *Fanden på flat mark. Historier frå Kviterussland.* Oslo: Det Norske Samlaget, 2009.

Tudor, Daniel and Pearson, James: *North Korea Confidential.* Rutland, Vermont: Tuttle Publishing, 2015.

de Waal, Thomas: *The Caucasus. An Introduction.* Oxford: Oxford University press, 2010.

Weatherford, Jack: *Genghis Khan and the Making of the Modern World.* New York: Broadway Books, 2004.

Westlie, Bjørn: *Fangene som forsvant. NSB og slavearbeiderne på Nordlandsbanen.* Oslo: Spartacus, 2015.

Wilén, Broge: *Eckerö Post- och Tullhus.* Self-published: Stockholm, 1988.

Wilson, Andrew: *Belarus. The Last European Dictatorship.* New Haven & London: Yale University Press, 2011.

Wolff, David: *To Harbin Station. The Liberal Alternative in Russian Manchuria, 1898–1914.* Stanford: Stanford University Press, 1999.

Wormdal, Bård: *Spionbasen. Den ukjente historien om CIA og NSA i Norge.* Oslo: Pax Forlag, 2015.

Yekelchyk, Serhy: *Ukraine. Birth of a Modern Nation.* Oxford: Oxford University Press, 2007.

INDEX

ERIKA FATLAND was born in 1983 and studied Social Anthropology at the University of Oslo. Her 2011 book, *The Village of Angels*, was an *in situ* report on the Beslan terror attacks of 2004 and she is also the author of *The Year Without Summer*, describing the harrowing year that followed the massacre on Utøya in 2011. For *Sovietistan: A Journey Through Turkmenistan, Kazakhstan, Tajikistan, Kyrgyzstan and Uzbekistan* (MacLehose Press, 2019) she was shortlisted for the Edward Stanford Lonely Plant Debut Travel Writer of 2019. She speaks eight languages and lives in Oslo with her husband.

KARI DICKSON is a translator from Norwegian of crime fiction, literary fiction, children's books, theatre and non-fiction. She is also an occasional tutor in Norwegian language, literature and translation at the University of Edinburgh, and has worked with B.C.L.T. and the Writers' Centre Norwich.